PRAISE FOR *THE TORONTO MAPLE LEAFS:*
THE COMPLETE ORAL HISTORY

"Eric Zweig captures what the Toronto Maple Leafs have meant to many hockey fans since their inception. I was particularly interested in the decades following their 1967 Stanley Cup victory … I also enjoyed reading about the present state of the Maple Leafs and … the rebirth and future of this franchise."

— Scotty Bowman, Hockey Hall of Famer and winning-est coach in NHL history

"A standout hockey book of Leaf fortunes and foibles, with a twist. Zweig calls on numerous chroniclers of Leaf history to make this one hum. Leaf Nation will love it."

— Brian McFarlane, bestselling author and former broadcaster

"To put it simply — and historically — the moment I began turning these pages, I felt precisely the same thrill as when I heard Foster Hewitt shriek *He Shoots! He Scores!!* on a big Don Metz goal in that classic 1942 playoff comeback. Eric Zweig wrote — and he scored!"

— Stan Fischler, hockey historian, broadcaster, and author

"Not just another history of the Toronto Maple Leafs, but generational work by one of hockey's premier historians, period. Supremely researched and presented, as one would expect of Eric Zweig."

— Howard Berger, former Leafs radio reporter and creator of BetweenThePosts.ca

"Eric Zweig has bled blue and white since he was seven years old. But this is far, far from just a fan's book. When you combine the abject fan with a fine historian and a writer's ear for grand storytelling, you end up with the book on the Toronto Maple Leafs, from past grandeur through years of debacle to today's future promise. A wonderful read."

— Roy MacGregor, bestselling author and *Globe and Mail* columnist

"The hundred-year history of the Toronto Maple Leafs is so rich in drama and event and personality — there are even some (long-ago) Stanley Cups in there, somewhere. Trust Eric Zweig to wrangle it all into such a full and compelling narrative, which he has done — just as the Leafs look like they're ready to dominate again."

— Stephen Smith, author of *Puckstruck: Distracted, Delighted, and Distressed by Canada's Hockey Obsession*

PRAISE FOR *ART ROSS: THE HOCKEY LEGEND WHO BUILT THE BRUINS*

"Painstaking research by one of the best in the business on one of hockey's most influential pioneers."

— *Toronto Sun*

"A fascinating read. In fact, when I started reading it I could hardly put it down until I completed it. What a pioneer Art Ross was ... a great story."

— Scotty Bowman, Hockey Hall of Fame builder and winning-est coach in NHL history

"A diligently researched portrait of a canny, controversial, colourful hockey icon. Recognition for a hockey genius long overdue. As Cherry would say, 'Two thumbs up, Eric!'"

— Brian McFarlane, bestselling author and former sportscaster

"It's high time [Art Ross's] formidable tale was told; Eric Zweig does it with a vim and an eye for detail that delights the fan in me as much as the historian."

— Stephen Smith, author of *Puckstruck*

"Zweig does fine work, breathing life into 100-plus-year-old details; his descriptions of Stanley Cup matches from the era of the rover and the '60-minute men' manage to evoke the excitement of those bygone times ..."

— *Winnipeg Free Press*

THE TORONTO MAPLE LEAFS

THE TORONTO MAPLE LEAFS

The Complete Oral History

ERIC ZWEIG

DUNDURN
TORONTO

Cover image: Bill Barilko (Michael Sr. Burns / Hockey Hall of Fame)
Printer: Webcom

Library and Archives Canada Cataloguing in Publication

Zweig, Eric, 1963-, author
    The Toronto Maple Leafs : the complete oral history
/ Eric Zweig.

Includes bibliographical references.
Issued in print and electronic formats.
ISBN 978-1-4597-3619-1 (softcover).--ISBN 978-1-4597-3620-7
(PDF).-- ISBN 978-1-4597-3621-4 (EPUB)

1. Toronto Maple Leafs (Hockey team)--History. 2. Toronto Maple Leafs (Hockey team)--Anecdotes. I. Title.

GV848.T6Z845 2017   796.962'6409713541   C2017-904768-X
                                        C2017-904769-8

1   2   3   4   5   21   20   19   18   17

 Conseil des Arts   Canada Council
du Canada   for the Arts

ONTARIO ARTS COUNCIL
CONSEIL DES ARTS DE L'ONTARIO
an Ontario government agency
un organisme du gouvernement de l'Ontario

We acknowledge the support of the **Canada Council for the Arts**, which last year invested $153 million to bring the arts to Canadians throughout the country, and the **Ontario Arts Council** for our publishing program. We also acknowledge the financial support of the **Government of Ontario**, through the **Ontario Book Publishing Tax Credit** and the **Ontario Media Development Corporation**, and the **Government of Canada**.

Nous remercions le **Conseil des arts du Canada** de son soutien. L'an dernier, le Conseil a investi 153 millions de dollars pour mettre de l'art dans la vie des Canadiennes et des Canadiens de tout le pays.

Care has been taken to trace the ownership of copyright material used in this book. The author and the publisher welcome any information enabling them to rectify any references or credits in subsequent editions.
— *J. Kirk Howard, President*

The publisher is not responsible for websites or their content unless they are owned by the publisher.

Printed and bound in Canada.

VISIT US AT

dundurn.com | @dundurnpress | dundurnpress | dundurnpress

Dundurn
3 Church Street, Suite 500
Toronto, Ontario, Canada
M5E 1M2

For my father, who introduced me to the game,
and for Leafs fans like him everywhere

CONTENTS

Foreword

LOVING THE LEAFS

Exactly seventy-five years ago I became a passionate fan of the Toronto Maple Leafs. I was ten years old, living in Brooklyn, following the New York Rangers and New York Americans, and for three years had been going to the "amateur" doubleheaders on Sunday afternoons at the old Madison Square Garden. But, for some unknown reason, my heart sought some other team to generate my sports passions.

Then it happened. On my tenth birthday, in March 1942, my parents gave me a pair of presents: one was a tiny brown Philco Transitone radio; the other a rather large scrapbook. Each would play a major part in my love for the Leafs.

One night, a few weeks after receiving my radio, I was turning the dial, and somewhere between New York stations WOR (710) and WJZ (770) I heard a rather piercing, yet captivating voice excitedly describing Game Four of the 1942 Stanley Cup Final.

This was my introduction to *Hockey Night in Canada*, and, most importantly, Foster Hewitt, who did as much as anyone to increase my love of hockey in general and, specifically, the Leafs. I loved the names and, better still, the nicknames: "Turk" Broda, "Bingo" Kampman, "Sweeney" Schriner, and "Bucko" McDonald suddenly became heroes along with my eventual role model, captain Syl Apps.

That this glorious hockey club was en route to four straight victories and the Stanley Cup — after losing the first three games — added to the glamour transmitted by my tiny Transitone radio and through the pages I pasted into my scrapbook.

Day by day I would clip hockey stories from the newspapers. There wasn't much in the New York dailies about the Leafs, but in 1946 I made a wonderful discovery. Sitting in the middle of Times Square, right across from the famed Paramount Theater, was a Big Apple anomaly: an out-of-town newsstand. I stopped and noticed that among the many cities represented, the stand featured the *Globe and Mail* from Toronto; and for only a quarter. I purchased the paper, turned to the sports section, and was thrilled to see not one, not two, but three stories about my Leafs. A day later I bought a subscription and soon received the *Globe* in the mail every day.

After devouring stories by the likes of Jim Vipond and columns by Jim Coleman, I pasted the pieces into my scrapbook; now I was *really* loving my Leafs. What a parlay; and with them en route to the first of three straight Stanley Cups — four out of five years — I followed them just like any kid in Etobicoke, Saskatoon, or Medicine Hat.

My idols were manager Conn Smythe, coach Hap Day, and players such as Ted ("Teeder") Kennedy, "Wild Bill" Ezinicki, Max Bentley, and Howie Meeker. Oh, I could go on and on with the names! To this day I could reel off the jersey numbers of the 1946–47 squad that upset Montreal in the Final. But most of all, I loved Bashin' Bill Barilko, the hardest hitter, and the guy who scored the Cup-winner in 1951. When Barilko and his buddy, Dr. Henry Hudson, disappeared after taking off in a plane for a fishing trip in northern Ontario near the end of that summer, I was crushed beyond all reason. And when a fellow named Hugh Bolton replaced Bashin' Bill on the blue line; that was more than I could take. I joined the Rangers Fan Club.

But deep down, my love for the Leafs — the Gashouse Gang of the 1930s before and Punch Imlach's troops later — never abated, nor did my appetite for reading more and more about those fellows wearing the royal blue and white.

That explains why I am so delighted that my journalistic pal, Eric Zweig, has produced this magnificent, insightful, and all-encompassing oral history of the Leafs I so much loved. To put it simply — and historically — the moment I began turning these pages, I felt precisely the same thrill as when I heard Foster Hewitt shriek *He Shoots! He Scores!!* on a big Don Metz goal in that classic 1942 playoff comeback.

Eric Zweig wrote — and he scored!

Stan Fischler
New York, New York
July 2017

Introduction

I grew up in Toronto and attended my first NHL game when I was seven years old. The date was December 30, 1970. It was a Wednesday night during the Christmas holidays. The Maple Leafs always seemed to play at home on Wednesdays and Saturdays when I was a kid. This night, they were playing the California Golden Seals. The Leafs won the game 3–1.

I'm sure it's no coincidence that all the players who would become my early hockey heroes did something good for the Leafs that night. Dave Keon scored just 33 seconds after the opening face-off. Garry Monahan (who autographed my cast when I broke my arm in the summer of 1973) got the second. Norm Ullman set up Paul Henderson for the third. But goalie Jacques Plante became my favourite of them all. The *Toronto Star* reported that Plante was "excellent" that night. That's certainly the way I remember it. "Plante had his moments …" said the *Star*, "and the youngsters in attendance because of the school holidays rocked the Gardens with their applause."

I was one of those youngsters!

My father took me to the game that night. My parents were both sports fans. So were all my cousins, aunts and uncles. It was easy for my brothers and me to become big fans, and we certainly did.

I remember being at another game with my father many years later. He looked up at the Stanley Cup banners hanging from the rafters and said, "No wonder I loved this team so much!" The Leafs had won the Cup the year my father turned seven in 1945, and then won it again in 1947, 1948, 1949, and

1951. Five championships in a seven-year span. By the time he turned 29 in 1967, they'd added four more. He didn't live long enough to see another.

I was alive for the Leafs' Stanley Cup victories in 1964 and 1967, but was too young to remember them. For me, hockey began the night of that first game with my father. To me, Jacques Plante *was* a Maple Leaf. I had no idea yet about his long and successful history in Montreal. Ullman and Henderson (who'd only been acquired by Toronto two years earlier) were, to me, every bit the Maple Leafs that Dave Keon was. On the other hand, Frank Mahovlich, who I would watch win the Stanley Cup on TV with Montreal in the spring of 1971, *was* a Canadien. In my mind, Montreal rookie Ken Dryden was a contemporary of Jacques Plante, while — when I finally learned of them — true contemporaries such as Terry Sawchuk (who had died just a few months before my first game) or Johnny Bower (who'd retired at about the same time) would seem as old to me as Georges Vezina or any other legendary name out of the past.

I loved the 1970s Toronto Maple Leafs — Darryl Sittler, Lanny McDonald, Borje Salming, Mike Palmateer — but unlike my father, as I grew up, the team got worse. Perhaps that's why I began to fall in love with their history. By the time Pat Burns, and then Pat Quinn, presided over the much-improved Leafs teams of the 1990s and early 2000s, I'd begun writing books about hockey history for adults and children, and was working with the small publishing company that produces the annual *NHL Official Guide & Record Book*.

Now, with strong new management and a host of young stars led by Auston Matthews and Mitch Marner, this book comes out as the Leafs may *finally* be poised for a return to greatness. It might still be a few years off, but at least it seems like there's reason to hope. I'd say the odds of Toronto winning the Stanley Cup five times in a seven-year stretch anytime soon probably aren't very good, but I'm guessing that most Leafs fans will settle for finally getting that first victory since 1967.

Here's hoping!

1917 to 1926:
The Arenas and St. Pats

1917–18

During the winter of 1916–17, Canadian soldiers were completing a second full year of fighting on the fields of Europe during the First World War. Canadian citizens were increasingly questioning why some fit young men were giving their lives overseas while others were being paid to play sports at home. Many amateur leagues suspended operations for the duration of the hostilities, and even though professional hockey was thought to be good for morale on the home front, attendance was dropping and teams were beginning to fold.

For the 1916–17 season of the National Hockey Association (NHA), a team of hockey-playing soldiers from the 228th Battalion was admitted to the league. Though based in northern Ontario, the team played out of the Arena Gardens (later the Mutual Street Arena) in Toronto. The soldiers did well on the ice and helped boost the box office takings in the cities they visited. When the Battalion was unexpectedly called overseas in February, however, the NHA had a real problem.

The 228th shared the Toronto market that winter with the hometown Blueshirts. At the time, it was considered important that there be two teams in Toronto to help make the long road trips by train from Montreal, Quebec City, and Ottawa worthwhile. Blueshirts owner Eddie Livingstone had never been popular among his fellow NHA owners. Faced with the loss of the 228th Battalion, the league decided to abandon Toronto entirely and play out the season with just four teams: the Montreal Canadiens, the Montreal Wanderers, the Ottawa Senators, and the Quebec Bulldogs. Livingstone's Blueshirt players were scattered among those four teams to help bolster their rosters.

Come the fall of 1917, the NHA was in serious trouble. During a series of meetings that November, the organization suspended operations.

Before the meetings got underway, the *Toronto Daily Star* reported on November 10:

> The NHA meeting will be held in Montreal to-night, and the upshot of the whole professional hockey tangle will be a four-club league, with Ottawa, Canadiens, Wanderers, and Toronto on the circuit.
>
> The Toronto Arena directors have purchased the Toronto franchise, and all players will go with the purchase. Quebec will drop out and a four-team league will be in vogue.
>
> The deal was closed yesterday, and the Toronto directors immediately wired Charlie Querrie, the Tecumseh lacrosse star and manager, asking him if he would undertake to manage the hockey club. Querrie replied that he would be willing to manage the club if given absolute control of the players and all matters pertaining to the playing end of the club.

Two days later, Elmer Ferguson of the *Montreal Herald and Telegraph*, wrote, "Canadiens, Wanderers, Ottawa, and either Toronto or Quebec will form [a] new league, although officials of the NHA today made solemn assertions that they knew nothing about it — their fingers probably being crossed at the time, however.

"It leaks out from Saturday night's meeting that the condition of Quebec is a trifle shaky…. On the other hand, with Eddie Livingstone out of any new league, there would be no further objection to the entry of a Toronto team."

Reports and rumours ran rampant in the weeks to come.

> "The management of the Toronto club has been offered to Charlie Querrie, who has not as yet made any definite arrangements regarding taking over the team, but it is probable that he will assume control as soon as the situation is cleared up….
>
> The proposed formation of the new league will likely stand in abeyance in view of the decision of Quebec to drop out…. Prospects for the new league, no matter what its composition, are not bright."
>
> — *Toronto Daily Star*, November 17, 1917

"The successor to the NHA will likely be known as the National Hockey League instead of the Eastern Hockey League. The former name is favoured and it is understood that the substitution of the league for association will overcome any legal difficulties that may arise from the similarity of the names."

— Tommy Gorman, *Ottawa Citizen*, November 20, 1917

"There seems to be a feeling that Quebec is 'stalling' for better terms and certain men, in connection with the pro hockey situation.... This is all to be decided at the meeting to be held Thursday or Friday, with the understanding that Toronto is still ready to plank in a new team.... If Quebec finally decides to drop out Toronto will get a franchise to make up the four-team schedule. That much seems certain at any rate."

— *Ottawa Journal*, November 21, 1917

The NHA would soon be replaced by the National Hockey League (NHL), but until the end of the meetings, which began on November 22 and concluded on November 26, it remained unclear whether or not Toronto would be included in the new league.

"During the past two or three weeks, there have been rumours and denials galore regarding the Quebec Club's hockey intentions this winter, but on the eve of the gathering of NHA clubs in Montreal tonight word, which can almost be taken as official, came from the Royal City to the affect that Quebec had definitely decided to suspend operations this winter.... Of course it is understood that with Quebec dropping out, the Toronto Arena Company will be given a franchise."

— *Ottawa Journal*, November 22, 1917

"Quebec Club Is Still Stalling/Nothing Done At Last Night's Hockey Meeting./Bulldogs Given Until Saturday to Decide Intentions."

— *Ottawa Journal* headline, November 23, 1917

"The pro hockey clubs will meet in Montreal again tonight, and it is confidently expected that the tangle, which now exists regarding the make up of the league for this season, will be straightened out. The Quebec owners, though they have been given every chance to make up their mind about operating this winter, are expected to drop out."

— *Ottawa Journal*, November 24, 1917

"The new senior professional hockey body to take the place of the National Hockey Association will come officially into existence this afternoon with a four-club schedule of two matches a week, the *Star* says. The new National Hockey League will be composed of Ottawa, Canadiens, Wanderers, and Toronto."

— *Montreal Star* story reported in *Ottawa Journal,* November 26, 1917

On November 26, the *Globe* announced: "The professional hockey league tangle was finally straightened out this afternoon at a conference of the clubs interested, when the National Hockey League, to take the place of the National Hockey Association of Canada, now suspended, came into existence.

"The five clubs which operated in the old body are represented in the new, but only four will operate this season. These four are Ottawa, Toronto, Wanderers, and Canadiens of Montreal. The Quebec club retains its place on the directorate of the new body."

In the days that followed, there was much stir about the new league. The *Toronto Daily Star* wrote on November 27:

> The inauguration of the new organization is a revival of the National Hockey Association, under the name of the National Hockey League, and was apparently a move to bring about a change in the ownership and management of the Toronto club more than anything else....
>
> The Wanderers, who are the weakest club in the league, on last season's form, have been given their choice to strengthen them up. Toronto is well supplied with players, while Ottawa have signed the majority of their men up, and Canadiens are in as good a position as a year ago. The only man they will lose will be Reg Noble, who played with them after the Toronto club was suspended, and afterwards reverted back to the Toronto club....
>
> All the players that wore the blue and white uniform last year will again be with the Toronto club. It is expected that the team will get down [to practising] about December 3.

Who's In Charge?

"While Ottawa and Canadiens may appear to shade the Torontos and Wanderers a trifle, still on the whole the four teams, on a paper at least, look to be pretty evenly matched, and the great battle for the championship should be in order from the first game.... Toronto will be a hard team to beat. Jimmy Murphy will have all of last season's outfit and some new ones. They are all youngsters and have speed and ginger to burn."

— Ottawa Journal, November 27, 1917

"Toronto is assured of good hockey if either 'Jimmy' Murphy or Charlie Querrie is at the helm. Today it looks as if Mr. Murphy had the call, as he is in Montreal for a final conference. Jimmy has been a national figure in sports for years. As a lacrosse player he had few equals and later he managed Toronto Lacrosse club when they won several championships."

— Toronto Daily Star, November 27, 1917

"After a meeting with the [Montreal] owners of stock in the Toronto Arena, James J. Murphy, the well-known lacrosse manager, has decided to accept the position of manager of the Toronto professional hockey team for this winter."

— Globe, Toronto, November 30, 1917

But the good news didn't last long.

"The Toronto Hockey Club is certainly having a stormy passage this fall.... [N]ow they are without a manager. As the schedule announces the opening game two weeks from tomorrow night, the club will soon have to get straightened away if they want to cut any figure in the race.... In the meantime, the extent of Jimmy Murphy's injury cannot be ascertained."

— Mail and Empire, Toronto, December 4, 1917

"I have not yet received notice that Mr. Murphy wished to resign. All I know I have read in the newspapers. Apparently, Mr. Murphy's illness is not of a serious nor permanent nature, and with contracts mailed out to all the players, I do not think there is any necessity to go casting about for a new manager just yet."

— A.G. Brooke Claxton, Toronto Arena executive, December 4, 1917

"James A. Murphy has definitely decided that he will not manage the Toronto Hockey Club, no matter what happens. The managers of the club are in a quandary as to who to secure. Charlie Querrie, who was named as a likely man, has also refused to accept the position...."

— Ottawa Journal, December 5, 1917

"I've got a new job."

— Charlie Querrie to reporters from the *Globe*, Toronto, December 5, 1917

"Querrie's decision to accept the appointment followed a short conference with Mr. A.C.B. Claxton, KC, of Montreal, representing the directors of the Toronto Hockey Club last night. Jimmy Murphy, who was expected to handle the local pro team this season, suffered an injury on Saturday that forced his retirement for this winter....

"Mr. Querrie has been in charge of the hockey at the Arena since it opened. He not only knows the game from A to Z, but he is familiar with all the angles in connection with it, and is very popular with the players ... 'Dick' Carroll, who has been connected with the Torontos for several seasons, has been appointed assistant manager. He, too, is well-liked by the Blue Shirt squad. Querrie will have a free hand in the running of the team and has called the first practice for five o'clock this afternoon."

— *Toronto Daily Star,* December 6, 1917

Building a Team

On December 7, 1917, the *Ottawa Journal* printed the following:

> Art Ross is trying out a number of amateur net guardians this season in the hopes that he may be successful in discovering or developing one of some class for his Wanderers. He may be lucky and then again he may not. If he is, his capture will be the first by an eastern pro hockey club in recent years. In fact, there hasn't been [a] high class goal tender developed since Clint Benedict of the Ottawas was tossed into the ring for inspection.
>
> For instance, Georges Vezina has been with Canadiens since professional hockey started. He is as good as ever today. At least he was when the 1916–17 season closed.
>
> Bert Lindsay, at present the only experienced net guardian in sight for the [Wanderers], has seen a dozen years of service. He has become very unsteady....
>
> Clint Benedict, the Ottawa star ... ranks with Vezina as the best in the east....
>
> Sammy Hebert subbed for Percy LeSueuer on the Ottawa team before Benedict broke in. Then he also subbed for Benny as well as playing for the Ontarios. He has been

playing for some time now but is just fair at his best. He will be with Toronto this year.

The same club will have [Art] Brooks, who showed very little the few games he played in last season. He ducks at the high ones.

The *Toronto Daily Star* reported on the first practice of Toronto's new team, December 7, 1917.

The Toronto pros had their initial workout at the Arena last night, and the players electrified the rail-birds with their speed. A good crowd gathered to see the boys in action, and they kept up the dizzy pace throughout the hour.

Brooks of last year's team and Wright, an Edmonton product, occupied the nets. In front of Brooks, "Ken" Randall and Jerry Coughlin formed the defence. Reg Noble, Corbett Denneny and Harry Meeking worked on the forward line along with Jack Marks, the Quebec right wing.

The players really displayed midseason form. The improvement of Meeking and Coughlin over last season was most noticeable. Noble's skates were giving him trouble, and he was unable to get into his stride as well as usual. Randall and Denneny had all their accustomed speed and pepper.

Brooks in the nets looked as good as ever. Wright will have to improve in order to make good in fast company as a goalkeeper. Hebert, [Alf] Skinner and [Harry] Cameron were among the missing.

Skinner announced that he has not come to terms with the new management as yet, and does not care to give up his position at present for hockey. He will no doubt be in line before long. Harry Cameron is in the same position as Skinner. He is still at his home in Pembroke, but is expected by Manager Querrie to report at any time.

The arrival of big [Harry] Mummery is awaited with interest by the other players who are greatly pleased at his joining the Torontos. He is a very effective player defensively and the locals can use him to good advantage.

Three days later, the *Daily Star* wrote:

> The chances are that Ken Randall, the defence player, will captain the Toronto professional hockey team this season. He has not been named yet, and manager Charlie Querrie refuses to confirm or deny the story that Randall is to lead the Blue Shirts.... If Querrie selects Randall he will have a good sane leader. The Lindsay boy is quiet and game, popular with his comrades, and he has plenty of experience. He has proven his "never-say-die" spirit in some pretty tough games in Montreal and Quebec, and if he only has the faculty of shooting the same spirit into his team mates he will make a good leader.

Charlie Querrie's "Wise Words to His Pro. Players" appeared in the *Toronto Daily Star* on December 13.

1. First and foremost, don't forget that I am running this club. It won't do you any good to tell your troubles to the public and the other players. If you have a grievance, tell it to me.
2. When practice is called at a certain hour, be there. If you are late we want to know why, and even then the "why" isn't an excuse.
3. You are being paid to give your best services to the club. Condition depends a lot on how you behave off the ice.
4. Remember that it does not require bravery to hit another man over the head with a stick. If you want to fight go over to France.
5. Time spent in the penalty box is time wasted. You are not expected to take all abuse without going back at your opponent, but do not be foolish.
6. Remember that there are generally five other players on a team with you. You are not expected to play the whole game.
7. You are not out on the ice to score all the goals. Combination with the rest of the players will probably result in more goals than individual play.
8. You will not be fined for doing the best you can. You will be punished for indifferent work or carelessness. If you are anxious to win all the time you will be a good player. Indifference or lack of "pepper" is one thing we never did like.

9. Remember it means as much to you to win the champion-
    ship as it does to me. If you do not play as well as you can
    you are not only hurting yourself, but the rest of the team
    and your supporters.

10. Do not think that you are putting something over on
    the manager when you do anything that you should
    not. You are getting paid to play hockey, not to be a
    good fellow.

11. If playing hockey is going to be your business in the win-
    ter remember that the wise man attends to his business
    and generally gets better results. Your future in the game
    depends on how you play the game.

12. It is the public who pay your salary. Show them the best
    you can and your chances of better financial results in the
    future will be good.

13. Don't always imagine you are getting the worst of it from
    the officials. Play hockey and they will see you secure an
    even break.

14. Don't knock your fellow players. Remember they might
    also have a hammer concealed somewhere and might be
    tempted to use it.

15. Play hockey, attend practices regularly, take care of
    your condition and you will not suffer any penalties.
    Remember the first paragraph and be sure to tell your
    troubles to me; I am an easy boss if you do your share. If
    you do not want to be on the square and play the hockey
    you are capable of, turn your uniform in to Dick Carroll
    and go at some other work.

They were ready to go.

The First Game

"Tomorrow night the National Hockey League brings up the curtain on
an expectant public in two cities. Canadiens, last season's champs, play
Ottawa at the local Arena, while the Torontos, under new management,
go to Montreal to meet Wanderers."

— *Ottawa Journal*, December 18, 1917

"The unexpected certainly happened last night in the National Hockey League. Toronto looked good enough to step into Montreal and beat Wanderers handily, but they didn't…. Bad goalkeeping certainly defeated Torontos in Montreal…. Surely Hebert and Brookes [*sic*] have rid their systems of about all the bad work they have in stock. They surely can never be quite as bad again."

— *Toronto Daily Star*, December 20, 1917

"Wanderers beat the Toronto Blue Shirts 10 to 9 in the opening game of the National Hockey League series last night, but if there had been a few minutes more to go, the result might easily have read the other way about, for Wanderers were fading toward the end, while the Blue Shirts, with youth in their favour, were smashing through the defences in a last effort to snatch victory out of defeat…."

— *Toronto Daily Star*, December 20, 1917

"I guess we looked pretty bad in the opener…. Our goal-tending was poor … [Wanderers] must have worn themselves out in that 10–9 contest, for they didn't finish the season."

— Charlie Querrie to Vern DeGeer, *Globe and Mail*,
Toronto, February 4, 1944

A Need in the Net

"Charlie Querrie and his Toronto pros make their debut to the [home] fans tomorrow night at the Arena. Eddie Gerard and his Ottawa team will be the Blue Shirts' opponents and the battle should be a hummer. The Senators always play fast hockey here. Manager Querrie thinks his team is the best in the league and if they get a fair article of goal-tending they should turn in a victory."

— *Toronto World*, December 21, 1917

"Sammy Hebert and Brookes [*sic*], the Toronto goalkeepers, say that they rid themselves of all the bad goalkeeping they had in their systems on Wednesday night at [Montreal]. If they did, the blue shirts will give Ottawa a lacing in the pro-league opener at the Arena tonight. Both boys were going nicely in practice yesterday…."

— *Toronto Daily Star*, December 22, 1917

"The Torontos made a most favourable impression in their opening NHL game at the Arena on Saturday night, when they administered a decisive trouncing to the Ottawas. The final count was 11 to 4.... The much-discussed weakness expected in the Toronto nets was not in evidence. Although four counters were registered against him, Brooks played a cool, collected game throughout."

— *Toronto Daily Star*, December 24, 1917

Toronto beat Georges Vezina and the Canadiens 7–5 in their next home game on December 26, but then lost 9–2 to the Canadiens in Montreal on January 29.

Toronto switched to Sammy Hebert for their next game and defeated the Senators 6–5 in Ottawa on January 2, but by then newspapers had been reporting for several days that Querrie was after a former Blueshirts 1914 Stanley Cup–winner and future Hall-of-Famer to replace Brooks and Hebert in net.

Hunting for Harry "Hap" Holmes

"Just who will occupy the nets for Charlie Querrie's Torontos tonight when they face the champion Canadiens is problematical. Brooks, who did so well on Saturday night, looks like the choice again tonight, but there is a chance that Harry Holmes, the old Toronto boy, who has been playing on the [West] coast, will be between the posts.... He wants to play with the Torontos, and so sought Manager Querrie. Querrie was cautious, and wired [Pacific Coast Hockey Association president] Frank Patrick for permission to use Holmes, but up to noon had not received any reply. He was in consultation with Holmes this morning, but because of the peculiar angle which has cropped up in the game he refused to make any announcement of the result. The 'joker' in the game is a wire from Sammy Lichtenhein, president of the Wanderers [who claimed he held the goaltender's NHL rights], offering to trade Holmes for Reg Noble. 'How can Lichtenhein trade a man he doesn't own?' asks both Querrie and Holmes. It's a cinch the Wanderer club will not get Noble, and Holmes says he doesn't want to play in Montreal."

— *Toronto Daily Star*, December 26, 1917

"A telegram to Lichtenhein elicited the information that he would waive all claim on Holmes if Querrie would let him have Reg Noble, the Blueshirts' star forward. Naturally Querrie cannot begin to see any such proposition.

"It is an involved affair and means that Toronto will, in all probability, be without the services of Holmes and that, although 'Sammy' cannot use him, the star goalkeeper is not in a position to sell his services without first consulting the eastern magnate. And Holmes is now wondering whether the term 'free agent' is not a choice bit of satire."

— *Globe*, Toronto, December 27, 1917

"If the Torontos had Harry Holmes they would just about clean up."

— *Toronto Daily Star*, December 27, 1917

On January 2, 1918, a fire destroyed the Montreal Arena in Westmount. The Canadiens moved across town to the Jubilee Rink in the east (French) part of the city. The Wanderers chose to drop out of the NHL, and the league completed the season with just three teams.

"The Wanderers are out…. This means that only Torontos, Canadiens and Ottawa are left and that the schedule will be rearranged. The blue shirts will get Harry Holmes and will be strengthened in their only weak spot."

— *Toronto World*, January 4, 1918

Hap Holmes gave Toronto the top-quality goaltending the team needed to contend with Montreal and Ottawa. Still, in the first half of the split-season schedule, the Canadiens took top spot with a record of 10–4–0 ahead of Toronto at 8–6–0. Ottawa (5–9–0) finished in third. In the second half, Toronto finished on top in a close race after posting a record of 5–3–0 to Ottawa's 4–4–0. Montreal fell to last place at 3–5–0.

1918 NHL Playoffs

The playoffs pit the winner from the first half of the season against winners of the second. Toronto faced Montreal in a two-game, total-goals affair on March 11 and March 13, 1918.

"The hockey week here opens tonight with the first of the NHL playoff series between Torontos and Canadiens. The Blue Shirts, with the exception of Reg Noble, are in excellent shape for the final struggle, and are confident that they will take a three- or four-goal lead to Montreal with them for the final game on Wednesday night. Noble has a bad knee, the result of a collision with Crawford at Ottawa. Total goals count in this series. The Montreal team came in today at full strength. Joe Malone and Didier Pitre, who were absentees at the last game, are both with the team, and tonight's struggle will be a red-hot one from gong to gong."

— *Toronto Daily Star*, March 11, 1918

The acquisition of Hap Holmes gave Toronto the goaltending it needed to compete with Ottawa and Montreal during the NHL's first season. Holmes spent the early part of his career in Toronto but mainly played in rival leagues out west before returning to the NHL from 1926 to 1928 with the Detroit Cougars (who later became the Red Wings).

Toronto handily won the opening game 7–3. Both teams then hit the road, travelling to Montreal for Game 2 on March 13.

"It is a fortunate thing, indeed, for Les Bons Canadiens that both matches of the NHL playoff series do not take place in Toronto.

"You'd never know the old club from its play on Toronto ice last night, compared with its dash and brilliance in games played before the friendly faces at Jubilee Rink. And, by the same token, you'd never recognize the meek and inoffensive team wearing the blue shirts which we've been accustomed to seeing in the rampaging, aggressive and chip-on-the-shoulder gang which rode roughshod over our habitants last night. Canadiens were outskated, outplayed and outguessed from the start."

— Elmer Ferguson, *Montreal Herald*, March 12, 1918

"A fall in the temperature here this morning made the chances of Toronto winning the championship of the NHL from Canadiens tonight look good, according to hockey experts. Last night a thaw set in, which made the ice at the Jubilee Rink like a mud-pile. The Canadien management believed these conditions would be distinctly to the advantage of the French team, which is the heavier. This morning's change in the weather reversed conditions.

"The Toronto team reached here this morning and were reported by Charlie Querrie to be all in good shape.... The betting was 2 to 1 in favour of Toronto winning the series and even money on tonight's game."

— *Toronto Daily Star*, March 13, 1918

"We figure that a strong offence is the best defence, and will go right out tonight and try to increase our lead on Canadiens. We won't try any three- or four-man defence, but will pitch in to get more goals. I don't look for a particularly rough game. It is true we checked up [Bert] Corbeau and [Joe] Malone hard at Toronto, but that was part of our plan of campaign, and we did not try to cut them down, or anything like that. We aimed to slow them up by straight bodychecking and I think we accomplished that. We will play the same style of game tonight. I don't think there's a chance in the world that Canadiens will overcome our four-goal lead."

— Charlie Querrie, *Toronto Daily Star*, March 13, 1918

"Montreal, March 13 — Torontos tonight won the championship of the NHL and the right to play the Pacific Coast League champions for the Stanley Cup when the Canadiens failed to wipe out the four-goal lead which the Queen City team secured on their own ice in the first of the home-and-home games Monday night. Canadiens won tonight's match by 4 to 3, leaving the complete score for the series Torontos 10, Canadiens 7.... The game was rough, with the Canadiens contributing most of the penalty list."

— *Globe*, Toronto, March 14, 1918

"It was only after one of the greatest exhibitions of gameness ever witnessed on a hockey arena that the Torontos are today wearing the NHL championship crown of honour....

"The attraction was billed as a championship hockey fixture with Torontos and Canadiens as the contestants, but the public who paid good money with the expectation of witnessing a hockey game were victimized, and should commence legal proceedings against the promoters for obtaining money under false pretences....

"Bullfighting is prohibited in Canada for the reason that it is considered brutal, but it is a regular 'pink tea' in comparison with what the Donnybrook served up to the fans at the Jubilee Ice Palace last night...."

     — Harvey Sproule, *Toronto Daily Star*, March 14, 1918

"Gameness, matchless gameness, has made the Toronto hockey team champions of the National Hockey [League]. The Blues stood up under one of the most gruelling, rasping, thrashings ever handed out to any hockey club. Battered, smashed, and cut, they refused to quit under the drive. For the entire first period, Canadiens hammered and battered these game youngsters, put Randall out of the game for keeps, cut [Jack] Adams' head to ribbons, battered [Rusty] Crawford from head to foot, sent Cameron hobbling off half through the period with one leg limp from a sweeping slash, broke the teeth of goalkeeper Holmes, knocked out Meeking and Skinner, and bumped every other opposing player on the ice — but Toronto did not quit.... It was the same system as Toronto used in their home city, but with improvements, for Canadiens made punishing play the issue in the early going and hockey the side-line, whereas the Blues presented a judicious combination of both, scoring goals as well as bumping the Habitants to a finish."

     — Elmer Ferguson, *Montreal Herald*, March 14, 1918

1918 Stanley Cup Series

In the early years of the NHL, the Stanley Cup was a battle between professional hockey's two top leagues, pitting the champions of the eastern NHL against the champions of the Pacific Coast Hockey Association (PCHA). This was a continuation of an agreement first reached between the NHA and the PCHA for the 1913–14 season.

"Vancouver hockey players are champions of the Pacific Coast today ... as a result of their win last night over the Seattle Metropolitans by a score of 1 to 0 in Seattle. The game was the second of a series of home and home games for the title, the first of which was played here on Monday night, the teams battling to a two-all draw. Vancouver won the series by 3 goals to 2....

"Today, the Millionaires leave for Toronto, where they will play Querrie's Blueshirts during the latter part of the month, defending the Stanley Cup against the eastern challengers....

"Great satisfaction was expressed by members of the team last night on Torontos winning the NHL championship. The world's series games will now be played on artificial ice, which will give the Millionaires a much better advantage than if the games were played in Montreal. The Millionaires are out to win, and if confidence counts for anything they will be world's champions as well as Coast champions after the Eastern series is over."

— *Vancouver World*, March 14, 1918

"In the forthcoming Stanley Cup series it looks a whole lot like 'summer' versus 'fall.' The Toronto team [has] youth on their side … Holmes in goal and Cameron and Randall on the defence are the only players who are over the 25-year-old mark. The Vancouver team is a long way from being so youthful. Cyclone Taylor, Hugh Lehman, Frank Patrick, and Si Griffis are a long way beyond the 25-year mark and Ran McDonald, Barney Stanley, and Speed Moynes cannot afford to give the quarter century mark anything in years. McKay and the Cooks are the youngest on the team and they have been voting for several years.... The western bunch is a clean-cut outfit and are in direct contrast to the battle-scarred champions of the NH[L]. They will step out on the ice tonight unmarked about the face, while Holmes will be sporting a beautiful black eye; Randall plasters on his forehead and chin; while Meeking, Skinner, Cameron, and Noble all have half healed cuts on their faces or heads. The condition of the two teams is an apt illustration of the difference between the kind of hockey played in the two leagues. The Blue Shirts are the Speed Kings of the NH[L], but they will have no margin of speed on the invaders unless it be toward the end when their youth and stamina may serve them and give them more speed in the dying moments. It looks right now like a tidy little series, though tonight's game may change the look of things."

— *Toronto Daily Star*, March 20, 1918

Ever since the National Hockey Association and the Pacific Coast Hockey Association (PCHA) had agreed to have their two champions meet for the Stanley Cup, the best-of-five series had rotated between a host city in the east and in the west in alternate years. The two leagues had very different rules, with the PCHA still employing a rover, but also allowing forward passing in the neutral zone while no forward passing was permitted anywhere on the ice in the NHA, or now in the NHL. League rules were alternated game by game, with the host league using its rules in games one, three, and five, and the visiting team playing under its league's rules in games two and four. No visiting team had yet to win the Stanley Cup under this arrangement. Playing under NHL rules in Game 1 on March 20, 1918, Toronto scored a 5–3 victory over Vancouver.

> "Toronto looks like a good team. Vancouver boys seemed nervous."
> — telegram from Frank Patrick to brother Lester on the morning after Game 1,
> reported in *Vancouver World*, March 21, 1918

> "Montreal, March 21 — President Calder of the NHL returned from Toronto this morning, where he witnessed the first of the Stanley Cup matches. He said the Torontos played their regular good game that they have been in the habit of playing at home this season and deserved their victory as being the best team on the ice....
>
> "He admits, however, that the Eastern rules, and the long journey from the coast, which always affects a Western team for a day or so after its arrival, were strong handicaps against Vancouver."
> — *Globe*, Toronto, March 22, 1918

Toronto did play a much rougher style of game during the Stanley Cup series, but Vancouver was able to win Game 2 (6–4) and Game 4 (8–1) under PCHA rules. Toronto won Game 3 by a score of 6–3 under NHL rules. Despite the fact that Game 5 would once again be played according to the NHL rulebook, the hometown fans were nervous.

> "The Stanley Cup is wavering in the balance, and tonight will tell the tale. Thursday night Vancouver … handed the Torontos an 8 to 1 lacing, evening up the score, two games each, so tonight's game under NHL rules will decide possession of the Cup. The Blue Shirts, of course, should have a big advantage playing the final under their own rules, but they made such a sorry showing Thursday … that the Cup challengers must be granted a whole lot more than a fighting chance to win."
> — *Toronto Daily Star*, March 30, 1918

The final game was a close one, but Toronto hung on to win 2–1. All three goals were scored in the third period.

A star of the 1918 Stanley Cup Final, Corb Denneny (left) played in the NHL with the Arenas and the St. Pats and was later back in Toronto when the St. Pats became the Maple Leafs. He's seen here with goalie John Ross Roach and Bert McCaffrey early in the 1926–27 season.

"[Corbett] Denneny, who has everything that goes to make up a star pro player but size, came through with the goal which won the Cup series for Toronto within nine minutes of the completion of an hour's play in the final game of the series at the Arena Saturday night. It was a sensational goal, in a sensational game, and to say that the crowd enthused over young Denneny is putting it mildly."

— *Toronto Daily Star*, April 1, 1918

"The surprise of the game … was the stellar work of little Corbett Denneny…. Displaying speed that was only eclipsed by [Vancouver's Mickey] McKay, and stick-handling ability that almost equalled that of the veteran [Cyclone] Taylor, Denneny was perhaps the most dangerous man on the Toronto team. Toronto's second goal, which clinched the game and the Cup, was due solely to Denneny's individual effort."

— *Globe*, Toronto, April 1, 1918

"Outside of Denneny's great work the outstanding feature was the marvellous work of Harry Holmes and Hugh Lehman, the rival goalkeepers. No better exhibition of goal-guarding has ever been seen in Toronto than this pair gave on Saturday night. They were both wizards. It was positively uncanny the way in which this pair came out and outguessed players who had penetrated the defences."

— *Toronto Daily Star*, April 1, 1918

"Too much praise cannot be paid to Harry Holmes for his exhibition in the nets. Harry has his eye on everything and he made many startling saves. The only score against him was one from close range, on which it was impossible to beat Taylor. His net guarding was one of the strongest points of the Toronto defence, and it certainly went more than half way in winning the honours."

— *Vancouver World*, April 1, 1918

"Today top salary for any player in the National Hockey League is $7,000, yet Charlie Querrie recalls that in 1918 the Toronto Arenas won the championship and the Stanley Cup, and the owners distributed less than that amount to nine puck-chasers. Harry Holmes got $700, Harry Cameron, $900, Harry Mummery, $600, Ken Randall, $450, Reg Noble, $750, 'Rusty' Crawford, $500, and Corbett Denneny, $550."

— Mike Rodden, *Globe and Mail*, January 13, 1937

"In 1917, the local professional club was handed to me by the directors, and with a team called Arenas won the Stanley Cup, much to everyone's surprise, including my own."

— Charlie Querrie to Jim Fitzgerald, *Toronto Telegram*,
reported in *Montreal Gazette*, February 24, 1944

1918–19

The lead-up to the NHL's second season was almost as confusing as the first, and once again Toronto was at the forefront of the troubles.

The first season had been a financial success in Toronto, and Eddie Livingstone wanted his share of the profits. When the management of the Arena Gardens refused to pay what Livingstone thought was fair, he launched a lawsuit, which dragged on as summer turned to fall.

More Trouble Behind the Scenes

"The annual talk of freezing Eddie Livingstone and his Toronto Club out of the [NHL] is rampant, according to a despatch supposed to be from Montreal. Charlie Querrie, manager of the Arena, was down in Montreal this week talking hockey, and the upshot was the divulgence of a scheme for a three-club league — Ottawa, Montreal Canadiens, and Toronto — with Percy Quinn's newly purchased Quebec team as the Toronto representative … Querrie says that the Arena has made no arrangements to operate any professional team or to give any pro team terms. He says the Quebec franchise may be owned by Livingstone for all he knows. The chances are, according to Querrie, that the Arena people will get a franchise in the NHL, as they did last year, and operate a team."

— *Toronto Daily Star*, September 6, 1918

Livingstone, meanwhile, was anxious to get his team back, and return to play in a restored NHA, which would hold a meeting in Montreal on September 28 — despite the fact that the representatives from the Canadiens, Wanderers, and Ottawa Senators were all now owners in the NHL.

"Professional hockey's annual harangue has commenced. The professional game finished last season in the courts, and it starts the campaign of 1918–19 with the commencement of further litigation. The NHA decided last Saturday to suspend and the NHL has not yet decided to operate. The teams have not as yet secured rink accommodations. There may or may not be professional hockey this season, but, of course, that is no obstacle to the litigants. It seems that there can be litigation without pro hockey, but little pro hockey without litigation...."

— *Globe*, Toronto, October 2, 1918

"Montreal, Oct. 3. — Charlie Querrie, Manager of the Toronto Arena, was in Montreal this afternoon in conference with the directors, who are all local men. When seen tonight Querrie disclosed some facts regarding the professional hockey situation in Toronto. In speaking of the suit alleged to have been instituted by the Toronto Hockey Club against the Arena Company, Querrie stated that the Arena company intended fighting the suit instituted by the same club in which it claims $20,000 as its share of profits of the Toronto Arena Hockey Club of last season....

"It has developed that when the National Hockey Association suspended operations a year ago all players were declared free agents and that when the Torontos leased players to the Toronto Arena Hockey Club they did not own them. This will be offered by the Arena Company in defence of the suit and their not paying the amount claimed. According to Querrie, the Toronto club was tendered a cheque at the close of the season for $6,900 and refused to take it, demanding $20,000....

"It is now likely that the National Hockey League will comprise four teams next winter, two in Toronto, with one in Montreal and the other in Ottawa. [Toronto native] Percy Quinn, by his purchase of the Quebec club, holds a franchise in the league with Ottawa and Canadiens, while it is likely that the Arena Company will be given a franchise again this winter."

— *Globe*, Toronto, October 4, 1918

The situation soon got even more confusing, with reports that Eddie Livingstone's Torontos and a team called the Shamrocks — the new name Percy Quinn had given to the Quebec club he'd purchased — were going to form a new professional league to be known as the Canadian Hockey Association, and had offered contracts to Montreal Canadiens star Newsy Lalonde and other NHL players.

NHL President Frank Calder and Canadiens president/owner/manager George Kennedy were in Toronto on October 8, 1918, and were quoted (Kennedy in particular) at length in the *Toronto Star* that day.

"The National Hockey League will operate this winter and it will have teams in Montreal, Ottawa and Toronto."

— Frank Calder

"Yes, and maybe two in Toronto."

— George Kennedy

"Let me tell you the situation: The NHL will operate this year with my team in Montreal, the Ottawa team in Ottawa ... and the Arena team here. If Percy Quinn cuts loose from E.J. Livingstone and shows us that he is free, he may be allowed, by the NHL, to transfer his franchise from Quebec to Toronto.... We would like to see a second team in Toronto and, for my part, I would welcome Percy Quinn."

— George Kennedy

"The Toronto Club and E.J. Livingstone do not contest a single player. Randall, Meeking, Skinner, Denneny, and Noble, the players he rented to the Arena Company last fall, were not his property at all. That is why the Arena people refuse to settle with him, hence his $20,000 suit. He agreed to rent them players he did not own. The NHA, which suspended that year, declared all players free agents, and the Arena people were free to hire them, irrespective of E.J. Livingstone or his club. The Arena people have a franchise in the NHL now and they own these players for this season unless they throw up the franchise."

— George Kennedy

It may well have been untrue that Livingstone did not have a claim on the Toronto players he provided to the Arena Company. When his suit was finally settled in 1923, he was originally awarded $100,000, which was later reduced to $10,000 on appeal.

In the meantime, it was still unclear who, if anyone, might operate a team in Toronto — and in what league — in 1918–19.

"Rumours and more rumours seem to be the situation with regard to professional hockey, but as far as the Arena is concerned, we have heard nothing in connection with the Canadian Hockey Association, or the National Hockey League, with the exception that Percy Quinn of the Shamrock Hockey Club applied for ice a couple of weeks ago.

"The Arena Gardens hold a franchise in the [NHL] until the next meeting, when they will return it to the league in compliance with their agreement of last year; and furthermore, I wish to state that the Arena will have no connection with any team during the coming winter outside of renting ice privileges. We will not rent ice to anyone for professional hockey until they show us a league which will provide good hockey, and in this connection it might be just as well to point out that last season the [NHL] provided the best season of hockey that the fans have enjoyed for many years, and if they operate again they will naturally receive the first consideration from the Arena officials."

— Charlie Querrie, *Toronto Daily Star*, October 10, 1918

"The annual meeting of the National Hockey League, which replaced the National Hockey Association last winter, will be held at the Windsor Hotel this afternoon, when the hockey situation may be straightened out. This at present is only a two-club league, Canadiens and Ottawa, as Wanderers forfeited their franchise a year ago, when they withdrew without finishing out their season, and the Toronto Arena Company was given a franchise for last winter only, according to Charlie Querrie, who managed the team and won the championship with it.

"When in town a short time ago, Querrie stated that the Arena Company might be given a franchise again this season … [but] so far as known, nothing definite regarding the hockey season has been done."

— *Montreal Gazette*, October 19, 1918

"Dear Sir:

We hereby make application for franchise rights to become a member and partner of the National Hockey League on terms to be mutually agreed upon.

Yours truly,

Toronto Arena Hockey Club
H. Vearncombe,
CEO, Treasurer"

> — *Minute Book of National Hockey League*, November 22, 1917,
> to November 7, 1925, Hockey Hall of Fame Collection, Toronto

"As a result of the annual meeting … a three-club schedule is assured for this season, and there is every likelihood that four clubs will compete for professional hockey honours during the coming year....

"Owing to the influenza epidemic, only three delegates attended the meeting, which adopted reports from last season and ratified the transfer of the Quebec franchise to Percy Quinn, of Toronto.

"The Quebec club, although it did not operate last winter, retained a franchise in the [NHL], and, with the sale of the club, the franchise goes to Percy Quinn, of Toronto, who has changed the name of the club to that of the Shamrocks.

"Whether Percy Quinn will operate the franchise in the [NHL] is still a problem, but it is likely that with no other league in sight, that there will be two teams in Toronto this winter, one to be operated by the Toronto Arena Company, who won the title last season and the other by the Shamrock Club....

"Charles Querrie, of the Toronto Arena Company, was one of the delegates at the meeting, and made formal application for a franchise this season, and was granted it which is an assurance of three teams, as Ottawa and Canadiens will also operate."

> — *Montreal Gazette*, October 21, 1918

As for Livingstone …

"What [Frank] Calder said was that the Toronto Hockey Club owned and controlled its players in the National Hockey Association, but the point is this — that [NHA] suspended and declared all its players free agents. Of course E.J. Livingstone objected, but all players were nevertheless declared free agents, and the Arena club last year signed up his players for one season. These players and their contracts were turned back to the NHL, and we purchased a franchise and the right to these players for $5,000 at the meeting last Saturday. That is how we claim we own them. This point is, of course, the crux of the dispute. If our position is upheld, we own them. If it isn't, why, of course, the Toronto Hockey Club controls their services."

— Charlie Querrie, *Toronto Daily Star*, October 24, 1918

Meanwhile, the Canadian Hockey Association was still trying to get off the ground well into November. With Percy Quinn's Shamrocks still said to be a part of the new league, Eddie Livingstone was attempting to sign up players — including those from his former Toronto club — and offering to pay them even if the league failed to operate.

"Believing that the public are about tired of the so-called professional hockey wrangle, I wish to make my position in this matter public once and for all.… Last year, as the public are aware, I conducted a hockey team which won the world's championship and the championship of the [NHL]. This winter, in company with Mr. [Hubert] Vearncombe, I purchased a franchise in the [NHL] and at a meeting of the Arena directorate last Saturday we were granted exclusive rights for professional hockey in Toronto.…

"As far as Mr. Quinn is concerned, I would personally like to see him and his Shamrocks as a fourth team [in the NHL], and in answering a letter from the Canadian Hockey Association refusing them ice privileges for professional hockey it was only what I was instructed to do by the Arena directors.…

"The Arena is in the hockey business to provide the best of hockey for the fans, and feel sure that the public were satisfied a year ago. There is nothing personal in my position as Manager of the Arena in regard to the matter of renting ice to anyone, but surely there is no one who could expect me to grant privileges that had already been contracted for."

— Charlie Querrie, *Globe*, Toronto, November 15, 1918

As it became more apparent in December that the CHA would not get off the ground, and the Toronto players began signing with the Arena club and turning out for practice, Livingstone threatened injunctions against the NHL.

"Toronto Dec. 19 — The boys who are practicing with the Arena squad have all accepted expense money and are going to stick to Charlie Querrie....

"The squad is going great guns in practice and looks like the outfit to beat in the NHL race....

"Today Eddie Livingstone of the opposition league was very wroth over the report from Montreal that President Calder had said that Percy Quinn was negotiating through a third party to get back into the league. 'Any negotiations we will have with the NHL will be in the nature of an ultimatum,' said Livingstone. 'We have them where we want them, and are going ahead with our injunctions and other legal proceedings.'"

— *Ottawa Journal*, December 20, 1918

"The hockey public can take it from me that there will be no interference by E.J. Livingstone, or those who are associated with him, in Monday's opening professional hockey game between the Toronto team and the Canadiens of Montreal.... He may annoy us, but he cannot stop us from playing, and there will surely be a game here on Monday night."

— Charlie Querrie, *Mail and Empire*, Toronto, December 21, 1917

A Troubling Season

"According to the Toronto Hockey Club, injunctions intended to prevent the playing of the opening game of the NHL here tonight have been secured against the Arena Gardens, Messrs. Vearncombe and Querrie, and players Randall, Skinner, Meeking, Adams, Cameron, Noble, and Corbett Denneny. Some of these writs have been served....

"In spite of what has been done to prevent tonight's game between Arenas and Canadiens, the Arena management appears confident that there will be no interference. The Arenas are in better condition than the Frenchmen, and Harry Holmes, the local player, who is property of the Pacific Coast League, will be in the net, permission having been secured on Saturday for his use by the Arenas."

— *Globe*, Toronto, December 23, 1918

"E.J. Livingstone says that the chances of tonight's NHL game being played are 100 to 1. If he will wager at those odds, he will find plenty of takers....

"The general consensus of opinion is that tonight's NHL feature will be played at the Arena in spite of the insinuations of E.J. Livingstone to the contrary. No action has yet been taken which will serve to stop the game, and it will be noticed that in all his statements Livingstone has not come out flat-footed to say that he will obtain an injunction to stop tonight's game."

— *Toronto Daily Star*, December 23, 1918

The game was played as scheduled, but the result was not what Toronto had hoped for.

"Charlie Querrie won a heat and lost one last night at the Arena. He won his argument with Eddie Livingstone, inasmuch as the scheduled National Hockey League fixture was played, but his team lost the game to Canadiens by 4 to 3....

"Blue Shirts were beaten by overconfidence. They went into the fray feeling that they could win any time they wanted to, and when they went to the front in the second period, after a scoreless first period, they grew careless, and that and a little luck, plus some good old experience on the part of Canadiens, put Querrie's crew on the short end of the score."

— *Toronto Daily Star*, December 24, 1918

"Being the best skaters and puck carriers doesn't count alongside of placing that little old puck in the net."

— Arenas coach Dick Carroll, *Toronto Daily Star*, December 24, 1918

"Hockey fans did not get much of a chance to survey the new pro rules last night. About the only thing they saw of the new 40-foot [forward passing] area at centre ice was the [blue] lines. Neither team has been drilled to use it. Outside of a couple of forward passes made by either side, no real legitimate use was made of it.... The fans want to remember that a forward pass must be started and completed with both puck and player inside the 40-foot [neutral zone] area. A couple of times last night players took the puck while the latter was on the line and they were over it or came out of the area to take a pass started forward within the area. Both plays are against the new rule."

— *Toronto Daily Star*, December 24, 1918

Toronto also lost its second game of the season 5–2 at Ottawa on December 26, but the team suffered an even greater loss after the game.

"Harry Holmes, the crack goalkeeper of last year's champion Toronto Hockey Team ... was recalled to Seattle, of the Pacific Coast League, after last night's game at Ottawa. He played two games for Charlie Querrie's Arenas this season and wanted to stay here. The Patricks were willing, but the Seattle players [whose goalie, Hec Fowler, of the previous season, had yet to return from First World War military service] wanted Holmes back. Holmes will be replaced ... by Bert Lindsay."

— *Toronto Daily Star*, December 27, 1918

"Two games down, Harry Holmes going to the coast, and Harry Mummery ill with the flu! Charlie Querrie's champions are certainly in a bad way. The boys in blue will have to buckle in and play some of the real hockey they should have left [in them] and climb out of the rut."

— *Toronto Daily Star*, December 27, 1918

After losing their third-straight game of the season 6–3 in Montreal on December 27, the Arenas returned home for a New Year's Eve game against Ottawa feeling that they were already facing a must-win situation.

"The Blue-Shirted Arenas might just as well gallop down Church Street and jump into the bay if they step off the ice at the Arena tonight holding the short end of the score against Ottawa.... Manager Querrie and Coach Carroll are giving the crew one more chance and if they don't make good tonight some of the boys will walk the plank."

— *Toronto Daily Star*, December 31, 1918

"Watch those boys of mine travel tonight. They are going to show that Ottawa team and the Toronto fans just what they are capable of doing. They realize just as well as the fans do that a defeat tonight by Ottawa will make the future road a rocky one."

— Arenas coach Dick Carroll, *Toronto Daily Star*, December 31, 1918

Toronto beat Ottawa 4–2, but then suffered three straight losses again, including a trouncing in Montreal on January 11 that was either 13–3 or 13–4 depending on the reports.

"The [defending] champions were having a rough time and after six losses in seven games manager Querrie finally swung his axe. For some reason, he had been unable to accompany the team on the road and the players were having a high old time."

— Charles Coleman, *The Trail of the Stanley Cup*, Vol. 1

"Either the players are not trying to win or they are in no condition to play, possibly a combination of both. One player on the club, an athlete noted for his conscientious efforts and who invariably gives his best, is quoted as having said that three members of the team have forgotten all thoughts of training rules and routine the instant they left Toronto, and on striking a 'wet' territory had promptly made a gallant effort to drown out the memories of a long drought in Dryville. However true this may be, Toronto certainly looked anything but a championship hockey team Saturday night."

— Elmer Ferguson, reprinted in *Toronto Evening Telegram*, January 13, 1919

The *Toronto Daily Star* reported on January 14, 1919:

Players Suspended By the Arena Club:
Athletes Misbehaving, and Cameron and Noble
Have Been Penalized

There are wigs on the green in the Arena Hockey Club over the miserable showing made by the Blue Shirts at Montreal Saturday night. Charlie Querrie is scouring the country for new players and is dangling tempting offers in front of star amateur eyes endeavouring to strengthen up the team. The team's bad showing in Montreal was due to a couple of the boys breaking training rules, and [Harry] Cameron and [Reg] Noble are now under suspension as a result. Manager Querrie says that unless the team comes through with a victory tonight over Ottawa the blow-up at Messines Ridge will be like a firecracker in comparison to the explosion in the lines of the Blue Shirts.

Toronto beat Ottawa 5–2 in its next game. Noble was reinstated, but Cameron was traded to the Senators. (He would return to Toronto the following season.) The Arenas followed up with an 11–3 win in Montreal, but then lost to the Senators 3–2 on January 23. Toronto was now just 3–7–0 on the season, and the troubles of the team — both on and off the ice, and behind the scenes — was killing fan interest.

In an effort to keep Toronto in the running (and to make sure the season would end soon enough to allow for a Stanley Cup playoff with the PCHA),

NHL president Frank Calder announced a revision to the schedule, reviving the split-season format of past years. The Canadiens were declared champions of the first half with a record of 7–3–0 and awarded a spot in the playoffs. A 12-game second half of the season would begin on January 25 to determine the other playoff participant. (If Montreal won again, they would be declared league champions.)

Toronto continued to play poorly.

"It must be admitted that the source of most of the difficulty in the Toronto Arena pro team is weak goalkeeping and poor caretaking by several members of the team. The carelessness and lack of stability on the part of several players started them on the downward path but now that the combination has been broken up and the boys are behaving, weak goaltending is killing their efforts. There is no doubt in anybody's mind but that Vezina and Benedict of Canadiens and Ottawa are much superior to Lindsay, the Toronto goal guardian. Lindsay is not a poor goaltender. He is a good goal guardian, but Vezina and Benedict are stars."

— *Toronto Daily Star*, February 5, 1919

The Arenas continued to lose, and attendance got worse. After dropping a 9–3 decision to the Senators on February 20, Toronto's record fell to 2–6–0 in the second-half standings while Ottawa improved to 7–1–0. The Arenas no longer had even a mathematical chance of making the playoffs and it became clear the team did not intend to play its final four games of the season.

"Rumors that have been in circulation for the past ten days that Arenas would not finish their schedule are well-founded, and it may be that last night's game at Ottawa will be the last the locals will participate in this season."

— *Globe*, Toronto, February 21, 1919

"Developments came thick and fast in [NHL] circles last night, following the defeat of the Toronto Arenas by the Ottawa Hockey Club at the Ottawa Arena. The Senators clinched the second half of the schedule beyond all doubt and it was decided to call it a season insofar as the Torontos are concerned. The Blueshirts returned home after the match and are disbanding today."

— *Ottawa Journal*, February 21, 1919

Harry Cameron played with the Toronto Blueshirts for their entire run in the National Hockey Association and would play for the Arenas and the St. Pats in the NHL. He's seen here as a member of the Saskatoon Crescents in the Western Canada Hockey League.

"I immediately got in touch with the Ottawa and Canadien clubs, and suggested that the playoff series should begin at once ... the best four games [out of seven] to decide the championship."

— statement by NHL president Frank Calder,
Montreal, February 21, 1919

The Canadiens defeated Ottawa four games to one in the NHL playoffs and headed west to face the PCHA champion Seattle Metropolitans for the Stanley Cup. The series, however, would be cancelled without a winner declared due to a re-occurrence of Spanish influenza, which had killed millions of people around the world in 1918 and now claimed the life of Montreal's Joe Hall. Toronto would return to the NHL for the 1919–20 season, but the team would be under new ownership and boast a new name.

1919–26

Eddie Livingstone finally got his day in court beginning on March 24, 1919, though the case would, in fact, linger through appeals for many years. Several of the players Livingstone claimed belonged to him were soon sold to other teams and new investors were found to purchase the club from the Arena Company ... but even that had its complications.

Sold, Renamed … and Renamed Again

"The team to represent Toronto in the National Hockey League will probably be known by a name other than Arenas. Yesterday Mr. Fred Hambly, Chairman of the Board of Education, bought the franchise and immediately telegraphed to President Calder asking permission to change the name to Tecumseh Hockey Club. It will be remembered that Tecumsehs operated in the NHA several years ago.

"The new owner lost no time in clearing the decks for the coming race. The franchise changed hands in the morning and in the afternoon the following officers were elected: Honorary President. Dr. Noble; President, F. Hambly; Managing Director, C. Querrie; Delegate to NHL, C. Querrie; Secretary-Treasurer, W.F. O'Connor.

"The Arena Company surrendered all rights and henceforth will have no connection with the club."

— *Globe*, Toronto, November 27, 1919

"A first schedule draft, subject to change, was drawn up at the annual meeting of the NHL on Saturday afternoon.... Ratification of the new Toronto club title [Tecumseh] was made by the meeting."

— *Globe*, Toronto, December 8, 1919

But a day later, the Toronto team changed hands again and got another new name.

"The pro hockey situation was cleared up yesterday, and the club reorganized. The paid artists will sail under the name of St. Patricks this season."

— *Toronto World*, December 9, 1919

"Practically the same interests which controlled St. Patricks hockey team in the Senior OHA last season has obtained control of the Toronto franchise in the NHL and will operate the pro team under the name of St. Patricks Hockey Club. Frank Heffernan has been signed as playing manager and will have entire control of the team. He will sign up the players and handle them on the ice."

— *Toronto Daily Star*, December 9, 1919

"The officers named are a combination of the old Arena club, the recently organized Tecumseh Hockey Club, [and] the St. Patricks Hockey Club."

— *Toronto Daily Star*, December 9, 1919

"Charlie Querrie, Manager of the Arena, and who is the accredited delegate of the St. Patricks Club to the NHL, stated last evening that the team would start practice not later than Monday next. He refused to divulge the names of the players expected to line up with the Irishmen, but promised some surprises."

— *Globe*, Toronto, December 9, 1919

1919–22

The Toronto team that took to the ice as the St. Pats in 1919–20 featured a much different lineup from the Arenas of the season before. Of the regulars, Reg Noble, Ken Randall, and Corbett Denneny were still on hand. Harry Cameron was back, but would soon be traded to Montreal (only to return to Toronto once again in 1920–21). Harry Mummery had returned to Quebec, who chose to ice a team once again that winter. Bert Lindsay was also gone, replaced in goal first by Howard Lockhart, then by Mike Mitchell, and finally by Jake Forbes. Other newcomers included two veterans of other professional leagues, Goldie Prodger and Cully Wilson, as well as a rookie named Cecil "Babe" Dye.

Dye was a Toronto boy. He was a slow skater, but had a bullet shot. He was also a multi-sport athlete who played top-level minor-league baseball while he became the top scoring star in the NHL. In addition, Dye was a top amateur football star, although likely never played for the Toronto Argonauts as is often claimed. As a ballplayer, he was probably good enough to play in the Major Leagues, and there are stories that Connie Mack of the Philadelphia Athletics offered him a $25,000 contract in 1921, although this likely happened two years later, as the *Globe* reported on September 8, 1923, that an A's scout was watching Dye play with the Buffalo Bisons after Mack had recently made a large offer for his services.

> "[Babe] Dye first attracted attention as a hockey player in 1917, when he starred at right wing for Aura Lee juniors, champions of the OHA. The next season he played for De la Salle, and they also won the honours. Last year, he played for St. Patrick's OHA senior team. He is also adept at baseball, football and lacrosse."
>
> — *Globe*, Toronto, October 28, 1919

> "Cecil H. Dye made the plunge into the professional ranks when he turned out to the St. Patrick's practice at the Arena today. Dye is an all-around athlete and is expected to make good at professional baseball. He should make good at pro hockey too, if he keeps his temper when on the ice."
>
> — *Toronto Daily Star*, December 16, 1919

The St. Pats played their first NHL game on December 23, 1919, losing to the Ottawa Senators 3–0, but the game was said to be a good one and was closer than the score indicated.

The next game was the St. Pats' first at home, on December 27, and they easily defeated a weak Quebec team 7–4. Dye scored his first NHL goal 12 minutes into the first period to give Toronto a 2–0 lead.

> "'Babe' Dye is the best of the amateurs who are breaking into the pro ranks. Though used only for short intervals, he did far better work than [anyone]."
>
> — Lou Marsh, *Toronto Daily Star*, December 29, 1919

The St. Pats were only a .500 team in their first season, finishing the first half of the split-season schedule with a record of 5–7–0, and the second half with a mark of 7–5–0. Ottawa finished first in both halves of the schedule, eliminating the need for an NHL playoff series, and then defeated Hap Holmes and the Seattle Metropolitans of the PCHA for the Stanley Cup.

The Hamilton Tigers replaced Quebec as the NHL's fourth team in 1920–21, but would be no match for Ottawa, Toronto, and Montreal. The Senators won the first half of the 1920–21 NHL schedule, posting an 8–2–0 record to finish comfortably ahead of the second-place St. Pats, who were 5–5–0. Toronto came on strong in the second half, boosted by the midseason addition of former Ottawa star Sprague Cleghorn. The St. Pats were 10–4–0, edging out the Montreal Canadiens who were 9–5–0. Babe Dye led all NHL players in goals this season with 35 during the 24-game schedule.

Though Ottawa had fallen to a 6–8–0 record during the second half and Toronto fans were optimistic, the Senators shut out the St. Pats 5–0 on home ice in the first game of their total-goal playoffs, and then won the second game 2–0 in Toronto to take the series 7–0. Ottawa went on to beat the Vancouver Millionaires to win the Stanley Cup.

The NHL abandoned the split schedule in 1921–22, deciding instead that the first- and second-place teams at the end of a full schedule would meet in the playoffs for the league championship. Ottawa was 14–4–2 through 20 games, but then lost four in a row to finish 14–8–2. Toronto needed three wins in their last four games to finish 13–10–1 and stave off Montreal (12–11–1) for second place and another chance at Ottawa in the playoffs.

1922 NHL Playoffs

"Tomorrow night at the Arena the two best professional teams in eastern Canada will cross sticks, when the St. Patricks and Ottawa play the first game of the National Hockey League playoff series. The Senators have been the 'top-dogs' in the pro league for two years, and they are ambitious to make it three titles in a row, and so take their place in history with the famous Ottawa Silver Seven, which in other years won the Stanley Cup for the Capital.

"Coach Green of the Ottawa team is reported as saying that the Senators will make every effort to win here, as they believe that on the hard [artificial] ice they can make a much better showing than on a slush covered [natural ice] surface at Ottawa. Many Toronto followers of the sport are under the impression that the Ottawa champions are invincible, but this pessimism is not shared by the local players…. [T]hey are firmly convinced they will turn them back in both the playoff games."

— *Globe*, Toronto, March 10, 1922

"Manager Taylor of the Arena Gardens expects to handle the largest crowd of the season at the NHL classic tonight between St. Patricks and Ottawa. There are a few tickets left, but it is expected they will be disposed of early in the day."

— *Globe*, Toronto, March 11, 1922

"St. Pats and Ottawa open the first of their home-and-home series for the NHL championship tonight. Total goals count. The Irish expect to take at least a two-goal lead to Ottawa for Monday's game. The Senators figure on beating the Irish right here, and they say if they don't pile up a lead here, they will be out of luck at home, for soft weather is predicted, and they admit the Irish are best on slow, heavy going [on a slushy surface].

"The Ottawa and St. Patricks have furnished great struggles here every time they have met this season. The games have been fast, full of clever hockey, and clean. Tonight's contest should be the same with even better hockey than has been exhibited by the two teams previously this season. As total goals count in the two games, the locals will be out tonight to score as many goals as possible against the barber poles to carry to Ottawa for the second game on Monday, and the Senators will not be satisfied with playing their famous defensive game all night.... If the St. Pats can get a three-goal lead tonight they will be in pretty fair shape for the final game."

— *Toronto Daily Star*, March 11, 1922

"Reg Noble, captain of the Toronto St. Patricks pro team ... will start at centre tonight in an effort to hold Frank Nighbor, the famous Ottawa mid-ice performer, in the first of the NHL playoff games at the Arena. Noble and Nighbor are both adept at the sweep and poke checks, but Noble is the sturdier of the two and he may shake the lathy Ottawa star up with a few body-checks and stop his speed."

— *Toronto Daily Star*, March 11, 1922

"Showing commendable battling spirit and unexpected strength, St. Patricks on Saturday night defeated Ottawa by 5 to 4 and thus gained the lead in the playoff series for the National Hockey League championship....

"[Trailing 4–3 late in the second period], the Irish fought back courageously ... before Dye finally took a pass from Cameron and scored [his second goal of the night] just as the period ended. Cameron raced down the centre at his usual fast pace, and, when about to be checked, passed to Dye, who was coming in at top speed. The sharp-shooter was slightly off his balance, but he secured possession, and with one of the most accurate shots imaginable, beat [Clint] Benedict. So rapid was the movement that the Ottawa net guardian never had a chance.

"The best hockey of the night was dished up in the last twenty minutes…. With less than four minutes to play, [Corbett] Denneny scored from a scramble near the net, and the Ottawa players claimed that the puck had not crossed the line. The goal umpire, however, was supported by the referee when he said that Denneny had scored."

— *Globe*, Toronto, March 13, 1922

"One goal up — and that one a disputed one — St. Patricks are down in Ottawa to play Ottawa [in] the NHL final tonight. Whether they can hold that lead or not is the question….

"Saturday's game was a beautiful contest all the way…. [W]hen it looked as if the game would end in a 4 to 4 tie, Denneny cracked the puck in a scrimmage, and as the disc wobbled on the line the goal umpire waved his hand.

"Goalkeeper Benedict was so incensed because he was of the opinion that his team had been given the worst of a close decision, that he tried to break the goal umpire's cage down with his war club, and massacre the official. He was dragged away, and then he and the whole team swarmed down to their own bench to make a protest. The protest had no effect. Referee [Cooper] Smeaton upheld the goal umpire, and so St. Pats are at Ottawa today with a one-goal lead, facing a thoroughly aroused and peevish squad of champions."

— Lou Marsh, *Toronto Daily Star*, March 13, 1922

The second game of the series in Ottawa was played on soft, slushy ice as expected. The Senators had the best of the play, and outshot the St. Pats badly, but could not put the puck past Toronto goalie John Ross Roach. The St. Pats spent much of the game firing the puck out of their end and all the way down the ice, which was not punished with a face-off in the offender's zone in this era. The game ended in a scoreless tie, which gave Toronto the championship by a total score of 5–4.

"One of the greatest crowds in history was disappointed at the result, and it was hard to believe at the finish that the Senators were out of the Stanley Cup finals. They played their hearts out in a great effort, and at the finish practically every member was ready to drop in his tracks. St. Pats were as badly off, and though they went wild with delight when the final whistle ended the suspense, it was the jubilation of their victory that gave them the added pep to demonstrate their feelings.

"In the opinion of the St. Patricks' management, Babe Dye was the next most effective player to Roach. The little right winger worked himself sick and when the final whistles sounded was in a state bordering on collapse. He was used more as a defensive force than on the attack, but this was following the policy laid down by [coach] George O'Donoghue and [captain] Reg Noble. O'Donoghue handled the Irish from the bench and showed excellent judgment in making the changes. A new power behind the throne has arrived in the NHL and O'Donoghue will take his place with ... the other [great] strategists who have gone before him.

"The Toronto team owing to the late start missed the midnight train and will not reach the Queen City before [this] evening at 6 o'clock. It is anticipated that a large crowd will be on hand at the Union Station when the conquering players arrive."

— *Globe*, Toronto, March 14, 1922

"Ottawa, March 14 — Ottawa hockey fans today have scarcely recovered from the defeat handed their favourites last night by Toronto St. Patricks for the right to meet Vancouver for the Stanley Cup. On every hand it is claimed that only the heavy going prevented the locals from winning handsomely. The *Journal* credits Charlie Querrie, manager of the St. Patricks, with an admission that it was the slow ice which beat out the Senators.

"The *Citizen* says today: It was the most heartrending game ever seen here. To the credit of the ex-champions, it may be said that they went down with flying colours and with all due respect to St. Patricks, only the most bias will say they are the better team....

"St. Pats have the best wishes of the Senators and hundreds of local hockey enthusiasts will be pulling for them to retain the much-coveted hockey trophy in the East when they meet Vancouver."

— *Globe*, Toronto, March 15, 1922

CELEBRATE "WAKE" OF OTTAWA TEAM:
Wailing and Weeping Greets Visitors to St. Pats' Dressing-Room

St. Patricks came back from Ottawa yesterday and received a right royal welcome from their numerous supporters who had gathered at Union Station to meet the team.... Mayor Maguire was on hand to let the conquering players know that Toronto appreciates what they have done and there were many other celebrities present who showed their admiration for the plucky band led by George O'Donoghue and Reg Noble.

The welcome at the station surprised the locals, but they were due for another unexpected event, a tribute to the esteem in which the 'pro' players are held by the Arena management. When the new champions reached the ice palace and entered their dressing-room they got the shock of their lives. In the centre of the room a coffin, supposed to contain the last remains of the Ottawa team, while wreaths ... were conspicuous. Bottles ... were used as candle-holders, while the Arena attendants played the Dead March in 'Saul'.... Long green streamers were used to decorate the interior of the room, and all in all, a striking picture was presented.... [T]here were other features which amazed the many visitors who flocked to the dressing room when they heard that the last rites were being performed at the expense of the Ottawa team.

— *Globe*, Toronto, March 15, 1922

1922 Stanley Cup Series

There was a lot of interest in the Stanley Cup series in Toronto. There likely would have been anyway, but the fact that Toronto had played Vancouver in 1918, and that a few former Toronto (and Toronto-area) players were members of the Millionaires, added to the excitement.

"Vancouver has a great net guardian in the veteran Hugh Lehman, but Toronto fans will never concede that the youthful John Ross Roach is not the peer of them all. At Ottawa the little fellow covered himself with glory, and the Senators blame him for their downfall. No recruit who ever broke into professional company attracted so much favourable attention in his first year as Roach has....

"'Babe' Dye, who has been ordered to report to the Buffalo International League baseball team tomorrow, will ignore the summons and will help his team in the upcoming series. At Ottawa, the little right winger with the fastest shot in hockey played the best game of his life....

"Vancouver may be a more powerful foe than the Senators, but from Reg Noble down to the last substitute the St. Patricks players believe that they will successfully defend the battered mug presented to Canadian hockey many years ago by Lord Stanley....

"[The] famed Millionaires arrived here yesterday afternoon at 2 o'clock, and they expressed their amazement that the Senators had met their match. The Westerners had expected to play against Ottawa and were eager to settle accounts for the defeats sustained at Vancouver last spring.

"The rival players are not unknown to each other ... and it will be remembered that the last time Vancouver played in the East they drew as their opponents the Torontos, practically the St. Patricks of today, and went back to the coast defeated.

"Having disposed of Ottawa, the local players do not fear Vancouver or any other team, and Reg Noble predicts that the Stanley Cup will remain in the East...."

— *Globe*, Toronto, March 15, 1922

In addition to comparing and welcoming home players, Toronto fans and sportswriters were intrigued by the differing rules between the NHL and PCHA, which would be alternated from game to game (as they had been in 1918). The NHL now permitted forward passing in the neutral zone, but PCHA rules allowed for a much larger passing area. And since OHA teams also called the Arena home and had their own rules about forward passing, there were going to be a lot of blue lines.

"Why the blooming thing will look like an American [football field] on ice. The players will think they are behind the bars or counting ties or something."

— Charlie Querrie, *Toronto Daily Star*, March 16, 1922

The PCHA had also introduced the penalty shot to hockey this season, though it worked much differently than the rules of today. In PCHA arenas a line was painted on the ice 36 feet in front of each net. The puck was placed on the line, and though a player could charge at the puck from any distance behind it, he had to shoot from the line. Instead of adding yet another line across the ice in Toronto, three dots would be spread out across the 36-foot distance. Torontonians were not impressed with the rule.

"I'll lay 5 to 1 any time anybody shoots at John Ross Roach from 36 feet out. If they beat him on penalty shots I'll eat the puck and the goal pads too."

— Charlie Querrie, *Toronto Daily Star*, March 16, 1922

Game 1, under NHL rules, was played on March 17, 1922.

"Vancouver and St. Patricks will meet here tonight in the first game of the Stanley Cup series, and the visitors from across the continent will start equal favourites with the locals. So impressive has been the all-around work of the Western champions that many local fans are conceding them the Canadian title; but, irrespective of this pessimism, the great majority of Toronto critics are behind the Irish to a man. The team that defeated the once invincible Ottawa machine will not need for support.... The struggle for supremacy between [former Toronto star Alf] Skinner and [Reg] Noble should be interesting, but unless Skinner has improved a whole lot he will not outplay Noble, who when right is without a peer in the hockey world. [Mickey] MacKay will be handicapped at left wing [instead of rover], but, irrespective of that, he should be able to hold his own against [Babe] Dye. The substitutes — [Ernie] Parkes, [Eddie] Oatman and [Charles] Tobin — outclass the local reserve men, and it is here that the championship will be won or lost.

"Interest in the series is at fever heat ..."

— *Globe*, Toronto, March 17, 1922

Playing on St. Patrick's Day did not prove to be a good omen for the Toronto team. Though Babe Dye put them on top less than two minutes after the opening face-off, Jack Adams [formerly of the Arenas] quickly got Vancouver even. The Millionaires led 3–2 after one period, and though Dye's second goal tied it 3–3 after two, Adams's third goal of the night late in the game gave the visitors a victory.

"Vancouver Millionaires got away to a flying start in the opening game ... when they beat St. Patricks by 4 to 3 and the battered and famous Stanley Cup is rocking on its base. The visitors from across the continent earned the verdict.... If anything, they were better than the score would indicate…. The Eastern rules bothered the visitors not one iota. They adapted themselves to the system with remarkable ease."

> — *Globe*, Toronto, March 18, 1922

"Vancouver will win three straight."

> — Alf Skinner, entering the dressing room after the victory, quoted in Puckerings, *Globe*, Toronto, March 18, 1922

"Reg Noble, who is in command of St. Patricks, stated last night that the NHL champions will not be handicapped greatly under PCHA rules…. Tonight's Stanley Cup game at the Arena should be one of the best of the year. There are any number of fans who believe that seven-man hockey is preferable to the abbreviated game."

> — Puckerings, *Globe*, Toronto, March 21, 1922

The St. Pats won the second game 2–1 on Babe Dye's goal at 4:50 of overtime, but a shot Dye missed in the second period also garnered a lot of attention.

"The outstanding incident … was a penalty shot awarded to St. Pats when Duncan tripped Dye as he was going to shoot. Dye teed up the bun on one of the blue marks, selected his best putter — and then failed to run down his 36-foot putt. He missed the net by ten feet amid the hoots of the crowd."

> — Lou Marsh, *Toronto Daily Star*, March 22, 1922

Still, with the series tied at one game apiece — and both teams' winning under the other league's rules — it was shaping up as a real fight to the finish.

"They are well matched — these Goliaths of professional hockey — and the games to come will be as bitterly fought as any in history."

> — *Globe*, Toronto, March 22, 1922

Vancouver won again under NHL rules in Game 3, beating Toronto 3–0. Harry Cameron was hurt that night, and Toronto received permission to borrow Eddie Gerard of Ottawa to take his place in Game 4.

Gerard played so well in a 6–0 Toronto victory to even the series that he was denied permission to suit up for the fifth and final game. Cameron returned, but it was a total team effort — and four goals from their best scorer — that made the difference in Toronto's victory.

Babe Dye is pictured here, likely outside the Arena Gardens, during the 1922–23 season wearing a patch noting that the St. Pats were world champions after their 1922 Stanley Cup victory.

"Helpless in the vise-like grip of the St. Patricks checkers, and unable to subdue 'Babe' Dye and his machine-gun shot, the Vancouver Millionaires, pride of the West, went down here last night in the Stanley Cup final game by 5 to 1. The victory of the NHL titleholders was clean-cut and decisive, and they left not the slightest doubt in the world but that they are the best professional hockey team in captivity."

— *Globe*, Toronto, March 29, 1922

"While everybody played superb hockey on the winning team, Roach in goal, Noble at centre, and Dye stood out. Roach was practically unbeatable, while Dye's shooting was the best ever seen in this burg. Noble's mid-ice checking was a mighty factor in making the Coasters' attack look cheap and weak. That trio broke the hearts of the invaders. Dye laid that old black bun on the target with terrific speed all night and scored four of the five goals. When he whipped it in it almost sounded like a ricocheting bullet."

— Lou Marsh, *Toronto Daily Star*, March 29, 1922

"The luck of the Irish! They said St. Pats were lucky to beat Ottawa for the NHL title. Maybe they were, but they weren't in beating Vancouver Millionaires. They were simply the better hockey team."

— *Toronto Daily Star*, March 29, 1922

"John Ross Roach, recognized as the greatest goalkeeper in the world. Roach has lived up to all expectations in the Stanley Cup series. Only a little fellow, weighing one hundred and twenty-five pounds, Roach nevertheless has shown that he has nothing to fear when competing against the best sharpshooters that professional hockey has produced. He gave a splendid exhibition of courage last night when, after being injured, he continued to play his usual game."

— *Globe*, Toronto, March 29, 1922

"Handsome is as handsome does, they say — Righto. The Vancs looked handsome but the Irish performed handsomely."

— *Toronto Daily Star*, March 29, 1922

"St. Pats did not win because they had the breaks. They won because they were the better team and they played the best hockey from end to end.... The Westerners played like a telegraph message all through the piece — in dots and dashes. They couldn't get anywhere simply because they were checked off their feet."

— Lou Marsh, *Toronto Daily Star*, March 29, 1922

"[Toronto] mayor Alf Maguire was as tickled as a schoolboy when the St. Pats won the Stanley Cup last night. Right away he arranged a banquet for the boys which will take place at the Carls-Rite tonight at 6:30."

— *Toronto Daily Star*, March 29, 1922

"At a banquet tendered [in honour of] the St. Patricks hockey team, professional champions of the world, at the Carls-Rite Hotel last night, the-players were given every reason to feel that the city of Toronto appreciates their achievements in retaining possession of the battered Stanley Cup. Mayor Maguire presided, and in an interesting address, he stated that St. Patricks had done a lot to advertise the Queen City, not only by their effectiveness on the ice, but also by the clean and gentlemanly way they did it. He believes that Toronto owes them a debt of gratitude for the good, clean and plucky battles they put up in the face of great odds ..."

— *Globe*, Toronto, March 30, 1922

Reg Noble began his pro career with the NHA's Blueshirts in 1916–17 and returned to Toronto when the NHL was formed. He was with the St. Pats until early in the 1924–25 season when he was sold to the Montreal Maroons.

"In the absence of William Foran of Ottawa, the chief trustee of Lord Stanley's Cup, the mayor presented the battered and scratched old silver jardiniere to Fred Hambly."

— *Toronto Daily Star*, March 30, 1922

"Frank Calder of Montreal, president of the NHL, turned Senator O'Brien's Cup, emblematic of the NHL, over to captain Reg Noble."

— *Toronto Daily Star*, March 30, 1922

"This cup was lost for some time and when I dug it up I found it was being used as a watering trough for a bulldog. May you and your team show the proverbial tenacity of the bulldog who drank out of it, in defending it."

— Frank Calder

"We will do our best to keep it here."

— Reg Noble

1923–26

The St. Pats were not able to keep the Stanley Cup or the O'Brien Cup in Toronto. The team fell to third place and out of the playoffs in the four-team league in 1922–23 and 1923–24. When the NHL added the Boston Bruins and Montreal Maroons in 1924–25, the St. Pats climbed to second place in the six-team league but were eliminated from the playoffs when they were beaten 3–2 and 2–0 for a 5–2 total score by the Montreal Canadiens.

New ownership took over the St. Pats prior to the 1924–25 season when Charlie Querrie helped to bring in movie theatre owner Nathan Nathanson and mining magnate J.P. Bickell to buy out Fred and Percy Hambly. On the ice, Babe Dye remained a bright spot for the struggling St. Patricks. He led the NHL with 26 goals and 37 points in 22 games played during a 24-game schedule in 1922–23. After finishing second in the NHL in goals scored in 1923–24, he was recognized by his teammates prior to the 1924–25 season.

> "'Babe' Dye, the noted sharpshooter, has been elected captain of the St. Patrick's professional hockey team, the election having taken place previous to the opening workout of the season at the Arena Gardens yesterday."
>
> — *Globe*, Toronto, November 12, 1925

Dye played 29 of 30 regular-season games for the St. Pats during the expanded schedule of 1924–25 and led the NHL with a career-high 38 goals and 46 points that season. He continued to play professional baseball as well, but the double duty was beginning to take its toll on his body and he scored 20 fewer goals in 1925–26. With his production declining and the St. Pats struggling financially as further NHL expansion into the United States made the relatively small seating capacity of the Mutual Street Arena an increasing problem, something was bound to happen.

> "Cecil ('Babe') Dye will play no more in a St. Patrick's uniform. The well-known sharpshooter's services were sold to the Chicago National League Club for a large price here on Saturday. Several clubs put in bids for the former goal-getting leader, but Chicago's offer was accepted.

The Toronto St. Pats of 1926–27.
Charlie Querrie is in the hat and
tie in the centre of the picture. Ace
Bailey (standing second from the left)
and Hap Day (seated third from the
left) would become big stars in the
years to come.

"Dye showed the way to National League scorers for several years, but illness and injuries wrecked his chances last season and he bulged the net only 18 times. This record, however, was remarkable, considering that he was used as a relief man most of the time."

— *Globe*, Toronto, October 18, 1926

In a rather roundabout way, Dye's trade to Chicago would play a big part in the future of NHL hockey in Toronto.

1927 to 1934: Conn Smythe and the Maple Leafs

1926–27: FROM ST. PATS TO MAPLE LEAFS

Conn Smythe was born in Toronto on February 1, 1895, and grew up in the city. He attended high school at Jarvis Collegiate, playing many different sports and helping his team win the city hockey championship in 1912. He later helped his University of Toronto hockey team reach the Ontario Hockey Association junior finals in 1914 and win the junior championship in 1915.

After service in the First World War, Smythe returned to Toronto and opened what would become a successful sand and gravel business. He also coached the varsity hockey team at the University of Toronto, which reached the Allan Cup finals in the spring of 1926. When the New York Rangers entered the NHL that fall as part of a league expansion to 10 teams, Smythe was hired to assemble the Rangers and then manage them.

Smythe built his team mainly from amateur players he'd seen while coaching and professionals who'd played out west. But there was one player he wasn't interested in, and he would always claim it cost him his job in New York.

"If I'd been a politician, I would have stuck with them. But I was no politician. The word was getting around that the Rangers couldn't be much, because so few of them had ever played pro hockey. I wasn't worried. I knew the calibre of the rest. But [Rangers president] Colonel [John] Hammond didn't. Babe Dye had been a big scorer with Toronto St. Pats for years. He was offered to me, and I turned him down. Colonel Hammond called me and practically ordered me to sign Dye. I refused. 'He wouldn't help this team one day,' I said. He wasn't my kind of player, too much the individualist, not enough of a team man....

"Anyway, after enough other big wheels in the NHL kept telling Hammond that he should have picked up Dye when he had the chance (instead of letting him be sold to Chicago), I guess he thought he'd better replace me with someone more likely to do what he was told."

— Conn Smythe, *If You Can't Beat 'Em in the Alley* (1981)

Smythe was replaced as Rangers manager shortly after the team started training camp at the Ravina Rink in the west end of Toronto. The story, however, was not reported at the time the way Smythe would tell it later.

"'Conny' Smythe, manager of the New York Rangers, severed his connection with the team Wednesday.... Col. Hammond, president of the Rangers, affected the change of pilots in the American club. Mr. Hammond, in explaining the change, said that the club and Conny Smythe are parting on the best of terms. Smythe finds that his position with the hockey team interferes with his contracting business, it was reported."

— *Winnipeg Tribune*, October 28, 1926

"It is rather surprising ... that the Rangers should make a change in management at this stage without giving Mr. Smythe an opportunity of managing the team that he has organized. Col. Hammond pointed out that no change would have been made if Mr. Smythe could have given his services to the club for the whole year instead of the winter months, which was according to the terms of the original contract."

— W.A. Hewitt, *Toronto Daily Star*, October 28, 1926

Smythe would recall being let go by the Rangers as his biggest disappointment.

"My biggest personal disappointment in hockey was when I assembled the first New York Rangers Club — in fact there were two complete teams; Rangers and Springfield — and I invited the Ranger president, Colonel Hammond, to see them play their first practice game in Toronto, my own hometown. And, Hammond's greeting to me was: 'Smythe, meet Lester Patrick, the Rangers' new manager!'

"That was the first inkling I had about being fired after having gathered those thirty-two players, including the Cooks, Boucher, Johnson, Abel and Chabot before the start of that season. I had got them for Hammond at a cost of less than $25,000 — and here I was fired before they played their first practice game."

    — Conn Smythe to Bill Roche, *Globe*, Toronto, November 26, 1938

It wasn't easy for Lester Patrick either.

"It was embarrassing for me. I did not know Connie Smythe up till this time — I had to come to Toronto and take over 26 or so strange players — and practically another man's job. And in spite of this, I want to say Connie Smythe has been my chief booster ever since."

    — Lester Patrick to Archibald Lampman, *Toronto Daily Star*, April 15, 1933

Smythe's dismissal by New York came at a time when Canadians were worried that Americans were taking over the game. His departure from the Rangers would soon be good news for fans in Toronto and all across the country.

"It is impossible to imagine what would have happened to professional hockey in Canada had Smythe stayed in New York."

    — Frank Selke, *Behind the Cheering* (1962)

After losing his job with the Rangers, Smythe offered his services as coach to the Toronto pro team, but was turned down. Soon, he was coaching again at the University of Toronto and — amidst reports the St. Pats would be sold to American interests and moved to the United States — trying to put together a syndicate to buy Toronto's NHL team.

"[Charles C.] 'Cash and Carry' Pyle wants to buy the St. Patrick Professional Hockey Club. The man who introduced professional tennis, and who is interested as well in professional football, wants to break into the hockey ring. Through a Toronto representative, Mr. Pyle several weeks ago asked the owners of the St. Patrick Hockey Club to name their price. They did, and while official figures are not available, it is understood they asked $200,000.

"That, according to information, was a little high for Mr. Pyle, and he hasn't accepted yet — [nor] has he rejected. But what is most important about the deal — if it does go through — is that Mr. Pyle will transfer the club intact to Philadelphia.

"If Mr. Pyle takes St. Pats team and franchise and moves it to Philadelphia, the fate of pro hockey in Toronto is doubtful."

    — *Evening Telegram*, Toronto, November 19, 1926

"There is nothing extraordinary about the alleged proposal of 'Cold Cash' Pyle to buy the Toronto pro hockey club and transfer the franchise and team to Philadelphia. That, it has been pointed out in these columns, is merely the trend of the times … it has become patent to everybody who has watched the machinations of the big money interests across the border that an all-United States league is inevitable, with a Canadian organization as kind of adjunct…. There are more convincing indications every day that pro hockey in Canada is destined to become very 'bush' compared to the major league or leagues bound to develop in the United States…. A big new arena with vastly increased seating capacity might enable the pro game to survive here, but with three artificial ice hockey arenas already operating in Toronto, the prospect for another is remote, at least."

— Frederick Wilson, *Globe*, Toronto, November 20, 1926

"I argued strenuously with everybody who would listen … that if Toronto lost its NHL franchise it might be a long time before we got another. [J.P.] Bickell assured me that if I could match the Philadelphia offer, they'd give me the edge. I didn't have more than a fraction of the money myself, but I pounded on doors and lined up some others. I also talked often with Bickell. He listened and finally he said, 'I've got about $40,000 in the club. If you can round up the $160,000 to pay off the others, I'll leave my

Conn Smythe is seated fourth from the left in this photo of the 1931–32 Maple Leafs. If Smythe hadn't put together a syndicate to buy the St. Pats in 1927, Toronto may well have lost its NHL franchise.

money in on the understanding that you'll take over the team.' I agreed. Late in January, I put down $10,000 for an option to purchase."

— Conn Smythe, *If You Can't Beat 'Em in the Alley* (1981)

"The deal by which the St. Patricks Hockey Club changes hands may be completed today, according to a statement made yesterday by one of the members of the syndicate of Toronto business men who have been negotiating to purchase outright the interests of the present owners of the local NHL entry....

The men who are behind the deal held a meeting Saturday afternoon, and following this it was stated that all arrangements were completed for paying over the first $75,000 on Monday morning. Owing to the fact that under NHL franchise agreement no further trades or deals for players can be made after Jan. 31, it was decided to take possession today, so that a couple of deals planned by the purchasers can be put through before Tuesday."

— *Globe*, Toronto, January 31, 1927

Still, it took another two weeks for the deal to get done

"On February 14 ... the new investors I'd rounded up met with the owners and we paid ... $75,000 and undertook to pay the remaining $75,000 in thirty days."

— Conn Smythe, *If You Can't Beat 'Em in the Alley* (1981)

With the Senators visiting Toronto on Saturday, February 12, Ottawa newspapers seemed to jump the gun on the sale of the St. Patricks.

"Toronto, Feb. 13 — Ottawas chased the persistent jinx which has camped on their trail in Toronto for three years, when they defeated Maple Leafs, as the former St. Pats are now known, by a score of 1–0 here Saturday night."

— *Ottawa Journal*, February 14, 1927

"St. Pats ceased their existence at 11 o'clock Saturday night. Today they become Maple Leafs, and it is stated that Charlie Querrie is counting $65,000 as his end."

— *Ottawa Journal*, February 14, 1927

"Seven years ago Harvey Spoule, Frank Heffernan, Percy Hambly, Paul Ciceri, and yours truly sat around a table in the Arena trying to make some assorted cards behave. Someone made the remark that the professional hockey club could be bought for $2,000. It was $400 apiece and it took a lot of time to persuade a couple of us to part with the four. For $2,000 we got some hockey sticks and a few gloves and a lease to play in the Arena. Then we bought a franchise in the NHL for $5,000 to be paid for when we made the price. Gradually the club went along until all that was left of the old guard was the Hambly boys, Ciceri and myself. Then the game grew until the Hambly boys could not attend to business and hockey too and they preferred their business and sold their interests to Messrs. Nathanson and Bickell, who were persuaded by the writer that they would have a lot of fun. After a couple of years' worry over players Mr. Nathanson decided that it was not so funny, and receiving an offer that pleased everybody the club was sold for close to $200,000. Quite a jump from two to two hundred, but with a team up near the top and franchises valued at $50,000, with hockey players at $20,000 it was not a bad deal for the buyers."

— Charlie Querrie, *Toronto Daily Star*, November 21, 1927

"We paid $165,000 for the old Toronto St. Patrick's franchise. It might have been worth $15,000."

— Conn Smythe, *Toronto Star*, February 2, 1977

"Good-Bye, St. Pats! Howdy, Maple Leafs."

— headline, *Globe*, Toronto, February 15, 1927.

"When the Toronto pro hockey team takes the ice at Arena Gardens on Thursday night against the New York Americans it will be under new name and colours.

"The name St. Patrick's will be used for the last time at Detroit tonight.

"The team will be known henceforth as the Maple Leafs of Toronto....

"New uniforms of white will be used with a green maple leaf on the breast and the word 'Toronto' underneath, something like the Canadian Olympic sweaters at Chamonix in 1924."

— *Toronto Daily Star*, February 15, 1927

"The transfer of the local professional hockey club to new interests should prove beneficial to the National Hockey League in Toronto. The new club embraces a very formidable list of shareholders including some of the leading young businessmen of Toronto. The intention is to get the Toronto public interested in the team as much as possible and to make the team a real Toronto aggregation with some home-town pride."

— W.A. Hewitt, *Toronto Daily Star*, February 14, 1927

"I was coaching both the Varsity Grads and the college team at the time. Alex Romeril handled the Leafs for me. We didn't set the world on fire at first because we really picked up only two big players from the St. Pat's — Hap Day and Ace Bailey....

"But we did a bit of wheeling and dealing to get things going. It wasn't that great at first. In the first full year as the Maple Leafs, we took in only $115,000 at the old Mutual Street Arena."

— Conn Smythe, *Toronto Star*, February 2, 1977

1927–30

Building a Better Team

After losing their final game as the St. Pats 5–1 to Detroit in Windsor, Ontario, on February 16, 1926, the Maple Leafs won their first game under their new name when they defeated the New York Americans 4–1 at home on February 17. Over the final 12 games of the 1926–27 season, the Maple Leafs went 6–5–1, but they still finished last in the five-team Canadian Division with a record of 15–24–5 (nine points out of a playoff spot) and eighth overall in the 10-team NHL. Conn Smythe took control as coach and GM of the Maple Leafs in 1927–28.

"Four new managers will pilot teams in the National Hockey League.... Two of the new pilots, Wilfred 'Shorty' Green, of the New York Americans, and Jack Adams, of the Detroit Cougars, have had playing experience of several years in the major leagues, but Barney Stanley, the new pilot of the Chicago Black Hawks and Connie Smythe, who will be in charge of the Toronto Maple Leafs, are making their first [NHL] appearances....

"Smythe is well known as the manager and coach of the University of Toronto sextet, international intercollegiate title holders.... The Toronto fans expect a great deal from [him] because of his success in the inter-collegiate ranks."

— Associated Press, November 1927

Still, the Leafs showed only modest improvement under Smythe, climbing up to fourth in the Canadian Division and finishing the 1927–28 season at 18–18–8 for 44 points, which left them six back of third-place Ottawa in the playoff race. Making things worse for Smythe, the New York Rangers won the Stanley Cup in only their second season.

"When I looked at what I had, I wished I hadn't signed all those hotshots from the sticks to Rangers contracts, and had saved a few for myself. Rangers won the Stanley Cup, which made it, in effect, my first Stanley Cup. When I was kidded about 'my' Rangers coming first and my Leafs last, I vowed publicly that I would put together another Stanley Cup team, this time in Toronto."

— Conn Smythe, *If You Can't Beat 'Em in the Alley* (1981)

"His beloved Leafs were having trouble in the National Hockey League.... And since no club would sell any good players to the Maple Leafs, Smythe's team failed to make the playoffs.

"One day when Conn was in a mood more despondent than usual, he asked Bill Christie and myself what we thought he should do about it....

"'I'll tell you [what],' I said. 'Just fire those old men you have playing on your team now. Replace them with these young bucks I have with me on the Marlboros. Do that, and you'll never look back!'

"Conn looked at me reproachfully. 'There are times when I think there's something wrong with your head,' he told me frankly.

Red Horner spent his entire NHL career with Toronto from 1928 until 1940. He led the NHL in penalty minutes for eight straight seasons beginning in 1932–33, but he was no goon. Horner was the Leafs' captain in his final two seasons.

"He must have given my suggestion some sober thought, however. He concluded he really had no other alternative. At any rate, I am sure that it was this Marlboros Club, and Conn Smythe's interest in it, that was to dramatically change the face of hockey in Toronto for many years to come."

— Frank Selke, *Behind the Cheering* (1962)

The first major acquisition Conn Smythe made from Frank Selke's Marlboros junior team was Toronto native George Reginald "Red" Horner, a hard-rock defenceman and future team captain and Hall-of-Famer.

"I was playing for the Marlboro Juniors, but I was playing for the Broker's League too. I was a clerk.... On Friday night, I played with the Marlboro Juniors. The Broker's League always played Saturday afternoons. I played Saturday afternoon with Solway Mills. Smythe was at the game and he came to me and said, 'Red, you've had enough of this amateur hockey. We want you to come with us!' Those were his words. This was just before Christmas in 1928. I said, 'Thank you very much, Mr. Smythe. When do you want me?' He said, 'Tonight!' I said, 'But I played last night and this afternoon!' He said, 'Well, that's nothing for you.' He said, 'I'll tell ya what I'm gonna do. I'll pay you $2,500 for the balance of the season.'

"I thought about it and it sounded pretty good because I was making $25 a week as a clerk at the Standard Stock Exchange."

— Red Horner, One-on-One Spotlight, Hockey Hall of Fame website (2003)

"Reginald (Red) Horner, defence man of the Marlboro Junior OHA team, turned pro on Saturday and signed with the Toronto Leafs. He played on Saturday night against Pittsburgh and held his own with the company. Horner is a Toronto boy, 19 years old and weighs 187 lbs. He has played two seasons in Junior OHA and was just starting his third. He started his hockey [career] with the North Toronto Midgets in the Toronto Hockey League."

— *Toronto Daily Star*, December 24, 1928

"Horner made an immediate hit with fans and was very effective too despite the fact that he had played games on Friday night and Saturday afternoon ... but was ill-advised to make the jump into the professional ranks at this stage. No player should be allowed to turn pro until he is 21 and is sufficiently matured to stand the wear and tear of the long pro campaign."

— W.A. Hewitt, *Toronto Daily Star*, December 24, 1928

Despite the loss of Horner from the Marlboros, the junior team was deep in talent and more than good enough to win the Memorial Cup in the spring of 1929. The Maple Leafs made the playoffs, too, and even won a round. Soon Conn Smythe had his eye on another talented Toronto-area youngster: Charlie Conacher.

"One of the most versatile players in junior hockey is Charlie Conacher of the Toronto Marlboros … Charlie is a younger brother of the famous Lionel Conacher, one of the best rugby players ever produced in Canada and at present a member of the New York Americans hockey team. When Charlie scored a goal past Holmes of the [Winnipeg] Elmwoods, putting his team two goals up on the western team [for the Memorial Cup], he immediately became the idol of thousands of hockey fans."

— Jimmy Thompson, *Toronto Daily Star*, April 12, 1929

"From reliable sources it has been learned that four of last year's Marlboro juniors stars will be playing as professionals when the next hockey season gets under way. The men slated for monied ranks are: Eddie Convey, who may sign with the New York Americans, and Charlie Conacher, Harvey Jackson, and Alex Levinsky, who are expected to line up with the Toronto Maple Leafs when Manager Conny Smythe takes pen in hand and opens up his interviews. Conacher, the best right-wing player in junior ranks last winter, may replace the late 'Shorty' Horne as a relief man to [Ace] Bailey. He is big and strong, and as a marksman, possessing speed and accuracy, he looms up as another Babe Dye. The New York Americans were also keen to secure Conacher's services. Conny Smythe, an astute business man who demands the best in a hockey way for Toronto, has made no statement regarding his plans, but it can be taken for granted that he will have a team out there worth cheering for when the snow begins to fall."

— Michael J. Rodden, *Globe*, Toronto, August 19, 1929

"Manager Conny Smythe of the Toronto National Hockey League Club generally 'gets his man,' and, therefore, no surprise was occasioned here yesterday when the official announcement was made that Charlie Conacher, younger brother of Lionel Conacher, had signed on the dotted line."

— *Globe*, Toronto, October 8, 1929

"'Red' Horner ... arrived in the city after a well-spent summer in the Northern woods. Although as mild-mannered as ever, the 'Redhead' looks fit and as hard as nails — rather an ominous outlook for opposing forwards. Horner is overjoyed at having his former team-mate, Charlie Conacher, lined up with the Leafs, as the pair were a very effective duo when attacking for the Marlboros."

— *Globe*, Toronto, October 16, 1929

"Although the death of 'Shorty' Horne deprived the Maple Leafs of an able right-wing substitute for 'Ace' Bailey, in Gordon Brydson, purchased from the Buffalo International Hockey League Club, and Charlie Conacher, local amateur star, Manager Conny Smythe possesses two players who should fill the gap ... Charlie Conacher is one of the brightest prospects developed in local junior circles for some seasons. He possesses a terrific shot, and should make good from the start."

— *Globe*, Toronto, October 22, 1929

The Maple Leafs began the 1929–30 season with a 2–2 tie on home ice against the Chicago Black Hawks, and Conacher did, indeed, make good.

Charlie Conacher (left), Joe Primeau (centre), and Busher Jackson (right) began playing together in December of 1929. The Kid Line would become the NHL's top-scoring trio during the early 1930s.

"Then Conny Smythe tossed young Charlie Conacher out with his relief line and the kid gave the congregation its first real chance to warm up when he sailed down his right wing, took a pass from [Eric] Pettinger, walked in around his check and smoked a sizzler past [Charlie] Gardiner for the first goal of the season."

— Lou Marsh, *Toronto Daily Star*, November 15, 1929

"Charlie Conacher's performance stood out. His shooting alone is worth the price of admission. A little more accuracy and he would have had two or three more counters."

— Bert Perry, *Globe*, Toronto, November 15, 1929

Conacher was soon playing right wing alongside a young Leafs centre (soon to be 24 years old) named Joe Primeau. They were teamed with left winger Harold 'Baldy' Cotton, a veteran at age 27, and yet *Toronto Daily Star* sportswriter Lou Marsh was soon referring to them as Conn Smythe's "Kid Line." Then, in December, another youngster from Toronto joined Primeau and Conacher, and the kid line was soon the Kid Line.

"Harvey Jackson, left-wing star of the Marlboros … yesterday signed to play with the Toronto Maple Leafs in the NHL. Jackson is 18 years of age, and will be the youngest player in the major professional circuit."

— *Globe*, Toronto, December 7, 1929

"The addition of Harvey Jackson, who will be used freely … lends interest to the contest. The Leafs will produce a second-string forward line tonight composed of Joe Primeau at centre and Jackson and Conacher on the wings. All are former Marlboros stars, and they will be out there to show that Toronto can produce some real hockey talent."

— Bert Perry, *Globe*, Toronto, December 7, 1929

The Leafs lost to Montreal 1–0 that night, but by the end of the month, the Kid Line would be a fixture after all three starred in a 4–3 win over Chicago.

"What pleases Horace H. Public the most is the fact that the Leafs' kid forwards — Conacher, Primeau and Jackson — delivered on target."

— Lou Marsh, *Toronto Daily Star*, December 30, 1929

There was no splitting up the threesome after that.

"The feature of [last night's 5–3 win over the Montreal Maroons] was the work of the ex-Marlboro stars. Jackson and Conacher worked well with Primeau and they provided some of the best attacking plays of the game.... That 'kid' forward line of Primeau at centre and Conacher and Jackson on the wings showed some pretty hockey."

> — Bert Perry, *Globe*, Toronto, January 2, 1930

Three nights later, when the Leafs beat the Canadiens 4–3 on January 4, 1930, the Kid Line earned headlines ... and capital letters!

"Kid Forward Line Leads Leafs to 4–3 Victory over Canadiens"

> — headline, *Toronto Daily Star*, January 6, 1930

"Canadiens, 3; Leafs, 4! Play that on your old tambourine and see how nice it sounds!! And it was the Kid Line which turned the trick!!! That is what makes Saturday night's victory down at the Arena Gardens such a sweet morsel."

> — Lou Marsh, *Toronto Daily Star*, January 6, 1930

"We didn't jell right off, but I knew before too many games that this was a pretty fair line. Harvey was a natural; he did things with the puck without having to think about them. As for Charlie, he was aware of every move he made and could tell you about each one. The pair of them had lots of fire and confidence, which I think helped me quite a bit since I needed both at the time."

> — Joe Primeau to Stan Fischler, *Those Were the Days* (1976)

The 1929–30 season marked the first time the NHL allowed forward passing in every zone on the ice, which was a big help to the Kid Line.

"It seemed to give me the confidence I needed. It certainly favoured me. All I had to do was get the puck, and if it wasn't Busher streaking up on on the left side yelling for a pass, it would be Charlie roaring down the right side."

> — Joe Primeau, quoted in Ed Fitkin, *The "Gashouse Gang" of Hockey* (1951)

Even so, Toronto's top scorers in 1929–30 were all well back of the league leaders and the team missed the playoffs again. The Maple Leafs record was just 17–21–6, their 40 points putting them in fourth place, 10 points behind Ottawa for a playoff berth. Still, the outlook was improving from a business standpoint.

"At the annual meeting of shareholders of the Toronto Maple Leaf Hockey Club, held yesterday at the offices of the club, President Edward W. Bickle presented his report of the year's activities, concluding with a detailed financial statement which was favourably received. Harmony was the keynote of the gathering, everyone present expressing confidence in the directorate of the team.

"During his address, Mr. Bickle pointed to the growth of the attendance figures of the National League games....

"Conn Smythe was re-elected managing director, his contract being extended for a further period of two years. Mr. Smythe has been responsible for the team's gradual improvement in a playing sense, while his business deals have been instrumental in solidifying the club in a financial way. In National League circles, Connie's judgement of young players ranks ace high, the Leafs being considered the best young club in existence."

— *Toronto Daily Star*, July 16, 1930

But Conn Smythe had his eye on a veteran player who would help to turn the team around.

1930–31

A King-Sized Deal

The Ottawa Senators had been the top team of the early 1920s, winning the Stanley Cup in 1920, 1921, and 1923 when the NHL had only four teams and still had to compete with other leagues for the top prize. Even after the NHL expanded to 10 teams in 1926–27 and became the only league to compete for the Stanley Cup, the Senators won it again that season. But with six of the league's teams now in the United States, and Toronto and Montreal both much larger than Ottawa, the Canadian capital was the smallest market in the NHL by far. In order to survive, the Senators began selling off their stars: Cy Denneny to Boston, Hooley Smith and George Boucher to the Montreal Maroons, Frank Nighbor to Toronto.

By the late summer of 1930, it was clear that the Senators were willing to entertain offers for King Clancy and teams had begun making inquiries about the Ottawa captain and star defenceman.

**"Ottawa Hockey Club Puts King Clancy on Market:
Offers Running up to $50,000 Made for Great Defence
Star Whose Contract Has Expired"**

— headline, *Ottawa Journal*, August 20, 1930

"It is true that many offers of trades and straight cash have been received for some of our star players. None so far has been accepted. It is well known that the team here has been operating at a loss for a number of years past. This company cannot refuse to consider the sale of one or two of its super stars, providing the price offered, whether it be cash or cash combined with players, is sufficiently attractive. So far that has not been the case."

— Major F.D. Burpee, president of the Auditorium Company, owner of the Ottawa Hockey Club, *Ottawa Journal*, August 20, 1930

"The real change in the Leafs came ... when we got King Clancy in the biggest deal ever made up to that time ... The Ottawa club in the NHL was in financial trouble. They needed money so badly they decided to sell their best player.... [Clancy] was not only one of the best defencemen in the league but one of the most colourful, lots of guts.... I had the right players, but we were still playing in the Mutual Street Arena, and even though we were filling it about half the time there weren't enough seats to give us the ready cash. With the Depression, the $35,000 Ottawa wanted was, it seemed, the one insuperable drawback."

— Conn Smythe, *If You Can't Beat 'Em in the Alley* (1981)

Meanwhile, other teams were making offers. The Maroons were offering $35,000 and right winger Jimmy Ward. Boston was also interested, but Ottawa wanted Lionel Hitchman in return. The New York Americans were offering $50,000 in a straight sale, while the Rangers were offering $60,000 for Clancy and Hec Kilrea.

"They tell me that Mr. Smythe had made up his mind that he couldn't afford the price Ottawa wanted for my services, but a day at the race track soon changed that. At the time he owned a horse called Rare Jewel who was anything but a world-beater. This day Rare Jewel went off at fantastic odds and Mr. Smythe had a bundle on him. The horse paid more than $200 for a $2 ticket ... [and] I guess he was feeling pretty pleased with himself and probably said, 'Maybe I'll take this money and get a couple of fellows to sign a note or two so we can buy that Irishman from Ottawa.'"

— King Clancy, *Clancy* (1968)

"Third Race — Coronation Stakes; $4,000 added; two-year-olds foaled in Canada; 6 furlongs: 1, Rare Jewel, 112 (Foden); 2, Froth Blower, 127 (Baker); 3, Roche d'Or, 122 (Maiben). Time–1.15.

— race results, *Globe*, Toronto, September 22, 1930

"Do you know how it feels to bet on a 100 to 1 long shot? Connie Smythe does. That was no 'hooey' about him betting $50-$30-$50 on his Rare Jewel in Saturday's running of the Coronation Stakes at Woodbine. That was Connie's bet and Connie is about $10,000 richer thereby, counting the winnings on his wager and the winner's portion of the purse."

— Charles "Horses" Ayres, *Toronto Daily Star*, September 22, 1930

"The Stanley Cup is the next objective. The next biggest thrill I would like to experience would be to see Charlie Conacher bang in the winning goal to give my Maple Leafs a Stanley Cup."

— Conn Smythe, quoted in the *Toronto Daily Star*, September 22, 1930

"Members of the Ottawa hockey team will commence indoor training next Monday night at the YMCA…. The future of King Clancy is still an open question. Another figure has entered the field for the services of the dashing Ottawa captain and it is none other than Conny Smythe, scrappy manager of the Toronto Maple Leafs."

— *Ottawa Journal*, October 7, 1930

"The Ottawa Hockey Club have given Conny Smythe … an option on the services of Frank ('King') Clancy, captain of the Ottawa team. The option holds good until October 15, a week from today, and Smythe and his *confreres* have been advised of the minimum price that Ottawa will take….

"By giving an option to Toronto it does not necessarily mean that Clancy will wind up there. The price demanded is a stiff one, and the terms as quoted to Smythe are such that he will have to 'come clean' or lose any chance to get the Ottawa captain."

— *Globe*, Toronto, October 8, 1930

"The Toronto club has an option on Clancy for $35,000 and two players from the [Toronto] club. The option expires on Wednesday, October 15. In the meantime, Connie Smythe intends to put advertisements in the newspapers asking the fans to express an opinion on the deal. And the club will be guided by what the fans say."

— *Toronto Daily Star*, October 8, 1930

"Toronto hockey fans have been asked by Conny Smythe to let the wide world know if they desire the Maple Leaf management to purchase the services of Frank ('King') Clancy, one of the most colourful players the sport has ever known. Smythe did not need to seek such a guarantee. Toronto wants Clancy, and the dashing Irishman will be on the local defence this coming season. The Toronto owners will exercise their option, without a doubt."

— Michael J. Rodden, *Globe*, Toronto, October 9, 1930

"That was a happy thought of Connie Smythe's to ask for an expression of opinion from the hockey fans on the King Clancy deal. Connie has advertisements in the newspapers today requesting the fans of Toronto and vicinity to write in and say what they think of the Maple Leafs paying $50,000 ($35,000 cash and two players) for the release of Clancy from the Ottawa club. 'King' is not only the most spectacular player in professional hockey, but one of the most useful. It is expected that he will, if secured, add the final punch to the attack of the Leafs and put them in the championship running. In any event, he should give them the fighting spirit and the leadership that is needed in a championship team. Clancy is a 60-minute man and a leader on the ice."

— W.A. Hewitt, *Toronto Daily Star*, October 9, 1930

"Fans — The Directors of the Toronto Maple Leaf Hockey Club, Limited, will make their decision on Friday regarding the purchase of Frank 'King' Clancy from the Ottawa Senators. What do you think of this deal? Write the hockey club's office, 11 King Street West.

C. Smythe, Managing Director"

"If Conny Smythe succeeds in his securing of 'King' Clancy for his Maple Leafs, our cup of joy will be filled. We have always said, and are still of the same opinion, that Clancy is the star of the Calder circuit. With Clancy and [Hap] Day the Leafs would have a crowd pleasing and sparkling defence. They are both spectacular and have speed to burn."

— Charlie Querrie, *Toronto Daily Star*, October 9, 1930

"I would offer more money for Clancy than for any other player in the league if I was manager of a club."

— former Senators star Eddie Gerard, *Ottawa Journal*, October 10, 1930

"The directors of the Toronto Maple Leaf Hockey Club unanimously resolve to exercise their option on player 'King' Clancy with Ottawa. The directorate also appreciate the tremendous enthusiasm and support displayed by the fans of Toronto and all Ontario in this matter."

> — official announcement handed out to the press
> on the night of October 10, 1930

"When I came out of work … to meet my dad … who picked me up after work in his Nash, he stopped the car and sat reading the *Ottawa Journal*. I asked him what was wrong; he handed me the paper and said: 'Have you seen this?'

"The headline said: CLANCY SOLD TO MAPLE LEAFS …

"I thought: What the devil! I'll go to Toronto for a few seasons and it might be fun."

> — King Clancy, *Toronto Star*, February 9, 1977

"Backed to the limit by the fans of Toronto, the Maple Leaf directors yesterday decided to purchase the services of Frank ('King') Clancy from the Ottawa Senators, the price being $35,000 in cash, while Ottawa also gets Art Smith, a smart young defence man, and Eric Pettinger, a centre player of ability. Conny Smythe is the man mainly responsible

King Clancy had been a two-time Stanley Cup champion and was one of the NHL's top defencemen when Conn Smythe acquired him to bring his winning ways to Toronto. Clancy remained with the team for most of the next 56 years.

for the completion of the deal.... Smythe has made good his promise, and he has shown his courage by setting a new high record in paying such a huge sum for Clancy."

— Michael J. Rodden, *Globe*, Toronto, October 11, 1930

"I paid ... $10,000 down and five cheques for $5,000 each, post-dated a week apart starting the following week."

— Conn Smythe, *If You Can't Beat 'Em in the Alley* (1981)

"You'd think a fellow coming to Toronto as I did might get a cool reception. Some of the boys might have said, 'Well, they paid a lot of money for this gabby Irishman. What do you say we let him do all the work? We'll soon know if he's worth $35,000 or not!' But they weren't that way at all. They took me in as if I were one of their own and gave me the biggest welcome any player can get when he moved from one team to another."

— King Clancy, *Clancy* (1968)

"Along with the celebrated Mr. Clancy on defense will be our own 'Happy' Day and 'Red' Horner. Day, as you know, is no mean hockey player himself and what a teammate he will be for Clancy. This 'Red' Horner can also add a lot of fireworks to any game. In fact, the Leafs' defence array should easily be worth the admission price."

— Charlie Querrie, *Toronto Daily Star*, October 29, 1930

"I rate ... King Clancy as one of the four best defencemen the game has ever known. Not a pretty skater, he covered the ice at a rapid long-striding gait; he could break faster than any rival; and had a hard, low shot. But his greatest asset, as I see it, was his tremendous will to win and the inspiration he was to his teammates."

— Frank Selke, *Behind the Cheering* (1962)

"If the Lord gave me any talents, it's the ability to spot a phoney at 1,000 yards and the ability to smell a thoroughbred — either a racehorse or a human. Thoroughbreds of any kind just smell like a thoroughbred. Clancy was one of the great ones."

— Conn Smythe, quoted in *Toronto Star*, February 9, 1977

"Considerable interest was displayed in the initial workout of the Toronto Maple Leafs at the Arena Gardens yesterday. Practically one-half of the seating space was occupied by interested fans, who came to see the players make their first appearance on the ice this season....

"The fans were intent on watching 'King' Clancy, and the former Ottawa star was given a big hand when he appeared on the ice. He made many of his famous sallies down the ice and appeared to work well with Day, who was moved over to the left side of the defence. Day also appeared to advantage and he and Clancy should make one of the speediest and quickest-breaking defence pairs in the NHL."

— *Globe*, Toronto, October 31, 1930

The Maple Leafs had a good year in 1930–31. Charlie Conacher led the NHL with 31 goals during the 44-game season and Joe Primeau topped the circuit with 32 assists. Neither, however, was elected as either a First-Team or Second-Team All-Star when the NHL handed out these honours for the first time. King Clancy did earn a berth on the first team, along with Boston's Eddie Shore. Toronto finished second in the Canadian Division with a record of 22–13–9 for 53 points and returned to the playoffs, although they lost their first-round matchup with the Chicago Black Hawks. It had been a successful season, and the future looked bright. Now Conn Smythe wanted to assure that he had a brand new building to house his hockey team.

1931–32
Maple Leaf Gardens

"When Smythe announced that he was going to build this place back in 1929, everyone told him he was crazy. The depression was on and there wasn't a dime to be had. But Smythe did it."

— King Clancy, *Toronto Star*, February 9, 1977

"In a few years, the Toronto Maple Leafs hockey team got too big for its britches. The Mutual Street Arena, which had been more than adequate to handle patrons of the St. Patricks professional hockey team, had a capacity of nine thousand.... At the prevailing prices, the best money the club could hope for from those seats was two hundred thousand dollars. This sum was much too small to enable the Maple Leafs to compete successfully with their wealthy rival clubs from Montreal and the United States.... The Maple Leafs had to have a new arena, controlled by the same people who owned the hockey team."

— Frank Selke, *Behind the Cheering* (1962)

"I had started to talk up the idea that we needed a bigger and better arena to play in.… I said, as a place to go all dressed up, we don't compete with the comfort of theatres and other places where people can spend their money.… We need at least twelve thousand seats, everything new and clean, a place that people can be proud to take their wives or girlfriends to."

— Conn Smythe, *If You Can't Beat 'Em in the Alley* (1981)

Ironically, before Smythe and the Leafs could announce plans for their arena project, another local group went public with plans to build an ice palace in midtown Toronto. But the Maple Leafs' boss wasn't interested.

"Questioned last night about the proposed new Arena, Manager Conny Smythe stated the present owners of the NHL franchise were fully alive to the need of a new arena here, and had been working for some time on a proposition which may be announced shortly. He did not know anything of any other plan than the one the hockey club is considering and did not think the club would be interested in any other.…

"When pressed for an opinion as to when the Maple Leaf Club would make an announcement of their plan, he stated he was not in a position to say. For some time past, however, it has been completing plans for a new hockey stadium here, and that these plans had advanced to the stage where a definite announcement would be forthcoming."

— *Globe*, Toronto, January 9, 1931

"If there is a new arena, it should be built on the waterfront. One has only to take a look at Mutual St. when there is a hockey game to see how traffic is impeded. You can imagine what would happen in the impeding of traffic on Spadina Ave. if there was a hockey arena built there."

— Alderman (and future mayor of Toronto) Nathan Phillips, reacting to
the Knox College arena plan, *Toronto Daily Star*, January 9, 1931

The Knox College arena never came to pass, but may have spurred the Maple Leafs into action, as Conn Smythe announced the team's plans just a few days later, on January 16.

"The Maple Leaf Hockey Club directors, at a meeting held today, considered a number of alternative suggestions for a new arena for Toronto. After due consideration, they have unanimously decided that they will sponsor and build an arena themselves. Details of finance, with a Board of

Directors representative of the best business elements of the city, will be announced within a few days."

— statement issued by Conn Smythe, January 16, 1931

"We have decided to go ahead with construction of a modern arena which will be suitable in every respect for hockey and all other sports, as well as for conventions and big displays such as motor shows."

— Conn Smythe, elaborating on the plans
in *Toronto Daily Star*, January 17, 1931

"The two sites under consideration have not been definitely announced as yet, but it is known that Yonge and Fleet Streets is one, while the other is said to be on College Street, not far from Yonge. Both are admirable for the purpose intended, and there is easy access to them from any part of the city.

"The present contract with the Arena Gardens does not expire until the end of next season. Under its terms, the Toronto club would have to forfeit $1,000 for every home game that was not played there. As there are twenty-two home games, this means a matter of $22,000 for the entire season. This, however, will not interfere with the Toronto club's plan to proceed with the new arena in time to play next season's games. It is felt that, with the extra seating accommodation which the new arena will provide, it will more than repay the club to have the building ready for next year's games."

— *Globe*, Toronto, January 17, 1931

"[Smythe] said he was in favour of the Yonge and Fleet streets site on city-owned reclaimed land. It was only four minutes' walk from King and Yonge and with the completion of the lake front boulevard there would be almost perfect motor approaches from both ends of the city. It was also easy [to] access from the Bay and Yonge streetcar lines, and all car lines running along Front Street."

— *Toronto Daily Star*, January 17, 1931

Though the naming of the board of directors promised in January did not occur until March 5, during February of 1931, shareholders of the Maple Leafs Hockey Club created a new company to be known as Maple Leaf Gardens Ltd., and Conn Smythe worked at wooing city council to get the proper building permits granted in a timely fashion.

"Conn Smythe, Managing Director of the Maple Leaf Club, appeared with Frank Selke at the committee meeting urging that speed in granting the permit was essential if they were to hold the backers of the scheme together...."

"'We ask that you let us have the permit so that we may get on with our work,' Mr. Smythe urged.

"Alderman Chamberlain — When do you propose to start building?

"Mr. Smythe — Just as soon as we can. I assure you it is no easy matter to raise a million and a quarter dollars these days; every two weeks you hold us up is vital.

"Alderman Hunt — We should not delay this one day; here is a proposal that will give work to many. Let it go on to Council subject to the approval of our officials.

"Alderman Wadsworth — Why all the hurry? They have had a year to come here with their plans; do not try to rush it through; it should go on to Council in the regular manner."

— *Globe*, Toronto, February 13, 1931

"The official announcement is made today of the plans and financing of the Maple Leaf Hockey Club for the erection of the new modern, up-to-date sports arena at Carlton and Church streets in time for next year's hockey.... Everybody recognizes the need of a larger arena so far as hockey is concerned, and the new Maple Leaf Gardens promises to be the last word in that respect."

— W.A. Hewitt, *Toronto Daily Star*, March 5, 1931

"According to the architectural plans ... the new home of the Maple Leafs ... will be an imposing structure indeed. It combines architectural beauty with all the modern equipment and conveniences that such structures require, and it will be a decided asset to Toronto.

"The ice surface of the new building will be 200 feet by 85 feet, which is twenty feet longer and five feet wider than the present Arena Gardens. The total seating capacity, according to the plans, will be 13,514. The promenade, including all rail seats, will accommodate 500; the amphitheatre, which includes the box seats, will seat 7,054. An additional 1,380 can be seated in the side galleries, while the top gallery will provide 4,600 seats.

"The main floor of the building will have space for several shops, a bowling alley and billiard parlour, gymnasium, spacious clubrooms for the Toronto players and visiting clubs. The main entrance will face Carlton Street. There will also be exits leading to Carlton, Church and Wood Streets. The whole structure will occupy a space of 350 feet running east and west on Carlton Street by 283 feet running north and south on Church Street....

"It is planned to have the building ready for the opening of the NHL season next November."

— Bert Perry, *Globe*, Toronto, March 5, 1931

"The splendid crowd that attended the Leaf-Chicago game last night testified to the popularity of the local team and the hold the game has on the public. This has been a record season for pro hockey in Toronto, the gate receipts exceeding $200,000 for the first time. The receipts would have been much greater had there been more accommodations, no less than 14 of the 22 home games being sellouts, in which thousands of more tickets could have been sold had the building been able to accommodate all those who wished to attend. This will be remedied this year with the building of the new Maple Leaf Gardens ... with over twice the seating capacity of the present Arena. Wrecking operations will commence on the build on the 1st of April, or as rapidly as the tenants move out, and construction work is scheduled to begin on May 1. The new arena is expected to be ready for hockey by November 1."

— W.A. Hewitt, *Toronto Daily Star*, March 20, 1931

Construction did not actually begin until June 1.

"Sir John Aird, one of the Maple Leaf Gardens Limited directors, called a meeting in his office to open the bids.... But when the bids were opened and read, and the amount of money we had in hand or promised or even hoped for, was totalled up, we were — as I recollect — a few hundred thousand dollars short. That wouldn't be much today. Early in 1931, it was a mountain.... I left the meeting to take a rest, trying to think what rabbit I could pull out of the hat now. Outside on a bench was Frank Selke."

— Conn Smythe, *If You Can't Beat 'Em in the Alley* (1981)

"I had a chance to discuss the matter with my fellow business agents of the Allied Building Trades Council of Toronto.... I still held the position of honorary business manager of the International Brotherhood of Electrical workers ... [and] at this meeting, every business agent of the union who worked in the building trade was present.... It was then I made one of the most important speeches in my life. 'Now, look here!' I said. 'Don't you realize the terrific blow this would be to the building trades if it falls through?' I asked.... 'Here is my proposal.... Every union in the building trades has hundreds of men out of employment. Many of our boys are on civic relief, with no hope of a job anywhere. So why not make the company an offer? Why not tell them that if they hire all union mechanics we will sign an agreement that each skilled worker, not labourers, will accept 20 percent of his wages in Maple Leaf Gardens stock? Most of these men are unemployed now; so they will at least get 80 percent cash, and they'll have the balance in stock certificates....' So the men took the stock. Some, unfortunately, sold it for what they could get when the job was finished. But most of the boys waited until it paid dividends, and put their money back in their pockets."

— Frank Selke, *Behind the Cheering* (1962)

"Directors yesterday granted the contract for the erection of the new Maple Leaf Gardens to Thomson Brothers, Toronto, whose tender was $989,297, the lowest of ten tenders submitted. This sum is exclusive of steel work, estimated at $100,000. Two American firms were among the nine other bidders."

— *Toronto Daily Star*, May 30, 1931

"In the end, the contractors who had submitted the low bid with a price shaved to the bone, Thomson Brothers, lost money on the deal.... Even though they were losing money, they were still doing the job. A lot of contractors would have come back to us and tried to renegotiate. I certainly admired Allan Thomson."

— Conn Smythe, *If You Can't Beat 'Em in the Alley* (1981)

"The first formal function in connection with the new Maple Leaf Gardens, now nearing completion at Church and Carlton streets, will be the laying of the corner-stone on Monday afternoon at 3:30.... Lieut. Governor W.D. Ross will perform the ceremony and J.P. Bickell, chairman of the board of directors of the Gardens, will preside. An inspection of the building will follow the ceremony and all shareholders are invited to attend."

— W.A. Hewitt, *Toronto Daily Star*, September 19, 1931

"I am glad that the idea of building a new sports arena in Toronto was initiated during my term of office as Lieutenant-Governor of Ontario and that it is my official duty, as well as my keen personal pleasure, to lay the corner-stone. Toronto is, and has been for years, a sports centre. Our position on Lake Ontario, our National Exhibition, our general enthusiasm for sports of all kind — amateur and professional — make this city the 'logical location' for a building worthy of our record, of our need and of our ambition....

"In the hope and expectation that Maple Leaf Gardens will play well its part in the development of good and clean athletic sports, I hereby declare its corner-stone to be well and truly laid."

— W.D. Ross, Lieutenant-Governor of Ontario, September 21, 1931

"The ceremony was followed by an inspection of the building which evoked the admiration and wonder of all beholders. The new gardens will be formally opened on November 12 with the first game of the NHL season. There is plenty of work yet to be done, but the contractors promise to complete the building on time."

— *Toronto Daily Star*, September 22, 1931

"From time to time we would wander over from the Mutual Street Arena to take a look at the progress they were making.... The players were all excited about moving over to play in the Gardens when it was ready for use. And believe me, when it was finished it was something to behold. When we moved in after playing in the Mutual Street Arena, it was like walking into a palace."

— King Clancy, *Clancy* (1968)

"Just because of the increased seating capacity of Maple Leaf Gardens over that of Arena Gardens, I am afraid that many local hockey fans figure that seats can be obtained at any time. If they are of that opinion, I am afraid many people are going to be disappointed if they try to obtain seats for Thursday's game next week. Indications point to a sell-out, and already the $1.50 seats have been bought up. The Maple Leaf Club is anxious that all its loyal supporters of past seasons be not disappointed in securing tickets, and it advises them that it will be unwise to delay until the day before the game. Professional hockey is creating more interest locally than ever before, and, judging by the way the tickets were taken up yesterday, when four wickets at the new Gardens were kept constantly busy from the noon hour on, I don't think there will be a ticket left for the opening night by Tuesday afternoon."

— Frank Selke, Maple Leafs business manager,
speaking to the press on November 7, 1931

"Good advice to all who attend tonight's premiere at Maple Leaf Gardens is to get there early. The doors will be open at 7:30 when the band concert will begin and the opening ceremonies will start an hour later.

"There will be plenty of interest for early-comers as they will get a real chance to see the new Gardens....

"For the benefit of thousands of radio listeners all over the country, Foster Hewitt will broadcast the game over CFCA and CKGW, the game being sponsored by General Motors Products of Canada."

— W.A. Hewitt, *Toronto Daily Star*, November 12, 1931

"The blue and white of the Maple Leafs team will be the prevailing colours tonight at the official opening of our new hockey playhouse, Maple Leaf Gardens.

"The only contrasting colour in the house, so far as the furniture is concerned, will be the red leather seats of the boxes. And these will be all hidden from view.

"Those who have not had an opportunity to see the magnificent building where we are to enjoy our hockey games this winter are in for a treat this evening. So come early and get a chance to look-see before the opening ceremonies.

"Tonight society in all its glory will be among those present. The brilliant jewels of the fair ladies, the colourful gowns, the rich evening wraps, will be of just as much interest to a large portion of the audience as the final score will be to the rest of those present."

— Alexandrine Gibb, *Toronto Daily Star*, November 12, 1931

"Bill Hewitt has requested me to deny the fiendish rumour that things are so high hat around the new Gardens that the peanut men will only be allowed to sell salted almonds!

"As a matter of fact, he intimated that special chutes would be found beneath each seat to convey peanut shells to the furnace room so that they may be used to provide heat. So any time you get a bit chilly buy yourself a new sack of peanuts and fire up your own seat.

"What a calamity it would be if Chicago Hawks knocked Leafs off at tonight's opener!

"Don't forget these are the same Hawks — only better — that kicked Leafs out of the Stanley Cup [playoffs] last spring and dang near cost us our new ice palace. They should call them the Capones for they have no respect for law, order or the eternal fitness of things.

"Some cynical fans twitter that tonight's game is as safe for Leafs as a girl in cotton stockings! The chatter is that it isn't on the books for the Leafs to be beaten in their first home game in the new ice palace — 'twoudn't be policy — in the bag — all that sort of 'wise' stuff....

"Tonight's game will not be won until the last gong has sounded — and then maybe not then. The Hawks are a better team than they were last season. And the Leafs should be!"

— Lou Marsh, *Toronto Daily Star*, November 12, 1931

Chicago did go on to defeat Toronto in that first game at Maple Leaf Gardens, winning by a score of 2–1. Chicago's Mush March scored the first goal early in the first period, before Charlie Conacher got the first Maple Leafs goal in the second. The Black Hawks won it on a goal by Vic Ripley scored early in the third. Newspapers all said the Leafs were over-anxious and lacked teammmwork, but most of the stories focused on the spectacle of the evening.

"Nothing finer in the world."

— NHL president Frank Calder on Maple Leaf Gardens, November 12, 1931

"Toronto passed a new milestone in its long and eventful hockey history last night.

"Before the largest crowd that ever attended a hockey game here, 13,542, according to the official figures, the National League season was ushered in at the magnificent new home of the Maple Leafs at Carlton and Church Streets. All that was lacking to make it a highly satisfactory occasion from every standpoint was a victory for the home team….

"Maple Leaf Gardens, rivalling Madison Square Garden, the Boston Arena Gardens, the Montreal Forum, and other huge arenas in the National Hockey League, proved a revelation to Toronto fans, who turned out on this occasion to pay tribute to the courage and enterprise of the men behind the Maple Leaf Hockey Club.

"With its row upon row of eager-eyed enthusiasts rising up and up from the red leather cushions of the box and rail seats, where society was well represented by patrons in evening dress, though section after section of bright blue seats to the green and grey of the top tiers, the spectacle presented was magnificent. The immensity of the hippodrome of hockey claimed to be the last word in buildings of its kind, was impressed upon the spectator, and those present fully agreed that Toronto had at last blossomed forth into major league ranks to the fullest extent."

— Bert Perry, *Globe*, Toronto, November 13, 1931

"The new Maple Leaf Gardens proved a revelation to the hockey public last night. Everybody expressed amazement and pleasure at its spaciousness, its tremendous capacity, its comfort, its beautiful colour scheme, and its adaptability for hockey and all other indoor sports with the spectators right on top of the action....

"It was a night that will live long in the memories of the fans, even if the home team lost."

— W.A. Hewitt, *Toronto Daily Star*, November 13, 1931

"The opening ceremonies, too lengthy for the impatient spectators whose primary interest lay in the hockey game to follow, included two massed bands who gathered on the ice while J.P. Bickell, President of the Maple Leaf Club, Hon. George S. Henry, Premier of Ontario, and Mayor W.J. Stewart spoke words of welcome to the citizens and players. Floral horseshoes presented to the Leafs by the City of Toronto municipal body, added to the picture presented, and after Captains [Cy] Wentworth of the Black Hawks and 'Happy' Day of the Leafs had spoken a few words into the microphone, Mayor Stewart dropped the puck for the opening face-off and the game was ready to begin."

— Bert Perry, *Globe*, Toronto, November 13, 1931

The 1931–32 Season and Stanley Cup Final

After the Leafs lost on opening night, they tied their next two games, and then lost two more, making them winless in five starts.

Conn Smythe decided the fault with the struggling Leafs lay with coach Art Duncan, who'd been hired the previous season. Duncan was fired on November 27, 1931, after a team practice at the Gardens.

"It is from the results to date — that is, the standing of our team with only two points, with the material available — that we are engaging a new coach. It is thought that a new man, with an unbiased view on the older players, will work to the advantage of the Maple Leafs, and for these reasons we are making the change, and not from any personal feeling between the club, Manager Smythe, and Mr. Duncan."

— club announcement, November 27, 1931

"Conn Smythe and I had been so engrossed in getting the new building ready for the opening that we had neglected the hockey team. We had simply left the chore in the hands of Art Duncan. Art was too soft-hearted to drive the players during practice. In consequence, they opened the season many pounds overweight and not ready for stiff competition."

— Frank Selke, *Behind the Cheering* (1962)

"[We] only managed to tie two games in our first [five]. That was difficult to fathom, considering the talent we had on the roster. Art Duncan, our coach, was replaced by Mr. Smythe for the sixth game against Boston…. Then Mr. Smythe made a decision that paid dividends. He called Dick Irvin in Regina and offered him the Leafs coaching job. Dick was a brilliant hockey man and a strict disciplinarian, Mr. Smythe's kind of fellow, all the way…. Dick spotted the trouble. We'd been having things too soft in practice, and he started to work us…. So we soon learned to carry out the instructions that were given us. Our play on the ice improved, but we still carried on in the dressing room."

— King Clancy, *Clancy* (1968)

"I well remember Dick walking in, bright and early, hours ahead of his appointment that morning…. 'What kind of man is Smythe, anyhow?' Dick asked me. I cannot think of any more difficult task than to give a character sketch of Conn Smythe. But I did the best I could. I told Dick that above everything else, Smythe was the Boss with a capital B. And if Dick felt he could work under strict discipline, he would no doubt have a happy time in Toronto."

— Frank Selke, *Behind the Cheering* (1962)

Dick Irvin quickly got the Maple Leafs on track and they were soon staging a season-long battle with the Montreal Canadiens for first place in the Canadian Division. Charlie Conacher led the league with 34 goals in the newly expanded 48-game season, while Joe Primeau topped the circuit with 37 assists, and Busher Jackson led the scoring race with 53 points. Jackson earned a First-Team All-Star berth at left wing, while Conacher (right wing) and King Clancy (defence) earned Second-Team selections. Primeau won the Lady Byng Trophy for sportsmanship.

In the end, Toronto finished the season in second place with a record of 23–18–7 and 53 points (which was nearly identical to their finish in 1930–31). They got revenge over Chicago by defeating them in the first round of the playoffs, and then knocked off the Montreal Maroons to advance to the Stanley Cup Final against the New York Rangers.

"For the first time since 1922, Toronto has a chance to win the historic Stanley Cup, but said chance seemed negligible until midway in the third period of Saturday night's thrilling game here against the gallant Montreal Maroons. The latter had taken a 2-to-1 lead when 'Hooley' Smith's bounding shot beat Goalkeeper Lorne Chabot, but 'Happy' Day got that one back …"

— M.J. Rodden, *Globe*, Toronto, April 4, 1932

"Down came 'Happy' Day, veteran captain of the team — Day, who is just beginning to really find himself and play the hockey that made him the idol of two years ago.

"Here he comes … top speed … all along … He swerves by the last defence man … He's inside with only [goalie Flat] Walsh to beat … He tricks Walsh into diving at him. He flips it by … HE SCORES! … HE SCORES!!

"THE GAME IS TIED!!!"

— Lou Marsh, *Toronto Daily Star*, April 4, 1932

"[A]fter nearly eighteen minutes of overtime play Bob Gracie scored the winning marker."

— M.J. Rodden, *Globe*, Toronto, April 4, 1932

"Gracias, Gracie! You're some hombre! And to think that you almost landed in Syracuse or Tulsa or some other burg down the river! Gracie certainly deserved the 'break' which gave him the hero's role. He has been coming steadily — yes, sensationally…. Gracie's goal qualifies as a well-earned goal, for he picked up his pass faultlessly, tore right on in and shot true and hard. There was plenty on the old pill when it left Gracie."

— Lou Marsh, *Toronto Daily Star*, April 4, 1932

"In defeating Maroons, a great money team, the Leafs earned brackets, but it was close, and a break either way might have decided it long before the teams went into overtime…. The Leafs will oppose Rangers at New York tomorrow night, and will undoubtedly get another acid test, but they are confident that they will not stop now until they have won the Cup."

— M.J. Rodden, *Globe*, Toronto, April 4, 1932

"It's going to be kids against veterans tomorrow night. Joe Primeau, Harvey Jackson, and Charlie Conacher are just fledglings alongside of Frankie Boucher and the Cooks. But through the regular hockey season the fledglings beat the veterans three games out of five, significantly what the Maple Leafs must do again to carry the mug home to Toronto."

— Harold C. Burr, *Brooklyn Daily Eagle*, April 4, 1932

"The New Yorkers are given the edge over the Toronto players because of the manner in which they disposed of the Montreal Canadiens … last week.… The Montreal players had been favoured to win the Stanley Cup for the third successive time and their defeat by the Rangers was something of an upset.

"Lester Patrick's players enter the game completely rested, while the Toronto stick-wielders are anything but full of pep. They finished up a hard series with the Maroons Saturday night and then made the long jump from Toronto to New York yesterday, and that train ride didn't add to their energy.…

"After tonight's contest the teams will move to Boston, where the second game will be played Thursday.

"The New Yorkers were forced off their home rink because the Garden has been leased for that night to a circus. The third game will be staged at the Maple Leaf Gardens in Toronto Saturday night. If fourth and fifth games are necessary they will be held in Toronto next Tuesday and Thursday."

— *Toronto Daily Star*, April 5, 1932

The Maple Leafs won the series opener 6–4, paced by a hat trick from Busher Jackson and some weak goaltending from 1922 St. Patricks Stanley Cup star John Ross Roach.

"When we played Rangers in the first game of the Cup finals at New York, we served fourteen or sixteen minutes in penalties, and from Goaler Chabot right out to centre ice every Leaf was like the Rock of Gibraltar while Rangers shot the works with their ganging. And we finished on top in the scoring at the end of a period that contained one of the greatest defensive stands and also one of the greatest sustained ganging attacks I have ever witnessed."

— Conn Smythe, recalling Game 1 of the 1932 Cup Final as his greatest thrill from a Leafs team to Bill Roche, *Globe and Mail*, Toronto, November 26, 1938

Playing in Boston for Game 2 after the circus took over Madison Square Garden, the Rangers scored two early goals, but the Leafs stormed back to score a 6–2 victory. King Clancy scored two goals and the Kid Line starred again, with Conacher scoring twice and Jackson once.

"Congratulations again. Citizens have no doubt of your ability to come through. Keep up the good work. Best wishes.

(Signed) W.J. Stewart, Mayor."
— telegram sent to the Maple Leafs in Boston, April 7, 1932

"It appears fairly certain now that the Stanley Cup is coming to this city. The Maple Leafs took another step towards the world hockey championship last night in Boston when they gave the New York Rangers their second straight beating in the final series and it only remains for the Leafs to finish off Lester Patrick's men here tomorrow night to bring the venerable battered mug to Toronto after an absence of ten years.... Only a miraculous recovery by the Rangers will prevent the Leafs winning the Stanley Cup now."
— M.J. Rodden, *Globe*, Toronto, April 8, 1932

"Just Sixty Minutes from Stanley Cup, All Toronto Hopes"

"Fourteen Thousand Inside Maple Leaf Gardens and Millions Outside Ready to Whoop for Joy if Leafs Down Rangers Tonight."
— front-page headlines, *Globe*, Toronto, April 9, 1932

"The honest sportsman who believes that the game is on the up and up asks: 'Can the Leafs make it three straight?' But right now the chiselers — the guys who are so tricky that they even put the slug on one another — are smugly enquiring, 'Will the Leafs make it three straight?' and a lot of them will be in there tonight in the Suckers Roundup betting that the same crowd of game athletes who stood up so gallantly under the Rangers' heavy assault in New York on [Tuesday] night ... and then skated the champs dizzy in Boston Thursday ... will toss off tonight's game.

"If you ask them what for, they will reply, 'The gate receipts,' and lay the digit along the beak.... It won't do you a bit of good to argue with them that the players get nothing out of extra gates ... that the players only share in the receipts of the first three games — that if the series goes into a fourth and fifth game that only the club owners, the league and the rinks profit.

"They only look at you pityingly ... and point out that the Leafs are owned by the same company which owns the new Gardens, and tell you that it is easy to make a sub-rosa split of the extra money after it is all over.

"'Mean to tell me that the Garden Company and the Leafs club are gonna pass up the 47 1/2 per cent of the gross gates which goes to the rink plus the 57 per cent of the net receipts which go to the owners of the winning club on its fourth and fifth games?' sweetly inquired one of these limburger-minded chislers…. There is no arguing with these gentry. They're simply born that way."

— Lou Marsh, *Toronto Daily Star*, April 9, 1932

"It was a three-out-five series, and Mr. Smythe, who certainly needed the money, stood to clear a bundle if it went the full five games…. We're up two in a row, and now we come back home for the third and perhaps final game.

"I remember so vividly Mr. Smythe coming into the room at the Gardens and saying to us, 'Fellows, if you win this game tonight you win the Stanley Cup. If you lose, it means at least one more game and another big gate here. Now, I want to make it perfectly clear what I want you to do. I want you to go out there and prove to the people of the world that hockey is played on a high plane, that it's strictly on the up-and-up. You show them there's no monkey business in our sport. I want you to win this hockey game tonight. If you lose, sure it's more money in the till for me, but I'm telling you I won't tolerate a loss tonight. I want a championship and I want that Stanley Cup!'"

— King Clancy, *Clancy* (1968)

On Saturday, April 9, 1932, in front of a crowd of 14,366, the Maple Leafs jumped out to an early 2–0 lead, were up 5–1 late in the third, and held on for a 6–4 victory to sweep the series.

"The capture by the Toronto Maple Leafs of the Stanley Cup … will send a reassuring thrill, not only through Toronto, but throughout all Canada. The centre of the hockey-playing population has been shifting southward so swiftly in recent years that there has been some wonder as to whether or not hockey pre-eminence would remain long in Canada. The laurels are in safe hands for another year. Canada is first. The Maple Leaf forever."

— *Globe*, Toronto, April 11, 1932

"I'm happy to be with the team to bring the Stanley Cup here for the first time since 1922. I want to thank you all for your support and to say 'hello' to my mother and dad. I hope they're listening in."

— Leafs captain Hap Day on the post-game radio broadcast

"Three cheers for the Leafs."

— Toronto mayor W.J. Stewart on the post-game radio broadcast

"It's the players who make a coach."

— Dick Irvin when asked about winning the Stanley Cup in Toronto
a year after leading Chicago to the Stanley Cup Final in 1931

"We are naturally disappointed with the three-game defeat. It is hard to offer any excuses, but I don't think that week's layoff did us any good. We caught the Leafs stepping out of a fine victory over Maroons. They were in full stride and I can't say that we were in our best playing form. We played our best, but we lacked the early scoring punch that helped us in the regular schedule and against Canadiens."

— Rangers star centre Frank Boucher

"The ten-minute ovation to the Leafs after the game testifies to their popularity.... Autograph hunters pestered the players for hours after the game."

— *Toronto Daily Star*, April 11, 1932

"[Hap] Day may have been a bit slow starting the season but he was right there at the tail end of the season to make good his opening night promise via the loud speaker that the Leafs would win the Stanley Cup."

— Lou Marsh, *Toronto Daily Star*, April 11, 1932

"Conny Smythe, manager of the world champion Maple Leaf hockey team, has commemorated the triumph of the club in a novel manner. Conny is also a race horse owner and has named three of the younger members of his stable Stanley Cup, Six to Four, and Three Straight.... The rest is up to the thoroughbreds. If they turn out good ones, there will be reason to remember the Leafs' victory for a long time."

— *Ottawa Journal*, May 12, 1932

"Moose Jaw, Sask., July 2 — Dick Irvin, famous coach of the Toronto Maple Leafs, world's hockey champions, who calls for speed and more speed from his hockey players during the playing season and who races pigeons as a hobby during the summer, was presented yesterday with a homing pigeon with a number he is not likely to forget. It is 646264-32, which is the score of the games between Toronto Maple Leafs and the New York Rangers when the championship was won. R.H. Long, of the Moose Jaw Racing Pigeon club, made the presentation. The bird with such numbers should prove a champion itself. The last two numbers, 32, stand for the year the bird was hatched."

— *Winnipeg Tribune*, July 2, 1932

1932–33

A Great Season, But a Tough Playoff

Toronto finished in first place in the Canadian Division in the 1932–33 season with a record of 24–18–6 for 54 points in the 48-game season. Busher Jackson had another big year, finishing second in the NHL with 27 goals and 44 points, and earning a Second-Team All-Star selection along with Charlie Conacher and King Clancy.

> "I couldn't see why Toronto Maple Leafs shouldn't keep on winning Stanley Cups year after year, now that we'd won the first one. And that next year … we would have won at least one more Cup if it hadn't been for circumstances that I don't think would be allowed to happen today."
>
> — Conn Smythe, *If You Can't Beat 'Em in the Alley* (1981)

To open the playoffs, the Maple Leafs faced the Bruins, who had won the American Division, in a best-of-five series to determine a direct berth in the Stanley Cup Final. Toronto hadn't won a game against the Bruins in Boston since 1929, and the streak continued when the Bruins won the opener on home ice with a 2–1 victory in overtime. Game 2 went into overtime as well, and Toronto came out on top when Busher Jackson scored at 15:03 of overtime. Lorne Chabot earned the shutout in a 1–0 victory. The rest of the series would be played in Toronto, and the Maple Leafs were confident.

> "Take a good look at your team. It's the last time you will see them in action this season."
>
> — Conn Smythe to Boston fans after Game 2

The series remained tight. Boston won Game 3 by a score of 2–1 in overtime, but Toronto bounced back for a 5–3 victory to tie the series once again. A Canadian-record crowd of 14,530 filled Maple Leaf Gardens for the finale on April 3, 1933. They witnessed what is still the longest game in Maple Leafs history, and the second longest in NHL history.

The game was scoreless through regulation time, although Boston had a goal called back in the third period. Toronto finally appeared to win it when King Clancy scored — in the fourth overtime session! — but that goal was called back too. When the game remained scoreless through a fifth overtime period, it appeared things might be settled by a coin toss, but having already played 160 minutes of hockey, the two teams were back on the ice for a sixth overtime period.

"I know I played 114 minutes of hockey that night and no one can say that a fellow who's played that much is as fresh as he was in the first ten minutes…. When we went into the dressing room there wasn't one player sitting up. We were spent, absolutely drained of energy. Between periods, we all [lay] out on the dressing room floor; we weren't worth a quarter. It was just a case of who was going to get a lucky break — who was going to score first. And it was Kenny Doraty, who picked up a pass from Andy Blair and threw the puck into the net. I can see the puck going in there yet; it never left the ice and went right into the corner of the net. I think Tiny Thompson was so tired he couldn't lift his stick to stop it…. It was one of the greatest victories I was ever in, but we didn't do any celebrating that night because we were too tired to move."

— King Clancy, *Clancy* (1968)

"There's Eddie Shore going for the puck in the corner beside the Boston net. Andy Blair is on for the Leafs now…. He's moving in on Shore in the corner. Shore is clearing the puck — Blair intercepts!

"Blair has the puck. Ken Doraty is dashing for the front of the net. Blair passes. Doraty takes it!

"He shoots! He scores!"

— Foster Hewitt's broadcast of the goal, quoted by William Houston, *Globe and Mail*, Toronto, May 5, 1993

The time of Doraty's winning goal was 4:46 of the sixth overtime period.

"Boys, you deserved that one! You kept coming and coming and coming."

— Conn Smythe, bursting into the Leafs dressing room after the game

"A wonderful game. The boys came through marvellously…. They are all feeling fine considering what they went through."

— Coach Dick Irvin, in the dressing room after the game

"It was a great game. All the boys showed wonderful stamina and the goal-keepers were brilliant. It was a tough series to lose, but we congratulate the Toronto team on their victory."

— Boston Bruins coach and GM Art Ross

"I remember Art Ross, the manager of the Bruins, coming over and kissing me. He was a dour, hard loser, but he was fair."

— King Clancy, *Clancy* (1968)

It was approximately 1:48 a.m. on the morning of Tuesday, April 4, 1933, when the game finally ended. Because the circus was once again moving in to Madison Square Garden, Game 1 in the Stanley Cup Final was scheduled for that same night in New York.

> "I know we left for New York at three or four in the morning and didn't arrive until the next afternoon. And to expect us to play that evening after the previous night's game had gone on for so long was asking a little too much…. However, this is the price of being a hockey player."
>
> — King Clancy, *Clancy* (1968)

> "[W]e didn't get there by train until 4:30 in the afternoon. We were totally exhausted and we lost to the Rangers, 5–1. We never recovered from that."
>
> — Joe Primeau to Frank Orr, *Toronto Star*, February 9, 1977

Even with the remainder of the series played in Toronto, and four days off before they had to play Game 2, the Leafs lost the next one 3–1. Ken Doraty scored the lone goal. He scored two more in a 3–2 victory that kept the Maple Leafs alive in Game 3, but the Rangers wrapped up the best-of-five series in four when Bill Cook scored at 7:33 of overtime to give New York a 1–0 victory. Toronto had two men in the penalty box at the time.

> "They got the breaks. We had to spot them two games after the Boston series, and it was too much to ask the boys to come back. At that we out-played them tonight. Two undeserved penalties gave them the game."
>
> — Coach Dick Irvin, in the dressing room after the game

> "We had the finger on us all season and we just had to take it, that's all."
>
> — King Clancy, in the dressing room after the game

> "You did well, gang. You played a great game and you couldn't do more; that puck just wouldn't go in."
>
> — Conn Smythe, in the dressing room after the game

> "My prophecy we would take the Cup has been fulfilled. We have the most crowd-pleasing team I have ever handled, and they sure deserved to win this series…. Toronto Maple Leafs are a bunch of battlers and as pleasing to watch as the Rangers. It was tough for them to lose, but somebody had to win."
>
> — Rangers coach and GM Lester Patrick after the game

"Primeau says the best Leaf team of the eight seasons he wore Toronto colours was the 1932–33 outfit which lost to the New York Rangers in the Stanley Cup finals when the Rangers scored in sudden-death overtime."

— Al Nickleson, *Globe and Mail*, Toronto, October 20, 1950

1933–34

The Ace Bailey Incident

Boston Bruins owner Charles Adams liked tough hockey players. Art Ross built Adams's team to reflect that philosophy. Conn Smythe had done the same thing in Toronto. Off the ice, Ross and Smythe hated each other, and their personal animosity was often reflected in the games between their two teams. The long, gruelling playoff series in the spring of 1933 had only increased the tension between the Bruins and Maple Leafs. Even so, the events at Boston Garden on December 12, 1933, were so terrible that no one could really have seen them coming.

The Bruins' great Eddie Shore had held out for a better contract in the fall of 1933 and missed the first two games of the season. Even after he returned, the team that finished first in the American Division in five of the last six seasons was spinning its wheels. The Bruins were 6–6–0 heading into the December 12 game against Toronto. The Maple Leafs were 9–2–1 and Boston fans hoped the visit by Toronto would bring out the best in the Bruins. It didn't.

"When I played, if you carried your stick above your shoulders you got a penalty. There were lots of fights and lots of tough bodychecking, but you never thought of going after a guy's head with your stick.... When I played we had a lot of tough players, but none of the stick stuff and boarding you see now. Lots of fights, though I was a lousy fighter. Just hung on until big Charlie [Conacher] arrived."

— Ace Bailey to Trent Frayne, *Globe and Mail*, Toronto, January 12, 1988

"I never thought I could get hurt. I was knocked out a bunch of times, but that doesn't hurt. I lost a bunch of my teeth, had my nose broke, cuts, broke my hands, fingers, but no, it never entered my mind that I could get hurt. I was on the ice the night in Boston when Eddie Shore cracked Ace Bailey's skull and ended Ace's career. But it didn't bother or scare me. I felt sorry for Bailey because he was a game player, but I thought it could never happen to me."

— King Clancy to Gare Joyce, *MVP* magazine, April 1986

Ace Bailey's life hung in the balance for several days after his head struck the ice when he was knocked down by Eddie Shore. A series of operations saved Bailey's life, but he never played hockey again.

"I'll never forget it. You know, I'm sure Shore hit the wrong man. He mistook me for Red Horner."

— Ace Bailey to Paul Hunter, *Toronto Star*, January 13, 1988

"Shore wasn't a vicious player, although he knew he was playing a rough game. He wasn't out there to maim anybody, but simply to make his living. He certainly meant to hit Ace as hard as he could, but I don't think he expected such drastic results."

— King Clancy, *Clancy* (1968)

"We were two men shy and the Bruins were pounding in, led by Eddie Shore."
— Ace Bailey to Trent Frayne for a Maple Leaf Gardens program, circa 1948–49
(quoted by Harold Kaese in the *Daily Boston Globe*, February 22, 1949)

"Hec Kilrea opened the second period with a brilliant exhibition of stickhandling, which he ended by driving a terrific shot at the Boston goalkeeper. If he had any of his mates up with him, a goal might have resulted. The Conacher-Primeau-Jackson line came on after three minutes and got into trouble when [Red] Horner and [Hap] Day went off [with penalties] almost together. The Bruins attacked their weakened foes with five men, but the Leafs managed to hold them back until they regained full strength.

"Then came five more minutes of furious slashing and [Toronto's Andy] Blair went off for hooking. The Barry line came on for the Bruins, and Day aggravated the Leafs' chances by interfering with Marty as he crossed the Toronto blue line. But again the three Leafs managed to turn back every Boston advance."

— *Globe*, Toronto, December 13, 1933

"Dick Irvin sent out King Clancy and myself and Ace Bailey up front to kill off the (two) penalties. Bailey was a very expert stickhandler, and he ragged the puck for a while."

— Red Horner in Ace Bailey Spotlight, Hockey Hall of Fame website (2007)

"Bailey had been stopping the Bruins' rushes while the Leafs were short-handed, and he had just checked Shore and taken the puck away from him and shot it down the ice."

— Frank Selke on the phone to Bert Perry of the *Globe*, Toronto, December 12, 1933 (reported in the paper on December 13)

The Leafs soon regained full strength, but Boston was still pressing.

"Shore came into our end with the puck; we had Horner and King Clancy on defence, and I was following from behind. When Shore got to Horner, Red checked him into the boards."

— Ace Bailey to Paul Hunter, *Toronto Star*, January 13, 1988

"Shore got his stick on the puck and made a nice rush deep into our end. Shore came down my side and I gave him a very good hip check."

— Red Horner in Ace Bailey Spotlight, Hockey Hall of Fame website (2007)

Some sources claim Horner had tripped Shore.

"As I recall, the play leading to the accident happened as Shore started a rush toward our zone. When he reached the defence, Horner stopped him with what seemed to be a trip, and Shore slid into the end boards."

— Joe Primeau to Stan Fischler, *Power Play* (1972)

Others say it was King Clancy who tripped Shore.

"Eddie Shore picked up the puck and made one of his famous sorties into the Toronto end. Shore is generally rated the best rushing defenceman of all time. Naturally, he was hard to stop.

"As he tried to round King Clancy at Toronto's right defence, Clancy tapped him on the front of his skates with his hockey stick. It was an innocuous trick, seldom frowned upon by referees."

— Frank Selke, *Canadian Weekly*, November 17–23, 1962

Sources also differ as to whether it was Horner or Clancy who then carried the puck up the ice.

"As Shore slipped to his knees, Clancy carried the puck into the Boston end. Ace Bailey automatically dropped into Clancy's place on the defence, while the King was hurtling pell-mell into the Bruin zone."

— Frank Selke, *Canadian Weekly*, November 17–23, 1962

"Horner recovered the puck and moved up the ice with it. Meanwhile, Ace took up Horner's position. Since Ace was tired, he leaned over to catch his breath."

— Joe Primeau to Stan Fischler, *Power Play* (1972)

"Red Horner broke it up. He dumped Shore into the boards and raced away with the puck. As he moved down the ice I stayed back at his right defense post."

— Ace Bailey to Trent Frayne, Maple Leaf Gardens program, circa 1948–49

"When Clancy started his rush, Shore made no attempt to rise. Instead he remained on his knees, with both gloved hands resting on the ice. I was sure he was hoping to attract the referee and thus get a penalty handed out to Clancy. So, instead of watching the play at that moment, we were all watching Shore. As Shore dropped his head to look at the referee under his right arm, [*Boston Globe* sportwriter] Victor Jones said to me, 'Shore is sure mad!'

"Realizing the referee was ignoring him, Shore arose and slowly started back for his end of the ice."

— Frank Selke, *Canadian Weekly*, November 17–23, 1962

"George Hainsworth in the Toronto goal … had the best view of what happened next — and he said Shore charged Bailey from behind."

— Conn Smythe, *If You Can't Beat 'Em in the Alley* (1981)

"Shore climbed to his feet behind me in a corner. Eddie loved to win and when Red dumped him, he was mad — mad at himself, mostly, I suppose, because he hadn't clicked.

"He started back down the ice and as he drew near me I guess he thought I was Horner.

"He skated by and, still sore at himself in particular and all the Leafs in general, he took a swipe at my skates as he went by."

— Ace Bailey to Trent Frayne, Maple Leaf Gardens
program, circa 1948–49

"Ace Bailey was tripped from behind by the retreating Shore. Bailey's head struck the ice with terrific force and he was unconscious."

— *Globe*, Toronto, December 13, 1933

"[Shore] caught my skates in such a way that my feet went completely from under me. I went straight into the air and landed full force on the back of my head."

— Ace Bailey to Trent Frayne for a Maple Leaf
Gardens program, circa 1948–49

"I'll never know whether Shore mistook Ace for Horner. In any event, Shore came up and ran into Ace from the back, it seemed, and Ace fell … and hit his head on the ice. Shore had given him a good shot from behind with his whole body."

— Joe Primeau to Stan Fischler, *Power Play* (1972)

"[Shore] was behind Horner and Bailey, who were then on Toronto's blue line, and he was headed in a direction that would take him halfway between them…. About 10 feet from the blue line Eddie changes his course.

"Ace Bailey, tired from his exertions, was leaning forward, resting his stick across his knees, watching Clancy battling a couple of Bruins for possession of the puck at the far end of the rink. Whether Shore mistook Bailey for Clancy, or whether he was annoyed by his own futility and everything in general, nobody will ever know. But we all saw Shore suddenly put his head down and rush at top speed. He struck Bailey across the kidneys with his right shoulder with such force that it upended Bailey in a backward somersault."

— Frank Selke, *Canadian Weekly*, November 17–23, 1962

But Selke had told the story somewhat differently at the time.

"Shore, skating back to his position, came up behind Bailey, charged him below the knees and lifted the Toronto player off his feet. Bailey came down on his head with a terrific impact and was knocked unconscious."

— Frank Selke on the phone to Bert Perry of
Globe, Toronto, December 12, 1933

Foster Hewitt, however, recalled it similar to the way Selke did in 1962.

"Shore slowly regained his feet and headed on a course that should have steered him safely between Bailey and Horner. However, without further provocation, Shore suddenly changed direction, picked up speed, and rushed headlong into Bailey. He crashed the unprotected Toronto player with such reckless force that Ace was hurled into a backwards somersault and landed on his head with a crack that was heard around the rink."

— Foster Hewitt, *Foster Hewitt* (1967)

"All of us in the press box heard a crack you might compare to the sound of a pumpkin crashed with a baseball bat."

— Frank Selke, *Canadian Weekly*, November 17–23, 1962

"I found out after a good many years that ice is a lot harder than a hockey player's head."

— Art Ross, *Toronto Daily Star*, December 13, 1933

"I saw Marty Barry coming up ice with the puck and I raced to get out of the Toronto zone before an offside was called. I had absolutely no premeditation. I had absolutely no animosity towards Bailey, and there was no malice in my heart."

— Eddie Shore, *Blueline Magazine*, April 1956

"I can't remember exactly what happened. Yesterday, Art Ross, Bruins manager, came in and told me his version of how the accident occurred. Horner and Clancy were out on a rush and [Boston's Marty Barry] was carrying the puck.

"Well, Art Ross said Shore was offside in our defense zone and he was skating back fast to avoid a penalty, and I was skating fast to protect Horner and Clancy's territory. I didn't see Eddie and he didn't see me, and we crashed, and that's all.

"I don't remember anything leading up to the play or anything about the game except what Ross told me. There never was any hard feeling between Shore and myself."
— Ace Bailey to reporters from his Boston hospital room, January 4, 1933

"Ace Bailey was a player whose qualities I never truly appreciated until I played with him in Toronto and discovered just how good a player he was. I was with the Leafs in Boston on December 12, 1933, when Ace played his last game. Believe me, it was one of the most unfortunate incidents — although I prefer to call it an accident — that ever happened in sport."
— King Clancy, *Clancy* (1968)

"Eddie Shore was always a tough campaigner, but he was sincere and a good fellow. He came into the [dressing] room [where Bailey had been taken to recover] with right hand outstretched, saying, 'I'm sorry, Ace. I didn't mean to hurt you.'

"Bailey was lying on his back, his face flushed. As Shore came to his side, he sat up. 'That's all right, Eddie. It's all part of the game.'"
— Frank Selke, *Canadian Weekly*, November 17–23, 1962

After the incident on the ice, Red Horner had rushed at Shore, punching him and knocking him to the ice. Shore struck his head and was bleeding badly.

Both Shore and Bailey were carried off the ice unconscious. It took seven stitches to close the cut to the back of Shore's head, but the injury was not as serious as it looked. Bailey, however, had suffered a fractured skull. It took several operations to save his life and weeks of recovery before he could leave hospital, but Bailey never played hockey again.

NHL managing director Frank Patrick investigated the game. He contacted lawyers in both Toronto and Boston. Fifty-one depositions were taken, involving every player in the game, as well as Boston sportswriters, prominent Boston citizens, and other spectators at the game. It turned out that only five Toronto players and four Boston players actually saw the collision, as most were watching the action further up the ice. Everyone agreed that despite the rough play, there'd been no indication of bad blood between Bailey and Shore prior to the incident, and even the players who saw them collide had sharp differences of opinion as to whether Shore had hit Bailey in an illegal manner. Patrick admitted it was impossible to know for sure. In the end, Shore was suspended for 16 games (one-third of the season) and Horner for six.

On February 14, 1934, the NHL staged a benefit All-Star Game at Maple
Leaf Gardens to raise funds for Ace Bailey and his family. Toronto faced a team
of two stars from each of the other NHL clubs that night. Shore had returned
to action by this time and was included on the All-Star Team. The Maple Leafs
won the game 7–3, but the most interesting aspect of the night occurred during the pre-game ceremonies when commemorative medals and windbreakers
were presented to all the players.

> "The first time [Shore] loosened up a bit was when Ace Bailey stepped
> out to make the presentations. The roar which greeted Bailey when he
> marched out so steadily and sure-footedly made Shore look up…. He
> came up as second man in the lineup to get his windbreaker."
>
> — Lou Marsh, *Toronto Daily Star*, February 15, 1934

> "It was a pretty dramatic meeting. As Ace stood there at centre ice, bare-
> headed and wearing glasses, Shore skated over to him and put out his hand.
> Ace gripped it and they both smiled, and the crowd went mad with cheering."
>
> — King Clancy, *Clancy* (1968)

Although this image is often
said to be Ace Bailey and Eddie
Shore shaking hands at the
Benefit Game in Maple Leaf
Gardens on February 14,
1934, it's actually from a game
at the Boston Garden on
March 6, 1934. The Leafs were
visiting the Bruins that night
and Bailey was in town for a
follow-up appointment with
his doctors there.

"They looked at each other for a moment, then clasped hands and talked quietly. What thoughts they had or what they said was never announced. But the cordial meeting of the two stirred the crowd into wild bursts of applause."

— Foster Hewitt, *Foster Hewitt* (1967)

"They sure warmed my heart. Please thank Toronto fans for those cheers. I appreciate them more than any others I ever received."

— Eddie Shore to reporters after the game

A capacity crowd of 14,074 paid a total of $20,909.40 for their tickets that night. All of the money was turned over to Ace Bailey.

Leafs Stars of the Early 1930s

"When we moved in [to Maple Leaf Gardens] back in 1931, a really fine hockey team was coming together. We had guys like Hap Day, Ace Bailey, Baldy Cotton and Lorne Chabot and then a gang of younger players came along — and what a bunch they were — Charlie Conacher, Joe Primeau and Busher Jackson."

— King Clancy, *Toronto Star*, February 9, 1977

"It was something very, very special to be a Maple Leaf in those years.... [T]here was an enormous team spirit and we were all very close friends. We spent a great deal of time on trains, which is very conducive to being close."

— Joe Primeau to Frank Orr, *Toronto Star*, February 9, 1977

"Charlie [Conacher] was my best friend. A great right winger and scorer. Tough as hell. He was a young lion, a battler. If you got in a squabble, he'd be the first one there."

— King Clancy to Gare Joyce, *MVP* magazine, April 1986

"King Clancy, that 165 pounds of energy who teams up with Happy Day on the Leaf defense ... has never failed in the dressing room to put his left sock and skate on first. One particular night, King became so enthused during one of his occasional outbursts that he slipped up on his superstition and put his right boot on first. When I pointed out his mistake, King was completely dressed and ready for the game, but he took off his skates and immediately donned the left one first."

— Charlie Conacher, *Globe*, Toronto, November 13, 1936

"There were many wonderful lines in hockey, but to me the most colourful of them all was Toronto's Kid Line of Conacher, Primeau, and Jackson. Joe Primeau was a very slight individual and a great play-making centre. He had quite a time with Charlie and Busher, who would both whistle at him when they were in the open and waiting for a pass. And it was up to Joe to give the puck to the fellow who had the best chance. I think he was one of the all-time greats as far as handling and passing a puck was concerned. I don't remember him giving a bad pass."

— King Clancy, *Clancy* (1968)

"Both Charlie and Harvey were keen and anxious and both would be hollering for the puck at the same time, so it was a job for me to keep them both happy by setting up plays for them."

— Joe Primeau, quoted by Stan Fischler in *Those Were the Days* (1976)

"We knew each other's plays so darn well."

— Busher Jackson to Bill Roche, *Globe and Mail*, Toronto, November 7, 1938

"I have no hesitation in saying that Charlie Conacher ranks as the greatest all-around athlete I have managed in my fifty years with sport…. Only Maurice Richard of the Montreal Canadiens ranks as a better hockey player [but] he never did stand out in baseball, football, or lacrosse, as Charlie Conacher did."

— Frank Selke, *Behind the Cheering* (1962)

"Harvey Jackson was … the classiest player I have ever seen…. Good looking as a movie idol, six-foot tall and weighing some 202 pounds, Jackson was as light on his feet as a ballet dancer. He could pivot on a dime, stickhandle through an entire team without giving up the puck, and shoot like a bullet either forehand or backhand. In fact, his backhand was the best I ever saw."

— Frank Selke, *Behind the Cheering* (1962)

"Harvey Jackson, one of the most spectacular players in the league, has his sticks taped a certain way, and if the trainer or assistant ever makes a mistake, the Busher will squawk to high heavens. In fact, I've seen Harvey use four or five sticks in one hockey game, and that, more or less, is the way this flashy left winger feels, and I don't think anything could change him."

— Charlie Conacher, *Globe*, Toronto, November 13, 1936

"[The greatest individual thrill I've had in hockey] came from a goal scored by Busher Jackson in Montreal back in the days when the Maroons had their big rough and tough team. Jackson got the puck in centre ice, and it so happened that the entire Maroon team was between him and their goal. I believe that the Busher stick-handled around and past every Maroon at least twice before he pulled out Goaler Benedict and then tossed the rubber into the net. I've seen all the stars in pro hockey for many years, but that was the greatest individual exhibition of skill I've ever witnessed."
— Frank Selke to Bill Roche, *Globe and Mail*, Toronto, November 29, 1938

"[King Clancy's] main forte was his ability to break fast, to come leaping off that blue line as thought it were a springboard, with the loose puck tossed out in front. He could pass on the dead tear, though not a graceful skater (he was almost running on his blades at times), and he had a wicked shot....

"It was that indefinable something — the competitive spirit — that made Clancy so valuable to the Leafs. And the God-given gift of fun in him that would bring them out of the doldrums with a whoop and a holler. That high-pitched sort of husky voice, his piping exclamations and his infectious grin."
— multi-sport star and legendary sportswriter Ted Reeve

"Hap Day was a great defenceman and a college man. He didn't talk a lot but everything made sense. You could tell that he would be a great coach, and he was. He understood the game and he'd communicate it."
— King Clancy to Gare Joyce, *MVP* magazine, April 1986

"He was a hard-hitting guy who didn't care for anybody when he got out on that ice. To his way of thinking, nobody was his friend because everybody that played against him was trying to take the money out of his pocket. This is the kind of player I liked to see. Horner ... wasn't a graceful skater, but how he could hit!"
— on Red Horner in King Clancy, *Clancy* (1968)

"Our Reginald Horner
Leaped from his corner
Full of ambition and fight;
He broke up the clash with a furious dash
While the stockholders shrieked with delight."
— Ted Reeve on Red Horner

"One of the present-day Leafs asked me not long ago about what he would have to do to get his picture on our dressing-room walls along with the six oldtimers. Those six are Day, Clancy, Primeau, [Frank] Finnegan, Bailey and [Baldy] Cotton. I told this lad there were no set specifications for that … that those six players had been so great over a long period of time that I simply had to put their pictures on the wall."

— Conn Smythe to Bill Roche, *Globe and Mail*, Toronto, November 26, 1938

"Life was certainly never dull with [Conn] Smythe around. He was always stirring something up. But Smythe was like all the owners at that time. Sure, he was interested in making money, but he had such a great love for the game of hockey, which always came first."

— Joe Primeau to Frank Orr, *Toronto Star*, February 9, 1977

"Smythe certainly speaks his mind, but he's fair. If he tells us to play a certain type of game, he expects us to follow out instructions. If we do so he's satisfied, whether we win or lose. If we win he gives us credit, and if we lose because we have done what he has told us, he is ready to take the blame.…

    "Another thing, if we get in a tough spot, whether it is a fight, an argument with officials, or anything else, Smythe is right on the job to back us up."

— Charlie Conacher to Tommy Munns, *Globe and Mail*,
Toronto, November 26, 1936

3

1934 to 1945: The Great Depression Gives Way to the Second World War

1933–34 AND 1934–35

Conn Smythe had overseen construction of Maple Leaf Gardens during the depths of the Great Depression and had built a team that not only won the Stanley Cup in 1931–32, but would remain a power in the NHL for years to come.

> "It is my conviction that this particular Maple Leafs team was the best in the League for the next few seasons. But it did not manage to win the Stanley Cup again until 1942, when Hap Day was coaching."
> — on the Maple Leafs following their Stanley Cup win in 1932 in Frank Selke, *Behind the Cheering* (1962)

> "You could see the effects of the Depression in the arenas that fall: only two thousand for the opener in Detroit; four thousand for our first game at Chicago. We didn't have that kind of trouble at home because we were winning and we were exciting, an unbeatable combination."
> — on the Maple Leafs of 1932–33 in Conn Smythe, *If You Can't Beat 'Em in the Alley* (1981)

> "We were lucky. An ordinary team would have failed miserably. To begin with, Conn's uncanny business acumen under the benign influence of J.P. Bickell guided us through the financial shoals; but the Maple Leafs hockey team provided the real stimulus. And Foster Hewitt's voice on the radio … every Saturday night made the entire Dominion a nation of hockey

addicts. The result was that, even in the worst years of the Depression, Maple Leaf Gardens paid its bills and earned a modest profit."

— Frank Selke, *Behind the Cheering* (1962)

The Maple Leafs finished first overall in the NHL in 1933–34 with a record of 26–13–9 for 61 points. Charlie Conacher led the league with 32 goals and 52 points. Joe Primeau topped all players with 32 assists and finished second in scoring with 46 points. The Leafs scored 174 goals this season. The next best team (the New York Rangers) scored only 120. Even so, Toronto was knocked out of the playoffs in the first round by the Detroit Red Wings.

The Maple Leafs of 1934–35 were even better, collecting a league-best 64 points on a record of 30–14–4. The team's scoring total dropped to 157 goals, but was still the best in the league by far. Charlie Conacher's 36 goals were the most ever in a 48-game season and he won his second straight scoring title with a career-best 57 points.

After defeating Boston to open the playoffs, Toronto faced the Montreal Maroons for the Stanley Cup. The Maple Leafs had finished 11 points ahead of the Maroons in the Canadian Division standings, but it didn't help them in the Final.

A star centre in his playing days, Dick Irvin became a successful coach in Chicago, Toronto, and Montreal from 1928 to 1956. He led the Maple Leafs to the Stanley Cup Final seven times in nine seasons from 1931–32 through 1939–40.

"[The biggest disappointment of any of my Toronto teams] came when the Leafs were ousted from the Stanley Cup finals in three straight by Maroons in '34–35."

— Conn Smythe to Bill Roche, *Globe and Mail*, Toronto, November 26, 1938

Coach Dick Irvin, in an interview with the *Globe and Mail* on November 25, 1938, also listed the loss to the Maroons in 1935 as one of his three biggest disappointments: "Our woes began in the first game when [Dave] Trottier scored to beat us 3–2 after more than thirty-three minutes of overtime…. Overtime goals in Stanley Cup playdowns are very nice to get, but very bitter to take. It never seems so bad to be beaten in a straight hour's playing."

Despite the disappointing loss, the team was back almost intact for the 1935–36 season. The offence declined to 126 goals that year, but was still the best in the NHL. Charlie Conacher and teammate Bill Thoms tied for the league lead with 23 goals, but Toronto slipped to second in the Canadian Division. Even so, the Maple Leafs reached the Stanley Cup Final for the fourth time in five years, but lost (this time to Detroit) for the third year in a row.

1936–37 AND 1937–38

Joe Primeau retired after the 1935–36 season. King Clancy retired early in the 1936–37 campaign, and goalie George Hainsworth would be let go. But by then the Maple Leafs already had new stars in place. Toronto dropped to third in the Canadian Division standings in 1936–37 and was eliminated from the play-offs in the first round, but a few key rookies ensured that the future was bright.

Syl Apps

"Syl Apps, Hamilton pole vaulter, has made up his mind not to try out this fall for the Hamilton Tigers football team…. Apps hasn't determined whether to sign a professional hockey contract with the Toronto Maple Leafs."

— *Globe*, Toronto, August 26, 1936

"I wasn't aware that Toronto was looking at me. They had their scouts out, of course, but things weren't so scientific in those days. I don't even remember who came over to Hamilton to talk to me about the team."

— Syl Apps in Jack Batten, *The Leafs in Autumn* (1975)

"In our circle, professional athletes were not looked upon as the right sort. But economic conditions were poor at the time and jobs were scarce.

Molly [Marshall, his girlfriend] told me the chance with the Leafs was a golden opportunity. I decided to sign although I was scared when I went to see Mr. Smythe."

— Syl Apps to Stan Fischler, *Those Were the Days* (1976)

"Sylvanus Apps loves hockey above all other games, but when Conn Smythe offered him a professional contract to play the game professionally, he was hesitant. Apps is black-haired, blue-eyed (handsome in a sort of Robert Taylorish way), suspicious of reporters. He is 21, weighs 175 pounds stripped, has excellent manners and some social address. He is the most boyish and 'I don't knowish' celebrity (he became famous when he joined this great Canadian hockey squad), that I have ever interviewed."

— Andy Lytle, *Toronto Daily Star*, October 28, 1936

"I didn't drink and didn't smoke but I used to do my share of swearing. That's where Apps has me beaten. He doesn't smoke. He never bends his elbow except to twist his stick over an opponent's wrist. The strongest language he ever uses is "By hum' and 'Jiminy Christmas.'"

— Hap Day on Syl Apps being the cleanest athlete he'd ever seen in
Stan Fischler, *Those Were the Days* (1976)

Apps made the team, and had proved his worth by the second game of the season when he scored his first goal.

"Apps proved beyond a shadow of doubt that he is made of the right stuff. He showed all kinds of dash and playmaking ability. And he mixed it up with all comers…. He was given a big ovation from the crowd and many slaps on the back from his mates for his first [goal with the] professionals."

— Don Cowie, *Globe*, Toronto, November 9, 1936

"Syl Apps will be judged the best rookie breaking into the NHL this year, without question, and to my mind, there is no better centre player in the whole league than the same lad right now."

— Charlie Conacher, *Globe and Mail*, Toronto, February 1, 1937

At the end of the season, Apps led the NHL with 29 assists in 48 games. With 16 goals as well, his 45 points had him just one behind Sweeney Schriner of the New York Americans in the league scoring race.

"That Syl Apps would be adjudged the best rookie of the National Hockey League season has been a foregone conclusion these past few weeks, but official announcement of the award calls for congratulations to Sylvanus, by Jiminy. Apps need have no regrets at not winning the scoring championship. It may save him plenty of grief next season. If he had finished on top, the self-appointed critics would have expected him to set the scoring pace from the outset of the 1937–38 campaign."

— Tommy Munns, *Globe and Mail*, Toronto, March 23, 1937

"Conn Smythe can sit back today and view with satisfaction the selections of the 'best rookies' in the National Hockey League, made this winter by writers in the NHL cities. No less than four of the first seven chosen were his Maple Leafs.

"An almost unanimous choice for top honours was Syl Apps, the 21-year-old Paris and Hamilton lad who rocketed to fame this, his first year in professional hockey. He was signed for his centre ice post upon his return

Gordie Drillon (left) and Syl Apps (centre) are seen here as well-established veterans with Nick Metz (right) in a picture taken at Maple Leaf Gardens on November 7, 1941.

from the Berlin Olympics last fall where he placed sixth among the pole vaulters of the world. Vaulting gave Apps a pair of wrists like corded steel and he came within an ace of snatching the scoring honours of the league. In the voting [for the Calder Trophy] he received 79 points out of a possible 81.

"Next to him came Gordon Drillon, another Leaf. Then in sixth and seventh places one finds Turk Broda and Jimmy Fowler."

— *Toronto Daily Star*, March 23, 1937

Gordie Drillon

Gordie Drillon began the 1936–37 season in the minors with the Syracuse Stars, but with the Maple Leafs struggling early, he was summoned to Toronto after just a few games. He had an assist in his debut in a 4–2 win over Montreal on November 26, and fit in quickly with the team. With Charlie Conacher missing much of the year with a wrist injury, Drillon proved to be an important addition.

"He was the best fellow to put the puck in the net I ever saw. He scored goals from every place on the ice. He had no special way of doing it — he could just score any time you asked."

— Syl Apps on Gordie Drillon in Jack Batten, *The Leafs in Autumn* (1975)

"Drillon looks like he's kissed Syracuse a long farewell."

— Andy Lytle, *Toronto Daily Star*, November 30, 1936

"Equally pleasing is the way Gordon Drillon is making good…. The Leafs have been exceptionally fortunate with their rookies. Apps, Fowler, Drillon and Broda all are making good in a very big way."

— Tommy Munns, *Globe and Mail*, Toronto, December 23, 1936

Drillon finished his rookie season with 16 goals and 17 assists for 33 points in 41 games. He had only one penalty all season. Not only was Drillon the runner-up to linemate Syl Apps for the Calder Trophy, but he finished second in voting for the Lady Byng as well. A year later, in 1937–38, Drillon led the NHL with 26 goals and 52 points and had just four penalty minutes. He won the Lady Byng that year, and remains the last Maple Leaf to lead the NHL in scoring. Syl Apps led the league with 29 assists and was second to Drillon in the scoring race with 50 points.

"[Dick] Irvin this evening paid a grand tribute to Gordon Drillon, the top scorer of the league. The Leafs coach told me that never once during the season had Drillon come off the ice to the bench and done any complaining about some mate not giving him a pass when he was in scoring position. Irvin also said that Drillon had never asked to be used out of regular turn, not even in the last few games when all the leading snipers were gunning for points.

"The fine spirit existing in the Leafs ranks was shown when Syl Apps, who was runner-up to Drillon for the league's scoring honours, bought ginger ale for the team in celebration of his linemate's triumph."

— Bill Roche, *Globe and Mail*, Toronto, March 22, 1938

Turk Broda

Veteran netminder George Hainsworth won the Vezina Trophy with the Montreal Canadiens the first three years the award was presented, from 1926–27 through 1928–29. He set an NHL record never to be broken during the 1928–29 season when he had 22 shutouts in a 44-game season. He won the Stanley Cup with the Canadiens in 1930 and 1931.

George Hainsworth's 22 shutouts and 0.92 goals-against average with the Montreal Canadiens in 1928–29 are NHL records never likely to be broken, but he was near the end of his career when the Maple Leafs brought in Turk Broda to compete with him in 1936.

In 1933, Conn Smythe traded Lorne Chabot to Montreal for Hainsworth. Hainsworth was 38 years old, but had three strong seasons with the Maple Leafs. He was 41 by the time the 1936–37 season started, and Toronto brought in a younger goalie to compete with him.

"The Toronto manager occupied the spotlight at yesterday's opening of the NHL annual conclave at Detroit when he announced the sale of one veteran Leaf and the accession of two minor leaguers. Smythe disposed of 'Handy Andy' Blair's services to Chicago Black Hawks for 'an unannounced cash consideration.' He also purchased Goalkeeper Walter Broda from Detroit Olympics, and drafted Centerman Murray Armstrong from the Philadelphia Ramblers. Experts who have seen Broda in action rate the goaler very highly. He scintillated in the Olympics' drive to the International League championship."

— Tommy Munns, Globe, Toronto, May 8, 1936

"Smythe purchased Walter Broda from Detroit, called off a $6,500 offer made tentatively some time ago for Earl Robertson, and laid $8,000 on the line for Broda. This is said to be a new high for minor league goalkeeping ivory."

— Toronto Daily Star, May 8, 1936

"When the Leafs said they wanted him, and once we knew we could get [Jimmy] Franks [to replace him with the Olympics] there was nothing for us to do but give Broda his chance at the majors. He is a great hockey player and deserves the promotion. We couldn't have given it to him here."

— Red Wings owner James Norris, quoted in
Ed Fitkin, Turk Broda of the Leafs (1950)

"Broda hasn't a nerve in his body. He could tend goal in a hurricane and never blink an eye. And you can blame any carelessness on youth. He'll outgrow that in a hurry."

— Red Wings coach and GM Jack Adams, quoted in Ed Fitkin,
Turk Broda of the Leafs (1950) (a similar quote has
been attributed to Conn Smythe)

"Facts are facts, and if there is sentiment in sport, there is very little of it when a manager is striving to put together a winning combination. There is, to judge by the glowing reports … of the ability of Walter ('Turk') Broda, a greater than even chance that the rookie goalie may beat Hainsworth in the competition which will determine which is going to be given the regular net assignment…. Hainsworth thinks that he can stave off this challenge of youth, else he wouldn't be at the Leafs' training camp now."

— Tommy Munns, *Globe*, Toronto, October 28, 1936

"Brilliant playing of some and more or less disappointing efforts by others have left several question marks hovering over the personnel of the Maple Leaf hockey team. The big problem is in goal, and the question being asked on all sides, Will it be Hainsworth or Broda?

"Coming out of a huddle with other officials of the club yesterday, Manager Conn Smythe announced that sixteen players, including an extra goaler, would be carried by the Leafs, and that Broda and Hainsworth would alternate until the better man was determined."

— Don Cowie, *Globe*, Toronto, November 4, 1936

"You will remember several years ago when Lorne Chabot and Benny Grant worked the same way. Between them they scored five shutouts in a row, before Grant finally cracked and Chabot earned the nod."

— Conn Smythe to the press on the Broda-Hainsworth battle

Broda started the season opener at home to Detroit on November 5, 1936. He gave up three goals in the third period and the defending Stanley Cup champion Red Wings scored a 3–1 victory. Two nights later, Hainsworth surrendered a pair of goals in the first period. After Toronto battled back to tie the game early in the third, a screened Hainsworth was beaten on a long shot with just 1:33 left and the New York Americans beat the Leafs 3–2. The next game was another home game, seven days later on a Saturday night.

"It is Turk Broda's turn to go in the Leaf net tonight. This week in practice he has looked better every time out, and he will be in there trying to score his first shutout in NHL company."

— Charlie Conacher, *Globe*, Toronto, November 14, 1936

Broda didn't get the shutout, but he did pick up his first of a club-record 302 victories in a 6–2 win over Chicago. Still, the Leafs continued to rotate their goalies.

"The goaltender job of our club is still as undecided as ever, and I'm glad it's Connie Smythe's job, not mine, to make a choice later on between George Hainsworth and Turk Broda."

— Charlie Conacher, *Globe and Mail*, Toronto, November 23, 1936

The decision came down just two days later.

"Conny Smythe, manager of the Toronto Maple Leafs, announced [last night] that George Hainsworth, veteran goalie, had been released outright.... Asked why the sturdy little netman from Kitchener ... was dropped, the Leafs manager said Broda was just as good as Hainsworth and about 20 years younger."

— *Globe and Mail*, Toronto, November 26, 1936

"Broda has the job and it's his as long as he can keep it."

— Conn Smythe

"If I'm lucky and good enough, I figure I've got ten good years ahead of me. But this league's a lot tougher than the minors. The guys are cleverer. They still fool me, but I'm getting better. They've got to fight for anything they get from me now. Pretty soon, I'll get tougher."

— Turk Broda, quoted in Ed Fitkin, *Turk Broda of the Leafs* (1950)

* * *

The Maple Leafs sold Hap Day to the New York Americans just before the 1937–38 season. Red Horner was entering his tenth season, but was still just 28 years old, and anchored a defence in front of Turk Broda that featured youngsters Jimmy Fowler, Reg Hamilton, and Bingo Kampman. With Drillon and Apps fuelling the NHL's best offence, Toronto returned to the top spot in the Canadian Division, and then defeated Boston to return once again to the Stanley Cup Final.

The Chicago Black Hawks had finished with just 37 points in 48 games on a record of 14–25–9 but still qualified for the playoffs in the American Division when the two-time defending Stanley Cup champion Red Wings crashed to just 35 points. Chicago shocked the Montreal Canadiens to open the playoffs, and then upset the New York Americans before going on to the final round, where they beat the Maple Leafs three games to one.

"Sixth in the National league and first in the World! Ladies and gentlemen, we give you the winners and new champions of all hockey — Chicago's irrepressible Blackhawks!

"Climaxing one of the outstanding comebacks in professional athletic history by defeating the Toronto Maple Leafs, 4 to 1, before 17,205 in the Stadium last night, they won the coveted Stanley Cup, emblematic of the world championship, for the second time."

— Charles Bartlett, *Chicago Tribune*, April 13, 1938

1939–41

By the start of the 1938–39 season, the NHL had lost the Ottawa Senators/ St. Louis Eagles, the Pittsburgh Pirates/Philadelphia Quakers, and the Montreal Maroons; reducing what had once been a 10-team league to just seven and ending the two-division format. Six of seven teams would make the playoffs, and although the Maple Leafs finished only third in 1938–39 with a losing record of 19–20–9, they eliminated the New York Americans and Detroit Red Wings to reach the Final once again. This time, they lost four games to one to the Boston Bruins in the first best-of-seven series for the Stanley Cup.

Conn Smythe made a big deal shortly after the end of the 1938–39 season, acquiring former two-time scoring champion Sweeney Schriner from the New York Americans in exchange for Busher Jackson, Buzz Boll, Jimmy Fowler, and Doc Romnes. Toronto also included Murray Armstrong in the deal.

"Smythe traded quantity for quality. He let Romnes go in the deal because he wishes to make room for Billy Taylor. The inclusion of Schriner at left wing and the injection of players like [Wally] Stanowski, [Hank] Goldup, Lex Chisholm, Taylor, and Don Metz complete the Leafs for the 1939–40 season. They're ready to [start training camp] right now....

"Smythe made the move deliberately to rid himself of some playing talent that wasn't standing up. Boll, Fowler, and Jackson were ticketed for disposal weeks before the season yawned to its conclusion. Romnes was used largely as bait on the hook Smythe cast to secure Schriner. The whole deal smacks of the Smythian determination to mix flaming youth with the steadying influences of experience."

— Andy Lytle, *Toronto Daily Star*, May 26, 1939

The Leafs' record improved to 25–17–6 in 1939–40, but they once again finished in third place. Toronto then won two playoff rounds to reach the Final again, only to lose, this time to the New York Rangers.

"In the years between 1933 and 1940 we were in the Stanley Cup final every year except 1934 and 1937, but never won it. I know now that I should have broken up the Kid Line around 1935 or so. I didn't have the guts.... Once in the mid-thirties Red Dutton offered me Sweeney Schriner for Busher Jackson. I thought of all the uproar that deal would have caused in the press and public, so I didn't do it, although I did get Sweeney Schriner later. He was the best left winger I ever saw. That includes everybody — Frank Mahovlich, Busher Jackson, Bobby Hull — everybody."

— Conn Smythe, *If You Can't Beat 'Em in the Alley* (1981)

The Second World War began just before the start of the 1939–40 season. Though it didn't impact the NHL right away, it soon would, as many players left to serve in the Armed Forces. Despite his age, the patriotic Conn Smythe was planning to enlist almost from the time war broke out, and this decision, according to Smythe, also led to a change in the Leafs' coaching ranks shortly after the Leafs lost the Cup to the Rangers.

"As far back as early 1940 I had spoken to the Gardens' directors about taking a leave of absence when the time came that I would be shipped out of Toronto. In 1940, Montreal Canadiens had finished last with Pit Lepine coaching. They wanted another coach badly. I called them and suggested Dick Irvin, my coach. That might sound strange. After all, we'd been in the Stanley Cup Final more often than not during Dick's years with Leafs. But I didn't think he was tough enough, without me backing him up, to do what needed to be done. Montreal was delighted at the chance to get Dick, and he took a step up in pay."

— Conn Smythe, *If You Can't Beat 'Em in the Alley* (1981)

But that's not exactly how Smythe told it at the time....

"Canadiens asked me a month ago for permission to make Dick an offer. I told them to come back again, after they completed their front-office reorganization. If I hadn't been sure the reorganization would give the next Canadiens coach a better chance to make a showing than the last two or three had, I'd have insisted that Dick stay here. As it is, I think Dick's stepping into a promising position."

— Conn Smythe, April 17, 1940, reported in the *Globe and Mail* the next day

"There are no strings attached to the departure of Irvin. He gave the Leafs nine years of valuable service. He would have been coach of the team again next winter if the Canadiens hadn't made him a tempting two-year contract offer at more money than we're paying him here. It's Dick's chance to handle a club on his own initiative as manager as well as coach."

— Conn Smythe, April 17, 1940

"I want to make it clear that the Canadiens approached me before they dealt with Irvin, asking if it were all right to offer him the job. The Maple Leafs club's reaction was that we hated to see Irvin go but we felt that the sorry condition in which the Canadiens had found themselves wasn't doing any team in the league any good.… After the wonderful job Paul Thompson has done this year in building up a last-place club at Chicago, I think Dick can do the same at Montreal."

— Conn Smythe, April 17, 1940

The departure of Dick Irvin gave Conn Smythe the chance to bring former Leafs star and long-time captain Hap Day back into the fold.

"Hap was everything I wanted. He could do things I couldn't: fire people; bench them; live always on what a man could do today, not what he had done a few years ago."

— Conn Smythe, *If You Can't Beat 'Em in the Alley* (1981)

"Sure, I feel pretty good about it. But I know now how George Selkirk must have felt when he took over Babe Ruth's spot in the Yankee outfield. Dick compiled an enviable record in the nine years he was in charge of the Leafs. Better than any other pro coach. So I've really got something to shoot at…."

— Hap Day, *Toronto Daily Star*, April 19, 1940

The Maple Leafs posted an NHL-best 28 wins under Hap Day in 1940–41 (28–14–6, 62 points) but finished in second place behind the Boston Bruins who had 67 points on a record of 27–8–13. When the two teams met in the playoffs for a berth in the Final, Boston won in seven games and then went on to sweep the Red Wings for the Stanley Cup.

The Maple Leafs offence in 1940–41 was led by Syl Apps, Gordie Drillon, Sweeney Schriner, Nick Metz, and Billy Taylor, though the attack was not as effective as it had been under Dick Irvin. Hap Day, a former defenceman, emphasized defence first.

"When I was a defenceman on Toronto, I saw all kinds of players in front of me, and I learned right then that it's defence that wins hockey games.... When you think of defence, you think of the two men, the defencemen, isn't that right? Wrong! Think of all six men doing the job on defence. I told my players if they worked as hard coming back as they did going down the ice, we'd be okay. Of course, you had to have the proper type of player to handle that approach — or make them into the proper type of player. A player's got to learn to keep his mind on defence, apply himself....

"Coaching offensively is too hard. A centre goes down the ice — he doesn't know what he's going do to with the puck. It depends on where his wings happen to go. You can give them a plan of attack, and then the situation for the plan may never come up in the game."
— Hap Day in Jack Batten, *The Leafs in Autumn* (1975)

"I was a good skater and puck-carrier from the beginning but I wasn't the world's best defensive player. [Day] never said much to me about it, but he somehow made sure you were checking."
— Syl Apps in Jack Batten, *The Leafs in Autumn* (1975)

Day also worked hard with Turk Broda to improve his technique.

"There's nothing like it to sharpen your eyes and co-ordinate your timing."
— Hap Day recommending handball to Turk Broda,
quoted in Ed Fitkin, *Turk Broda of the Leafs* (1950)

"There were other tricks up Hap's sleeve in his determination to improve Broda's netminding. During practice sessions at training camp — and they were longer and tougher with Hap cracking the whip — the new Leafs coach would order Turk to toss his stick away and for the next 10 minutes Broda would be subject to every type of hockey bombardment — long shots, close in shots, goalmouth plays. Broda speared screaming drives from all angles, booted out the low ones, began to block and fend and catch with greater dexterity. It was a bruising form of practice but the Turk was a willing worker and was improving under such unusual treatment. In the long run, it was to pay him rich dividends."

— Ed Fitkin, *Turk Broda of the Leafs* (1950)

Under Day, Toronto posted the best defensive record in the NHL in 1940–41, giving Turk Broda the Vezina Trophy in a tight race with Boston's Frank Brimsek.

"I'm glad he won it. He's played grand hockey for us all winter."

— Hap Day, quoted in Ed Fitkin, *Turk Broda of the Leafs* (1950)

1941–42

The Great Comeback

Toronto finished in second place again in 1941–42, this time behind the Rangers, but they beat New York in a best-of-seven series for a direct berth into the Stanley Cup Final against Detroit.

"We had reached the finals by upsetting the New York Rangers and we were confident we could whip Detroit. Even the fact that Toronto hadn't won the Cup since 1932, which might have indicated we were jinxed, didn't upset our confidence."

— Syl Apps to Stan Fischler, *Those Were the Days* (1976)

"The Wings will come out roaring. Unless we can out-thump them, they will lick us again as they have done before."

— Conn Smythe prior to the 1942 Final, quoted in
Ed Fitkin, *Turk Broda of the Leafs* (1950)

"We had decided before that series that Toronto, with Apps and a powerful club, would be a problem. It was [coach and GM] Jack Adams' idea that we should fire the puck into their end of the rink and go and try and check the Leafs before they could get started. I never did like the idea of it, but we had a meeting and decided on it."

— Detroit's Syd Howe to the *Ottawa Journal*, June 8, 1965

"Detroit's style had us buffaloed. That was the first time any club ever shot the puck into the end zone and flooded in after it. There was no centre red line then, and the Detroits would simply get the puck across their own blue line and let it go into our end. Then they'd race in and get to it before we did."

— Hap Day to Stan Fischler, Those Were the Days (1976)

The Red Wings scored 3–2, 4–2, and 5–2 victories to take a 3–0 stranglehold on the series.

"There's nothing we can do. Everything is going their way."

— Turk Broda after Game 3

"We felt we were licked, but we were determined to win the fourth game and avoid a clean sweep and get back to Toronto. The main thing was to come home with one victory. The Stanley Cup wasn't even on our minds at that point; we just didn't want to get shut out in four straight."

— Syl Apps to Stan Fischler, Those Were the Days (1976)

"We had tried that [dump and chase] style of play back in 1936–37 but it wasn't until 1941 that we really put it to use in earnest…. It went well for three games [against Toronto] because we had a terrific forechecker in Johnny Grosso on a line with Sid Abel and Eddie Wares. I was with Mud Bruneteau and Carl Liscombe. But the Leafs caught on after three games and did a record-breaking job in their comeback."

— Detroit's Syd Howe to the Ottawa Journal, June 8, 1965

"I told them [the Maple Leaf Gardens directors] about Detroit's style. And I told them our star defenseman Bucko McDonald was simply tired out. He had played wonderful hockey for us but he was just tuckered out and couldn't cope with Detroit's shooting tactics. I said the same thing about [Gordie] Drillon. He was a great scorer but his style wasn't suited to that shoot-and-skate stuff."

— Hap Day to Stan Fischler, Those Were the Days (1976)

After Game 3, Hap Day benched Gordie Drillon and Bucko McDonald and inserted Don Metz and Hank Goldup instead. Day also employed a new piece of counter-strategy.

"That Detroit club invented something that's common now, shooting the puck in from centre and then forechecking like hell. It had us completely buffaloed. But Hap Day, our coach, had the answer in time for Game 4.

Coach Hap Day is seen here with Les Costello, Vic Lynn, and Teeder Kennedy in the dressing room at Maple Leaf Gardens after eliminating the Boston Bruins in their 1948 semifinal series.

We'd simply fire it right back out, which was also a new wrinkle. Some of the new faces were faster guys. And we just killed Detroit from then on."
— Bob Goldham, a 19-year-old Toronto rookie in 1942, quoted by Jim Proudfoot, *Toronto Star*, April 19, 1993

Toronto bounced back for a 4–3 victory in Game 4. The Red Wings were incensed by the officiating, and Jack Adams was accused of punching referee Mel Harwood on the ice after the game. He was suspended for the rest of the series, which returned to Toronto for Game 5 on April 14. The Leafs made another roster move, inserting 18-year-old Gaye Stewart into the lineup.

"In the fifth game we had a picnic. We beat Detroit 9–3 and, all of a sudden, everybody on the club realized we could still win the Cup."
— Syl Apps to Stan Fischler, *Those Were the Days* (1976)

Back in Detroit again for Game 6, the Leafs scored a 3–0 victory to send the series back to Toronto for Game 7.

"I'm no mastermind. My team just went out and played and, really, I thought we were lucky. That first goal by Don Metz turned the trick."

— Hap Day to reporters after Game 6 (April 16)

"We got the breaks in the first three games, now they're getting them. Since they changed their lineup, the Leafs have a great club. But we're going to give 'em a battle; it won't be any set-up."

— Detroit's Ebbie Goodfellow, coaching in place of
Jack Adams, to reporters after Game 6

"Since [the shakeup to the lineup] the boys have really been playing great hockey, but I wouldn't say how that final game is going to go in Toronto on Saturday because the teams are too evenly matched."

— Hap Day to reporters after Game 6

A record crowd of 16,218 was on hand for Game 7 on April 18. Maple Leaf Gardens had been under siege all day from those hoping to get tickets.

"It's a madhouse."

— MLG switchboard operator, *Toronto Daily Star*, April 18, 1942

"I wasn't able to call my wife. The incoming calls were so many I couldn't get a line out to save my husbandly neck."

— Frank Selke, *Toronto Daily Star*, April 18, 1942

There would be no further tinkering with the roster for Game 7.

"We will sink or we will swim to the Cup tonight as we were."

— Hap Day, *Toronto Daily Star*, April 18, 1942

Toronto fell behind 1–0 early in the second period, and Detroit nursed the slim lead until Sweeney Schriner scored at 6:46 of the third.

"It was a blind shot. I didn't know I had scored until I heard the crowd shouting, and then saw the light go on. It was the biggest light I ever saw in my life."

— Sweeney Schriner, after the game

Pete Langelle put Toronto ahead at 9:43, and Schriner clinched the 3–1 victory with his second goal at 6:13.

"I'll never forget the last minute of that game, skating around with a two-goal lead and the knowledge that Detroit couldn't win it now. We were champions. It felt wonderful."

— Syl Apps to Stan Fischler, *Those Were the Days* (1976)

"Come on out, Conn, you waited long enough for this Cup. Come and get it."

— Leafs captain Syl Apps, calling out to Conn Smythe after accepting the Stanley Cup from NHL president Frank Calder

"Shake, Dave, shake. That was a grand game you played for us, and you did it. Should have had three more goals."

— Syl Apps, extending his hand to Sweeney Schriner in the dressing room

"It took a great hockey team to beat us. We weren't kidding ourselves that the Stanley Cup was just around the corner, even after taking three in a row. With three well-balanced lines firing at us all the time, we realized the big wallop was liable to come from any direction, and it seems the punch came from all directions."

— Detroit's Ebbie Goodfellow after Game 7

"It was our coach who won the Stanley Cup. And when I say that I know I'm speaking for the entire team. It was his counsel and guidance that put us where we are today.

"Most of us waited a long time for this thrill. Some of us seven or eight years. A few of us only a few weeks. To me it was one of the greatest thrills, and I think the rest of the players feel the same way.

"I know I am speaking for all the players when I say our coach was the big factor in our final triumph. He praised us when we deserved to be praised and he criticized us when we needed to be criticized. And it was our coach's influence that carried us to the top."

— Syl Apps at the victory dinner at the Royal York Hotel

"One thing I know is the Leafs have one of the two greatest captains in history in Syl Apps. The other was Hap Day, now our coach."

— Conn Smythe at the victory dinner at the Royal York

"I want to thank the Gardens directors for allowing me to continue as coach of the Leafs for a second season. It allowed me to experience the greatest thrill of my athletic career. My part was a very small one. The play-ers made the big contribution. They came out of the series the fightingest bunch in the history of hockey."

> — Hap Day at the victory dinner at the Royal York

"I have never, before or since, played in such a tough series."

> — Nick Metz, looking back on 1942, *Globe and Mail*, Toronto, April 13, 1949

Amid all the celebrations, Toronto's Stanley Cup victory was not a sweet one for Gordie Drillon, who would be traded before the next season. Though he never said so publicly, Drillon's wife had been ill for some time and she underwent a serious operation shortly after the final game.

"I had been dreaming about that Stanley Cup ever since I was a kid. It grew and grew in my mind each season. But when the series was finished out, and I wasn't even on the bench, that Cup grew smaller and smaller. Just a shattered dream, I guess.

"Simply couldn't stand it, so Mrs. Drillon and I went home after the second period. Heard the last period on the radio.

"I tried to take the whole affair with my chin up. I didn't play well in the first games against Detroit, but I had thought I would get back into uniform before the series was over, even as an extra forward.

"One of the toughest touches came after the fifth game here in Toronto. A bunch of hoodlums appeared at our apartment house about midnight, tossed stones at the windows, and put on a wild, hooting demonstration.

"Even the kids in the neighbourhood got to booing me as I walked down the street. And only a few weeks previously I had been a pal to many of them.

"Nobody knows what I've gone through in the last few weeks. Why, even a $1,000 bonus that had been promised to me for making the Second All-Star team was taken away. It wasn't Conn Smythe's fault. The Major made good on every verbal agreement we ever had together.

"So I'm going back to Moncton. I won't be back with the Leafs next winter."

> — Gordie Drillon, quoted by Vern DeGeer,
> *Globe and Mail*, Toronto, April 28, 1942

1942–43 AND 1943–44

Conn Smythe was already in the Canadian army at the time the Maple Leafs won the Stanley Cup in 1942. He came down from Camp Petawawa, near Ottawa, in order to be at Game 7 and the victory dinner that followed, but he would soon be stationed overseas.

Beyond the loss of Smythe from the day-to-day operations of the team, the Leafs had not felt any significant effects on the ice. That would change by the time Toronto opened training camp in the fall. In the months following their Stanley Cup triumph, the Leafs lost Bob Goldham, Ernie Dickens, Bingo Kampman, Wally Stanowski, Nick Metz, Don Metz, Pete Langelle, Johnny McCreedy, and a few other players in their system to the army, navy, and the air force. Stars such as Syl Apps, Turk Broda, Billy Taylor, and 1943 Calder Trophy winner Gaye Stewart would all be lost to military service after the 1942–43 season.

Like all other NHL clubs in what became a six-team league in 1942–43 with the loss of the New York/Brooklyn Americans, the Leafs would have to get by during the rest of the war with younger players (below the age of 20), or older, married men and others exempt from military service (often because of hockey-related injuries). With an eye toward replacing the offensive talent that would be lost to the team in 1943–44, the Maple Leafs made a deal for a 17-year-old future franchise player in the spring of 1943.

Come on, Teeder!

"I told Dick Irvin that the Maple Leafs were desperate for bodies to fill the lineup, and that we could give up the rights to [Frank] Eddolls for the rights to Ted Kennedy. After weeks of negotiation and a lot of hesitation, Gorman and Irvin finally consented to make the trade. Fearing they might change their minds ... Happy Day and I completed the transfer of Eddolls to Montreal without taking the time to consult Smythe....

"[We] received a cable from France ordering us to cancel the deal. It was ignored, and Ted Kennedy developed into as effective a hockey player as the Maple Leafs ever owned. But the deal spelled *finis* to my usefulness as an assistant to Conn Smythe."

— Frank Selke, *Behind the Cheering* (1962)

"We know we are giving up a strong defence player to deal with Kennedy, but we won't be shy of defence material after the war and we do need attack strength now."
— Hap Day, quoted in *Toronto Daily Star*, March 1, 1943

"We are taking a gamble. We think Kennedy is a coming star."
— Frank Selke, quoted by Andy Lytle in *Toronto Daily Star*, March 1, 1943

Kennedy played two games for Toronto late in the 1942–43 season, but suffered a groin injury and didn't see action in the playoffs, where the Leafs were eliminated in the first round by the Detroit Red Wings.

"To keep up [Kennedy's] morale, I had him sit with me, and I was dumbfounded by his mature observations on the game as it progressed. I remember telling sportswriter Ed Fitkin that I thought we might have acquired a superstar."
— Frank Selke, *Behind the Cheering* (1962)

As an 18-year-old in his first full season (1943–44), Kennedy was second on the team with 26 goals, and added 23 assists for 49 points in 49 games. In 1944–45, he led the Leafs with 29 goals and 54 points.

"In some ways it is difficult to make comparisons between rookies of today and 10 or 15 years ago. Players didn't often break into the NHL until after they were 20. And there were naturally more good players around than we find in these wartimes. But you can't take anything away from Ted. For a 19-year-older, I think he's an outstanding player for any company."
— Hap Day, quoted by Vern DeGeer, *Globe and Mail*, Toronto, February 8, 1945

Day believed Kennedy was the best teenage hockey player since Busher Jackson.

"Kennedy isn't as good a skater as Busher, and Busher was the more sensational player. But Ted is a better stickhandler. In fact, I'd say he is one of the best stickhandlers of the past two decades."
— Hap Day, quoted by Vern DeGeer, *Globe and Mail*, Toronto February 8, 1945

John Arnott was a vocal Leafs fan who modified his shout "Come on, Peter!" for Pete Langelle to "Come on, Teeder!" for Kennedy and his childhood nickname.

"Ted is my idea of the perfect hockey machine. He never stops trying."
— John Arnott, quoted in Ed Fitkin, *Come on Teeder!* (1950)

"My Christian name is Theodore, but I came from a small town and boys names were either Bill or Jack or Joe. For the other players it was too much to pronounce my name so they abbreviated it. One of the local reporters heard them saying 'Teeder' so that's how it appeared in the newspaper and it spread from there. The only one who called me Theodore was my mother."
— Teeder Kennedy, Legends Spotlight, Hockey Hall of Fame website

Rookie Record

Gus Bodnar was 20 when he joined the Maple Leafs for the 1943–44 season. According to most records, he had collected 10 goals and 29 assists for 39 points in just nine games in the Thunder Bay Junior Hockey League in his hometown of Fort William, Ontario, the year before.

"I thought I was pretty big stuff. I had my hair long and all slickered down with goo. I figured I was about the hottest rookie ever to hit the pros, even though I weighed only 145 pounds."
— Gus Bodnar discussing his first Maple Leafs training camp with Frank Orr of the *Toronto Star* (reprinted in Bodnar's obituary, *Globe and Mail*, Toronto, July 9, 2005)

On October 30, 1943, Bodnar set an NHL record that still stands for the fastest goal from the start of a career.

"Gus Bodnar, a resourceful young puckchaser from the Port Arthur hockey country, cut out the scoring pace for a band of 13 newcomers that bowed into National League competition at Maple Leaf Gardens Saturday night.

"Bodnar tossed home two goals, assisted in another, as Toronto Leafs rolled to a handy 5–2 decision over New York Rangers in the opening game of the 1943–44 campaign.

"It took Bodnar just 15 seconds to ring the scoring gong in the first period of play with Elwin Morris and Bob Davidson...."
— Vern DeGeer, *Globe and Mail*, Toronto, November 1, 1943

"I faced off and we scrambled for the puck for a few seconds. I finally got it, went straight down the ice, split the defense, went in, pulled [Ken McAuley] out and flipped the puck in."

— Gus Bodnar at a Brampton sports dinner, February 7, 1957 (reported by Jim Vipond, *Globe and Mail*, Toronto, February 9, 1957)

The 1943–44 season featured more rookies than ever before, but almost from the start 20-year-old Gus Bodnar and 29-year-old Canadiens goalie Bill Durnan were considered the best of the bunch. Bodnar led all rookies with 22 goals and 62 points, but Durnan was one of only two netminders to play all 50 games during the season. He led the Canadiens to a record of 38–5–7, boasted a league-best 2.18 goals-against average, and won the Vezina Trophy by a wide margin. (He would also lead Montreal to the Stanley Cup.) Still, sportswriters went with Bodnar by a fairly wide margin in voting for the rookie of the year.

"It certainly is a surprise, a most welcome surprise. I figured that perhaps Durnan would get it."

— Gus Bodnar's comments when informed he had won the Calder Trophy, *Globe and Mail*, Toronto, March 20, 1944

1944–45

Among the many players the Maple Leafs lost to war service, goalie Turk Broda was likely the hardest to replace. Goaltending had become even more difficult during the 1943–44 season after the NHL introduced the red line at centre ice to allow for more passing and faster offensive play.

"It's an unwise hockey coach in any company that doesn't realize that good goal tending is the basis for a hockey team. Without a sound man in the nets, the best defence and the best forward lines in the country have trouble winning hockey games. Yet plenty of Stanley Cups have been won with mediocre defensemen and mediocre forwards."

— Hap Day at Maple Leafs training camp in St. Catharines, October 14, 1943

Former Maple Leaf goaltender Benny Grant had last seen action in the NHL back in 1933–34, and had last played in the minors in 1941–42 when Toronto lured him out of retirement to open the 1943–44 season. He didn't pan out. With Bill Durnan starring in Montreal, the Leafs later acquired former Canadiens goalie Paul Bibeault through a loan arrangement. Toronto hoped to obtain Bibeault again in 1944–45, but no deal could be worked out while the Leafs were in training camp in the fall of 1944 (Montreal would later loan Bibeault to Boston) so Toronto's goaltending position was up for grabs.

Frank McCool

Frank McCool became a goalie for the same reason many others of an earlier generation did.

> "How did I come to be a goal-keeper? That's easy. I wasn't a good skater and that's the only position where I could stand and still play. I didn't learn to skate until I was in grade nine when I was 13. I played a lot of lacrosse, baseball, and football as a school kid in Calgary and was captain of those teams. When they got a hockey team together, I was made captain of that squad too. The captain had to play, so it was the net spot for me. There I could hold on to the goal posts when the ankles shimmied."
> — Frank McCool to Frank Ayerst, *Toronto Daily Star*, October 21, 1944

McCool went on to play junior hockey in Calgary and later played two seasons of U.S. college hockey at Gonzaga in Spokane, Washington, from 1938 to 1940. He spent two years in the army, where he played hockey with service teams until he was discharged due to a medical condition: Frank McCool suffered from stomach ulcers.

The New York Rangers signed McCool in the fall of 1943, and he was a strong candidate to make the team, but problems with his ulcers left him unfit to play. He returned to Calgary, where he spent the winter working as a sportswriter. A year later, in September of 1944, the Maple Leafs expressed interest.

> "Rangers had McCool but he had tummy ulcers last season. So they let him go for [Ken] McAuley.... Now McCool's an army reject [and] his ulcers aren't ulcing so he may be what the circumstances compel Leafs to regard as the best of prospects."
> — Andy Lytle, *Toronto Daily Star*, September 12, 1944

McCool went to the Leafs training camp in Owen Sound, Ontario, along with goalies Pat Boehmer, Bob Gillson, Leo Sargent, and Harry McQueston. And though there was still talk of landing Paul Bibeault, the 26-year-old McCool quickly established himself as the team's best option, and one who didn't take his position lightly.

"I've discovered that hockey is a serious business. Every time I feel like laughing, I remember what those ulcers did to me last year. That wasn't funny."
— Frank McCool to Frank Ayerst, *Toronto Daily Star*, October 21, 1944

"We are quite pleased with the showing of Frank McCool from Calgary in goal at the training camp at Owen Sound and we don't propose to make any further offers for Bibeault."
— Frank Selke to reporters, October 23, 1944

"If the rest of the league has as much trouble batting that puck past McCool as I had, then Day doesn't have to worry about the Toronto nets."
— Mel Hill of the Leafs after McCool led the Blue team to an 8–2 victory over the Whites in the Leafs' annual Blue and White game, October 25, 1944

McCool won the Leafs goaltending job and led the team to six straight wins to open the season. "I've been pretty lucky so far," he told Canadian Press reporter Fraser MacDougall after his fourth win.

The Leafs only won six of their next 16 games, but were still 12–8–2 at the end of December. Montreal — who had lost very few of their pre-war team to military service — would romp to another first-place record that season, with Detroit a strong second, but McCool kept Toronto comfortably in a playoff spot all year.

"Don't sell that boy short. He's not the best goaltender to look at. He has a nervous style that is deceptive. But he gets results and that's what counts."
— former star Bruins goalie (and fellow Calgary native) Tiny Thompson on Frank McCool, *Globe and Mail*, Toronto, January 1, 1945

"Every game was a life-and-death struggle for Frank. He sipped milk in the dressing room between periods to calm his fluttering stomach. There were times when he took sick during a game — but one thing about him, he'd never quit."
— Leafs publicity man Ed Fitkin on Frank McCool

"McCool hasn't much chance for the Vezina trophy for goalies because Bill Durnan of the Canadiens has that safely in hand. But Frank's work entitles him to some honour and I would call him the season's best newcomer."
— New York Rangers coach Frank Boucher to an Associated Press reporter, March 9, 1945

When the NHL trophy winners were announced on Friday evening, March 16, 1945, Frank McCool was indeed named the NHL's best rookie.

"Frank McCool, the modest young man who had successfully fought off the bees in his tummy, as well as enemy snipers, all season for Toronto Leafs, has been awarded the Calder Trophy by vote of sports writers, as the best rookie in the league. This is a remarkable climax to the one year career of a youth who, until he enlisted and did a stint in goal for army teams, was scarcely known as a player outside of his hometown of Calgary."
— Andy Lytle, *Toronto Daily Star*, March 17, 1945

"Award of the Calder Trophy to Leafs' Frank McCool won't arouse any arguments. McCool tapered off for a few games recently, but has been a standout all season with Leafs, and is being counted on to shine in the playoffs."
— Bill Westwick, *Ottawa Journal*, March 17, 1945

Syl Apps in his army uniform shakes hands with Frank McCool during the 1944–45 season.

The 1945 Playoffs

The Maple Leafs finished the 50-game 1944–45 season in third place in the six-team NHL with a record of 24–22–4 for 52 points. They were well back of the first-place Montreal Canadiens, who had 80 points on a record of 38–8–4. Maurice Richard became the first player in NHL history to score 50 goals this year, while his centre, Elmer Lach, set a new single-season record with 54 assists, led the league with 80 points, and won the Hart Trophy as MVP. Lach, Richard, and their left winger, Toe Blake, finished 1–2–3 in the scoring race and were all named to the First All-Star Team, as were Canadiens defenceman Butch Bouchard and goalie Bill Durnan, who did win the Vezina Trophy. Montreal would be Toronto's playoff opponent in the semifinals. The Canadiens were heavy favourites, but the Maple Leafs were ready for them.

"The greatest team in twenty years."
— Coach Dick Irvin on the 1944–45 Canadiens

"From what I've been able to observe in recent weeks, Dick has been doing all the talking and we've been doing all the fighting. If we have no injuries, we'll win the first round."
— Conn Smythe, Canadian Press report, March 17, 1945

"If Frank holds up, we may surprise a great many people."
— Hap Day on Leafs goalie Frank McCool and Toronto's chances against Montreal, quoted in Ed Fitkin, *Come on Teeder!* (1950)

With Teeder Kennedy shutting down Elmer Lach and scoring the game's lone goal with 22 seconds remaining, Toronto scored a 1–0 victory in Game 1 and then made it two straight in Montreal with a 3–2 victory two nights later. Toronto had a 3–1 series lead when Montreal exploded for a 10–3 win back home in Game 5.

"Ten of the 12 goals Leafs have scored against us [in this series] have been tagged with luck. Now it's our turn. I don't think we'll look back."
— Dick Irvin after Game 5

"There won't be any repetition of the scoring avalanche. We were outskated, outchecked and outplayed…. They were good and we were bad."
— Hap Day the day after the Game 5 loss

Toronto bounced back at Maple Leaf Gardens, winning Game 6 by a score of 3–2 to take the series 4 games to 2. It was a thrilling game that saw the Canadiens score at 15:26 of the third period to cut into a 3–1 Leafs lead. The game ended with a scramble in front of the Toronto goal and Toe Blake firing the puck over a wide open net with just 27 seconds remaining.

"Another finish like that and Leafs will need a new coach. Those last two minutes seemed like a lifetime."

— Hap Day after the game

"We shouldn't have beaten Montreal, but Frank McCool was great…. He saved us, really, because Montreal still had a bunch of their originals playing. They should have beaten us badly."

— Wally Stanowski, quoted in *The Goaltenders' Union* (2014)

"It's the old victory tune. The team that won't be beaten, can't be beaten — and that's us."

— Conn Smythe on eliminating Montreal, quoted in
Ed Fitkin, *Come on Teeder!* (1950)

"I call it the Series of the Deflected Puck. I've never handled a club that had such a rotten string of luck. Half the Toronto goals were deflected past Durnan by our players. If we'd had some of that luck we would have won in a gallop."

— Dick Irvin after Game 6

"I'd rather be lucky than rich."

— Hap Day, when informed of Irvin's remarks

The Maple Leafs advanced to face the Red Wings for the Stanley Cup. Detroit had finished second in the regular-season standings with a record of 31–14–5 for 67 points. They'd been particularly good against Toronto, posting a record of 8–1–1 in their 10 head-to-head matchups.

"We'll win this series. We'll win it because we've got too good a fighting team to lose. The boys proved that against Montreal and they'll prove it to Detroit. We beat Montreal because we blanketed their big line most of the time. Now we'll have to blanket the Wings' aces. Hap wants to gamble on using our best players the most, and I'll back him up. That means we'll have only two forward lines operating most of the time, our Big

Six [Gus] Bodnar, [Sweeney] Schriner, [Lorne] Carr, [Teeder] Kennedy, [Bob] Davidson, and [Mel] Hill. This is a fighting team we have, and as I've said before, a fighting team is never beaten."

> — Conn Smythe on facing Detroit for the 1945 Stanley
> Cup, quoted in Ed Fitkin, *Come on Teeder!* (1950)

"I put it up to the players, and they're right behind me. I feel we've got two able-bodied forward lines but I told them I didn't want anybody out there who felt worn out. Not one player has complained of overwork."

> — Hap Day, quoted in Ed Fitkin, *Come on Teeder!* (1950)

Not only did the Maple Leafs open the series with three straight wins, Frank McCool posted three straight shutouts as Toronto won 1–0, 2–0, and 1–0 again.

"I have never witnessed a greater display of moral courage than McCool has shown us all season."

> — Frank Selke, quoted by Andy Lytle, *Toronto Daily Star*, April 12, 1945

"It doesn't look like the puck is ever going to go in for us again. I thought we deserved to win but were outlucked. We'll have to take the series the hard way."

> — Detroit GM Jack Adams after Detroit fell behind three games
> to nothing, quoted in Ed Fitkin, *Come on Teeder!* (1950)

"They aren't that good. We have to win four straight and we can do it."

> — Detroit's Mud Bruneteau, quoted in Ed Fitkin, *Come on Teeder!* (1950)

The Red Wings stayed alive with a 5–3 win in Game 4, and then scored a 2–0 win in Game 5.

"We've got them on the run. The Leafs look tired and we're skating faster. Toronto's been trying to hang on with two forward lines and now they're hanging on the ropes."

> — Jack Adams, quoted in Ed Fitkin, *Come on Teeder!* (1950)

Game 6 was a tense one. Scoreless through regulation time, Detroit evened the series with a 1–0 win on a strange goal at 14:15 of overtime.

"The very first time I skated on the Gardens ice for a practice, I found myself thinking I better be good because Toronto has seen a lot of mighty fine goalers in their nets — Broda, Lumley, Bower, Rollins and, yes, Sawchuk. And it had been a Leaf goaler, Frank McCool, who gave me the very first inkling I had about the extreme pressure a major league goaler experiences in the playoffs in 1945....

"That McCool came up with three consecutive shutouts, and the newspapers were full of stories about him battling severe ulcers during the playoffs ... but what impressed me most was what happened in the sixth game. Detroit had rallied for two wins and the sixth game went into overtime with the score 0 to 0. First it was [Harry] Lumley making a big save in the Detroit nets, then McCool kicking out a hot one in the Toronto nets. I was listening so hard that I was afraid to breath for fear I'd miss the sudden death goal. Finally it came. Detroit scored — I don't remember who got the goal — but even as a kid goalie I suffered for McCool. I could imagine him that night trying to sleep, thinking and thinking about the save he didn't make."

— Jacques Plante, *The Jacques Plante Story* (1972)

"You'd think Jacques had enough pressure memories of his own without having to agonize over mine of a quarter-century ago. But how right he is about that overtime goal. Would you believe that I still fret over it?

"Eddie Bruneteau was the guy who got through our defence and fired for the corner of the net. The puck was a few feet wide of the net but I should have remembered — right there in my own Gardens' rink — that the boards at that spot gave off a fast rebound. Bruneteau picked up the rebound, shot, and scored. Maybe I was tired and not as alert as I should have been but I might have intercepted the puck coming back off those boards...."

— Frank McCool in Jacques Plante, *The Jacques Plante Story* (1972)

On the road in Detroit for Game 7, Hap Day surprised the Red Wings by employing a third forward line in this game featuring Art Jackson, Nick Metz, and Don Metz. Mel Hill got Toronto on the scoreboard at 5:38 of the first period and the Maple Leafs held the lead until Murray Armstrong scored for Detroit at 8:16 of the third. Toronto's Babe Pratt scored a power-play goal at 12:14, just 19 seconds after a penalty to Syd Howe, and the Maple Leafs held on for a 2–1 victory and the Stanley Cup.

"It was a great show our boys gave. I am proud of every one of them. During the long season haul we frequently had to put on a show. We always had the material but sometimes it wasn't available. In the playoffs we adopted a defence style that was designed to bring us the championship. That is what people expect of us. We were able to come through."

— Hap Day after Game 7

"He won a championship for us against Detroit three years ago by gambling that [Gordie] Drillon and Bucko McDonald should be benched. He gambled on a two-forward line system against the Red Wings in the series just ended, and his judgement was vindicated."

— Conn Smythe on coach Hap Day after Game 7

"If I were to single any one for individual praise I would have to say that of all the team, McCool has come farthest since Owen Sound. At Detroit last night when it was all over McCool came up to me and said, 'Thanks, coach, for sticking with me.' I think of all the boys, he got the greatest kick out of achieving Stanley Cup eminence in his rookie year."

— Hap Day, quoted by Andy Lytle, *Toronto Daily Star*, April 23, 1945

"That final series lasted 16 days but it seemed like an eternity. I couldn't keep anything down — not even the ulcer pills. But I was so much on edge even slow starvation didn't keep me from going through the motions. I've never ceased to be grateful to the three major referees of the day — King Clancy, Bill Chadwick, and George Gravel — for the way they helped relieve my tension by doing extra skating when they saw I was getting up slow."

— Frank McCool to Andy O'Brien, *Weekend Magazine*,
vol. 11, no. 4, January 28, 1961

Frank McCool was the best story of Toronto's 1944–45 season, but he was not the team's only star.

"There are few great hockey players in the NHL today. Kennedy is assuredly and emphatically one."

— Andy Lytle, *Toronto Daily Star*, quoted in Ed Fitkin, *Come on Teeder!* (1950)

"We've never had a better centre than Kennedy, and he's only 19! He scored 29 goals during the regular season and seven more in the playoffs.

Defensively, he's much more rugged than Apps or Taylor. He's a strong skater, too, with a change of pace that neither Syl nor Billy had. And Bodnar clearly demonstrated in the playoffs he could stand up under punishment against heavier and stronger opponents."

— Conn Smythe, *Globe and Mail*, April 26, 1945

But in truth, it was a total team effort that brought Toronto the Stanley Cup that season.

"I don't think folks really appreciate how much team spirit contributed to this championship. We've never had a team with more of it. And I'm sure there are plenty of boys overseas, as well as folks at home, that are proud of the players that have carried the banner of the Maple Leafs so effectively."

— Conn Smythe, quoted by Vern DeGeer, *Globe and Mail*,
Toronto, April 24, 1945

4

1946 to 1951:
The First Leafs Dynasty

1945–46 AND 1946–47

With the Stanley Cup win in April, followed by the end of the war in Europe that May, and the surrender of Japan in August, the summer of 1945 was certainly a good one in Toronto. The return of so many players from military service generated high hopes for the Maple Leafs as they entered the 1945–46 season, but things didn't work out.

Frank McCool had signed a $3,000 contract for the 1944–45 season. He also got a $1,000 signing bonus and collected $3,200 in other bonuses and playoff money. Prior to the 1945–46 season, he agreed to a new contract paying him $4,500, but then decided he wanted $5,000. When he didn't get it, he sat out the start of the season. The Leafs had a 3–10–1 start in the first five weeks of the season and never recovered, even after McCool agreed to terms before later being replaced by the return of Turk Broda.

The homecoming of other veterans from the war didn't do enough to offset a poor season by Teeder Kennedy, who played only 21 games due to another groin injury and had just 5 points. Toronto finished the season in fifth place with a record of 19–24–7 and went from Stanley Cup champions to missing the playoffs.

"[A] lot of us were coming back from war service — I was gone two years — and there was the feeling that we were going to be home-free in the league, what with all the veterans returning. But everybody forgot that it took half a season to get our bearings again. That's the way it was

Turk Broda seemed to play his best when it mattered most. He had a 60–39 record with a 1.98 goals-against average in 101 career playoff games and played on five Stanley Cup champion teams during 13 full seasons in Toronto.

with me. I'd hardly been on skates those two years, and I had a terrible time settling down."
　　　　– Syl Apps on the team's poor performance in 1945–46 in Jack Batten, *The Leafs in Autumn* (1975)

"When the Maple Leafs were having their long run of success, nobody bothered to credit me with any great part in the triumphs. But now, when we failed to make the playoffs for the first time, I was naturally selected to be the goat."
　　　　– Frank Selke, *Behind the Cheering* (1962)

Conn Smythe had shipped overseas in the fall of 1942. He was badly wounded in action in the summer of 1944. After weeks in hospital, he'd been sent back to Canada that September.

"He [Smythe] was always up to date on everything that was going on in Toronto even after he had been seriously wounded in France."
　　　　– Frank Selke, *Behind the Cheering* (1962)

Smythe kept tabs on the team while he recovered at home, and often commented on the goings on — particularly during the 1945 playoffs — but he was still not part of the day-to-day management. As the team struggled during the 1945–46 season, Smythe began to speak out more and more as he looked to take back a more prominent position with the team.

"We had no one feeding 'em in at the bottom for about five years. Our machine was good enough to run on its own power for four years, but it finally ran out of steam."

— Conn Smythe to Gordon Walker, *Toronto Daily Star*, March 30, 1946

But Smythe wasn't really being honest. Frank Selke had taken great pains to sign younger players during the war years.

"Conn Smythe had me on the carpet publicly and in the press. He was adamant; it was my selection of reserve material that led to the team's downfall.

"In reply I tried to explain to him that our veterans had now aged to a point where they could no longer play good hockey on successive nights. With a continuous Saturday-Sunday night schedule, this was disastrous in itself, and enough to cause our downfall.

"I produced a copy of a letter I had written to Ed Bickle some years before. I'd pointed out that all the good eighteen-year-old boys were joining the Services, and I asked permission to steal a march on the other clubs by signing as many of the most brilliant sixteen-year-old boys, whose parents would consent, to Maple Leaf options. My point was that they would be at their best at the end of the war, and very valuable to us....

"With Ed Bickle's approval, this had been done.... Despite my misunderstanding with Conn, I am sure the idea was a wise one."

— Frank Selke, *Behind the Cheering* (1962)

Selke resigned from the Maple Leafs at the end of May in 1946 and would soon take over operations of the Montreal Canadiens. Back in charge in Toronto, Smythe would use many of the young players Selke had signed to launch a Maple Leafs' youth movement.

"We've got to rebuild immediately. There are too many old men on our team. What we need is youth, fighting youth, kids with spirit. This rebuilding job isn't going to be easy. It may take us two years, and it may take us five."

— Conn Smythe on rebuilding, quoted in Ed Fitkin, *Come on Teeder!* (1950)

REBUILDING WITH YOUTH

On August 15, 1946, the Leafs announced that there would be separate training camps for the Leafs and Pittsburgh Hornets of the American Hockey League in St. Catharines starting on September 23, while the Tulsa Oilers of the United States Hockey League (USHL) would start camp in Kingston. Prior to this, the Leafs would run a week-long "hockey school" (what would now be called a Prospects Camp) in St. Catharines starting on September 16. The best from the hockey school would be invited to the team's main training camp.

"I should have figured it out years ago. Youth is the answer in this game. Only the kids have the drive, the fire, and the ambition. Put the kids in with a few old guys who still like to win and the combination is unbeatable."
— Conn Smythe on the plan to go with younger players in 1946–47

"Any player, whether he trains with Pittsburgh or Tulsa, will be moved up to the Leafs if he convinces us he is doing a better job than his same number on the Varsity squad."
— Hap Day, quoted by Jim Vipond, *Globe and Mail*, Toronto, August 16, 1946

"You have to keep your material pouring through or you club will dry up. This year we have youngsters coming through from Oshawa, St. Mike's, Marlboroughs, and the west coast. By the end of the season we should have a first-rate club on hand for the following season."
— Conn Smythe after the first day of the Leafs hockey school, quoted in the *Toronto Daily Star*, September 17, 1946

That week-long hockey camp would sprout players such as Garth Boesch, Vic Lynn, and Howie Meeker, all of whom made the Leafs straight away.

"I'll never forget that Sunday morning when Syl Apps, Bob Goldham, Wally Stanowski, Turk Broda, Gus Bodnar, Bud Poile, Gaye Stewart, Teeder Kennedy, and others arrived at the same hotel I was in. These were people I had listened to and watched play all my life; they had been my heroes. The next day, we were all going on the ice together. For a twenty-two-year-old guy just back from overseas, it was a hell of a thrill."
— on advancing to main camp from rookie camp in 1946–47
in Howie Meeker, *Golly Gee It's Me* (1996)

Bill Barilko was also there, and would be called up from the minors during the 1946–47 season. Tod Sloan would arrive a few years later. And other future Leaf stars would prove that Hap Day was as good as his word.

"I was with Pittsburgh [and] we had an exhibition game against the Leafs in Hamilton, so naturally I got my skates sharpened. I went all the way from Niagara Falls, where Pittsburgh was training, to St. Catharines, where the Leafs were, because I wanted Tommy Naylor, the Leaf guy, to do the sharpening. He'd always done it for me from the time I played junior hockey at St. Mike's in Toronto. The other guys on Pittsburgh waited to get their skates sharpened by the guy who worked at the Hamilton rink. Well, that night we skated out on the ice and I was the only player on Pittsburgh who could stand up. The Hamilton guy was incompetent or something, and he buggered up the blades on the other players' skates…. I must have played fifty minutes that night, and I looked like an all-star compared to everybody else. After the game, Hap Day comes over to me and says, 'Never mind going back to Niagara Falls. Just get on our bus.' I climbed on, and I wasn't out of the NHL for the next twelve years."

— Gus Mortson in Jack Batten, *The Leafs in Autumn* (1975)

"Good blend — that's what management got for us in 1947 and '48. New young fellows, old players, good goal scorers and good strong body-checkers. We had wonderful balance on those teams."

— Syl Apps on the Leafs youth movement in
Jack Batten, *The Leafs in Autumn* (1975)

"Most of those men weren't rookies in the real sense. They weren't green. Meeker, Boesch, some others — they'd matured in the army. I knew they'd measure up. They'd been through real battles."

— Hap Day on the rookies in 1946–47 in Jack Batten,
The Leafs in Autumn (1975)

Smythe was critical of the 1945–46 Leafs, not because they had missed the playoffs a year after winning the Stanley Cup, but because they had the fewest penalty minutes of any team in the NHL. He vowed that would never happen again, and he put that point across when he addressed the team hopefuls a few days into the main training camp.

"Conn told the boys of the tradition behind the Maple Leafs, stating that they were representing Canada in the NHL and were idols of young and old from coast to coast. He stressed the rebuilding program that is being carried out this year and told the players that he wanted a fighting team filled with a desire to mix it with anyone. He further stressed the importance of team spirit and co-operation and hoped that any time a member of the team was illegally attacked on the ice, his mates would rally to his aid."
— Jim Vipond, *Globe and Mail*, Toronto, September 27, 1946

"It took Conn Smythe no more than 10 minutes to make the 20 hockey players aware of what was expected of them this season. In a brief, forceful address on club policy, he warned them, from the oldest veteran to the youngest rookie, that there will be a one way ticket to the minors for any players who get shoved around and takes it numbly.... 'If they start shoving you around, I expect you to shove them right back, harder,' he cried. 'If one of our players should get injured by illegal tactics of the enemy, I expect the players on our team to see that the man responsible doesn't get away with it.'"
— Gordon Walker, *Toronto Daily Star*, September 27, 1946

In his own autobiography, Conn Smythe admitted that he couldn't remember when he first uttered his famous motto about beating them in the alley. No one appears to have quoted him saying exactly that at training camp in 1946, but it was readily apparent he wanted a tough team.

"I've tried to explain a hundred times what I meant when I said: 'If you can't lick 'em in the alley, you can't beat 'em on the ice.' I did not mean that you scare the other guy, but that you show him there is no fear in you."
— Conn Smythe to Bob Pennington, *Toronto Star*, October 1, 1973

One of the best things to come out of Leafs training camp in the fall of 1946 was a trio that would be dubbed "The New Kid Line."

"Hap Day put us on the ice in the first day of practice ... [Teeder] Kennedy wasn't a skater, didn't have the legs, but he was very competitive and a heck of a puck-handler. With him, you had to have two guys who could skate.... If anybody could make the two of us into something, it was Kennedy. [Vic] Lynn was a good hockey player. He was always looking for a fight. Vic'd cut you from ear to ear if he had half a chance. But boy oh

boy, he could skate. Me, I could skate and I could check. I couldn't pass....
It worked for us as long as Kennedy had the sense to get up ahead of the
play and cross the line before Vic and me.... [W]ith Kennedy firing the
puck to us young scooters, we could pop away at the net.... He was a great
passer. He kept Lynn and me in the league."

— Howie Meeker on playing with Lynn and Kennedy
in Jack Batten, *The Leafs in Autumn* (1975)

These be the choicest of summary words:
Kennedy, Meeker and Lynn.
Trio of Leaflets, fleeter than birds,
Kennedy, Meeker and Lynn.
Thoughtfully clicking on passing plays,
Doing tricks with the puck that amaze,
Words becoming a popular phrase,
Kennedy, Meeker and Lynn.

— Gordon Walker of the *Toronto Star*, spoofing
Tinkers to Evers to Chance

Gus Mortson and Teeder Kennedy stand behind Vic Lynn and Bud Poile. Lynn and Mortson
were among an impressive crop of rookies who joined the Maple Leafs in 1946–47.

"If you couldn't play hockey with Kennedy, you couldn't play hockey with anybody. He was probably as great a competitor as has ever played the game, and certainly by far the toughest competitor on our team. He had great hockey sense and great puckhandling and passing skills."

— Howie Meeker, *Golly Gee It's Me* (1996)

As training camp continued, Conn Smythe tried to be realistic about his team's chances in the upcoming season, but couldn't quite hide his optimism.

"The Maple Leafs will suffer plenty of defeats this season. We'll win plenty too."

— Smythe to reporters, quoted by Canadian Press, October 2, 1946

"At training camp ... Smythe made another of his daring moves. With Apps and Kennedy back in form, he traded centre Billy Taylor to Detroit for Harry Watson, a solid left wing player, who gave the team experience and ballast. But, mainly, he decided to go with kids."

— Frank Selke, *Behind the Cheering* (1962)

Still, it would be an old Leafs veteran who was the key.

"If Turk stands up, we may surprise a lot of people."

— Conn Smythe on the team's chances in 1946–47,
quoted in Ed Fitkin, *Turk Broda of the Leafs* (1950)

"Most of us thought his team might be one year away; but they surprised us all."

— Frank Selke, *Behind the Cheering* (1962)

With Broda, Apps, Nick Metz, and Wally Stanowski of the 1942 Stanley Cup team all returning to pre-war condition, Teeder Kennedy as good as ever (and still only 21 years old), and the new crop of rookies blending in nicely, Toronto went 7–3–1 to start the season and was in first place with a record of 20–6–4 at the halfway point of the newly expanded 60-game season.

Montreal's Maurice Richard scored 45 goals and led the NHL with 15 more than anyone else in the league by season's end, but Kennedy (28), Apps (25), and Howie Meeker (27) all ranked among the top 10. Meeker would win the Calder Trophy as rookie of the year. His five-goal game on January 8, 1947, went a long way toward helping him claim the honour. Were the Leafs inflating Meeker's totals that night to boost his Calder credit? For some, the dispute lingered on for years.

Meeker and Stanowski

"Howie Meeker, the spirited little hockey player with the crew haircut, who two years ago lay in a military hospital in England, his legs shattered with many shrapnel wounds, wondering if he would ever skate again, went on a wild scoring spree to net five goals and pace the league-leading Toronto Maple Leafs to a one-sided 10–4 victory over the Chicago Black Hawks at Maple Leaf Gardens last night.

"In so doing, the 'Stratford Flash' … virtually wrapped up the Calder Trophy as the outstanding rookie of the year."

— Jim Vipond, *Globe and Mail*, Toronto, January 9, 1947

"Wally Stanowski, the Leafs' most improved player, was originally credited with the first and third Toronto scores. However, the whirling dervish of the ice lanes was the first to admit that, although he did the shooting, the puck, in both instances, was directed into the net by Meeker. Official Scorer Bill Graham made the corrections at the end of the second period, following a protest lodged by Coach Happy Day. Stanowski was given assists on both scores, and also picked up an assist on Toronto's second goal, scored by Don Metz in the second period."

— Jim Vipond, *Globe and Mail*, Toronto, January 9, 1947

"Three good ones and two of the other kind. First goal, Stanowski shot the puck from their blue line and I was in a crowd at the front of the net. The puck went in between my legs, and when it did, I gave it a tap into the goal. They announced over the public address that Stanowski scored that one. Well, okay, in the second period I put two more in the net and I sat down on the bench and I said, 'That's three for the night.' Hap Day heard me and said, 'What do you mean three?' I told him I put Stanowski's in and Hap, a real heck of a man, gets the scoring changed to me. So, what do you know, Joe Klukay sent me into the clear for an easy tap-in and another shot of Stanowski's hit my leg and bounced past the goalie. Three good ones and two others, and they all look the same on paper."

— Howie Meeker in Jack Batten, *The Leafs in Autumn* (1975)

"I scored two of them. The first goal was, pretty much, standard. The puck went in and I came back to the bench and Hap Day, our coach, tapped me on the shoulder and said, 'We are going to give that one to Meeker.'

"The second goal that I scored took a funny hop. It hit the ice a couple of times ... and then went in. So he gave that one also to Meeker."

— Wally Stanowski to Joe O'Connor, *National Post*, January 30, 2015

"I know both the disputed goals were carom shots and it was hard to see who actually did the scoring at the time. Later when I checked with all parties concerned, I gave the proper credit to Meeker."

— Leafs official scorer Bill Graham, *Globe and Mail*, Toronto, January 15, 1947

"Say, you got them talking about you all over the circuit. [Art] Ross, [Jack] Adams and the others are all saying how they wish they had you in their hometown."

— Canadiens coach Dick Irvin to Maple Leafs' official scorer Bill Graham, reported in the *Globe and Mail*, Toronto, January 15, 1947

"President Clarence Campbell of the National Hockey League is of the opinion 'dressing-room awards' of scoring points should be kept 'to an absolute minimum.'

"The president's opinion was expressed in a recent letter to Bill Graham, official scorer in Toronto, who, during a game Jan. 8, awarded two goals to Toronto's Howie Meeker that previously had been credited to Walter Stanowski. The reversed decision came after the close of the second period, following a conference among players and officials....

"Campbell said today he wrote Graham largely to point out the duties of scorers, and that there was nothing wrong in what Graham did. He said a referee's information, or even that of a team captain, might often be valuable and acceptable to an official scorer."

— Canadian Press story, January 27, 1947

"They were lying. They were building Meeker up for the rookie award. Eventually he won it, with the five goals there — he made it."

— Wally Stanowski to Joe O'Connor, *National Post*, January 30, 2015

"Those were two horse-s*** goals.... The only reason I was standing in front of the net was because Wally's shot couldn't break a pane of glass. If he had any spit on his shot, he would have scored a million goals."

— Howie Meeker to Joe O'Connor, *National Post*, January 30, 2015

"He should have admitted the fact. I wouldn't talk to him anyway. I never did like him that much."

> — Wally Stanowski to Joe O'Connor, *National Post*, January 30, 2015

"If Wally wants to take a goal back, he can take one, and I'll take four. What's the difference?"

> — Howie Meeker to Joe O'Connor, *National Post*, January 30, 2015

The Debut of Bashin' Bill Barilko

Bill Barilko had been much in demand after the Leafs hockey camp in the fall of 1946. The Pittsburgh Hornets wanted him in the AHL. Scout Ernie Orlando, who had first tipped off the Leafs on Barilko, thought his development would be better served with the Tulsa Oilers in the USHL. In the end, Barilko was sent to the Hollywood Wolves of the PCHL, who were actually a Pittsburgh farm club. There, he would hone his skills playing with former NHL MVP Tom Anderson.

When injuries hit the Leafs at the end of January, the team began to slump. When they fell into second place behind the Canadiens in early February, Conn Smythe made the call for reinforcements.

> "In a sort of 'It's okay, kids, Daddy's here to fix things' message from New York, Smythe yesterday let it be known to a gasping public that the Leafs have help coming on the run from Pittsburgh and Hollywood. From the Hornets he plucked left-winger Sid Smith, only this winter hoisted from the Quebec Aces, and from the Wolves of Hollywood he fingered Bill Barilko, 19-year-old Timmins-born defence player, who showed fair form in the pre-season scramblings at St. Catharines."
>
> — Joe Perlove, *Toronto Daily Star*, February 3, 1947

> "Smythe said the decision to bring in two untried youngsters was in keeping with policy laid down at St. Catharines to rebuild a championship team with young players. What Barilko and Smith lack in experience they, like the six rookies who have become regular members of the Leafs machine, will make up in enthusiasm and fight, the managing director predicted."
>
> — Jim Vipond, *Globe and Mail*, Toronto, February 3, 1947

"He's green, but he's willing and he learns fast."
— Tom Anderson on Barilko, quoted in Ed Fitkin, *Turk Broda of the Leafs* (1950)

"Bill Barilko, a good-looking husky up from Hollywood, checked into the Leafs' hockey camp yesterday to bolster an injury-depleted defense corps, and Coach Happy Day lost little time in acquainting the newcomer with the three remaining healthy members of his biffem and bashem brigade ... Jim Thomson, Gus Mortson, and Wally Stanowski."

— *Globe and Mail*, Toronto, February 4, 1947

Barilko made his debut in Montreal on February 6, 1947. The Leafs lost 8–2 that night, but the young defenceman made his presence known.

"Bill Barilko, up from Hollywood Wolves, played on defense and was a bright spot in the Toronto cause with his ability to hit the opposition. Twice in the last period he sent big Butch Bouchard flying."

— Jim Vipond, *Globe and Mail*, Toronto, February 7, 1947

"He rocked a few of the boys. They kept their heads up when he was on the ice."

— Harry Watson on Barilko's first game, in Kevin Shea,
Barilko: Without a Trace (2004)

The Leafs finally snapped their six-game-winless streak (a tie and five losses) back in Toronto two nights later with a 5–2 win over Boston that was capped off by Barilko's first NHL goal.

"It was rookie night as the Toronto Maple Leafs ended a six-game winless streak with a 5–2 victory over Boston Bruins before 13,804 fans at Maple Leaf Gardens Saturday night. Six of the seven tallies came from the sticks of five freshman pucksters; four of them making their NHL debuts as far as Toronto was concerned. Howie Meeker, the aggressive little playmaker from New Hamburg, paced the Toronto scoring parade with two goals and two assists, while Bashing Bill Barilko and Toronto-born Sid Smith each scored once.... Barilko played as though he intended staying in the NHL for a long time. He has the ability to hit an opposing player squarely and handed out several jolting checks. He sent Milt Schmidt flying over his shoulder and on another occasion showed nice timing in combining with Wally Stanowski to take Joe Carveth out of the play."

— Jim Vipond, *Globe and Mail*, Toronto, February 10, 1947

"I'm going to make hockey my career. So I'm sure going to give everything I have to stay up here with the Leafs. It's a different, tougher game than any I've ever played — but getting a couple of goals to start sure helps the old confidence."

— Bill Barilko to Allan Nickleson, *Globe and Mail*, Toronto, February 18, 1947

Barilko would later score one of the most famous goals in hockey history, but it wasn't his offence that he became known for.

"Better at giving the hip than anybody in the league. A guy'd come down the ice with the puck and he'd think he was safely past Billy. Then, all of a sudden — wham! Billy'd catch him with the hip. Billy could move sideways quicker than any defenceman. That was his ace."

— Bill Ezinicki on Barilko in Jack Batten, *The Leafs in Autumn* (1975)

"He was quite a hitter. After all, you have to be a good hitter to get the nickname Bashin' Bill."

— Harry Watson recalling Barilko for *Hockey Digest* magazine

The 1947 Playoffs

The Leafs never again saw first place in the standings during the 1946–47 season, but they finished comfortably in second place with a record of 31–19–10; their 72 points eight back of first-place Montreal but nine up on third-place Boston. With the playoffs approaching, the team was confident.

"[We are] strictly the team to beat. Make no mistake about that. We play a tough, aggressive game, just the sort that goes best in a playoff where the players have no reason to save themselves. They know if they lose, they're out."

— Conn Smythe, Canadian Press report, March 14, 1947

"We had ten really tough hockey players, most of them true NHL calibre. The tougher it got — and that is the key — the better the guys played."

— Howie Meeker, *Golly Gee It's Me* (1996)

Toronto opened the post-season against fourth-place Detroit and scored a 3–2 overtime victory in Game 1. After being crushed 9–1 in Game 2, the Leafs bounced back with 4–1, 4–1, and 6–1 wins to take the series in five and advance to the Final, where they'd face Montreal.

"In the Stanley Cup final, I found myself opposed to my old buddy, Hap Day, and the very team of boys [whose] recruiting had cost me my job."

— Frank Selke, *Behind the Cheering* (1962)

The 1947 Stanley Cup Final between Toronto and Montreal marks the true beginning of the long-time rivalry between the Leafs and the Canadiens. Toronto had led the league in penalty minutes that season, and though they were more tough than dirty, Frank Selke had been critical of them all season. Selke accused the Leafs defence of using "wrestling tactics" and was incensed when Elmer Lach suffered a fractured skull after a hard hit from Don Metz in Bill Barilko's debut game on February 6.

It was the first all-Canadian Stanley Cup Final since the Montreal Maroons beat Toronto in 1935. The first-place Canadiens, who'd won the Stanley Cup in 1946, were favoured to win it again this year, but the series was bound to be close.

"Canadiens — in eight games."

— Montreal goalie Bill Durnan's light-hearted prediction, *Montreal Gazette*, April 8, 1946

"We'll give them our best, and it is possible it may be good enough."

— Conn Smythe to reporters before the series

It wasn't in Game 1, as the Canadiens opened with a 6–0 victory.

"At least they couldn't play much worse."

— Hap Day, expecting his team to play better in Game 2, Canadian Press, April 9, 1947

"Leafs will be better. In fact they're apt to be hot. Look how they came back after Detroit walloped them 9–1 in the semifinal. The only game we don't want to lose is the last one."

— Dick Irvin, expecting the Leafs to bounce back in Game 2, Canadian Press, April 9, 1947

"A Montreal hockey writer quoted Bill Durnan as saying 'How did that club ever get into the playoffs?' Durnan, never a pop-off, said no such thing, but the Toronto press played it up to the limit. Conn Smythe,

Coach Hap Day celebrates with Syl Apps and Turk Broda, who were the heroes of Toronto's 2–1 overtime victory over Montreal in Game 4 of the Stanley Cup Final on April 15, 1947.

who was the game's most articulate rabble rouser, inflamed his team to such a pitch that the Maple Leafs won the next three games."
— Frank Selke, *Behind the Cheering* (1962)

The Leafs won a rough Game 2 by a score of 4–0. Maurice Richard and Bill Ezinicki got into a stick-swinging brawl that resulted in The Rocket being suspended for Game 3, which the Leafs went on to win 4–2. Game 4 was key, and after each team allowed an early goal, Turk Broda and Bill Durnan staged a goaltenders' battle that wasn't broken up until Syl Apps scored for Toronto at 16:36 of overtime. Montreal stayed alive with a 3–1 victory at home in Game 5, but Toronto wrapped up the series in six games with a come-from-behind 2–1 victory at Maple Leaf Gardens on Saturday night, April 19.

Montreal had jumped in front after just 25 seconds, but Teeder Kennedy and Howie Meeker set up Vic Lynn for the tying goal early in the second period. Meeker set up Kennedy for the winner on a screened shot with just 5:21 remaining in the third.

The Stanley Cup was coming back to Toronto.

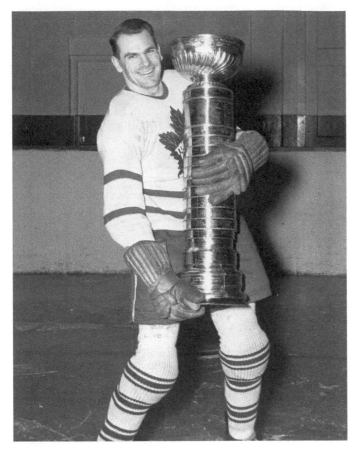

Proud captain Syl Apps displays the "Stovepipe" Stanley Cup after Toronto's 1947 victory.

"We had to beat a real team of champions to become champions, make no mistake about that. But if you want to know why we won, I'll give you three reasons. First, there was the coaching of Hap Day, who ran the team and made the decisions; second, there was the play of our old champions, by that I mean the veterans of other championship teams; third, there was the play of the kids who wanted to be champions."
— Conn Smythe in the dressing room after
Game 6, Canadian Press, April 21, 1947

"That's what you call taking them from the eggcup to the fighting-cock stage all in one season. I knew me and Hap could do her when we left St. Kitts with this gang of rookies."
— Leafs trainer Tim Daly after Game 6, *Toronto Daily Star*, April 21, 1947

"*Y-a-h-o-o-o.* We did it, Tim! We won her! We're the champs."
— Maple Leafs defenceman Jim Thomson to trainer Tim Daly
after entering the dressing room following Game 6

"You did it, Teeder. You're the baby, the guy who tied the can to them."
— Vic Lynn and Howie Meeker in the Leafs dressing room after Game 6

"He won the Cup for us two seasons back. We fell apart when he was shelved by injuries last season, and he came back to lead us home this term. His was as fine an individual performance as I've ever seen."
— Hap Day on Teeder Kennedy in the Leafs dressing room after Game 6

"Broda won that game for the Leafs in the first period when he beat [Toe] Blake and [Billy] Reay on those breakaways. Old Toe seemed to freeze on his shot. Turk made him look like a rookie."
— former Leaf Ace Bailey in the dressing room after Game 6

"They sure owe it all to you, boy."
— Red Wings coach and GM Jack Adams to Turk Broda in the dressing room
after the Stanley Cup win over Montreal, Canadian Press, April 21, 1947

"He was a bloody marvel sometimes, stood on his head, especially in those clutch games, key moments. What a goalie! Turk Broda was by far the best goaltender then and as good as any that ever played the game — particularly in big games."
— Howie Meeker, *Golly Gee It's Me* (1996)

"The boys kept themselves in wonderful shape all season and I think that was a big factor in our winning the title."
— Syl Apps, quoted by Jim Vipond, *Globe and Mail*, Toronto, April 22, 1947

1947–48

During the summer of 1946, Hap Day had announced that Syl Apps was planning to retire after the 1946–47 season. Conn Smythe convinced him to return for at least one more year, but Smythe was worried about the team's depth at centre. What would happen if Apps got hurt? What would happen after he retired?

The team opened the 1947–48 season with a record of 3–1–2 through November 1, and the next day Smythe pulled off a blockbuster trade. The

As defending Stanley Cup champions, Toronto hosted the first official NHL All-Star Game on October 13, 1947. Former Leafs King Clancy (who served as the referee), Charlie Conacher, Hap Day, and Busher Jackson line up with current Leafs Syl Apps, Turk Broda, Wally Stanowski, and Gaye Stewart. (Bobby Bauer of the Boston Bruins can be seen in the All-Star uniform in the background.)

Maple Leafs sent a complete forward line of Gus Bodnar, Bud Poile, and Gaye Stewart, along with defencemen Ernie Dickens and Bob Goldham, to the Chicago Black Hawks for rookie Cy Thomas and a centre who had led the NHL in scoring the past two seasons and had won the Hart Trophy as MVP in 1945–46.

The Max Bentley Trade

"Smythe was smart. When he had an idea he checked it out with more than one person. At the beginning of the 1947–48 season, he knew he wanted another centre and he came to me and asked me who was the best centre in the league who wasn't on our team. I went back in my mind — which centre had caused the most trouble for us? Max Bentley, I told Smythe. He didn't take my word for it. He got several opinions. I know one day when Montreal was in Toronto for a game, he went to their practice in the afternoon and called Bill Durnan, their goalie, over to the boards and asked him the same question. He got the same answer. So he traded for Bentley, and that was a great trade."

— Hap Day in Jack Batten, *The Leafs in Autumn* (1975)

"I really didn't think I could get Max because I didn't think [Bill] Tobin would part with him. When I was in Chicago, I talked about Max with the waitresses at the hotel, the clerks at the desk, the taxi driver, and many others, and they all said the same thing — that Tobin wouldn't trade Max, he was too popular."

— Conn Smythe, quoted in Ed Fitkin, *Max Bentley* (1951)

"He was kidding me. We were kidding one another and he finally said he'd give me four or five players for Max. I don't want to get rid of players and the Bentleys are definitely not for sale.

"I had been talking about buying [Bob] Goldham and Smythe said to make him an offering price. I said $15,000. He said it wasn't enough. How high would I go? So I said $25,000. Smythe said he wouldn't consider it.

"If I took him up on what I considered a rib about Bentley what, then, would he give me? He might give me five guys from Tulsa. I've got enough of that kind now. I'm still ready to give $25,000 for Goldham. But I don't think Smythe is serious about parting with any players."

— Chicago president and GM Bill Tobin, *Toronto Daily Star*, October 28, 1947

"Certainly I'm serious about the five for Max Bentley trade. I have given five in the past for one 'good one' and it always worked to our advantage…. Leafs need a first-class centre man to round them out as a championship contender and I think Bentley would be the man."

— Conn Smythe, *Toronto Daily Star*, October 28, 1947

The deal was announced on November 3 and was all over the newspapers the following day.

"Our purpose in making the deal relates to the centre ice problem. If anything were to happen to Apps we would be desperate. I feel it's quite a gamble but that it's worth it because we're getting the league scoring leader for centre duties. With Apps, Bentley, and Kennedy to centre our lines and Nick Metz as a utility player to spell them off, I think we'll have the strength down the middle that a championship team needs."

— Conn Smythe, *Globe and Mail*, Toronto, November 4, 1947

"We got the league's top scorer plus a promising rookie. What have the ones we gave away accomplished? Well then, Mr. Smythe made a very smart move."

— Hap Day, *Toronto Daily Star*, November 4, 1947

"We've drawn on all our reserves and we're hoping the trade doesn't weaken either club. It should help Chicago and benefit the whole league. I want to emphasize there has been no dissatisfaction with any of our players. They've been very fine. I hope this trade will give Goldham the chance to be the great star he should be."

— Conn Smythe, *Globe and Mail*, Toronto, November 4, 1947

"There's a guy with the greatest shot in hockey. A flick of the wrist, and brother, it's gone! He lets it go ankle-high, close to the post, and a goalie hasn't a chance. Boy, with Bentley on our side, I ought to win the Vezina hands down."

— Turk Broda, quoted in Ed Fitkin, *Turk Broda of the Leafs* (1950)

"What a surprise I received. They don't usually include rookies in these big trades."

— Cy Thomas on being traded to Toronto with Max Bentley, *Globe and Mail*, Toronto, November 4, 1947

Teeder Kennedy (left) and Syl Apps (right) pose with Max Bentley (centre) shortly after his arrival in the big trade with Chicago.

"It was quite a shock.... All I can say about that move is that I will do my best to make Hawks a better team."

— Gaye Stewart, *Toronto Daily Star*, November 4, 1947

"I just heard it on the radio, then the phone rang. It was Poile. We both said, 'Hello, Chicago' in the same breath. I think it's a break. With Chicago I'll get regular play and am confident I can prove I belong.... I had a hunch I'd be hitting the trail shortly."

— Gus Bodnar, *Toronto Daily Star*, November 4, 1947

"I was certainly surprised, but I think it's for the best. We'll get Chicago back in the playoffs or bust our gussets. I'm glad I hadn't found a permanent spot to live; moving won't be so tough on the little woman. Anyway, I like [coach Johnny] Gottselig and hear Chicago is a nice spot to live."

— Bud Poile, *Toronto Daily Star*, November 4, 1947

"[I was] reluctant [to break up the Bentley brothers but] it had to be done because we needed fresh blood and no other club wanted any of our players except Max Bentley."

— Chicago coach Johnny Gottselig, *Globe and Mail*, Toronto, November 4, 1947

"I didn't have to go to Toronto if I didn't want. Mr. Tobin, the Chicago president, called me and Doug into his office for a talk this one day. I'd heard rumours about a trade but I never dreamed it'd be me. Mr. Tobin said it was up to [me] whether I went or not. He said it'd help Chicago a lot, getting five top players like that. So I thought, well, I'll go. One person was very disappointed when he heard about the trade — my dad. He heard it on the radio. He wanted me and Doug to stay together. Maybe I should have phoned him right away so he wouldn't've heard it on the radio."

— Max Bentley in Jack Batten, *The Leafs in Autumn* (1975)

"I think it's a good break for me. Doug took it badly at first, but when we talked it over we realized it was for the best. The way the rest of the league has been shadowing us this season we have not had much chance to score goals; now some of the pressure may be lifted and we both will do much better."

— Max Bentley, *Globe and Mail*, Toronto, November 4, 1947

"Max did more things with the puck than anyone I've ever seen. He had difficulties breaking into our system, but he kept the puck so much of the time he was on the ice, it didn't matter."

— Hap Day in Jack Batten, *The Leafs in Autumn* (1975)

"I thought I knew about the fundamentals, but I got to Toronto and I learned from Hap Day there was more to hockey than I ever dreamed of."

— Max Bentley in Jack Batten, *The Leafs in Autumn* (1975)

The Regular Season ... And Syl Apps

From the middle of December until the end of the season, the battle for first place in the NHL was a two-team race between Toronto and Detroit. It was still up for grabs as the scheduled neared its end, but Syl Apps made it clear this was going to be his last season no matter what.

"Professional hockey is about to lose one of its finest players. Syl Apps, clever centreman and captain of Toronto Maple Leafs, has decided to retire in favour of a business career. He will hang up his hockey tack for keeps at the end of the Stanley Cup playoff series. Ted Kennedy will succeed the popular veteran as captain of the Toronto team. Apps ... told [Conn Smythe] of his decision while in Montreal for the Canadiens game. Smythe informed newsmen on the train journey home."

— Jim Vipond, *Globe and Mail*, Toronto, March 13, 1948

"I'd like to become as great a hockey player as Syl Apps and as great a captain, and to gain the same respect that everyone holds for Syl. He's really a wonderful fellow."

— Teeder Kennedy, quoted in Ed Fitkin, *Come on Teeder!* (1950)

"[Smythe] ran the team like an army. Discipline counted, officers must show leadership on the battlefield, that sort of thing. He demanded respect for his captains. And look at the captains he chose. Hap Day was a disciplinarian. Syl Apps led an exemplary life. There was a tradition of top guys and you had to adhere to standards when you were captain. It was Smythe who set the standards."

— Teeder Kennedy in Jack Batten, *The Leafs in Autumn* (1975)

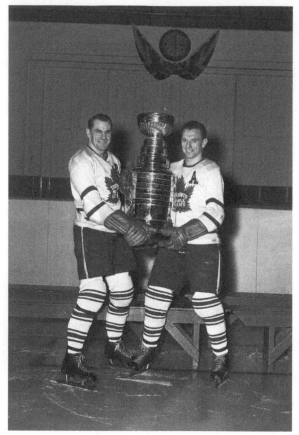

Syl Apps hands the Stanley Cup, which had been remodelled that year, to Teeder Kennedy in 1948. Apps would also hand off the "C" to Kennedy as the Leafs' new captain.

Apps had 195 career goals at the time of his retirement announcement, leaving him just short of the goal he had set for himself at the start of the season with only four games left on the schedule.

> "Yes, I would like to finish with 200 goals. It would be very nice, but I have my family to think of and I cannot go on playing forever, so I have made up my mind to retire at the end of this season…."
>
> — Syl Apps, *Globe and Mail*, Toronto, March 13, 1948

The Maple Leafs won their last four games of the season, including a home-and-home sweep of Detroit on the final weekend to clinch first place.

As usual, it was a total team effort in Toronto, with defence first. The Leafs allowed the fewest goals on the season, earning Turk Broda the Vezina Trophy. The strong core of centres led the team's offence. Apps scored a hat trick on the final night of the season to establish career highs with 26 goals and 53 points, and reach 201 goals in total. Max Bentley also had 26 goals, while Teeder Kennedy added 25.

"Apps is invaluable to the Leafs and to the league. I hope he reconsiders his retirement."

— Hap Day, *Globe and Mail*, Toronto, March 23, 1948

"I've often wondered if I'd have retired at the end of that year if I hadn't scored those goals in Detroit.... You didn't play hockey as long then. It didn't pay like it does now, and you had to get out and start a career."

— Syl Apps in Jack Batten, *The Leafs in Autumn* (1975)

"It was nice to get number 200, but it didn't compare with the thrill of our winning four straight against Detroit in 1942."

— Syl Apps to Stan Fischler, *Those Were the Days* (1976)

The Maple Leafs finished the season in first place with a record of 32–15–13 for 77 points. In the end, they were five points ahead of Detroit, who finished 30–18–12.

"Broda was the key and Day was the guy who turned the key, made everything work. In 1947–48 we had enough skill on the ice to win any game we all really wanted to win."

— Howie Meeker, *Golly Gee It's Me* (1996)

The 1947–48 season marked the first time in history that the Maple Leafs had won the Prince of Wales Trophy for topping the league standings (they've only finished first overall twice, doing it again in 1962–63). But this was not the prize the team had its sights set on.

"Right now, I feel as if we've finished one job and have to do another good job to make the first one complete. Now we've got to keep the Stanley Cup."

— Bill Ezinicki, *Globe and Mail*, Toronto, March 22, 1948

The 1948 Playoffs

The Stanley Cup quest got off to a good start when the Maple Leafs dispatched the Boston Bruins in five games in the semifinals.

"For Toronto Maple Leafs comes now the test of greatness.... [O]nly a really great hockey team can win the Stanley Cup one season and retain it the next. That's the task for which the Leafs are preparing. It's the reason their victory rejoicing after eliminating the Bruins was comparatively moderate in tone."

— Tommy Munns, *Globe and Mail*, Toronto, April 5, 1948

Toronto faced Detroit for the Stanley Cup and won the first three games 5–3, 4–2 and 2–0. But not everyone thought the Leafs were deserving of their big lead.

"I see by the Detroit papers that we shouldn't even be playing in the same rink as the Wings. Well, we've got nothing to say. We're doing all our talking through our actions on the ice."

— Jimmy Thomson, *Globe and Mail*, Toronto, April 13, 1948

Game 4 was set for April 14. Everyone was aware that Toronto had come back from a similar deficit against the Red Wings in 1942 and had almost let Detroit do the same to them in 1945.

"Most jittery person in the Toronto camp is Coach Hap Day. He has been having nightmares, day and night, always with the spectre of Detroit making a comeback, as did the Leafs against the Wings in 1941–42."

— Jim Vipond, *Globe and Mail*, Toronto, April 14, 1948

"Tomorrow night Leafs play the first contest in a four-game series. That is going to be our approach. I think the boys can end it all here in Detroit, but if they lose, they will still have three more chances to win a single game."

— Conn Smythe, *Globe and Mail*, Toronto, April 14, 1948

It turned out there was nothing to worry about as the Maple Leafs cruised to a Stanley Cup sweep with a 7–2 win in Game 4.

"There never was any doubt about it from the start to the finish."

— Detroit GM Jack Adams, congratulating Hap Day after the game

"We couldn't do anything about it."

— Red Wings coach Tommy Ivan

"I waited a long time for this. A Stanley Cup championship at last."

— Max Bentley, quoted in Ed Fitkin, *Max Bentley* (1951)

"Atta boy, Max, from the bottom to the top in one season."

— unknown teammate to Max Bentley, *Globe and Mail*, Toronto, April 15, 1948

"Strength in depth was the Leafs' victory weapon."

— NHL president Clarence Campbell

"Best we ever did in Chicago was finishing third one season. I have seen some great hockey teams since I turned pro but this Toronto team is the best of them all."

— Max Bentley, *Globe and Mail*, Toronto, April 16, 1948

"As coach Hap Day put it so well, we may not have the all-stars in our team, but we have the world champions…. We had the murderers' row of hockey with three 25-goal centre men. We had good goalkeeping and we had a good defense. With that batting order, we were hard to beat. This is the greatest team I ever had. They have never failed me, and for the first time in my life I did not have to give them a pep talk during the final series. I have had some great stars on other teams, but I've never had a team like this."

— Conn Smythe, *Globe and Mail*, Toronto, April 15, 1948

"The best team in Leafs' history" was a thought that those involved with the 1947–48 Maple Leafs kept coming back to over the years.

"I would have to like that club against any I could name. Of course, I admit I'm not completely unbiased."

— Conn Smythe, selecting the 1947–48 Maple Leafs as the greatest team he was ever connected with, *Toronto Daily Star*, April 27, 1960

"I think the 1948 team compares with any club in history. Our centre ice strength emphasizes the kind of club this was. We had Syl Apps, Teeder Kennedy, Max Bentley, and Nick Metz. Very few clubs ever had four centremen of that ability. Our defence was also tops. We had Garth Boesch and Bill Barilko as one pair, Gus Mortson and Jim Thomson as the other. They were great…. Then we had Turk Broda in the nets and there has never been another playoff goalie like the Turk."

— Hap Day to Frank Orr, *Toronto Daily Star*, January 8, 1963

"Those Leaf teams in the 1940s, they were way ahead of their time, the ideas they had…. As soon as the puck was dropped, everybody had something to do. On other teams, guys would stand around waiting for a pass. On our team, guys had a job to do before a pass ever came near them. If the faceoff was in our end, the centre got the draw back to a defenceman, he carried it up the ice, and the forwards' job was to take out the other team's forwards. They ran interference for the puck-carrier. They couldn't actually hit the other player — that'd be a penalty — but all they had to do was get in between them and the guy carrying the puck and the job was as good as done. It was just like football. That's what we made hockey — a team game. [On defence], never play the puck, always play the man. All teams do that today, but we were the first to really work at it."

— Gus Mortson in Jack Batten, *The Leafs in Autumn* (1975)

"They don't mention us too much, do they? But Smythe said, in his opinion, and it wasn't for publicity, that the 1948 team was the best team that ever played."

— Teeder Kennedy to Ken Campbell, *Toronto Star*, February 4, 2000

"All we ever hear about is the '67 team. They were great hockey players, but it's kind of nice for us to be recognized."

— Harry Watson to Ken Campbell, *Toronto Star*

The Maple Leafs and Red Wings have at it during Game 2 of the 1948 Stanley Cup Final. Detroit's Ted Lindsay is #7, Toronto's Turk Broda is #1, Toronto's Garth Boesch is #18, and Detroit's Pete Horeck is #11.

1948–49

Though he knew it would be difficult to replace Syl Apps, Conn Smythe had been optimistic about the future after winning the Stanley Cup in 1948.

> "We'll have a good club for several years to come at least. These are kids and yet they are veterans. They take the playoffs in stride, just as if it was another game. After all, they're playoff veterans. Kennedy has been in four or five, Thomson and Mortson have been mixed up with playoffs, junior and pro, for six or seven years. So has Ezinicki. If Watson plays next year the way he has played in the playoffs he'll be the greatest left wing in the league. Yep, everything looks good."
> — Conn Smythe in the *Toronto Daily Star*, April 16, 1948

But after Nick Metz followed Apps into retirement, and Wally Stanowski was traded away (for Cal Gardner, who was expected to replace Apps), Smythe was unhappy with the calibre of rookies looking to make the team in 1948–49 and was singing a different tune come the fall.

> "I thought it was the weakest [rookie] camp we've had! What I mean is, I haven't found anyone who looks like he can replace Syl Apps, Nick Metz, or Wally Stanowski, even after a lengthy seasoning period…. I don't think there are many top-flight rookies in this gang…. They may surprise me. I hope so! I don't know whether the NHL is getting better or the calibre of rookies falling off."
> — Conn Smythe to Red Burnett, *Toronto Daily Star*, September 13, 1948

Hap Day wasn't much happier with the main training camp either, feeling that the veterans' conditioning was below what he expected to see.

> "I want to see them in action against other NHL teams before I say anything."
> — Hap Day, *Globe and Mail*, Toronto, September 23, 1948

Smythe still wasn't sure what the Leafs had on hand when the season was set to face off on October 16.

> "I agree with the statement of [Rangers coach Frank] Boucher that the first could be last and the last could be first. Last year, with the greatest club we ever had, we had to go right to the last two games of the season to get into first place."
> — Conn Smythe in the *Toronto Daily Star*, October 16, 1948

"Day has a tricky job as he has ever had in his life. We are going to ask him to perform a miracle."

— Conn Smythe, *Globe and Mail*, Toronto, October 16, 1948

"Our team is thin in depth. You can't get anywhere without depth. Injuries decide the last three places in the league. If we run into injuries, we may be fighting it out for one of those three places. If we can make four rookies into four major leaguers in one year, we may run one-two."

— Conn Smythe, *Toronto Daily Star*, October 16, 1948

"We've got something no other club has. In the first place, we've got the best coach. He knows what he's trying to do and no one is pulling against him…. Secondly, we have the best team spirit we've had in years. I'm counting on those two things to keep us in there."

— Conn Smythe, *Globe and Mail*, Toronto, October 16, 1948

"Hap Day thoroughly understood the team and the individual talents needed to win, and man, oh man could he get the three most important ingredients out of his talent: hard work, discipline, and respect."

— Howie Meeker, *Golly Gee It's Me* (1996)

"It's going to be a very tough race all the way through the schedule. I've done all I can to get them in shape; now it's up to the players themselves."

— Hap Day, *Globe and Mail*, Toronto, October 16, 1948

The Leafs lost their season opener 4–1 at home to Boston, and then lost the next one on the road in Montreal 5–0. Though they won three of their next four, the season never really got on track. Injuries did prove a challenge to the team's depth, and they struggled along in fifth place for much of the season.

"That's the difficult part — getting a team ready mentally. For physical conditioning, nothing but hard work is the key. But mentally, well, you might have the situation where a team has won the year before, and if you get on them to do it again, they might say, 'What? D'you expect us to win every year?' And a lot of times they may think they're playing well out there on the ice, but you know they're really terrible. When a mental lag comes, it hits the whole team at once."

— Hap Day in Jack Batten, *The Leafs in Autumn* (1975)

"The fans shouted their disapproval of the Leafs' goal mouth efforts in the third period, making Captain Ted Kennedy the particular target of their wrath. They booed when Kennedy skated out to take over the face-off duties in a last-minute ganging attack with Broda off the ice and repeatedly jeered the game playmaker with such cries as 'Go on back to Port Colborne, Kennedy' or 'Take Kennedy off the ice, Day.'

"And that was the unsportsmanlike treatment given one of the greatest competitors in modern hockey. No one will deny that Kennedy has been having a bad year, but he is a player who gives everything all the time and it was only a few short months ago the same fans were hailing him as their favourite."

— Jim Vipond, *Globe and Mail*, Toronto, March 14, 1949

The team finished the season under .500 with a record of 22–25–13 for just 57 points, but they managed to finish in fourth place and make the playoffs.

"Anybody who knew us, knew the Leafs were much better than we showed.... We weren't a below .500 club really. Anybody who considered us that was way out of their minds."

— Howie Meeker, *Golly Gee It's Me* (1996)

Still, the second-place Bruins expected to come out on top when Toronto took on Boston in the semifinals.

"We'll win, but it'll be a long, rough, tough series. You don't knock two-time champions off the throne without a struggle."

— Bruins coach Dit Clapper as the series was set to begin in Boston on March 22, 1949

"We should win it. I think we have the better club, but it'll be rugged. They've been rough for us all season. We're going to have to beat them to the opening punch here. If we don't, they're liable to upset us."

— Bruins captain Milt Schmidt

The Leafs won the series opener 3–0 and went on to defeat the Bruins in five games.

"Maple Leafs are gaining stature with every passing game, looking more like last season's champions each time Hap Day turns them loose. They could be building up to the grand crescendo — their third straight Stanley Cup. They're moving into the finals for the third straight year in excellent physical and mental condition. Other than bruises there isn't a casualty in camp and they've regained the win-complex."

— Red Burnett, *Toronto Daily Star*, March 31, 1949

"They fought us right to the wire and I'm glad we're finished with them…. All our lines have been coming through for us at the right times."

— Hap Day after beating the Bruins

"That's $1,500 they can't take away from us."

— Turk Broda, on the $1,000 bonus for winning the semifinal series and the guarantee of at least $500 more for reaching the Final

"It's sure nice to win your first NHL playoff series."

— Ray Timgren

"You ain't seen nothing yet. Wait'll the next series. That's when the real shooting starts."

— Turk Broda to Timgren

With the Red Wings and Canadiens hooked up in a tough series before Detroit finally won in seven games, the Leafs had eight full days off before the Stanley Cup Final began on April 8. They held workouts in St. Catharines to stay in shape. No team in NHL history had ever won the Stanley Cup three years in a row, and Toronto was going to have to do it against a Detroit team that had romped to first place in the NHL standings with 75 points on a record of 34–19–7.

"It's going to be a tough series. We don't want to go out on a limb, but we'll sure be trying to take 'em in four straight, as we did last season."

— Bill Barilko and Gus Mortson, *Globe and Mail*, Toronto, April 7, 1949

"I'm not going to predict how long the series will last or who will win, and I'm not going to say what the games will be like until after the first test and I see whether we are playing for the Lady Byng Trophy or the Stanley Cup."

— Conn Smythe, *Globe and Mail*, Toronto, April 7, 1949

"Newspapers [in Detroit] predict a hard-hitting series and Cup fever really is starting to hit the Motor City. Wings haven't won … since 1943, have been beaten twice by Leafs in the finals since then. Coach Hap Day would give no indication of any plans to stop the scoring threats represented by the big three line of Gord Howe, Ted Lindsay, and Sid Abel."

— Al Nickleson, *Globe and Mail*, Toronto, April 8, 1948

The Maple Leafs won the first game of the Stanley Cup Final 3–2 in overtime when Joe Klukay tipped in a setup from Ray Timgren at 17:31 of the first extra session.

"The puck came over in an arc and just caught the top corner. Klukay tipped the puck on Timgren's pass."

— Red Wings goalie Harry Lumley, quoted by Al Nickleson,
Globe and Mail, Toronto, April 9, 1949

"That's only my second playoff goal."

— Joe Klukay, quoted by Red Burnett, *Toronto Daily Star*, April 9, 1949

The Leafs followed up with a 3–1 win in Game 2, and then came home to Toronto and won Game 3 by the same 3–1 score.

"Sure, the Leafs are ahead 3-0 in games. But we're still playing one at a time and we've still got to win one."

— Hap Day, quoted by Al Nickleson, *Globe and Mail*, Toronto, April 14, 1949

"If we play like we did in the last two periods, I think we'll win…. But if we play like we did in the first period, we'll lose. We were sloppy at the start."

— Teeder Kennedy, quoted by Al Nickleson, *Globe and Mail*

"End it soon, kid. I can't stand much more of this."

— Conn Smythe to Max Bentley, quoted by Al Nickleson, *Globe and Mail*

Toronto completed the sweep in Game 4 at Maple Leaf Gardens, winning 3–1 yet again.

"I don't know what to say. This is a wonderful thrill — one of the three greatest thrills of my life. We owe a great deal to Mr. Smythe and Mr. Day for being here and to you fans for standing by us. We must have been an awful strain on you because there were times when even we didn't think we were going to get into the playoffs. But here we are, and there's the Cup. That's all I can say."

> — Leafs Captain Teeder Kennedy, accepting the Stanley Cup from Clarence Campbell, quoted in Ed Fiktin, *Come on Teeder!* (1950)

"You did it! You did something never done before. You've taken that cup three years in a row."

> — Conn Smythe to the Leafs upon entering the dressing room after Game 4, quoted by Al Nickleson, *Globe and Mail*, Toronto, April 18, 1949

"You're seeing a Happy Day at night. I want to thank the boys for the way they played for me."

> — teetotaller Hap Day, dipping a finger into the champagne-filled Cup, quoted in *Toronto Daily Star*, April 18, 1949

"I don't know why you guys are so excited at winning the Stanley Cup. We do it every year."

> — Leafs trainer Tim Daly, quoted by Al Nickleson, *Globe and Mail*

Coach Hap Day shakes hands with NHL president Clarence Campbell after the Leafs swept Detroit in 1949. The players clearly visible are Teeder Kennedy, Bill Barilko, Sid Smith, Harry Watson, Gus Mortson, and Bill Ezinicki.

The Maple Leafs were the first team in NHL history to win the Stanley Cup in three straight seasons, and also the first to win it six times overall. They were the first to sweep a best-of-seven series in the Final in two straight seasons and the first club to win nine straight games in the Stanley Cup Final dating back over three years. Hap Day had coached the Leafs to five Cup titles and had been captain of the team in its first one back in 1932. Don Metz had played for five Cup winners in Toronto (although he saw limited action in this one), while Turk Broda and Teeder Kennedy had played for four. Broda was once again the hero of the 1949 Cup victory as Toronto only scored three goals in each of the eight games they won during the playoffs.

"Conn Smythe not only made the shrewdest deal of his career when he bought Turk Broda for peanuts from Detroit Red Wings in 1936, but he stole several Stanley Cups from the Norris interests and insured the same number for the Maple Leafs."

— Red Burnett, *Toronto Daily Star*, April 18, 1949

"Last year's team [1947–48] came through every time it was necessary, while this team came through only in the playoffs. That is important, but the players must remember they must come through for the fans right through the schedule."

— Conn Smythe, quoted by Jim Vipond, *Globe and Mail*, Toronto, April 27, 1949

1949–50

The Maple Leafs got off to a much better start this season, enjoying a record of 7-4-3 for 17 points after their first 14 games. However, in a nine-day stretch from November 19 to 27, Toronto suffered five losses and a tie in six games. Some sort of shakeup was in order.

Broda's Battle of the Bulge

In a story that broke on the evening of November 29, 1949, Conn Smythe decided that the problem with the Maple Leafs was that Turk Broda and a few other players were overweight.

"We are not running a fat man's team. Broda is way overweight at 197 pounds. He is off the team until he shows some common sense. He has been ordered to reduce to 190 pounds....

"Garth Boesch is out of condition at 195 pounds. He has been ordered to pare off three pounds or else. Harry Watson must get down from 205 to 200 and Sid Smith from 183 to 180. Vic Lynn weighs 189 pounds, the same weight Jack Dempsey fought at for the world's heavyweight title. How does he expect to keep up with the pack in that condition?…

"They all have a stock excuse that they are not playing enough to keep in shape. What are practices for?…

"We are starting Gil Mayer [in goal] on Thursday night and he'll stay in there even if the score is 500 to one against him and I don't think it will be…. Broda is just the first change. There may be more after tomorrow's workout…. I'm tired of that bunkum about relaxed athletes. The only place in hockey for a relaxed athlete is on the train going back to the minors and that's where all relaxed athletes in hockey end up."

— Conn Smythe, quoted in *Toronto Daily Star*, November 29, 1949

"The players were warned when they signed their contracts that we weren't going through the same ordeal as we did last season. This team is the highest paid in the league. The players are paid almost $1,000 a man higher than the lowest-paid club and I expect my dollar's worth."

— Conn Smythe, *Globe and Mail*, Toronto, November 30, 1949

"It seems to me I've been eating nothing but apples and killing my thirst with oranges. For my evening meal I had a lean steak with spinach. No potatoes, no bread. And a cup of tea. No cream. No sugar."

— Turk Broda, quoted in Stan Fischler, *Power Play* (1972)

"I don't know what to do. I think Walter [Turk] is just one of those persons who is naturally inclined to be stout. I'm going to stop him from taking 40 winks after dinner, that could be putting on a few pounds. Instead, Turk will just have to go for a walk. However, I think he'll have to work it off the hard way, by working overtime in the gymnasium. That's where he is right now."

— Mrs. Turk Broda to Red Burnett, *Toronto Daily Star*, November 30, 1949

Broda was in the green seats at Maple Leaf Gardens when Gil Mayer faced the Red Wings on December 1, 1949. Detroit beat Toronto 2–0.

"I must have lost a pound or two just watching and I never was so nervous. I could see mistakes, I could see plays coming, and I couldn't do anything about it but sweat."

> — Turk Broda to reporters after the game

"I had a three-hour workout at the gym and I've had nothing but two glasses of grapefruit juice and three soft-boiled eggs all day. For dinner, I had a dash of grapefruit. I'm going home to bed and not having anything, except a pinch of fruit juice before [tomorrow's] practice."

> — Turk Broda explaining how he'd already lost
> 7 ½ pounds and was down to 189 ½

"Meanwhile, the other four Leaf 'fatties' appeared to be winning their 'Battle of the Bulge.' Under orders to be at a stipulated poundage by Saturday noon, Garth Boesch, Harry Watson, Vic Lynn, and Sid Smith were well on the way."

> — Al Nickleson, *Globe and Mail*, Toronto, December 2, 1949

Broda was down to 187 1/2 after the Leafs' practice on December 2 prior to their Saturday night game at home to the Rangers. All the others were under weight, too.

"I could eat dogmeat."

> — Garth Boesch to reporters after the December 2 practice

"I'm going to have a small steak. And I'm so thirsty I could drink a rink full of water."

> — Turk Broda to reporters, after having the steak okayed by Conn Smythe

"There may be better goalies around somewhere, but there's no greater sportsman than the Turkey. If the Rangers score on him I should walk out and hand him a malted milk, just to show him I'm not trying to starve him to death."

> — Conn Smythe to reporters after the Friday practice

There would be a final weigh-in on Saturday at noon, but it appeared all the Leafs would make the cut.

"I think that's my business, but I might fine them $500."

> — Conn Smythe when asked what punishment there
> might be for any player not making weight

Broda and the others all made weight. Turk returned to action and starred while earning a shutout in a 2–0 win over the Rangers at Maple Leaf Gardens. The next night in Detroit, Broda was brilliant once again as the Leafs beat the Red Wings 2–1 despite being outshot 30–15.

> "I have to fast to be fast....
>
> "I sure felt faster than when I was 197 and it's hard to realize that was only a week ago. I really felt like moving. In fact, I feel so good that I'm going to keep up this exercise and light-food business."
>
> — Turk Broda, *Globe and Mail*, Toronto, December 6, 1949

The Leafs won four straight after Broda's return, yet they continued to struggle through December, falling to 12–18–6 after a 5–0 loss to Detroit on New Year's Day. The Leafs had dropped into fifth place, only two points ahead of last-place Chicago, but a strong finish saw them climb into third with a record of 31–27–12. With 74 points, Toronto was just three back of second-place Montreal, but well behind Detroit, who led the league for the second straight season with a record of 37–19–14 for 88 points.

The 1950 Playoffs

The Leafs faced the first-place Red Wings in the semifinals to open the playoffs. Toronto had beaten Detroit in 11 straight playoff games, eliminating them for three straight seasons, including two seasons in a row in the Stanley Cup Final. The Red Wings figured they were due.

> "Barring injuries, we can do it. We've got the team this year."
>
> — Detroit GM Jack Adams before the series

But Turk Broda, who'd recorded a career-best nine shutouts during the regular season, blanked Detroit in a 5–0 Toronto win in Game 1. Still, the biggest story of the game was the injury to Gordie Howe, who suffered a fractured skull. The Red Wings claimed that Teeder Kennedy had hurt Howe on purpose.

> "I saw Howe lying on the ice with his face covered with blood and I couldn't help thinking what a great player he was and how I hoped he wasn't badly hurt. Then Detroit players started saying I did it with my stick. I knew I hadn't, and as I've always regarded coach Tommy Ivan as a sensible, level-headed man, I went over the to Detroit bench and told him

I was sorry Howe was hurt and I wasn't responsible."
— Teeder Kennedy, quoted in Stan Fischler, *Power Play* (1972)

"They said he severely hurt himself. I've heard since then that it was certainly a serious injury but not nearly as critical as the Detroit press or Red Wings management made it out to be. Either way, the propaganda really killed us."
— Howie Meeker, *Golly Gee It's Me* (1996)

"Why did Kennedy come over to me and apologize?... I'm not saying that Kennedy did it intentionally, but I'm saying it was caused by his stick. It was a butt-end and he's not the only guy who throws butt ends."
— Red Wings coach Tommy Ivan to reporters after the game

"Everybody saw that Howe ran himself into the boards. For heaven's sake, Gravel, the referee, had his hand up to signal a charging penalty to Howe, and when Howe hit the boards, he almost landed in Clarence Campbell's lap. He was sitting right there and saw everything, the president of the league.... [But] Jack Adams, the Detroit general manager, was so emotional. He was from the old school of letting your emotions run away, and he stirred up a fuss, blaming me and the rest of it."
— Teeder Kennedy in Jack Batten, *The Leafs in Autumn* (1975)

"Kennedy, as a right-handed player, had the butt part of his stick right to the fence as he was going up the ice. He was being checked from his right. The injuries to Howe were on the right side of his head. Kennedy had stopped to avoid the check, and Howe went in front of him."
— NHL President Clarence Campbell

"Jack Stewart carried the puck into the Toronto end and was checked by Kennedy, who carried the puck into the centre zone right close to the fence on the players' bench side. I turned to follow the play, and Stewart was trying to check Kennedy and was right close to him. Just as Kennedy crossed the Toronto blue line, I saw Howe cut across toward Kennedy, skating very fast. Just before Howe got to Kennedy, Kennedy passed backhanded and stopped suddenly. Howe just brushed him slightly and crashed into the fence and fell to the ice. Stewart fell on top of him. Play carried on for a few seconds, as Toronto had the puck."
— report of referee George Gravel

"It seems that every time the Leafs go out to defend the championship, they have to defend their right to play. Loose accusations against players have no place in the game. Neither has rough hockey. Kennedy always has been a great and clean player."

— Conn Smythe, quoted in Stan Fischler, *Power Play* (1972)

"The people of Toronto know that absolutely no blame in any way can be attached to you for the accident to Gordie Howe. They are 100 per-cent behind you all the way and know you will go on and continue to play wonderful hockey and lead the team to the Cup. We regret very much the injury to Gordie Howe as he is a great player, but at the same time we know that he was the aggressor in attempting to crash you on the boards."

— Toronto Mayor Hiram Walker, quoted in Stan Fischler, *Power Play* (1972)

The Red Wings rallied around the injury to Howe, but Turk Broda kept the Maple Leafs in the series, posting three shutouts in the first six games as Toronto pushed Detroit to the limit.

"[Broda is] the greatest playoff goalie in [NHL] history. He's been turn-ing in sensational games since 1936. Some other goalies have a good year or two and then faded. He just keeps going along in top playoff form year after year."

— Conn Smythe during the series, quoted in
Ed Fitkin, *Turk Broda of the Leafs* (1950)

"Nobody. I think Broda is in a class by himself. The closest to him, in my mind, was [Boston's] Tiny Thompson, but you have to put Broda on top by any measurement."

— Conn Smythe, when asked who else he would rank with Broda

Broda nearly made it four shutouts in the series, but the Leafs lost Game 7 1–0 on a goal by Leo Reise Jr. at 8:39 of overtime.

"We should have beaten them. What the heck, they didn't have Howe — that was enough reason for us to win. But some of the guys were upset … and we lost it in seven games."

— Teeder Kennedy in Jack Batten, *The Leafs in Autumn* (1975)

"We'd still be out there if I could have got a look at that puck. I never saw Reise's shot until it hit the net and bounced out between my feet. I looked down and there it was — and gone was the Cup and 1,000 beans."

— Turk Broda to reporters after Game 7

"Turk was never greater than in this series. He kept us in there from the start."

— Hap Day to reporters after Game 7

"You've got nothing to be ashamed of. For four years you played like champions. That's quite a reign and I'm proud of you all."

— Conn Smythe to the team in the dressing room

The Leafs would bounce back to win the Stanley Cup again in 1951, meaning Toronto could have won five straight championships; something only the Montreal Canadiens (1956 to 1960) have ever done in NHL history.

"It should have been five Cups in a row. It would have been — we would have won the Cup in 1950 — if it hadn't been for the Howe incident. We whipped them that first game in Detroit … [b]ut the Howe thing took a lot of starch out of our guys."

— Teeder Kennedy in Jack Batten, *The Leafs in Autumn* (1975)

"With any luck at all, we could have won five in a row. Detroit went on to play the New York Rangers, and I'm telling you, we had the Rangers' number all year. We would have won five in a row."

— Sid Smith on losing to Detroit in 1950 in Kevin Shea, *Barilko* (2004)

1950–51

Within a few days of Toronto being eliminated by Detroit, the Maple Leafs were making plans for the future. Tod Sloan, who'd been a part of the rookie camp back in the fall of 1946, would return to Toronto for the 1950–51 season after a loan to Cleveland of the AHL. He'd become a big part of the offence. Tim Horton and George Armstrong had made brief appearances for Toronto during the 1949–50 season. Both would be given a chance to make the team in 1950–51, but each was still a few years away.

"We had only two 20-goal men last season (Max Bentley and Sid Smith). During the playoffs we did not get a single goal from a left-winger. [This] may indicate that our forwards were helping the defence to such an extent that they had little time for goals. If that is the case, our defence needs tightening."

— Conn Smythe, *Globe and Mail*, Toronto, April 28, 1950

Smythe was also planning for the day when Turk Broda would retire, and expected to see him share the workload with Al Rollins, who'd been purchased from Cleveland in November of 1949 and made two brief appearances in 1949–50. At age 36, Broda would be the oldest player in the NHL in 1950–51, and it would turn out to be his last full season.

"[Broda is] the greatest team player I ever had. However, I will recommend to the board of directors that we pay Turk a normal year's salary next season and work an understudy in for about 30 games."

— Conn Smythe, *Globe and Mail*, Toronto, April 28, 1950

Front Office Changes

But the biggest change Smythe would make involved himself. With health problems resulting from his war wounds making it more difficult for him to carry out his duties as general manager, he planned to promote Hap Day.

"I want it clearly understood that it would not be a case of kicking Hap upstairs. I have talked the whole matter over with him and offered him a two-year contract with the option of promotion to assistant general manager. I will not be able to travel as much as I used to and I need a competent man to take charge and visit such scattered cities as Pittsburgh and Winnipeg to look after our interests. I feel that Hap, who has established a remarkable record as a coach of world champions, is the man for the job and worthy of the promotion. Hap and I have an agreement that he will fit into either the managerial or coaching spot as I see fit."

— Conn Smythe, *Globe and Mail*, Toronto, April 28, 1950

On May 26, 1950, the directors of Maple Leaf Gardens implemented the suggestions of president Conn Smythe and appointed Hap Day to assistant manager of hockey.

"Day will be our minister of supply. He will be directly responsible for the results attained by all our minor league clubs and will keep a supply of young players flowing to the Leafs."

— Conn Smythe on Day's promotion

"The fans have been wonderful and I want to thank them. I hope in some way to be able to keep giving them the best hockey team in the league."

— Hap Day on his promotion

At the same time Day's promotion was announced, the Leafs also named former star Joe Primeau as their new coach. Primeau had been coaching at St. Michael's College in Toronto since the 1945–46 season and had led St. Mike's to the Memorial Cup in 1947. During the 1949–50 season, he'd also taken on coaching duties with the Toronto Marlboros Senior A team and led them to the 1950 Allan Cup.

"I had always hoped but never figured I'd wind up coaching the Leafs. I couldn't see how I ever could step in, the way Hap Day was winning championships. When I read that article in the Calgary paper [speculating while he was in town for the Allan Cup that he was to become the Leafs' next coach] it was a real shock. It was the first indication I had that I was being considered as a possible replacement for Hap."

— Joe Primeau, quoted in Ed Fitkin, *The "Gashouse Gang" of Hockey* (1951)

"Primeau will have complete charge of the Leafs. Both [he and Day] will report directly to me."

— Conn Smythe to reporters

"Joe Primeau had the [coaching] job but he just followed the system that Hap'd put in place. Joe was too nice a guy to coach…. He was a hell of a worrier. A couple of seasons later, '52–53, the team missed the playoffs and it just about killed Joe. That's when he quit. Not a moment too soon."

— Howie Meeker in Jack Batten, *The Leafs in Autumn* (1975)

"We'll miss Hap's technical ability and experience, but are counting on Primeau's enthusiasm to make up for that loss. If it does, both the Gardens and the fans will be happy."

— Conn Smythe, a few days before the opening of training camp, in the *Toronto Daily Star*, September 13, 1950

Bill Barilko was optimistic heading into the new season.

"We should have a better balanced club all the way around. But Detroit is still the team to beat. Despite the loss of Garth Boesch, I think our defence

Coach Joe Primeau (left) sits with Max Bentley (centre) and the new manager of the baseball Maple Leafs, Joe Becker (right), in the dressing room at Maple Leaf Gardens on February 7, 1951.

will be as good as last year. Bill Juzda and I proved we could work well together and Hugh Bolton will help considerably."

           — *Toronto Daily Star*, October 5, 1950

Conn Smythe also had a few predictions, and told the media:

> It's a question of how many boys become men. Gradually, each year, we are losing men, like Syl Apps and Garth Boesch, who have been around a long time and taken the gaff. Regardless of where we finish — and we have the largest ticket sales in history — the customer will get his money's worth. A club coached by Joe Primeau is always an offensive one. We expect a very exciting season here in Toronto.

Exciting Season, Entertaining Playoffs

It was, indeed, an exciting season in Toronto in 1950–51. The Maple Leafs set new club records with 41 wins (41–16–13) and 95 points, which wouldn't be broken until the 1990s. Max Bentley (66 points), Teeder Kennedy (43 assists), Tod Sloan (31 goals), Sid Smith (30 goals), and Cal Gardner (23 goals) led the offence. On defence, Jimmy Thomson, Gus Mortson, Bill Juzda, and Bill Barilko all missed some games due to injuries but anchored a crew in front of Turk Broda and Al Rollins that allowed the fewest goals in the NHL. Rollins played in 40 games and was the recipient of the Vezina Trophy. Still, it was Detroit — led by Gordie Howe's league-leading 43 goals and 86 points, and rookie sensation Terry Sawchuk in goal — who finished in first place and set new NHL records with 44 wins and 101 points.

The Leafs were only 3–7–4 against the Red Wings in head-to-head match-ups during the regular season, but their coach was still optimistic heading into the playoffs.

"I'm not down about our chances. We can take Detroit or any other team if everybody, from the bench out, makes use of every possible advantage. We must get ourselves in fighting trim, and sharpen and smarten ourselves up mentally as well as physically. When everybody gets back on the beam we'll be all right."

— Joe Primeau, *Globe and Mail*, Toronto, March 9, 1951

The Maple Leafs faced the Bruins in the semifinals to open the post-season. Al Rollins started in goal but was hurt early in Game 1, and Turk Broda took over. Boston won the first game 2–0 and the second ended in a 1–1 tie after 20 minutes of overtime due to a Toronto curfew that did not allow games to be played on Sunday. After that, the Leafs won four straight with Broda collecting two shutouts and allowing just five goals overall in six games.

"I don't remember anything like it. He's the greatest playoff goalie of them all. I don't see how those All-Star selectors reach down and pick out some-one else almost every season. Then Broda comes along in the playoffs and plays Santa Claus — in reverse."

— Conn Smythe on Turk Broda after the Maple Leafs eliminated Boston

In the Final, the Maple Leafs would not be facing the Red Wings. Detroit was eliminated in six games by a Montreal team that had finished 36 points behind them in the standings with a record of only 25–30–15. So it would be the Maple Leafs and the Canadiens for the Stanley Cup.

"If Canadiens continue to play like that they will win everything. But it's a shame to see a team like the Red Wings go out."

— Detroit GM Jack Adams in the *Montreal Gazette*, April 9, 1951

"[T]he Leafs have a powerful club. Look at their super scorers and the way they breezed through Boston…. We'll try to win a game. Our club considers it an honour that we are good enough be playing against the great Maple Leafs for the Cup."
— Dick Irvin, who had predicted Montreal would beat Detroit in six games, sarcastically suggesting why he was not making any predictions against Toronto

"Now that they've beaten Detroit, I know they'll be in there against us, and Irvin will have them flying. So far as I'm concerned, we're still underdogs."
— Conn Smythe to reporters the day before the Stanley Cup Final opened

"What? Did he really say that? Well, well, that's the first time I ever knew Smythe to admit that his own club is no better than the other fellow's."
— Dick Irvin's reaction

Toronto outplayed Montreal in Game 1 at Maple Leaf Gardens, but needed a goal by Sid Smith at 5:51 of overtime to score a 3–2 victory. Bill Barilko had saved the game moments earlier with a headlong dive to get his stick in front of a shot fired by Maurice Richard.

"We didn't play a good game, and they beat us only by that [overtime] goal."
— Canadiens captain Butch Bouchard after Game 1

"We can beat them right in their own back yard. If that's the best they can do they're not so hot."
— Canadiens coach Dick Irvin after Game 1

Montreal won the second game 3–2 when Maurice Richard scored at 2:55 of overtime. The Canadiens were confident going back home.

"The series is now three of five. We have three of the possible five games here in Montreal. There's our edge. We had to win one in Toronto to put us in line for the Cup."
— Dick Irvin to reporters the day before Game 3

Canadiens goalie Gerry McNeil was the star of the series through the first two games. The Leafs were concerned that the veteran Broda was looking tired, and switched to Al Rollins for Game 3. Toronto won it 2–1 on an overtime goal at 4:47 by Teeder Kennedy, but …

"The real credit goes to Rollins."

— Teeder Kennedy after Game 3

"I was so weak when the old captain shot that winner that I couldn't holler, although I wanted to shout and shout. And my leg didn't bother me a bit. I had an idea I was going to play tonight but neither Turk nor I knew definitely until we got to the rink an hour before game time."

— Al Rollins after Game 3

"I gave the game away when I missed three chances to score."

— Maurice Richard

"If I was as lucky as the Maple Leafs I'd be a millionaire."

— Dick Irvin

"It's hard to believe we won that one."

— Max Bentley to Teeder Kennedy

Game 4 was another overtime win for Toronto, 3–2 again on a goal by Harry Watson at 5:15. The Maple Leafs now led the series three games to one.

Game 5

The teams headed back to Maple Leaf Gardens with Toronto looking to clinch the Stanley Cup at home on Saturday night, April 21, 1951.

"We don't want to return to Montreal. We have to be ready, because its a cinch those Canadiens are going to throw their best shot."

— Joe Primeau to reporters prior to Game 5

Toronto carried the play throughout the game, but Gerry McNeil once again played brilliantly for Montreal. Maurice Richard put the Canadiens ahead 1–0 midway through the second period, but Tod Sloan evened the score just three minutes later. Montreal went ahead again early in the third on a goal by Paul Meger, and McNeil was making sure the lead stood up. Joe Primeau pulled Al Rollins at 18:33 of the third, and the Canadiens just missed an empty-net goal. Rollins returned to his net at the next whistle, but with a faceoff in the Canadiens end at 19:21, Primeau removed him again.

"I was worried about pulling goalie Al Rollins at the end of the game, but it was the only thing to do."

— Joe Primeau after the game

"The best I remember, the biggest thrill, was when we won the Stanley Cup in 1951. We were ahead of Montreal three games to one and the fifth game was at the Gardens and we were behind in it by a goal with around half a minute left. I had the puck in the Montreal end … Butch Bouchard, their defenceman, rushed at me, and I flipped the puck over his stick to [Sid Smith]. The goalie — Gerry McNeil … he turned toward Smitty and Smitty slid the puck to [Tod Sloan]. The net was wide open for him to tap it in. Tie game. The fans hollered so much I think the noise lasted fifteen minutes. I never heard anything like it. Seemed it must have kept up right through the intermission before the overtime, that loud crowd noise, and then Barilko scored right away [at 2:53] to win the Cup. That was the best."

— Max Bentley in Jack Batten, *The Leafs in Autumn* (1975)

"Watson comes back fast at centre ice. Skating down the left wing into the corner. Shoots, and hits the side of the net. Here's right in front to Meeker! Meeker went by the net. Centres out in front. McNeil fell. In front again! Watson shoots. He shoots. He scores! Barilko! Barilko has won the Stanley Cup for the Leafs. Barilko shoots it into the net while McNeil was left all by himself. The Toronto Maple Leafs are the world champions."

— Foster Hewitt's radio play-by-play of Bill Barilko's Stanley Cup–winning goal

"I still get [photos of] the Barilko goal mailed to me from fans, from all over the place, asking for my autograph. It's my claim to fame. What bothered me at the time was people saying Barilko shot from the blue line. I was a little happier when I saw the picture. He was almost at the net."

— Canadiens goalie Gerry McNeil to the *Montreal Gazette* in 2002

"Barilko was supposed to stay on the blue line, but he saw the puck coming out, so he just roared in and took a slap at it…. McNeil had gone down on the ice and Barilko was on his way, too. He tripped over Cal Gardner's skate as he took the shot and his momentum carried him towards the goal. He put his arms out and was totally horizontal above the ice, bracing for the fall. We picked Barilko up off the ice and began to celebrate our victory."

— Harry Watson, quoted in Kevin Shea, *Barilko* (2004)

"Conn Smythe and Joe Primeau were always warning him [about carrying the puck in deep]. They kept saying they were going to fine him $500. Then he scored that big goal."

— Bill Barilko's sister Anne Klisanich to Lance Hornby,
Toronto Sun, April 20, 2011

"Like Dagwood catching a bus."

— Conn Smythe describing Barilko's dash and dive to score the winning goal

"While we were in Montreal for the third and fourth games, I had been after Barilko for what we call 'getting caught up in the slot.' This meant he'd skate up when our forwards pressed the puck up into Canadiens' end of the rink and stay there too long and consequently get caught up-ice when Montreal captured the puck. This was poison against skaters like Rocket Richard and a few others…. I said, 'Bill, if you get caught up their once more, I'm going to fine you $100, and $100 every time after that' and I meant it.

"So Barilko started playing it pretty cautious, and then, of course, our fifth game went into overtime and who was on the ice but Bill…. [When he scored] I was so exuberant that I jumped the boards and ran onto the ice. Barilko was just getting up off the ice when I reached him. He looked up at me and remembered that I had been harping on him about playing back. 'Well,' he said, 'I guess you didn't want the hook on me that time did you?'"

— Joe Primeau in Stan Fischler, *Those Were the Days* (1976)

Primeau's Championship Hat Trick

"If any one person deserves credit more than any other, it's our coach, Joe Primeau. If you think it was tough for me to succeed Syl Apps as captain, think what a tough job it was for Joe to succeed a man like Hap Day as coach."

— Teeder Kennedy speaking to the crowd at Maple Leaf Gardens (MLG) over the public-address system during the post-game ceremonies

"It has been a wonderful season, and winning the Cup is a thrill I never dared to dream of. I've never had a finer bunch of fellows to work with."

— Joe Primeau speaking to the crowd at MLG over the public-address system

The Leafs celebrate with the Stanley Cup in 1951. The players clearly visible are Cal Gardiner, overtime hero Bill Barilko, Sid Smith (behind Barilko's shoulder), Bill Juzda, coach Joe Primeau, Turk Broda (also in a suit), and Fern Flaman.

"That year was a tremendous one for me because I had won the Stanley Cup and previously the Memorial and Allan Cups, which gave me a 'hat trick' among the major hockey trophies."

— Joe Primeau in Stan Fischler, *Those Were the Days* (1976)

The Last Goal He Ever Scored

"We just out-Irished them, that's all…. Pure Irish luck."

— Conn Smythe's reaction to beating the Canadiens in four out of five games that all had gone into overtime

But the Leafs good luck wouldn't last for long. Nearing the end of a busy summer, on Friday, August 24, 1951, Bill Barilko and Dr. Henry Hudson, a dentist in Barilko's hometown of Timmins who piloted his own seaplane, flew to Seal River off of James Bay for a fishing trip. After a successful weekend, they stopped off at Rupert House during their return trip on Sunday, where they were warned of an approaching storm. Though they were invited to stay, Barilko and Hudson were anxious to get home to Timmins, where they were expected late that afternoon. So they took off for home. No one ever saw them alive again.

"It seems unbelievable, one minute we were carrying him off the ice on our shoulders and the next minute he was gone."

— Bill Juzda, *Globe and Mail*, April 27, 1987

"Everyone love him. He such a good boy. I say to him, Billy … Billy don't go. Please no go fishing. He die for fishing. Oh … I make such mistake."

— Faye Barilko, Bill's mother, to Rick Drennan,
Sunday Star, Toronto, January 10, 1982

"We were all sitting around waiting for him to come home that Sunday. We had this farewell party planned because he was leaving for Toronto right after the fishing."

— Barilko's best friend, Leo Curik, to Rick Drennan, *Sunday Star*, Toronto

"Knowing Bill, we thought he'd decided to stay an extra day because the fishing was so good. Hudson had promised me the next trip, but I had to go out of town for a few days, when I got back, he said Bill was going."

— friend, fellow-Timmins native, and NHL star Allan Stanley
to Rick Drennan, *Sunday Star*, Toronto

No one was really worried at first when Hudson's plane didn't return on Sunday. Concern began to grow by Monday afternoon, and the news hit the papers in Toronto on Tuesday. Soon, the largest air search in Canadian history was mobilized.

"We stared into bush for six straight hours at a time. It was bush, bush, bush … everywhere. By the second week we were losing hope."

— Emile Klisanich, husband of Bill's sister Anne, who was a spotter
in one of the planes, to Rick Drennan

There was still no sign of the men or the plane when the Maple Leafs began training camp in late September. Most team members held out little hope that Barilko might still be found alive, but there was one fellow northern Ontario native who thought it might still be possible.

"It's a shallow lake and very rough most of the time. I figure they might have landed on it when the gasoline ran out, that the plane might have sunk and they managed to swim to one of the islands. It's just a hunch, but I haven't seen anything said of a search being made around that lake and I think it well worthwhile. They might have been following the Ontario Northland Railway line down in the dusk. At Cochrane, the CNR line crosses the ONR. They might have got mixed up and followed the CNR line east to Abitibi Lake, where they were forced to ditch, instead of continuing along the ONR line."

— Gus Mortson, reported by Al Nickleson, *Globe and Mail*,
Toronto, September 24, 1951

Stories began to spread that Barilko (who's family was of Russian decent) had defected to the Soviet Union, or that he and Dr. Hudson had been smuggling gold out of the north. People still held out hope that Barilko might be found alive. In October of 1951, Conn Smythe offered a $10,000 reward to the person who found him … or recovered his body.

"I wrote Conn Smythe to tell him where Barilko could be found and I also told provincial police. I've consulted the cards many times and the answer is always the same. [They crashed in the third lake from their takeoff point at Rupert House.] The trouble is the plane was circling, and I don't know whether the lake is north, south, or east."

— Toronto psychic Madame Laurence to Don DeLaplante,
Globe and Mail, Toronto, November 29, 1952

But it would take until the beginning of June in 1962 before the wreckage of the plane and the bodies of Bill Barilko and Dr. Henry Hudson were finally found. The discovery was made just a few weeks after the Maple Leafs had won the Stanley Cup that season — their first in the 11 years since Barilko went missing.

"The year after he disappeared, we had an exhibition game in Timmins and a few of us went to see Mrs. Barilko. She still believed he was alive. I remember her saying, 'They think they've seen Bill in California.' It must have been 11 years of hell."

— Barilko's teammate Sid Smith to Rick Drennan

"She aired his clothes out every year."

— Barilko's sister, Anne Klisanich, on her mother to Rick Drennan

"All 11 years I not miss one day. I no cry for my Billy. One day, Friday, I go to church. I get on my knees and pray. I say, please God, please tell me one way or other, where my Billy?"

— Faye Barilko to Rick Drennan

"When it came to body-checking and going down to block shots on his goal, Barilko had no peer during my time."

— Teeder Kennedy to John Melady, *Overtime, Overdue* (1988)

"When Bill was on the ice, he was fearless. If the accident hadn't happened, he would have been one of the greatest."

— Max Bentley to John Melady, *Overtime, Overdue* (1988)

"He was a great team man. He wasn't looking for individual glory. Hockey was fun for him, and he loved the team and the guys. It was no coincidence that we won four Stanley Cups while he was with the team. He made a big contribution to those clubs."

— Gus Mortson in Kevin Shea, *Barilko* (2004)

"The loss of Bill Barilko will be felt a great deal more than anyone realizes."

— New York Rangers GM Frank Boucher, quoted in
Stan Fischler, *Power Play* (1972)

5

1952 to 1961: Tough Times Finally End When Imlach Era Begins

1951–52 TO 1955–56

Struggling to score goals through most of the 1951–52 season, the Maple Leafs still boasted a strong defence in front of Al Rollins, who was now their main man in the nets. (Turk Broda was on call all season, but played only in the last game before making two appearances in the playoffs.) The Leafs finished in third place with 74 points on a record of 29–25–16. Toronto was only four points behind second-place Montreal, but both were a long way back of Detroit, who once again finished in first place with a record of 44–14–12. The Red Wings swept the Maple Leafs out of the playoffs in the semifinals, and then swept the Canadiens to win the Stanley Cup.

> "If a horse goes to the track too often, you don't get the best racing out of it. Our fellows have been whipped and whipped for a long time. I should think that a change of scenery would be part of the answer, so someone will be getting some good hockey players."
> – Conn Smythe contemplating changes after the Leafs' playoff loss in 1952

1952–53

Just before the start of training camp in September of 1952, Toronto traded Al Rollins, Gus Mortson, Cal Gardner, and Ray Hannigan to Chicago for goalie Harry Lumley. Lumley had a big year in 1952–53, leading the NHL with 10 shutouts (he would lead again with 13 the following year), but the Maple Leafs

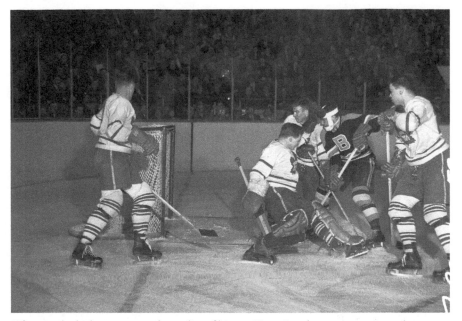

Often overlooked even among the goalies of his era, Harry Lumley put up great numbers in his four seasons in Toronto. Here, he's surrounded by teammates Jimmy Thomson, Gord Hannigan, and George Armstrong. The Boston player is Johnny Peirson, who is wearing headgear to protect a broken jaw.

were getting old. Injuries — particularly a shoulder separation that sidelined Teeder Kennedy for nearly half the season — didn't help. Nor did the fact that a depressed Max Bentley left the team for a time. (He would be with the Rangers in 1953–54).

Toronto was in a tight battle with Boston and Chicago for the last two playoff spots in 1952–53, but in the end the Maple Leafs' 67 points (27–30–13) left them in fifth place, two back of the Bruins and Black Hawks and out of the playoffs for the first time since 1946. Within a day of the season ending, there were predictions that coach Joe Primeau would retire.

"Joe has the coaching job until he gives it up. We're 100 percent satisfied with the results produced by him. I felt it would be a miracle if he got the team in the playoffs, and he just missed by two points after having only half a team much of the time."

— Conn Smythe to reporters, March 23, 1953

But Primeau had a growing cement-block business that was demanding more of his time, and he made his departure from the team official on March 24. There had been rumours during the Stanley Cup Final back in 1951 that Primeau was planning to leave the Leafs then. They'd been denied at the time, but ...

"It's true that Joe wanted to retire, but I wouldn't let him. It wouldn't have been fair to the next coach. Joe's successor would have been expected to win the Stanley Cup again, with a club that was on the downgrade. If he didn't win it, people would have said he couldn't be much of a coach, because Primeau had won in his first shot."

— Conn Smythe, reported by Milt Dunnell,
Toronto Daily Star, March 25, 1953

No formal announcement of the next Leafs coach was made, but everyone knew it was going to be King Clancy, who'd led Toronto's Pittsburgh farm club to the Calder Cup championship in the AHL in 1952 and had them back in the finals again in 1953.

"I'm overjoyed. I never dreamed I'd ever be coaching the Leafs. I'll do my best to live up to the record established by guys like Hap and Joe.... Conn told me I'd have a chance to coach the Leafs some day if I made good at Pittsburgh. It's wonderful to hear that I made it. Yes, sir, it's wonderful with me."

— King Clancy, March 25, 1953

1953–56

Midway through the 1954–55 season, Hap Day took over as general manager with Conn Smythe staying on as president and managing director of Maple Leaf Gardens. Youngsters such as George Armstrong, Tim Horton, and Ron Stewart showed promise for the future, but the Leafs were a long way behind the Red Wings and Canadiens when it came to talent. Toronto finished third in the six-team NHL standings in 1953–54 and 1954–55, and dropped to fourth in 1955–56.

"I spent three seasons behind Toronto's bench, getting into the playoffs each year, but I didn't perform any miracles.... Unfortunately, we were trying to find our way back into contention at a time when the Detroit Red Wings were pure dynamite and the Montreal Canadiens were gearing to become a powerhouse. You know, we met those Red Wings in three consecutive semifinal rounds but each time they knocked us right out of the playoffs."

— King Clancy, *Clancy* (1968)

"King is such a real Irishman that he believes in leprechauns. I always thought he figured they would win for him when he was coaching. He really depended on luck in the games and felt it was more potent than masterminding…. His coaching record may not have been as illustrious as his playing record, but in my opinion he was a great coach."

— Hap Day on Clancy as coach in *Clancy* (1968)

"No one else in hockey but Clancy could have put the Leafs in the playoffs. The King loved people, loved life, loved the game and the players. He was a fun, bubbly character. He loved horses, the track and the payoff window. What a man, what a pleasure. The players would walk on nails for Clancy."

— Howie Meeker, *Golly Gee It's Me* (1996)

"I was never cut out to be pacing up and down behind a bench, and I never thought I had the right temperament for it. But I enjoyed trying to buoy up the players and get them into the right mood for a game."

— King Clancy, *Clancy* (1968)

1956–57

The Maple Leafs were getting younger, with future stars such as Bob Baun (age 20), Bob Pulford (21), and Frank Mahovlich (19) among six players under 22 to make their debuts this season. Dick Duff was only 20, but he was already in his second full season and playing on the top forward line with 26-year-old George Armstrong and Tod Sloan. Twenty-three-year-old Ed Chadwick took over in net and played all 70 games, as he would again in 1957–58. But this youth movement would not provide the immediate results that the one 10 years earlier had. The 1956–57 season would prove to be a trying one, with the Leafs falling into fifth place with a record of 21–34–15. Their 57 points left them nine back of a playoff spot for which they had never truly been in contention.

Coaching Change

The Maple Leafs announced on April 2, 1956, that King Clancy would not be back as the team's coach for the 1956–57 season.

King Clancy, by then the team's assistant general manager, shakes hands with Dick Duff in the dressing room after Game 6 of Toronto's semifinal against Detroit in 1960. Carl Brewer can be seen behind Clancy's head. George Armstrong is bent down untying his skates.

"I'm tickled to death to get out from behind that bench. I was going to quit at the end of the season anyway. I haven't been able to eat or sleep for weeks. Coaching is the roughest job in the world. It's worse than refereeing."

— King Clancy, after the announcement that he'd
been promoted to assistant general manager

The announcement of a new coach would not come immediately. Howie Meeker, who had coached the Senior A Stratford Indians in 1953–54 and had led the Leafs' AHL farm club in Pittsburgh to a championship in 1954–55, was currently in his second season with Pittsburgh. Turk Broda was about to coach the Toronto Marlboros to their second straight Memorial Cup title, and former New York Ranger Alf Pike was coaching the Winnipeg Warriors. All three were possible candidates.

"We have three teams in the playoffs at present. Marlboros, Pittsburgh, and Winnipeg are still active. Therefore, I don't think it would be wise to say anything about players or a coach until after the playoffs ... Meeker, Alf Pike, and Turk Broda are all eligible. We could pick any one of them, but at the moment it is all speculation."

— Hap Day to the press, April 2, 1956

It was soon clear that Hap Day had recommended to Conn Smythe that he hire Howie Meeker as the Leafs' new coach. Smythe and Meeker met at Maple Leaf Gardens on April 12, 1956, to discuss the job.

"The result of the interview with Meeker will determine if he will coach [the] Leafs. There will be no announcement until I have talked to him."

— Conn Smythe

The announcement came later that same day, and Meeker, at 32, became the youngest coach in Maple Leafs history.

"This is a great honour, one I never dreamed I would get. It is a challenge to follow in the footsteps of great Maple Leafs like King Clancy, Joe Primeau, Hap Day, and a coach with Dick Irvin's record. I guess I'm the happiest guy in Canada at the moment."

— Howie Meeker at the press conference to announce his hiring

"Howie is a real Maple Leaf. I'm happy with the way things have turned out."

— Conn Smythe at the press conference

"I intend to make my own decisions during a hockey game. I know how to run a team and I know how to get the best out of my men. However, I'll welcome advice from Mr. Smythe and Mr. Day.... I would be a foolish young man not to ask for their help."

— Howie Meeker

"I have a one-year contract and that's the way I want it. If I can't make good in a season then I don't belong in the NHL."

— Howie Meeker

But Meeker soon realized that he was in a tougher situation than he'd thought.

"During that season as coach I knew that at age thirty-two or thirty-three and just three years removed from playing, my decision to coach the Leafs had been a major mistake. Sure, I knew how to teach systems both offensively and defensively, I knew when the player was giving sufficient physical effort, and I knew how to put defensive pairs and forward lines together. My problem was I didn't know how to handle the temperamental NHL men. It was tough to threaten, tougher to whip, and even harder to bench my former buddies."

— Howie Meeker, *Golly Gee It's Me* (1996)

Kennedy's Comeback

Though he was still just 28 at the time, Teeder Kennedy had completed his 11th season in the NHL in 1953–54 and planned to retire. Like Syl Apps, Kennedy was convinced to come back for one more season, and so he returned in 1954–55. He had just 10 goals that year, but his 42 assists ranked third in the NHL and his leadership was a key reason why the Maple Leafs even made the playoffs. When results of the voting for the Hart Trophy were announced, Kennedy easily outpolled teammate Harry Lumley as well as Maurice Richard, Jean Beliveau, and Doug Harvey of the Montreal Canadiens, to be named the NHL's most valuable player.

"It comes as quite a thrill, one of the biggest I've had in hockey. But I believe it should have been Harry Lumley. Leafs would have been down the drain without him. And I'm not just being modest."

— Teeder Kennedy to Red Burnett, *Toronto Daily Star*, May 6, 1955

"Kennedy deserves the Hart. I hate to think of us without him. He was the guy that made our club tick."

— Harry Lumley to Red Burnett

"I think it was a fitting climax to a great career."

— Conn Smythe to Red Burnett

Despite his Hart Trophy win, Teeder definitely had no plans to change his mind and return to the Leafs in 1955–56.

"I retired because I'd had enough. When you're young, hockey's a lark. After a few seasons, it changes. It's a pick-and-shovel job. And you're under pressure all the time. That gets tiring."

— Teeder Kennedy in Jack Batten, *The Leafs in Autumn* (1975)

But with the Leafs struggling during the 1956–57 season, Kennedy began to reconsider.

"Howie was the coach and he kept bugging me to come back and help out."
— Teeder Kennedy in Jack Batten, *The Leafs in Autumn* (1975)

"We have been hit hard by injuries this season. If most of the boys can get back soon I won't be needed. But if I can get into shape and help, I am willing to do anything I can, as right now I'm worried that we might drop right out of the bottom of the league."
— Teeder Kennedy to Jim Vipond, *Globe and Mail*,
Toronto, November 29, 1956

By January, Teeder was ready to test himself against NHL competition.

"Kennedy feels he has gone as far as he can go on workouts; that he now needs actual competition to prove whether or not he can regain his former stature as a player. He will play against Red Wings tomorrow night, Rangers in New York on Wednesday and Canadiens in Montreal on Thursday. After those games Ted will make up his mind whether or not he can take his place as a regular in the NHL despite his long layoff."
— announcement from Leafs GM Hap Day, January 5, 1957

"I feel I am ready to do a job for the Leafs. I'm not saying I can play as well as when I retired in 1955. But I am convinced that I can help the team. What I need now is actual playing to get to top condition."
— Teeder Kennedy

"As little as two weeks back I was afraid Teeder couldn't make it. But he's shown enough this past week to convince me he's ready to take his place in the lineup and improve this club."
— Howie Meeker

The three-game stint convinced Kennedy that he could still play.

"I went to see Hap Day … and told him I was ready. 'Well, Teeder,' he said, 'there's no way we can pay you what you were making when you quit.' 'Come on, Hap,' I said. 'Don't give me that.' That was Hap — always the company man. I couldn't blame him, but I didn't play till I got as much as I'd been paid before I retired."

— Teeder Kennedy in Jack Batten, *The Leafs in Autumn* (1975)

"He still had the spirit, toughness and work ethic; the puck and head skills were there, but he had absolutely no skating legs. Throughout his career, if Kennedy's skating had matched any other of his skills he would have set records even Gretzky would have found tough to beat."

— Howie Meeker, *Golly Gee It's Me* (1996)

Kennedy played 30 games during the 1956–57 season. He had six goals and 16 assists but could not rescue the Leafs from fifth place.

"I got myself in shape…. It's all very well to be in good shape, but it's a different matter to get into the swing of hockey after you've been away. It took me a while, and, well, we didn't make it. That's the long and the short of it."

— Teeder Kennedy in Jack Batten, *The Leafs in Autumn* (1975)

The Debut of Frank Mahovlich

With Teeder Kennedy on the way out for good, future hopes were pinned on a new young player. On March 20, 1957, 19-year-old Frank Mahovlich was called up to the Maple Leafs for the final three games of the regular season. He would play that night against Montreal and then in two weekend games against Detroit. In his third full season in Junior A as a member of the St. Michael's Majors of the OHA in 1956–57, Mahovlich had led the league with 52 goals in just 48 games and added two goals and seven assists in four playoff games.

"I asked Hap to play 10 forwards, five defensemen and a goalkeeper for this game. The only stipulation I made was that Mahovlich was to be one of the forwards. I want to get a good look at what we have."

— Conn Smythe

"I don't see how he can miss. He can do everything and I have never seen a junior who lays down a better pass."

— King Clancy

"His name might be Moses."

— Hap Day

"He certainly looks like the fellow who will lead us out of the hockey wilderness. It may not be next year, but it will be, before he's many years older. I had him out there against Jean Beliveau and Henri Richard and he didn't look out of place."

> — Howie Meeker after Frank Mahovlich (who was then playing centre) made his debut against the Canadiens

"Mahovlich played as if he'd been in the league all season. He'll be murder on rival defences and goalies in a couple of seasons."

> — Montreal defenceman Tom Johnson after Frank Mahovlich's debut against the Canadiens

The Leafs lost all three games to close out the season, but Mahovlich scored the lone goal in a 4–1 loss to Detroit in the final game. He would be in the NHL to stay in 1957–58.

Jimmy Thomson and the NHLPA

Jimmy Thomson had been a regular on the Leafs defence since 1946–47. Always a defensive defenceman, Thomson was still only 29, yet had not been at his best in recent years. But he was looking solid in training camp heading

Frank Mahovlich holds up three pucks after scoring a hat trick in Toronto's 5–4 victory over Montreal on Christmas Day in 1957.

into the 1956–57 season. Before a pre-season game in Boston on October 11, Thomson was elected captain of the Leafs in a team vote.

"James Richard Thomson is a proud man, and his appointment as captain of the Maple Leafs will, we feel sure, result in his having one of the best years of his hockey career…. His selection as captain comes as no great surprise. While the swing is to youth with the Leafs, the steady hand of a campaign-hardened veteran is needed and Thomson can provide that hand."
          — Jim Vipond, *Globe and Mail*, Toronto, October 12, 1956

"He has been terrific in camp and he has his old drive back."
          — Coach Howie Meeker on Thomson's election as captain

But it would be a trying season for Thomson, who did not seem to have Conn Smythe's approval even before his involvement in an NHL Players' Association became known later in the season.

"On the ice, Jimmy set a great example. But Conn Smythe let everybody know he strongly disagreed with our selection of him as captain. It broke Jimmy's heart because he'd lived and died for seven or eight years with the Toronto Maple Leafs. So he came to me one day and said, 'Howie, give the C to someone else,' but I talked him out of it."
          — Howie Meeker, *Golly Gee It's Me* (1996)

Still, when talk of Teeder Kennedy's comeback heated up, it was expected that he would wear the "C" when he returned.

"The players wanted Kennedy to return in the same status as when he left. Jimmy Thomson requested that Kennedy succeed him as captain and I think it was a nice gesture on Thomson's part."
          — Hap Day after Kennedy signed his contract on January 11, 1957

Meanwhile, Thomson had been working behind the scenes to help organize an NHL Players' Association. When news of the organization was announced on February 11, 1957, Detroit's Ted Lindsay had been elected president; Montreal's Doug Harvey, Boston's Fern Flaman, and Chicago's Gus Mortson were vice presidents; Bill Gadsby of the Rangers was treasurer; and Jimmy Thomson was secretary. Conn Smythe, who spoke for all the NHL owners, seemed to take the Players' Association as a personal attack.

"Conn Smythe ran the league back in those days. He told some [of my] old teammates, 'Mortson can forget about coaching in this league when he's done playing.' I understood that my involvement with that original players association cost me any chance of getting a job in hockey when I retired as a player. [But] I knew Jimmy Thomson with the Leafs, my old defence partner, had to put up with a lot worse back then just being in the same building with Smythe."

— Gus Mortson to Gare Joyce, *Globe and Mail*, Toronto, December 31, 1994

In a press conference covering a number of topics carried over the radio on March 17, 1957, from New York where the NHL governors were meeting, Conn Smythe took responsibility for what he called "a year of failure" by the Maple Leafs. But he also spread the blame around.

"I am making it doubly clear, this, which I consider a year of failure is my complete responsibility. Five principle factors, in my opinion, have influenced the club this year and also in the future."

— Conn Smythe, March 17, 1957

The five factors Smythe listed were: (1) the president, (2) the manager and coach, (3) the Players' Association, (4) the quality of individual players, and (5) the operation of the club. He also announced that Jimmy Thomson would not be playing during the final three games of the season. Smythe said the benching would allow the team to see some younger players in action, but he also took a shot at Thomson's role in the Players' Association.

"I find it very difficult to imagine that the captain of my club should find time during the hockey season to influence young players to join an association that has no specific plan to benefit or improve hockey."

— Conn Smythe, March 17, 1957

"Detroit's players belong to the same association and it didn't seem to hurt them any."

— Jimmy Thomson responding to the third of Smythe's five factors

When pressed for more comments a few days later, Thomson admitted that he resented his loyalty to the team being called into question because of the Players' Association.

"I will never play again for the Leafs. It would be impossible for me to play for a team that questioned my loyalty. After what happened during the past six weeks, I wouldn't feel right about playing for the Leafs. There's been a lot said about my loyalty. At no time have I been disloyal to the team. When I had a good season I asked for a raise. When I had a poor season, I expected a cut."

— Jimmy Thomson to reporters, March 25, 1957

"I never thought of Thomson being disloyal on the ice. But what I said in [my press conference] still goes."

— Conn Smythe, March 25, 1957

"The only difference between Thomson and me is he thinks he *is* a great hockey player and I think he *was* a great hockey player."

— Conn Smythe on Jimmy Thomson, *Globe and Mail*,
Toronto, August 17, 1983

During the summer of 1957, Thomson's contract was sold to Rochester in the AHL — even though he'd said he would not report to the minors. Later, his rights were sold to the perennial last place Chicago Black Hawks, where Detroit had also banished Ted Lindsay.

"It is nice to know that somebody still wants you."

— Jimmy Thomson to Red Burnett, *Toronto Daily Star*, August 6, 1957

"Many times [over the] years I have had reason to be proud of my association with the players of the Toronto Maple Leafs, but never more than to the eighteen gentlemen who withstood the challenge of ownership, who put the game and the players before individual persecution."

— Howie Meeker, *Golly Gee It's Me* (1996)

Sun Sets on Hap Day

Jimmy Thomson was not the only person who was upset at what Conn Smythe had to say in his radio press conference from New York. Hap Day had not liked what he heard either.

"Whoever signs my players next year will have to understand that there must be 100 percent loyalty to the Maple Leafs organization. That they will play when, where and whenever they are told."

— Conn Smythe, March 17, 1957

"We have a spartan system and we may be out of date. We prefer to go after the body instead of the puck. We have stressed defensive and not offensive. Our system may be open to question."

— Conn Smythe, March 17, 1957

"Chicago had its bloody St. Valentine's day massacre. [Toronto] may have had its St. Patrick's day purge. The St. Valentine's victims fell under machine-gun fire in a grimy garage. The St. Patrick's Day targets are not even sure they've been hit. But if they do develop rigor mortis, it was caused by unheated words poured into a microphone in one of [New York]'s cheeriest suites — the club quarters of the Hotel Commodore. Not even a fleck of blood soiled the thick carpets as Conn Smythe, the little pistol of Maple Leaf Gardens, fired what sounded like lethal shots into the breasts of his crew-cut lieutenant, Howie Meeker, and the practically thatchless second in-command, Hap Day, a hockey associate of 30 years. Neither of them cried out in pain. And they uttered nary a word of protest. They weren't even asked to speak, and Smythe made it plain he didn't want them quizzed by the press and radio within hearing. If the newshounds had questions — and they had plenty — Smythe asked that it be done privately, for the obvious reason that he didn't want a public trial of his coach and general manager after he already had announced they would be asked to explain their positions to the board of directors for their part of what Smythe described bluntly as 'a season of failure' on the part of the Leafs.

"Day and Meeker sat grim-faced through the conference while Smythe softened what seemed to be a studied failure to give either of them a vote of confidence by saying: 'The president's position [Smythe's own job] is as vulnerable as any other.' During a question-and-answer session, he agreed it was possible there could be a change in the presidency. Asked whether he had a successor in mind, Smythe replied, somewhat vaguely, that there were dozens of young men in Toronto who could make a success of the job.

"In the opinion of this listener, there was little doubt that Smythe, Sr. had one particular young man in mind — his son, Stafford Smythe, overseer of the Marlboro farm system, and partner of his father in the sand and gravel business. The younger Smythe frequently has voiced dissatisfaction over the handling of young players whom Marlboros have sent up to the Leafs. Staff Smythe was on hand for yesterday's huddle, but was not asked for comment....

"Obviously, Day would be doomed with Staff Smythe as boss — and Hap, doubtless, would resign if Staff took over."
                    — Milt Dunnell, *Toronto Daily Star*, March 18, 1957

"I feel like a corpse that has been dismembered in public."
                    — Hap Day's lone comment after Conn Smythe's press conference

"I'm amazed to read reports in the papers that Hap and Howie are on the way out. Where do you guys get those ideas? Now you know why I had that press conference tape recorded. Everything's on the record and I defy anybody to show me where I suggested anything of that nature. I stressed for the past week that nobody would lose their heads, but apparently you newspapermen didn't believe me. You fellows alone evidently decided that it would be Bastille Day."
                    — Conn Smythe to Toronto reporters, March 18, 1957

On Saturday, March 23, 1957, during the last home game of the season at Maple Leaf Gardens, Smythe went on the radio from coast to coast to make announcements he had been keeping from the press all week. Smythe said that he had signed George Armstrong to a new contract for 1957–58 and had named him captain. He said that he would recommend to the Maple Leafs board of directors that Howie Meeker be retained as coach and that King Clancy stay on as assistant general manager. He also addressed Hap Day's situation.

"I can't do anything until Hap lets me know if he is available. If he tells me he is available, then we'll sit down and talk it over from there."
                    — Conn Smythe

Smythe met with Day at Maple Leaf Gardens on March 25, 1957. After an association that had seen them together in some capacity for 28 of the last 30 years, their discussion lasted less than three minutes.

"Mr. Day says he is not available for next year. This puts a crimp in my plans. I thought that Hap and King and Howie and myself could do a good job next season."
                    — Conn Smythe to reporters after meeting with Day

"I have no comment to make at this time. Mr. Smythe will tell you about it."
                    — Hap Day to reporters after meeting with Smythe

"Hap asked me if there was any significance about my asking whether he was available for next season. Then — you'd better get that from Hap. He'll tell you."

— Conn Smythe

"I asked what he meant by asking me if the job was open would I be available. I told him I didn't understand that. He told me there was no use discussing next year's plans if I wasn't available. I said if that's the case, then I'm not available."

— Hap Day

"It's a sad day for me. Mr. Day going out isn't going to be the goat [for this season of failure]. I'm taking the blame. He's an honest workman and an honest guy. Once again, I have to take the blame for Day's departure. Anything good about a man can be said about Day."

— Conn Smythe

Hap Day held his own a press conference at the Royal York Hotel on March 27.

"I feel no rancor because I'm not connected with the Gardens anymore. The move was of my own volition. I may have just beaten the gun but I did beat it."

— Hap Day

"It was the first time in my years with the Leafs that I had been asked a question about my so-called availability. I didn't want to start negotiations on that basis."

— Hap Day

"I repeat what I said before. The inference I took from that press conference [on March 17] was that I had been publicly dismembered. That I was walking the plank."

— Hap Day

"I was always more than pleased to accept any advice Mr. Smythe had to offer.... It is the manager's prerogative to make suggestions if he feels they are necessary."

— Hap Day

"I think he's the smartest man in hockey…. At least he is now that I'm out."
— Hap Day on Conn Smythe

"The system was that when the Maple Leafs had the puck, they did their best to put it in the other team's goal and when the other team had the puck, they did their darndest to keep them from scoring. If that system is wrong, then my system was wrong."
— Hap Day defending what Smythe had referred to as his outdated, spartan system

"I understand the new system is to play 100 percent offensive hockey. All I hope is that players like Gordie Howe will let you do it."
— Hap Day

"The future looks good for Leafs. They have the best young players in hockey coming along. When they will reach fruition, I don't know."
— Hap Day denying that he gave up the job because the team's future was bleak

1957–58

A month after Hap Day left the team, no one had yet been hired to replace him as general manager; nor had Howie Meeker been confirmed as the coach for the 1957–58 season. Rumours were spreading that Meeker would, in fact, be bumped up to general manager and that Billy Reay would be brought in from the Montreal Canadiens to take over as coach.

"Billy Reay? Don't tell me they've got him on the chopping block now? Yes, I've considered Reay. I've also considered [Alf] Pike, [Turk] Broda, and [Bob] Goldham and half a dozen others."
— Conn Smythe on the coaching speculation, reported in newspapers on April 26, 1957

"I asked Meeker if he was available. He said he was. So he'll be with the Maple Leaf organization next year."
— Conn Smythe

Though he had yet to name a coach or GM, Smythe announced a huge shakeup in the Leafs organization on May 9, 1957. Smythe would remain on as president, but beginning on September 1, he would step away from the running of the team and concentrate solely on the operations of Maple Leaf Gardens. The Maple Leafs hockey team would be run by a committee of seven men, headed up by Conn's son Stafford Smythe and comprising John Bassett, George Gardiner, Jack Amell, William Hatch, George Mara, and Ian Johnston — though he would soon be replaced by Harold Ballard, who, for now, continued to work with the Toronto Marlboros junior team as he had since 1940. The committee would come to be known as the Silver Seven.

"I am going to sign the players, the coach and the manager, in order to hand over to the committee a complete parcel. Then, they will be free to hire, fire, and make whatever changes they see fit if the team does not meet with their approval. I felt I should turn over a working organization to the new committee, rather than have them step in cold with the job of signing a coach and manager."

— Conn Smythe, May 9, 1957

"He still knows more about hockey than any of us. It should make it easier for all of us. Our job will be to give the fans the best possible type of hockey and I know we have the nucleus of players in our organization to do it."

— Stafford Smythe

But Stafford Smythe did have his own opinions.

"As far as I'm concerned, you can develop a system and stay with it until it goes sour. I think that's what has happened in our case and that's why I'm in favour of bringing in a man from outside the Maple Leafs organization to coach the club.... It's time we [have a system that puts] a little enjoyment back in the game for the players.... I think Tod Sloan, George Armstrong, Bob Pulford, Bob Nevin, Ken Girard, and Frank Mahovlich have the ability to star in the NHL. Sloanie and Army have been hampered by too much regimentation."

— Stafford Smythe

"I have received permission from Montreal Canadiens to interview [Billy] Reay. He is definitely a candidate. It might be a good idea to bring in an outside man but I don't know if Reay is interested."

— Conn Smythe on a possible new coach

"Howie will be in our organization."

— Conn Smythe on his old coach, Howie Meeker

On May 13, 1957, Conn Smythe announced that he had hired Billy Reay as coach and Howie Meeker as general manager.

"I knew about the problems both on and off the ice that Hap Day had. I also knew that as general manager I'd have to take advice and interference not only from Connie but also from Stafford, a young man with an ego as big as all outdoors and not an ounce of class or hockey sense. The thought scared me."

— Howie Meeker, *Golly Gee It's Me* (1996)

The new Leafs coach patterned his methods on that of an old Leafs coach, but it wasn't Hap Day or Joe Primeau. It was Dick Irvin, whom Billy Reay had played under for eight seasons in Montreal.

"I try to capitalize on a player's strong points, rather than in trying to build up his weak ones. I feel that if a man is an offensive specialist he should work at the business of perfecting that art. If he is a defensive player he should work at that phase of the game. Few men are good at both jobs. Then, if you blend your offensive and defensive material properly you come up with a balanced club."

— Billy Reay to the Toronto press upon being hired as coach of the Leafs

Meanwhile, Howie Meeker's first job as GM was to get Frank Mahovlich's signature on a contract.

"The story hit the newspaper and I don't think it was on the street a half-hour before Connie [Smythe] was on the phone. He was steaming mad and he tore a strip off my back. 'You're saying all these complimentary things about this young kid and that's going to cost us money. You can't say anything at all, how bad you want him, how good he is, or anything. Just shut up.'"

— Howie Meeker, *Golly Gee It's Me* (1996)

Though terms were not announced in the newspapers at the time, according to Meeker, the Leafs original offer to Mahovlich was an $8,000 bonus and $8,000 a year for three seasons. When Mahovlich asked for $12,000 Meeker countered with $9,000. They soon agreed on a $10,000 bonus and $10,000 a year for two years.

"It's a good contract. Frank's satisfied, and we think he can earn it. He can be a great one, but that's strictly up to [him] and what he puts into the job."

— Howie Meeker to reporters, May 13, 1957

It proved to be a difficult summer for Meeker as general manager, but he tried to put a positive spin on things.

"We have no slogans or large promises to offer the fans. But I can assure you we won't play defensive hockey. We played and practised too much defence last season. It was a mistake. We didn't have the material for it. I'm convinced you have to have good, smart, experienced men before you can play it tight and win. We lack those men, but we do have youth and legs. That means we have to place extra emphasis on offence because I think it is easier to attack than defend.

"But before going any further, I'd like to make it clear Billy Reay is coaching this team and will be allowed to carry out his own theories. He believes you should work on a player's strong points rather than his weak ones and I'm in 100 percent agreement. We're also going to put a little fun back in the game for Leafs players. I used to have fun when I was a player here and we won Cups. I see no reason why it can't happen again.

"Last season became a drudge. We had too many workouts and too many meetings. I'm convinced that's why we'd run out of steam in the third period of those Sunday games. The boys were bushed from too much hockey."

— Howie Meeker in the *Toronto Daily Star*, August 22, 1957

But behind the scenes, things weren't going well. Despite repeated requests over the summer, Meeker received no input from either Conn or Stafford Smythe.

"I knew then I was on the outside looking in and that sooner or later I was gone."

— Howie Meeker, *Golly Gee It's Me* (1996)

Meeker explained some of the problems to Kevin McGran at the *Toronto Star* many years later (November 4, 2006): "I would have liked to have had an opportunity to do the job, but under Stafford I couldn't because he knew it all."

Meeker told McGran that he'd been anxious to sign Johnny Bower and Allan Stanley (who both signed with the Maple Leafs a year later), as well as Johnny Bucyk, but that Stafford Smythe insisted he come to terms with former

Marlboro Hugh Bolton, who was thinking about retirement after having been injured for most of the 1956–57 season.

"He did nothing about getting Bucyk, he did nothing about getting Bower, and did nothing about getting Stanley. We got nose to nose. He gave me a shove and I hit him between the effing eyes."

— Howie Meeker to Kevin McGran

After less than five months on the job, it was announced that Meeker had stepped down to take a position with the Maple Leafs' public relations department.

"He didn't have the experience needed for that kind of job and needs to learn more about it. We don't have the time to let him gain that experience. We have a team to put over right now. The general manager has to deal with experienced men like Jack Adams and Tommy Ivan and that's tough at any time, but especially when we're an underdog team.

"The only thing was that as far as I was concerned, he didn't have the necessary experience for the job. That would be no handicap if this were a team where everything was cut and dried. But with so much to be done, we had to take action right away."

— Stafford Smythe, October 3, 1957

"I haven't switched any position. I was just relieved of the general manager's job, that's all…. There were a number of incidents that forced the issue. I'm certainly not going to complain, but I'm sorry Stafford Smythe saw fit to make the remarks he did. If that's the way he wants to get rid of me, enough people will understand. It just vindicates the way I've been feeling over the last two months. Let's just say a lot of things don't add up right. However, first of all, I'm interested in the Leafs having a good hockey club and if I was the reason they weren't going to have a good team, then I'm glad it happened."

— Howie Meeker, October 3, 1957

The Maple Leafs most decidedly did not have a good season in 1957–58, finishing last in the six-team standings with a record of 21–38–11. The team was decent at scoring goals, finishing in the middle of the pack with 192, but they were the worst by far at preventing them, with 226 goals against. Among the few bright spots was the playing of Dick Duff, who led the team in scoring with 26 goals and 49 points. Frank Mahovlich scored 20 goals and beat out Bobby Hull of the Chicago Black Hawks for the Calder Trophy as rookie of the year.

1958-59

The Maple Leafs had emphasized speed, youth, and offence in 1957–58, and it had not gone well. As the head of the Silver Seven, Stafford Smythe had become the defacto general manager after Meeker was let go. After a season in last place, he appeared ready to consider the addition of a few key veterans to Toronto's lineup. In June of 1958, the Leafs picked up Johnny Bower from Cleveland of the AHL in the Intra-League Draft. The team also purchased Bert Olmstead from the Montreal Canadiens and then claimed him in the draft.

"When Hap Day and Howie Meeker persuaded Teeder Kennedy to do a comeback with the Leafs in the middle of the '56–57 season, Staff Smythe, then overseer of the Marlboro shinny holdings, complained: 'They're sacrificing youth in favour of an old man.' Kennedy was [31] at the time. Smythe's latest moves to rebuild the now last place Leafs include … drafting Bert Olmstead, who will be 32 by training camp time [and the] drafting of goalie Johnny Bower, officially 33, whom the Rangers sent back after two or three flings in the NHL. Conclusion: Either Leafs have no more youth to hold back — or Staff has changed his mind about veterans since assuming chairmanship of the big team."

— Milt Dunnell, *Toronto Daily Star*, June 5, 1958

Bert Olmstead

Bert Olmstead was a veteran who'd played in the NHL with Chicago and Montreal since 1948 and helped the Canadiens win the Stanley Cup in 1953, 1956, 1957, and 1958. A tough player and talented playmaker, he had starred with Jean Beliveau and Maurice Richard. But knee injuries had slowed him down, and so Montreal made Olmstead available to the Maple Leafs. He would be instrumental in turning Toronto around … but he was not the easiest person to get along with.

"He's a hard, hard loser, real mean when he loses, a proud son of a gun. He'll help whatever centre he plays with."

— Leafs coach Billy Reay, reported by Scott Young,
Globe and Mail, Toronto, June 12, 1958

"In Bert Olmstead, we welcome a fighter to our team."

— Conn Smythe at a hockey luncheon for the team prior to the opening of training camp, September 15, 1958

George Armstrong, Frank Mahovlich, and Bert Olmstead in October of 1958.

"No hockey player ever demanded more of himself than Bert Olmstead, and he demanded almost as much from his teammates."
— Leafs teammate Billy Harris, *The Glory Years* (1989)

"If Olmstead did publicity for Santa Claus, there wouldn't be any Christmas."
— Long-time minor league hockey star Eddie Dorohoy, quoted in an obituary for Bert Olmstead, *Globe and Mail*, Toronto, November 27, 2015

Drafting Johnny Bower

Johnny Bower would also be instrumental in Toronto's turnaround, but there were no guarantees the Leafs would actually get him. Drafting him was one thing. Signing him would prove to be another.

"I was sitting in the press box in [Cleveland], watching because I had three cracked ribs, when Bob Davidson asked me what I would think if Toronto drafted me that summer."
— Johnny Bower looking back to 1958 in *Canadian Magazine*, January 7, 1967

"I kept telling them I couldn't help them but they warned me if I didn't sign they would suspend me."

— Johnny Bower, *Canadian Magazine*, November 7, 1964

At his age, Bower didn't want to leave the security of playing with the Cleveland Barons. Barons GM Jim Hendy made it clear that Bower wanted a two-year contract from the Maple Leafs, plus moving expenses, and that he would expect to receive his full salary for two years even if he was injured.

"I want to make it clear that Bower is a good goalie and is in good shape, but I believe he is two years older than the record book indicates and he'll come awfully high for two years' service."

— Jim Hendy to the press, reported in newspapers on June 4, 1958

"I know he can play in the NHL. He proved that by setting a goals-against club record his one season with Rangers. He's always been the best in the minors."

— Leafs coach Billy Reay to reporters, August 13, 1958

Signing Bower would become the job of the newest addition to the Maple Leafs front office during the summer of 1958.

Punch Imlach Comes On Board

"George (Punch) Imlach will join the ... Maple Leafs next month as assistant manager on a two-year contract, it was announced last night. He will be responsible to Staff Smythe, chairman of Leafs' hockey committee of seven.

"A former outstanding junior and senior player here, Imlach last season was general manager of the Springfield Indians. The Indians gained the final playoffs in the American League for the first time in 17 years and showed the most successful financial year in club history.

"Prior to his AHL tenure, Imlach took Quebec Aces to the Quebec Hockey League title on six occasions and reached the finals in the two other seasons he was there. He is a former Toronto Marlboros [senior] player.

"The appointment, said Smythe, in no way affects the status of King Clancy, who remains as an assistant manager. Clancy also will continue in a public relations capacity."

— *Globe and Mail*, Toronto, July 11, 1958

"We didn't have a very good team in the late 1950s, so that management brought in a fellow named George (Punch) Imlach to help us get straightened out.... He was a bold, confident fellow and he was brought into the organization in the same capacity as me — assistant general manager. We both laughed about our titles because we were assistants to nobody — there was no general manager."

— King Clancy, *Clancy* (1968)

"I came here with my eyes wide open.... This is going to be a tough uphill battle, but we'll make it. I wouldn't be at this desk if I wasn't positive of that fact. We'll grab any players we think will help the big team or the minor pro clubs."

— Punch Imlach, as reported by Red Burnett,
Toronto Daily Star, August 21, 1958

"Johnny Bower has signed a two-year contract with Toronto Maple Leafs of the National Hockey League. Assistant manager Punch Imlach, newest member of Leafs front office battalion, flew to Saskatoon earlier this week to conduct negotiations. He returned triumphantly yesterday with the signed document."

— Rex MacLeod, *Globe and Mail*, Toronto, August 28, 1958

"[Guyle] Fielder was my first signing assignment, and I flopped there. But on the way back [from Seattle] I stopped on the prairies in Saskatoon, and signed Johnny Bower, whom we'd drafted from Cleveland. That was a good day's work for the Leafs. Also, I had talked my new bosses into having the Leafs play exhibition games, including one in Quebec City against Boston.... But the big bonus of that exhibition trip to Quebec was the deal for Allan Stanley."

— Punch Imlach, *Hockey Is a Battle* (1969)

Optimism for the New Season

Coach Billy Reay expected better things from the Maple Leafs in 1958–59.

"We don't expect to work miracles and none are needed to put this club into the playoffs. It will take hard work on our part and that of the players. I'm in a much better spot than I was at this time last year. Then I was fresh on the scene and didn't have a true picture of the ability of my players....

To make matters worse we lacked depth to repair the unexpected gaps that cropped up in our ranks. Add to that the fact that our players had been guaranteed a full season under the new system to play their way on or off the team. It was like handing some of them a year's salary on a silver platter. This time they'll be fighting instead of singing for their suppers.

"If they're not hungry enough to battle all-out for their jobs, we don't want them around. I hope to have a dog-eat-dog camp. We'll carry both Johnny Bower and Ed Chadwick for goal. But there will be at least eight defencemen battling for five jobs and up front there'll be some 16 fellows chasing 11 jobs if present plans materialize....

"No one is picking on Ed [Chadwick] or underestimating him. But I will say that I wasn't pleased with the excess poundage he'd picked up the last time I talked to him. He'll have to prove he's better than Bower to start in goal. But both will see action. I am firmly convinced one goalie can't stand the continual shelling of 70 games in the NHL. I feel that if we had been able to spell Chadwick last season we might have won a dozen games we lost."

— Leafs Coach Billy Reay to reporters, August 13, 1958

"I look for a 25 percent improvement. I expect 12.5 percent more goals and I figure on 12.5 percent less against us. That's not asking too much. I won't be surprised if we finish in second place."

— Billy Reay to reporters at the opening of the Leafs training camp in Peterborough, September 15, 1958

Six new players would be in the lineup when the Leafs opened the new season at Maple Leaf Gardens against Chicago on October 11, 1957. Among them were veterans Johnny Bower, Bert Olmstead, and Allan Stanley, as well as rookie Carl Brewer.

"We're a little better team over all than the one of last season. We could finish as high as second. More guys on the club feel they're National Leaguers now."

— Billy Reay, after the Leafs last practice prior to the season opener

Poor Start Leads to Change

The Leafs lost their opening game 3–1 to Chicago, and then dropped two more before recording their first win. By November 21, 1958, they had a record of 5–9–1.

"I told them the team obviously wasn't playing for Reay. I thought he wasn't tough enough on them; that he was trusting them to do things and they were letting him down. They asked me what I would do about it. I said I wasn't the general manager; I was only the assistant general manager. In a way, I put it up to them."

— Punch Imlach, *Hockey Is a Battle* (1969)

"Maple Leafs have won five of their first 16 hockey games. So yesterday, in a sweeping move, they announced the promotion of George Imlach from assistant general manager to general manager. So meteoric has been the rise of this young hockey executive that it is conceivable he might make it to president if the Leafs lose a few more games."

— Rex MacLeod, *Globe and Mail*, Toronto, November 22, 1958

"The committee is not satisfied either with the performance of the players through lack of consistency or with coaching for lack of consistency. It will be Imlach's problem to correct this."

— Stafford Smythe, announcing Imlach's promotion, November 21, 1958

"Changes have to be made and they will be made. Now that I'm solely responsible for this hockey team I intend to make them. There won't be any ducking the issues. If I'm going to be shot, I'd sooner be shot as a lion than a lamb."

— Punch Imlach to reporters, November 21, 1958

With two ties and two losses in the next four games, rumours about the next move focused on Billy Reay.

"Maple Leafs coach Billy Reay was given as much chance for survival as a Thanksgiving Day turkey after the club bowed to the flying Red Wings 3–2 here last night. Billy, who has been carved up by the experts more than the 20-pound gobbler that Wings general manager Jack Adams and his friends polished off prior to the game is suffering from a lack of horses. Latest rumour is that general manager George Imlach will handle the Leafs from the bench with Bert Olmstead acting as playing-coach."

— Red Burnett, *Toronto Daily Star*, November 28, 1958

"That week, we had two games with Detroit, Wednesday in Toronto and Thursday in Detroit — the U.S. Thanksgiving. Early that week I went into the office I shared with Billy Reay and I said, 'Look, we're going to have to tell these guys that if something isn't done, if they don't start playing hockey, there's going to have to be a change.' In a way, I was trying to warn him."

— Punch Imlach, *Hockey Is a Battle* (1969)

Reay was fired exactly one week after Imlach took over as GM.

"I knew I was through after we lost in Detroit Thursday. Actually I had known it long before, back as far as training camp. If I had only thought of it at the time I could have named the day."

— Billy Reay on his firing, November 28, 1958

"It wasn't a move I enjoyed doing. But it had to be done. I still think Billy is a good hockey man. Nobody knows more about the game. But he hasn't been getting anything out of the players lately. There was no spirit or drive on the team. It looked to me like the coach was to blame."

— Punch Imlach to reporters

"Some of you guys, in fact, most in this room will be playing for your fourth coach in just over three years. If you don't soon start playing the hockey that I know you are capable of playing, we will have no alternative but to start trading players instead of changing coaches."

— Billy Harris, recalling what Stafford Smythe said to the team after Reay's firing, *The Glory Years* (1989)

"The players gave us a complete vote of confidence. That's what we were hoping for. They seemed to agree that something had to be done. Now, with the air cleared, they have assured me they will try to play better hockey."

— Punch Imlach to reporters, November 28, 1958

"This team is much better than its record shows. Wait and see. The only thing they lack is the BIG player, the Howe or the Bathgate. But they should still be able to beat teams like Detroit, New York or Boston."

— Billy Reay

With Imlach taking over the coaching job on what he thought was an interim basis, the Leafs lost their first game 2–1 to Chicago on November 29, but then had three wins and two ties in their next five.

"I still looked at myself as only a fill-in coach for the hockey team then. Certainly if they'd gone out and lost the first six games with me behind the bench, that would have been it — I'd have had to hire a coach. But even when I talked to Alf Pike about coaching the Leafs, the hockey committee seemed to want me to coach. Especially Harold Ballard, I think."

— Punch Imlach, *Hockey Is a Battle* (1969)

Negotiations with Alf Pike fell through on December 12 when the Winnipeg Warriors refused to let him go without receiving players in return as compensation.

"After the Pike deal didn't work, I didn't look anymore. I was caught up in trying to get out of last place."

— Punch Imlach, *Hockey Is a Battle* (1969)

"This team has convinced me it can play hockey for me. I thought it would take longer to get them moving, but they have surprised me with their hustle…. We could be in third place after a few more games."

— Punch Imlach announcing his intentions to stay on as coach of the team, December 12, 1958

"By the time 1958–59 showed up, we had a confident team. We had been guys looking for a little direction; a little confidence. Imlach gave that to us…. He might have rubbed the other teams and the other coaches the wrong way, but he made us a confident team. We knew what it meant to wear the Maple Leaf sweater."

— Dick Duff, Legends Spotlight, Hockey Hall of Fame website

King Clancy felt the Leafs were going to make the playoffs under Imlach. One reason for his confidence was the play of rookie defenceman Carl Brewer.

"That kid doesn't play like a rookie. He acts like a fellow who had been around this league for years. The only thing he can't do well is shoot the puck, and that will come. For my money, he plays like a defenceman should. He can carry the puck; always takes a look before passing it; knows how to block an attacker and is mean. He's learned in half a season what it usually takes a defenceman years to learn. On top of that, he's a throwback to the old days. Plays hockey as if he enjoys every minute of it. I think he'd play for nothing if he had to. I always rated Red Horner as the top

Marlboro defence grad of all time, but this kid is better than Red. He's not as big or rough, but he is a better skater, better stickhandler and more mobile than Horner was and is just as mean. He's one of the reasons why I think this club will make the playoffs. The other is Imlach. Punch has done a terrific job."

— King Clancy to Red Burnett, *Toronto Daily Star*, January 13, 1959

At that point, the Leafs were 8–7–6 in 21 games under Imlach as coach. Toronto's 22 points in that stretch was better than any other team in the NHL except the first-place Montreal Canadiens, who had 31 points in 20 games on a record of 13–2–5.

"I'm going to make the playoffs with our present personnel. I'm tired of all this trade talk. Look at our record since I took over and you'll see why I have confidence in this club."

— Punch Imlach to Red Burnett, *Toronto Daily Star*, January 13, 1959

But as late as March 10, the Leafs trailed the Rangers by seven points in the race for fourth place. New York still had seven games to play to Toronto's six. Both teams lost the next night, leaving Toronto seven points out with just five games to go. But Imlach still believed.

"Sixty-five points will get us fourth place and a five-game winning streak will put us there."

— Punch Imlach before the Leafs played their final five games

"Imlach can crow all he wants. But it will be the same this year as last. The Rangers will make it; the Leafs won't."

— Rangers coach Phil Watson

"I played five straight games to begin the month 2–2–1 as we quit the cellar. Eddie [Chadwick] took over for a 6–2 loss to Montreal March 11, then Punch decided to ride me the rest of the way. And what a ride it was! We were seven points behind the New York Rangers for the final playoff spot with five games left to play. I couldn't believe we were going to get in the playoffs, but Punch always stressed during the run that we were going to make it. 'We're going to get in the playoffs,' he'd say. 'I know we're going to get in. You guys can do it if you want to do it. Put your heart and soul into it and you'll make it.'"

— Johnny Bower, *The China Wall* (2006)

The Leafs beat the Rangers 5–0 at Maple Leaf Gardens on Saturday night, March 14, and followed up with a 6–5 win in New York on Sunday. Suddenly, Toronto was only three points out with three games to go. Toronto won against Montreal and Chicago while New York split games with Boston and Detroit, leaving the Leafs just one point back on the final night of the season, March 22. When the announcement was made that the Rangers had lost 4–2 to the Canadiens in New York, the Leafs rallied for a 6–4 win in Detroit. The victory gave Toronto the 65 points Imlach had predicted it would take to make the playoffs.

> "Even a week before the season ended, you could have got a hundred to one against us even making the playoffs. I remember hearing later that Conn Smythe had said to someone on Toronto's hockey committee, 'What did you get, did you get a coach or a madman?' This because I'm saying, 'we're gonna make it, we're gonna make it.'"
>
> — Punch Imlach, *Hockey Is a Battle* (1969)

> "Just making the playoffs was a story in itself. A lot of old-timers will never forget the windup to that…. The league printed a list of possible playoff matchups and we weren't even mentioned. Imlach used this oversight to motivate his players."
>
> — King Clancy, *Clancy* (1968)

Imlach had more predictions for the playoffs.

> "I'm serious when I say that we can beat Boston in six games. I don't think there's been a better hockey team in this league than we have for the past few weeks. The fact that we made the playoffs proved it."
>
> — Punch Imlach on the eve of the playoffs

But he wasn't taking all the credit for the team's success.

> "Enough of this Imlach nonsense. I'm no miracle man. The players deserve all the credit. I just had faith in them and they didn't let me down. If we'd lost, they'd have been blamed for not being good enough. I was certain they were good enough or I wouldn't have made all those statements about making fourth place. But they had to make those promises good or I'd have looked like the world's biggest blowhard."
>
> — Punch Imlach before Game 1 in Boston

The Leafs lost the first two games of the series in Boston, but enthusiasm was still high when they returned home for the first NHL playoff game in Toronto in three years. And the coach and GM was still getting the praise.

"Imlach is tremendous behind the bench. He seems to sense when a change is needed and 99 percent of the time makes the right change. He is also a great teacher, which is borne out by the improvement in our young players since he took over as coach."

— Conn Smythe before Game 3

The Leafs bounced back to beat the Bruins in seven games, but they weren't good enough to deny the Montreal Canadiens their fourth straight championship.

"We gave Canadiens a real battle in the Stanley Cup finals. They beat us four games and we beat them one, but every game was close. If we'd had just a little bit of luck here or there we might have made it all the way from last place to the Stanley Cup.... But that season was still the greatest thrill of my life."

— Punch Imlach, *Hockey Is a Battle* (1969)

1959–60

The Maple Leafs made very few changes heading into 1959–60. Johnny Bower was now firmly entrenched as the number-one goalie and Ed Chadwick was dispatched to the minors. Defensively, Tim Horton, Bob Baun, Carl Brewer, and Allan Stanley carried the bulk of the load, with Stanley leading all NHL blueliners with 10 goals this season. Bob Pulford and George Armstrong led the offence, although their numbers were a long way back of those put up by top NHL scorers Bobby Hull, Gordie Howe, Bronco Horvath, and Andy Bathgate.

The Leafs climbed to second place with a record of 35–26–9 for 79 points, but were well back of the Canadiens, who had 92 points. When Toronto and Montreal met again in the Stanley Cup Final, the Canadiens scored a four-game sweep for their fifth straight championship. A Stanley Cup title in Toronto was still a couple of years away, but the Maple Leafs added a key piece of their future 1960s dynasty during the 1959–60 season.

The Red Kelly Trade

"There was a background to this situation.... Seven months before, in the previous summer, Jack Adams had called me.... He'd had a last-place team the previous spring and was looking around for ways to make sure it didn't happen again.

"'How'd you like to make a deal for Kelly?' he asked me.

"'Sure, I'd like to make a deal for Kelly,' I said.

"It turned out he was having trouble signing him. When a general manager is signing players after they'd finished last the year before he doesn't figure he should get too many arguments. He was getting arguments from Kelly.

"So Jack and I starting coming up with names, for a deal. I mentioned Marc Reaume. He'd been our fifth defenceman the previous season, once we got straightened away with Horton-Stanley, Brewer-Baun combinations....

"Well, deals don't happen all at once. You talk and think, talk and think.... But that was a tip-off about the way Jack was thinking about Kelly."
— Punch Imlach, *Hockey Is a Battle* (1969)

Before Red Kelly was traded to Toronto, Detroit had tried to deal him to New York, along with Billy McNeill for Bill Gadsby and Eddie Shack. But Kelly didn't want to play for the Rangers and decided to retire. So did McNeill.

"The Rangers were visiting Detroit, and after the game I was told to go to the office and see Jack Adams and owner Bruce Norris. They told me I was going to the Rangers for Bill Gadsby and [Eddie] Shack. I was shocked, and I remember saying the first thing I could think of: 'I'll think about it.' And I also remember Bruce Norris saying, 'What do you mean you'll think about it? You be ready to report to the Rangers tomorrow morning when they catch a train.' Again, I said I'd think about it, and I did.... The next morning I called the tool-refurbishing company I'd started working for that summer and asked if I could have my job back. They said sure and when. I said right now, and I took it."
— Red Kelly in Ross Brewitt, *Clear the Track* (1997)

"The best way to describe the way I feel today is 'hurt.' Hurt that the Red Wings would decide to trade me after more than 12 seasons with them. Hurt that I have to leave the game that has been my whole life when I think I could be useful for two or three years yet. But a fellow has to quit some time and now looks like a good time for me.

"Being traded has always been in the back of my mind, because it's happened to others — Ted Lindsay, for one. My feelings were hurt, but I've been preparing myself for something like this. Five years ago, I'd have accepted the deal and gone to New York. But I'm 32 now and you can't go on forever....

"I'm skating strong and I can still keep up with any player I've seen. So I might be able to stick around for two or three years more. But what would happen then? I'd quit anyway. So it might as well be now."

— Red Kelly writing in the *Toronto Daily Star*, February 5, 1960

"My concern is for the welfare of the players. I don't want any player to make a hurried decision that he might regret. If Kelly and McNeill stick to their decision the NHL then will place them on waivers. This is a big decision and it must be given very thorough consideration. There is nothing so urgent that it must be done today. I am giving both players a chance to get over the initial disappointment. The league will take no action until Saturday."

— NHL president Clarence Campbell, February 6, 1960

"I can't understand it. It's a matter of living up to a contract. The players have a moral responsibility. They're both fine boys and I hope they change their minds. After all, where are they going to make that kind of money?"

— Red Wings GM Jack Adams, February 6, 1960

"A deal of defence player Marc Reaume for veteran Red Kelly is likely to be offered Jack Adams, general manager of the Detroit Red Wings, if Kelly agrees to play for Toronto. Kelly, a star with the Wings for a dozen years, announced his retirement from hockey last Friday, rather than be traded to New York Rangers.

"Since then, King Clancy, assistant general manager of the Leafs, has asked Kelly whether he would report to Toronto if a deal could be worked out. Clancy had Adams' permission to approach the redhead.

"Kelly has promised to consider the proposal. Should he concur, Leafs would attempt to do business with Detroit. Adams was quoted in Detroit as saying he would be willing to make a deal for one of Toronto's good young defensemen. Reaume is young (26) against Kelly's 32. Whether Adams would consider him good enough would remain to be seen."

— *Toronto Daily Star*, February 8, 1960

"So far I haven't changed my mind from what I started out to do. I said I would sooner retire than be traded. I'm flattered that Leafs want me but I don't really know what I will do."

— Red Kelly, February 9, 1960

"That Clancy's a real Irishman. I enjoyed talking to him and I guess that's what Imlach had in mind. Clancy told me that Imlach could probably do a better selling job but I told him, 'you're doing okay, Clancy.'"

— Red Kelly

Shortly after eleven o'clock on the night of February 9, 1960, Punch Imlach — after meeting all day with Red Kelly at Maple Leaf Gardens — announced that he and Jack Adams had agreed to trade Kelly for Marc Reaume. Though NHL president Clarence Campbell said the deal may require league approval first, Imlach didn't plan on waiting.

"As far as I'm concerned, he's my player and he'll be in uniform tonight. Kelly belonged to the Wings and Marc Reaume belonged to us. We swapped. It's as simple as that. Kelly hadn't signed any retirement form and had been given a week to think over his decision to quit."

— Punch Imlach to Jim Proudfoot, *Toronto Daily Star*, February 10, 1960

"As a kid, I always wanted to play for Toronto. But that was before I went to Detroit."

— Red Kelly to reporters after the trade was announced

"I know we have a darn good hockey player — one who'll help us a lot."

— Punch Imlach

"What the heck, I've spent two seasons on the bench here. I think I'll have a better chance to play regularly in Detroit."

— Marc Reaume

"I'm tickled to death with the trade. I've got a defenceman who's six years younger, who wants to play here, and who'll do some hitting for us."

— Jack Adams

"If Red Kelly gives Leafs as much mileage as have the other good veterans — Bert Olmstead, Allan Stanley and Johnny Bower — the deal is a very good one."

— Scott Young, *Globe and Mail*, Toronto, February 10, 1960

Kelly had been the first winner of the Norris Trophy in 1954 and was an eight-time All-Star (six selections to the First Team, two to the Second) as a defenceman in his 12 full seasons in Detroit, but in Toronto he would play centre and be one of the Maple Leafs' top scorers.

"When I had the contract talk with Imlach, we talked most of the day and then it went until midnight before we agreed. Nothing was ever said about where I was going to play or anything until after I agreed to come to Toronto. Toronto was playing Montreal the next night. They had to fly my skates in from Detroit for that game. After I signed, I told Punch, 'I've been off skates for ten days or so. I'd hate to make a mistake out there and cause a goal,' and Punch said, 'Red, how would you feel about playing centre?' I said, 'Great! No problem.' I didn't care where I played as long as I was playing hockey. He said, 'If we're going to win the Stanley Cup, we're going to have to go through Montreal. I need somebody to check Beliveau.' He said, 'How would you feel if I started you against Beliveau?' I just said, 'Fine. Great. Love it!'"

— Red Kelly, Legends Spotlight, Hockey Hall of Fame website

1960–61

Red Kelly had a strong season at centre for the Leafs in 1960–61, establishing career highs with 50 assists (which ranked him second in the NHL) and 70 points while winning the Lady Byng Trophy for sportsmanship.

"Kelly is a different type of Lady Bynger. He isn't the kind that shies away from a check or ducks a battle in the corners."

— Punch Imlach after Kelly was announced as the leader in Lady Byng voting at the halfway point of the NHL season, January 25, 1961

Toronto battled Montreal for top spot in the NHL throughout the season. In the end, the Leafs finished a close second with a record of 39–19–12 for 90 points while Montreal was 41–19–10 for 92 points. Johnny Bower had a great season in goal and finished second in voting for the Hart Trophy at year's end. Red Kelly was also a big reason for the Maple Leafs' success, but he and Bower were not the only reasons.

Goal scorers Bert Olmstead, Allan Stanley (two), Red Kelly, and Larry Regan flank coach
Punch Imlach after Toronto's 5–4 win over Detroit in Game 5 of their Stanley Cup semifinal
on April 2, 1960.

Dave Keon Wins the Calder

Dave Keon was 20 years old and had yet to play any professional hockey when
he attended the Leafs training camp in September of 1960. Keon had previously been invited to a Red Wings hockey school when he was 15 years old,
but his parents wanted him to remain closer to home in Noranda, Quebec.
He was playing for the Noranda Lions juvenile team when Leafs scout Vince
Thompson saw him.

> "You'd better grab this Keon kid now. Otherwise he'll come back to
> haunt you."
>
> — Vince Thompson to Leafs' chief scout Bob Davidson, quoted
> by Leo Monahan in the *Sporting News*, February 25, 1967

"I hustled up to Noranda to see Dave and I agreed with Thompson's opinion. We took over sponsorship of the Lions for $1,000. This gave us the right to all the players, including Dave. I think that was the best $1,000 we've ever spent."

— Bob Davidson to Leo Monahan, *Sporting News*

Keon honed his talents over four seasons of junior hockey in Toronto with the St. Michael's Majors.

"I discovered early in my career that if you keep checking, eventually the other team will make a mistake and you can capitalize on it.... Father Bauer at St. Mike's figured out a checking style for a fellow my size. He told me to maneuver my body so that the opposing player had to commit himself. Not only did I check the player this way, but I also took him out of the play. Quite often the fellow I check takes a penalty too."

— Dave Keon to Leo Monahan, *Sporting News*

Still, few people expected Keon to make the team when the Leafs opened training camp in Peterborough before the 1960–61 season.

"We weren't counting on him at all. He'd been a good junior, but in a pro tryout at Sudbury he hadn't been impressive. But from the way he played in training camp, there was no way he could be kept off the team."

— Punch Imlach, *Hockey Is a Battle* (1969)

"Dave Keon, 20-year-old speedster from St. Michael's Majors of the Ontario Hockey Association junior A series, probably will be in Toronto Maple Leafs lineup when the National Hockey League season opens. With little more than a week of training camp completed here, Keon has not only been the most impressive rookie in camp — he has also been the Leafs' most accomplished centre."

— Rex MacLeod, *Globe and Mail*, Toronto, September 16, 1960

"As of now I would think Keon can make the team. He has also been responsible for a big improvement in Dick Duff's play. And Duff keeps giving Keon pointers. They play well together. This might work out better than we expected."

— Punch Imlach at training camp

"Bert Olmstead was the first guy who said to Punch Imlach, 'This little guy can make it happen.' ... Hey, he was a different guy. You know, when he was captain, he was living in his own apartment and he didn't even have a goddamn phone. Didn't want to hear any beefs from the boys.... But he was a good little player."

— Eddie Shack on Dave Keon in Ross Brewitt, *Clear the Track* (1997)

Keon and Bob Nevin both made the team as rookies in 1960–61. Nevin had 21 goals and 37 assists, while Keon had 20 goals and 25 assists with just six penalty minutes. Keon's better two-way play helped him to win the Calder Trophy as rookie of the year with Nevin finishing in second place.

"They say a jinx follows Calder trophy winners. I'm sure that won't catch Keon. He'll be an outstanding centre, as good as Canadiens' Henri Richard, when he matures.... They warned me Keon would run out of gas about the 40-game mark. They said he flattened in the stretch as a junior. We had to nurse him a little but he never flattened out."

— Punch Imlach, April 29, 1961

Keon would be a huge contributor to the Leafs' success in the future, but the biggest story in Toronto during the 1960–61 season was Frank Mahovlich's pursuit of the NHL's single-season goal-scoring record.

Mahovlich Shoots for The Rocket

After scoring 20 goals in his rookie season and 22 the following year, Frank Mahovlich scored just 18 goals in 1959–60. He had three goals in the Leafs' first nine games in 1960–61, but then scored a hat trick in an 8–4 win over Chicago on Saturday, October 29, and netted the game-winner the next night in a 3–1 victory over the Rangers in New York. Suddenly, with seven goals in 11 games, putting him on an early pace for more than 40, reporters began to take an interest.

"[Red] Kelly has been a great help to me. He's a swell playmaker, the type of guy who digs the puck out of corners and lays it right on your stick."

— Frank Mahovlich to reporters after Toronto's
3–1 win over the Rangers, October 30, 1960

By December 18, 1960, Mahovlich had scored 29 goals in 32 games. The NHL's single-season record was still Maurice Richard's 50 goals set in a

50-game season back in 1944–45. With a 70-game season, Mahovlich seemed a cinch to break the record.

> "I know a bit more about playing hockey. I'm fortunate to work with Red Kelly and Bobby Nevin on my regular line and have Bert Olmstead beside me on the power play."
>
> — Frank Mahovlich on his sudden scoring prowess

> "When Mahovlich wants to go, nobody stops him."
>
> — Terry Sawchuk on Frank Mahovlich in 1960–61,
> quoted in Scott Young, *The Leafs I Knew* (1966)

Mahovlich kept on scoring, and after the Leafs beat the Bruins 4–1 on Christmas Day, he'd scored a goal in seven straight games and had 31 goals in 34 games overall. Talk of breaking Richard's record intensified.

> "I'm out there to help the team win and it takes the whole team to do it. Personal records are made only by the help of others."
>
> — Frank Mahovlich

Maurice Richard was in his first year of retirement in 1960–61, and with the Leafs in Montreal on January 25, he was asked what he thought about the possibility of his record being broken. "Naturally I'd rather see someone on the Canadiens do it first, but what does it matter? Records are meant to be broken, aren't they?"

Mahovlich now had 37 goals in 46 games. Scoring 50 in 50 would be all but impossible. What did Richard think about his record being broken during a 70-game schedule? "The record is for most goals in a season, not in so many games. After all, Joe Malone once scored 44 goals in 22 games."

> "Every goal that Frank Mahovlich scores now is an occasion. Each time, his friends, and even some of the perverse ones who wish him no good at all, come to their feet as inexorably as if their pants had just caught fire. It is impossible to avoid being conscious of those dwindling few goals between the number Mahovlich has this season and the fifty Rocket Richard scored in the 1944–45 season, the NHL record."
>
> — Scott Young on Frank Mahovlich for a column in 1960–61,
> and quoted in Young's book, *The Leafs I Knew* (1966)

But goals were getting tougher to come by, and after being held without one in Toronto's 1–1 tie in Chicago on February 5, 1961, Mahovlich had 41 in 53 games.

"I still think I can do it. I have 17 games left and if I can get a hat trick or two, I can make it. But it has been tough lately, so I guess I'll just have to work harder."

— Frank Mahovlich

"By now he was really under the microscope from the press and the fans, and if he didn't score they were all over him, calling him a bum. He skated with the big, effortless stride, and they'd complain he wasn't working hard enough."

— Bob Baun, *Lowering the Boom* (2000)

At the end of February, Mahovlich had scored 45 goals in 62 games. He had broken the previous Maple Leafs record of 37 goals shared by Gaye Stewart (in a 50-game season in 1945–46) and Tod Sloan (in a 70-game season in 1955–56) and had scored more goals in a season than any left winger in NHL history. By March 5, Mahovlich was up to 47 goals through 65 games. He needed four goals in five games to break Richard's record.

"[He has a good chance,] but those goals will be the toughest he ever scored."

— Maurice Richard on Mahovlich

"I don't know [what my chances are]. I just have to have a good night, that's all. However, I have to have one. It's more important for the Leafs to win a game than for me to score a goal. And there's no secret to scoring — just put the puck in the net."

— Frank Mahovlich, March 9, 1961

"I suggested ways and means he might use to make it a little easier for himself. He's being held and hooked by everyone in front of the net.... Although he's been a marked man the last five or six weeks, it's not getting him down. He's not giving up and is very unselfish on the ice. He's had opportunities galore to score yet tosses the puck around to guys he's playing with.... I think he'll break the record."

— King Clancy, March 9, 1961

Over the last five games, though, Mahovlich would score just once and finished the season with 48 goals. At the same time, Montreal's Bernie Geoffrion — who'd been coming on fast since the middle of February — exploded for seven goals in a four-game span to pass Mahovlich and reach 50 goals through 68 games. But even Geoffrion failed to break Richard's record, as he was held scoreless during the Canadiens' last two contests.

"People have often asked me what Frank did that season that he didn't do later for Leafs. Well, I'll tell you one thing — he was aggressive.… Frank has always been one of the most naturally talented and skilful players in the game … [b]ut the 1960–61 season was the only one he spent with the Leafs when he really played up to his potential. That year, if he couldn't go around a guy, he'd go over him.… That year he was as good a left winger as ever played the game."

— Punch Imlach, *Hockey Is a Battle* (1969)

After the tight, season-long battle for first place between Toronto and Montreal, the playoffs proved a huge disappointment for both the Leafs and the Canadiens. Toronto fell in five games to Detroit, while Montreal dropped a six-game series to Chicago. The Black Hawks then beat the Red Wings in six games to win the Stanley Cup for the first time since 1938. The Maple Leafs drought only dated back to 1951, but it was about to come to an end.

6

1962 to 1969:
New Leafs Dynasty ...
Until Expansion

1961–62

The biggest change to the Maple Leafs this season was in ownership, as Stafford Smythe, Harold Ballard, and John Bassett bought control of the team from Conn Smythe in November of 1961.

On the ice, Punch Imlach believed he had the team to beat for the Stanley Cup despite the playoff disappointment against Detroit the previous spring. He made very few changes to the roster. For defensive depth, the Leafs acquired Al Arbour from Chicago, but Toronto relied mainly on Tim Horton, Allan Stanley, Bob Baun, and Carl Brewer.

> "I don't think there ever was a better defence corps than the pairings of Stanley and Horton, and Brewer and Baun. Montreal had Doug Harvey and Tom Johnson, but they didn't have another defenceman who could touch us. Today's NHL rosters carry six or seven defencemen, but I don't think there's a team in the league that could come up with four as good as we were."
> — Bobby Baun, *Lowering the Boom* (2000)

Offensively, Frank Mahovlich had another big year, ranking among the NHL leaders with 33 goals and 71 points and earning a Second-Team All-Star selection. As Imlach had predicted, Dave Keon suffered no sophomore jinx, collecting 26 goals and 35 assists while playing strong defensive hockey. He was named a Second-Team All-Star at centre. With just a single penalty all season, he also won the Lady Byng Trophy for the first of two straight seasons.

The Maple Leafs would drink from the Stanley Cup four times during the 1960s.

"Keon could be the man to take over from Kelly when Red decides to quit…. He can become as good as Canadiens' Henri Richard, one of the greatest little men in Hockey."

— Punch Imlach, *Weekend Magazine*, December 23, 1961

A few key injuries, to Johnny Bower and Red Kelly, hurt the Leafs somewhat, but they finished the season comfortably in second place with 85 points (37–22–11), although a long way back of the first-place Canadiens who were 42–14–14 for 98 points.

With no chance to move up or down in the standings, the Leafs took their foot off the gas pedal, and went winless (0–3–2) over their last five games, finishing the season in a slump.

Semifinal versus New York

"We haven't been playing well lately. Everybody knows that. As a matter of fact, since we clinched second place we've been awful. That can change, of course. It's happened before this season."

— Punch Imlach to reporters on the off day between the end of the regular season and the start of the playoffs

"Last season we were extended to the wire, didn't lose the duel for first place to the Canadiens until the last weekend of the season. We had nothing left and Wings kicked our teeth in. I think we'll be fine for this series, and we're not underestimating Doug Harvey and his men."

— Leafs captain George Armstrong

The Maple Leafs would be facing a Rangers team that had made the playoffs for the first time in four years under playing coach and former Montreal Canadiens star Doug Harvey. Toronto was 9–4–1 against New York during the regular season and had won all seven meetings between the two teams at Maple Leaf Gardens.

"I think we can surprise a lot of people. I know we'll be underdogs but that has never hurt any team. I think we're coming back to our peak. It doesn't bother me in the least that we lost seven games in a row in Toronto during the season. That can't go on forever."

— Rangers GM Muzz Patrick

But the streak continued in the playoffs with the Maple Leafs winning the first two games at home, 4–2 and 2–1. The Rangers got back in the series with two straight wins at Madison Square Garden and then returned to Toronto for game five. In a brilliant goaltending battle in which New York's Gump Worsley made 56 saves, Toronto won 3–2 at 4:23 of the second overtime period to take a 3–2 series lead on a somewhat controversial goal by Red Kelly.

The play for the winning goal began when the Rangers' Andy Bathgate tried to fire a long pass out of his zone to teammate Camille Henry …

"But the puck hit [Red] Kelly's skate, bounced high in the air and landed right in front of [Frank] Mahovlich."

— Andy Bathgate

"One instant I was at centre ice and the next I was inside the Ranger blue line with the puck on my stick. Don't ask me where it came from. It all happened so quickly."

— Frank Mahovlich

"When Mahovlich shot, I took it right here [his left shoulder]. It bounced into the air and Kelly took a whack at it on the way down and I fell to smother it. But I couldn't feel it anywhere."

— Gump Worsley

"I couldn't see the puck and I don't know whether [referee Eddie] Powers saw it or not. Powers told me he saw some of it, but the rules say the entire puck must be in view for play to continue."

— Doug Harvey

"I thought I had smothered the puck long enough for a whistle. But it was a judgment call and referee Eddie Powers didn't blow the note I wanted."

— Gump Worsley

"I figured I was down there long enough and nothing was happening so I lifted my head — and that's where the puck was. Under my head. When I lifted my head, 'Ole!'"

— Gump Worsley

"He moved a little and it squirted loose. He thought he had it smothered."

— Red Kelly

"Kelly is the type of player who takes advantage of a good opportunity and when I lifted my head, he poked the puck into the net."

— Gump Worsley

"Will this take the starch out of them?"

— unidentified voice in the Leafs dressing room

"Well, it won't do them any good."

— Punch Imlach

It certainly didn't as Toronto cruised to a 7–1 win in Game 6 to wrap up the series. When Montreal fell 2–0 to Chicago the next night, the defending champion Black Hawks upset the Canadiens in six games and would face the Maple Leafs for the Stanley Cup.

The Final

"[Leafs] have the size, speed and ability to handle Black Hawks. They are going into the finals healthy and at their peak. They won't be stopped."

— Boston Bruins coach Phil Watson

"Some of my guys are beginning to wonder when people are going to accept them as mighty good hockey players.... What more do people want? We have the league's scoring leader in Bobby Hull, two centremen who are magicians, Stan Mikita and Red Hay, and a great goalie in Glenn Hall. Sure, we have a bruising defence, but you can't name one successful team that hasn't had one. If any team wants to get tough with us, we can beat any of them in that department. But we'd like people to realize that we're a damn good hockey team too."

— Black Hawks coach Rudy Pilous arriving in
Toronto to begin the Stanley Cup Final

"Chicago can't win in Toronto and that's all the edge Leafs will need. Otherwise the teams are pretty closely matched."

— Canadiens coach Toe Blake

As with the Rangers' series, home ice did prove to be a key in the early going. Toronto beat Chicago two straight at Maple Leaf Gardens to open the series, but then the Black Hawks won two in a row at Chicago Stadium to tie it up. Johnny Bower was hurt in the first period of Game 4, lunging to stop a shot from Bobby Hull, and left with the Leafs trailing 1–0. They would lose 4–1, although no one was faulting backup goalie Don Simmons, who had to come in cold out of the stands.

"When I went for it, I stretched to get my foot behind my glove, to give it some backing when I caught it…. But when I went down, I could feel something snap. I thought all the muscles were going right up to my stomach, the way it felt."

— Johnny Bower, describing how he was hurt

Bower tried to play through it for the next seven minutes or so, and was beaten for the first goal of the game when Hull tipped in a shot from Stan Mikita. Did the injury bother him on the play? "A little. I knew that the pass was going across there but I couldn't throw myself over fast enough on that leg to get there."

A few minutes later, he limped to the Leafs bench and pulled himself from the game. "I just couldn't move fast. I had to get out of there. I just have to rest now. We've got a good goalie in Donnie [Simmons] anyway. It's a tough place to put the kid in, but he'll have more confidence in the next two games."

"I see no reason why Simmons can't handle the goaltending assignment…. He'll be better tomorrow at home. He'll know ahead of time that he's on deck and won't be brought in from the stands cold."

— Punch Imlach

"I don't know if Bower will be able to play in Toronto Thursday or not. If he doesn't, the Leafs may be more inspired and just that much tougher. They will play better defensively as a team to help [Simmons]. It could work against us more than if Bower were in the net — who knows? Then again, Simmons won't be taken lightly. He stoned us with Boston."

— Black Hawks coach Rudy Pilous

Simmons would play the rest of the series in goal for the Maple Leafs, and with the fifth game scheduled back in Toronto, the home-and-home aspect of the series was on everyone's mind.

"I guess both teams are a bunch of homers. We win two at home, then they win two at home. It's okay with me if it keeps up that way."

— Punch Imlach

"After squaring the series, we are up mentally. We have a little more zip going for us. We have adjusted to their style now. We are feeling we have some breathing room. But we've got to beat them in Toronto."

— Rudy Pilous

"We have Leafs on the run. If we can retain our strength, and I'm sure we will, we'll win in Toronto tomorrow."

— Bobby Hull

"We'll take over again in Toronto. I don't find them as tough as New York Rangers. We bounced back after losing the third and fourth games in that series and we'll do it against Hawks. We've come too far to fold."

— Tim Horton

Toronto didn't put up much of a defensive effort in front of Don Simmons in Game 5, but they had the offence in fine form and scored an 8–4 victory in a sloppy game.

"Hockey is a game of mistakes. We made twice as many as the Leafs as the score indicates."

— Rudy Pilous

After scoring just once in their two losses in Chicago, the Leafs had changed tactics a bit in this one.

"[Glenn] Hall drops to his knees a lot and is hard to fool with low shots or by deking. So we tried throwing them up high and it worked."

— Dave Keon

Even so, most experts expected Chicago to win at home again in Game 6 and force a seventh game.

"We played good games in Chicago during the season, a couple of our best, but I'm making no predictions. We only need one more win and I don't care where it happens. You fellows laughed at me when I stressed the importance of home ice and fans to these teams. Now, maybe you'll believe me."

— Punch Imlach

Champions!

Game 6 was played in Chicago on Sunday evening, April 22. Even playing on the road, the Leafs were the better team in this one. But the better team doesn't always win. Glenn Hall performed brilliantly in the Black Hawks net (Don Simmons faced only half as many shots), and the game was scoreless after two periods. At 8:56 of the third period, Bobby Hull put Chicago ahead 1–0. Dick Duff blamed himself for a giveaway, but the Toronto deficit didn't last long. Bob Nevin tied the game at 10:29, and a few minutes later, with ex-Leaf Eric Nesterenko in the penalty box for the Hawks, Duff himself scored at 14:14 on a setup from two of the longest-serving Toronto players, Tim Horton and George Armstrong.

"The score was 1–1. George Armstrong gave the puck to Tim Horton and Horton passed to me. I was about 20 feet out. I had to turn around because the puck was behind me. I spun around and sent the puck into the net."

— Dick Duff, recalling his winning goal a few years later

The Leafs made the lead hold up and won the game 2–1. For the first time since Bill Barilko's overtime goal in 1951, Toronto had won the Stanley Cup.

"This club has ability, guts, and desire, the ingredients that go to make up a championship team. I knew when they skated out for the game that they'd come back winners. You could sense it. I called them to win the Stanley Cup back in September and they didn't let me down."

— Punch Imlach

"I thought if we got the first goal we'd win it. When they got it, it didn't stop us."

— Bert Olmstead

"I really drove that winning goal home. I saw a little net as Hall came rushing out and I just put everything I had in the shot. This team has come a long way and we've got a lot of guys around that other people didn't think were good enough to win a Stanley Cup."

— Dick Duff

"The Leafs played good, solid hockey. You can' take that away from them. They earned everything they got."

— Black Hawks goalie Glenn Hall

"I wouldn't swap my team for any in the league."

— Punch Imlach

Coming Home

"When we won the first Cup, we were in Chicago Stadium wahooin' and having a beer in the downstairs dressing room, and Imlach comes in, all cranky and pissed off like we just lost. Then he says, 'If you aren't on the goddamn bus in 15 minutes, you won't be on this team next year.' No congratulations, no nice going, or anything. What a crabby bastard. He wouldn't even loosen up and have a beer with us."

— Eddie Shack in Ross Brewitt, *Clear the Track* (1997)

"We had a few cocktails, and Imlach says, 'If you're not on the bus in five minutes, you won't be on the team next year!' Holy smokes, eh!"

— Frank Mahovlich, *The Big M* (1999)

Punch Imlach had vetoed the idea of staying over in Chicago and ordered the players to get dressed and head for a late plane to Toronto. "They'll enjoy their celebration at home more than here. They all must be as tired as I am and I could sleep standing up. I don't think I could have lasted another game. I'm going to sleep for a month."

The Leafs arrived back in Toronto around 3:30 am on Monday morning. There were about 2,000 fans at the airport to greet them. The celebration there lasted more than an hour. Imlach carried the Stanley Cup with him. George Armstrong presented the puck that scored the game-winning goal to Imlach's wife.

"Mrs. Imlach asked for it two weeks ago. She said she wanted the puck that won the Cup and I said I'd see that she got it. I suppose Dick might like to have it. I know I would because I assisted on that big goal. But a promise is a promise. And I know that the goal meant as much to Punch as it did to us, maybe more."

— George Armstrong

On April 25, 1962, the Leafs were given a ticker-tape parade ending in a civic reception at Toronto City Hall. Police had expected a crowd of about 20,000 people, but between 50,000 and 60,000 lined the streets.

"Beating Chicago in the Stanley Cup Final wasn't as tough as this."

— George Armstrong on trying to move through the crowd

"I don't think that in the history of Toronto we've had such a large crowd around City Hall."

— Toronto mayor Nathan Phillips

"Even the Queen never got a crowd like this."

— Metro chairman William Allen

Six Weeks Later

On June 6, 1962, a local newspaper from Cochrane, Ontario, published the following report:

> The skeletons of Toronto Maple Leaf hockey player Bill Barilko and Timmins dentist Dr. Henry Hudson were found today amidst the wreckage of their yellow Fairchild 24 aircraft about 45 miles north of here in muskeg bushland.
> Barilko and Dr. Hudson disappeared Aug. 26, 1951, on a return flight from Rupert House to Timmins. The wreckage was first sighted last Thursday by Gary Fields, a pilot for Dominion Helicopter Service Ltd., Toronto. Mr. Fields again located the smashed plane at about 11:00 a.m.
> Land and Forests Minister J.W. Spooner said in Toronto tonight there could be no doubt the two skeletons were the remains of Barilko and Dr. Hudson. The skeletons were still in the seats of the plane and were held in place by seat belts.... [R]elatives of the long-missing pair were

notified immediately. Letters of the plane's registration number were clearly identified....

The April before the crash, defenseman Barilko scored the winning goal in the Stanley Cup finals.

Olmstead Ousted

"Bert was really the key to our success. He was a real student of the game ... [and] Bert was the only one who'd stand up to Punch. Bert would watch Punch at the chalkboard and just shake his head; finally he couldn't contain himself any longer and said something like, 'No, that's not the fucking way!' And to Punch's credit, he looked right at Olmstead and said, 'Well, then, you show us the way.' And Bert would walk up to the board and go through the sequence of what was going to happen on the ice, especially in the offensive zone."

— Bobby Baun, *Lowering the Boom* (2000)

"He was a player whose spirit and professionalism had meant a tremendous amount to us ever since he joined the club. He was especially good — the best in the league — at working in the corners. You have to have courage as well as skill to work the corners well, with defensemen trying to cream you into the boards. Bert was so tricky in corners that defensemen were almost afraid to commit themselves against Olmstead for fear they'd find themselves in there with him but with the puck out in front and into the net."

— Punch Imlach, *Hockey Is a Battle* (1969)

Given his importance to the team, the end of Bert Olmstead's tenure in Toronto after the 1962 Stanley Cup victory sounded something of a sour note.

"When I think of our dressing room celebration in Chicago, I remember looking at Bert Olmstead and Dave Keon. Bert, at age 35, was subdued, tired, hurting, and relieved that it was over. Dave had just turned 22, and was elated, energetic, and his boyish smile revealed that a dream had come true for him. Bert never again put on his hockey equipment. Dave played for another 20 seasons."

— Billy Harris, *The Glory Years* (1989)

"When you win the last game you play, you'll never go wrong."

— Bert Olmstead, acknowledging to reporters that he would likely retire

There were those at the time who didn't believe Olmstead really planned to retire, but he had made it known that he had coaching aspirations. Though he denied reports that he considered himself in line for the coaching job when Punch Imlach gave it up, there were stories about growing tensions between the two men.

> "Imlach, even with success, was insecure, and his treatment of Olmstead reflected that…. The Major [Conn Smythe] commented that Olmstead 'had the qualities to be the next Maple Leafs coach.' Coach Imlach, I think, heard this loud and clear and reacted by dealing Olmstead away."
>
> — Billy Harris, *The Glory Years* (1989)

The Leafs didn't literally deal away Olmstead, but they did make him available to other teams in the Intra-League Draft in early June. Olmstead claimed he had not been made aware of the decision until he was selected by the New York Rangers.

> "I didn't see how they could protect an old man like me but I thought they might convince other clubs that I was too old to be useful."
>
> — Olmstead on being drafted, June 7, 1962

> "I talked to a Ranger representative and there was some mention of an opportunity to coach. But I didn't hear a firm offer and I didn't make a firm commitment."
>
> — Olmstead after being drafted

> "Imlach will hold on as coach as long as possible and then, when he becomes strictly general manager, he'll hire a coach he can manipulate."
>
> — Bert Olmstead, June 7, 1962

Olmstead decided he would not report to the Rangers and he retired before the 1962–63 season. He later coached with the Vancouver Canucks of the Western Hockey League from 1965 to 1967 and returned to the NHL after expansion as the coach and general manager of the Oakland Seals (AKA California Seals) in 1967–68.

1962–63

Heading into a new season as defending champions, the Leafs coach and general manager had a lofty goal in mind — something the team hadn't accomplished since the 1947–48 season. "Finishing first and winning the Stanley Cup is one thing we haven't done. I'd like that," said Imlach.

But there were distractions. Toward the end of training camp, on the eve of the NHL All-Star game that would pit the defending Stanley Cup champion Maple Leafs against an NHL All-Star team, a story came up that would briefly dominate the headlines. Frank Mahovlich had been a holdout and Punch Imlach was having difficulty signing him.

A Million for Mahovlich

"The Leafs management should have taken care of all that business before camp started. My father and I had talked about it and we thought we'd just see what they'd offer. I had been making $15,000 and was looking for a good raise. I wanted $25,000 or $30,000, which was peanuts, but you couldn't get any more because they'd say, 'Gordie Howe only makes this much,' or 'Jean Beliveau is only getting $25,000.' They'd use that against you…. When it came time for them to make an offer, their offer was maybe a thousand-dollar raise. It was ridiculous. I just got up and said, 'To hell with you guys!' I didn't even want to argue with them it was so ridiculous … And I walked out on them."

— Frank Mahovlich, *The Big M* (1999)

Mahovlich was still unsigned on the night of Friday, October 5, 1962, when the annual NHL All-Star dinner was held at Toronto's Royal York Hotel. Harold Ballard was complaining to Chicago Black Hawks owner Jim Norris about the trouble with getting Mahovlich to sign his contract.

"Punch and I walked into a suite of rooms at the Royal York Hotel, where a whole bunch of people were talking hockey. We no sooner walked in the door when Harold Ballard grabbed us and said, 'Listen, Jim Norris just offered me a million dollars for Frank Mahovlich."

— King Clancy, *Clancy* (1968)

"Jim Norris got into it about the value of money with Harold Ballard and some other Leaf directors. It evolved into Norris offering the Leafs $1 million for Mahovlich, who was worth every penny of it."

— Tommy Ivan, Black Hawks GM at the time, quoted by Frank Orr, *Toronto Star*, March 31, 1990

"As general manager, I'd make that deal. But as coach I couldn't because the million dollars can't play left wing for me."

— Punch Imlach, *Hockey Is a Battle* (1969)

Punch's reaction was recorded somewhat differently at the time by Gordon Campbell of the *Toronto Star*, who was in the suite with Ballard and Norris and taking notes.

"You're a witness," Norris said to Gordon Campbell.

"Okay. Count me in. Is your million dollars in Canadian or U.S. currency?" Campbell asked.

"In Canadian. Will you take it?" Norris asked Harold Ballard.

"Yes," was his reply.

With that, Norris took a sheet of hotel stationary from a desk in the room. *"I will pay $1,000,000 for Frank Mahovlich,"* he wrote.

Ballard and Jack Amell both signed the paper, but Punch Imlach refused to shake hands with Norris on the deal.

"I'll recommend that it be accepted, though I don't think Mahovlich is worth that kind of money."

— Punch Imlach, quoted by Gordon Campbell

If Harold Ballard, shaking hands here with former Leafs great Turk Broda, had had the control of the team he would have later, Frank Mahovlich would have been sold to Chicago for $1 million.

"Ballard and Amell didn't have the power to make the deal. Nobody did without clearing it with me, unless I was fired first. But they wrote 'accepted' on the paper and signed it for the Leafs hockey committee. Then Norris took out his roll and said, 'How much earnest money do you need?' Ballard said, 'You're good with us, you don't have to pay anything down.' But Jim insisted on peeling off a thousand dollars in U.S. bank-notes and giving them to Ballard."

— Punch Imlach, *Hockey Is a Battle* (1969)

"I have $1,000 in my pocket right now confirming the deal, and Norris will be in Maple Leaf Gardens [Saturday] morning with the other $999,000."

— Harold Ballard to Ted Damata, *Chicago Tribune*, October 6, 1962

"Punch did not sign the paper, but he said, 'My advice is to sell him.' I have Jim Norris' $1,000 down payment and he has signed the paper to consummate the deal."

— Harold Ballard, reported in the *Toronto Daily Star*, October 6, 1962

"I don't know about that, but you can't turn down a million dollars."

— Harold Ballard, when asked if he thought the sale
would cost the Maple Leafs the Stanley Cup

"Jim Norris has made an offer of $1,000,000 for Mahovlich. I will not consider such a deal at a party. If he would like to meet me in my office at noon [on Saturday] and make the same offer, I am interested."

— Stafford Smythe, quoted by Jim Vipond,
Globe and Mail, Toronto, October 6, 1962

The next morning, Norris had a cheque made out and delivered to Maple Leaf Gardens.

"I was the guy who delivered the check. You don't forget having a million dollars in your pocket. At the time, it was more money than anybody had ever paid for an athlete."

— Tommy Ivan to Milt Dunnell, *Toronto Star*, July 3, 1994

"I was walking into the office, and Tommy Ivan was walking out with a check. The papers wanted to take a picture, but he was angry and walked right by."

— Frank Mahovlich, *The Big M* (1999)

"The Leaf guys got cold feet on the deal."
— Tommy Ivan, quoted by Frank Orr, *Toronto Star*, March 31, 1990

Stafford Smythe announced that he had no authority to conduct such a large transaction until he had conferred with his board of directors.

"There was some further conversation, but they wouldn't accept the check."
— Tommy Ivan to Milt Dunnell, *Toronto Star*, July 3, 1994

It wasn't reported at the time, but Milt Dunnell would later write that Stafford Smythe had spoken to his father about the deal around 3:00 a.m. on Saturday morning. Conn Smythe was apparently concerned that the Leafs would be taking advantage of Norris when he was drunk because no hockey player was worth $1 million … and that if any player actually was, he should be playing in Toronto and not Chicago.

"I don't know if the late Jim Norris was kidding or not when he offered a million bucks for Frank six years ago, but I know this: If we had gotten him, we'd really have cranked some firepower on the left side."
— "Hockey with Bobby Hull," *Toronto Daily Star*, March 9, 1968

"It might have started out [as a gag], but Norris got serious. The check I carried very nervously was a good one — and it wouldn't have bounced, either. If the Leafs had taken it, I suppose the Big M would have been a Blackhawk."
— Tommy Ivan, quoted by Frank Orr, *Toronto Star*, March 31, 1990

Meanwhile, as Stafford Smythe was meeting Tommy Ivan, Frank Mahovlich had been making his way to Maple Leaf Gardens to meet with Imlach and Clancy. "[They said to me] 'Come on in — here's what you wanted, sign here,'" said Mahovlich in *The Big M* in 1999. "It was all cut and dried. They didn't want to discuss it. They just said, 'Sign here.' I didn't know I was worth a million dollars. I never had a chance to think about it, everything happened so fast. By the time I got to the rink … they had me signed. And I thought I won the argument. Well, I didn't really win. When I found out what I was worth, I should have been getting $100,000 instead of $25,000."

The Leafs beat the All-Stars 4–1 that Saturday night, and then opened the season on Wednesday, October 10, with a 3–1 victory in Chicago. Jim Norris continued to insist that Mahovlich should now be his property, but the next day, Toronto formally turned down the deal.

"I have had a long meeting with John Bassett and Harold Ballard, my partners in control of Maple Leaf Gardens to discuss the Mahovlich matter fully. We have unanimously agreed not to accept the offer of $1,000,000 for this player."
                                                — Stafford Smythe, October 11, 1962

"It is with regret we have been informed that Stafford Smythe and his directors have rejected our offer. Evidently, they value Mahovlich as highly as we do."
                                                        — Jim Norris, October 11, 1962

"From 1962 on, I had trouble with management. I never really felt comfortable with the team after 1962. It was a real drag on me. My relationship with Imlach suffered and it never got repaired."
                                                    — Frank Mahovlich, *The Big M* (1999)

Strong Season and Another Stanley Cup

On the ice, Frank Mahovlich had another big season for the Maple Leafs in 1962–63. He led the team, and ranked among the NHL leaders, with 36 goals and 73 points. Red Kelly and Dave Keon also had good offensive seasons, while a strong defence nearly saw Johnny Bower claim the Vezina Trophy.

"When I look back on our team, one guy would lead one night, and another guy would pick up the flag and go another night. We had five or six great leaders, Red Kelly, Allan Stanley, and so on. But some nights, our leaders were different people, and that's what makes a great team."
                    — on the 1962–63 season, Frank Mahovlich, *The Big M* (1999)

With a ten-game unbeaten streak (seven wins, three ties) down the stretch, Toronto finished atop the NHL standings in the tightest race in league history. Only five points separated first-place Toronto (35–23–12, 82 points) from fourth place Detroit (77 points), with Chicago finishing second (81 points) and Montreal third (79 points). The Leafs actually lost their last two games of the season, but there was no cause for concern heading into the playoffs.

"They were pressing for 10 games to earn the pennant and if our streak had to end, this was the right spot.... They'll bounce back for the opening of our Stanley Cup semifinals against Montreal Canadiens at home tomorrow night."
                            — Punch Imlach on the off day between the end of
                                        the season and start of the playoffs

The Leafs won three straight to open the series against the Canadiens and wrapped it up in five games. Johnny Bower recorded two shutouts as Toronto's strong defence frustrated Montreal. But there was some frustration in the Leafs' camp, too.

"Young fellow, you listen closely to that man Imlach. He doesn't do it in exact words, but he says 'I won, they lost, we tied.' Between you and me and the gatepost, he makes it sound like he doesn't need us players at all."
— Tim Horton to a reporter during the Leafs' semifinal series

When Detroit beat Chicago in six games, it would be the Leafs and Red Wings for the Stanley Cup. Detroit had a slight edge on Toronto during the regular season with seven wins and a tie in their 14 games, but oddsmakers made the Leafs strong favourites in the Final.

"Leafs will be favourites and rightly so, but if Wings keep hustling the way they did against us, they'll put up a tremendous argument. An upset wouldn't surprise me a bit. Wings are perfectly capable of pulling it off."
— Chicago coach Rudy Pilous

"I don't know where the experts came up with that 'lead-pipe cinch' routine. I'm plenty worried about Wings. They gave us trouble all season. They can skate, they never stop checking, and they've got Gordie Howe."
— Leafs captain George Armstrong

"Leafs will win because they have the better third line. I think Wings can match any two lines Imlach can toss out, but they haven't a third line to compare with his."
— former Maple Leaf and current Bruins scout Baldy Cotton

Every game in the series was a tight, defensive struggle, but the Leafs prevailed in five to win the Stanley Cup.

"I hope we can win it again next year."
— Johnny Bower in the dressing room after Game 5

"I'll be back if they want me. Got to go for three in a row you know."
— Allan Stanley after Game 5

Dave Keon was a big part of all four Stanley Cup victories in the 1960s. Here, he accepts the Conn Smythe Trophy from Harold Ballard as MVP of the 1967 playoffs.

"I'm not certain. I'll give it some serious thought, but right now I'm looking forward to a vacation."

— Red Kelly

"Is there a practice tomorrow?"

— Eddie Litzenberger to Punch Imlach

1963–64

The Maple Leafs did not look like a team capable of winning a third straight Stanley Cup title for much of the 1963–64 season. Once again Johnny Bower was strong in goal behind a defence led by Tim Horton and Allan Stanley,

The Leafs' Carl Brewer and the Rangers' Andy Bathgate sit together during the era when NHL rinks had only one penalty box. They would soon be sitting together on the same bench as Toronto teammates.

although Bobby Baun and Carl Brewer lost a lot of time to injuries, which led to more action for Kent Douglas and Larry Hillman. Still, the biggest concern was a slumping offence that was struggling to score goals.

Fifty-five games into the 70-game season, Toronto had managed a record barely above .500 at 24–21–10. The Leafs were in third place, but their 58 points had them just four up on fourth-place Detroit while Montreal and Chicago were battling for top spot with 71 points apiece.

> "We had the same team that had finished first the previous spring and had manhandled Montreal and Detroit in the playoffs. But by midseason I knew we were in trouble.... I became more and more convinced that we weren't going to win a Stanley Cup that year, or even come close, unless I shook up the hockey club.... I felt I had to do something right at the core of the team to get these guys going again. And that's when I started seriously thinking again about a trade I had been trying to make off and on for a few years — to get Andy Bathgate from New York."
>
> — Punch Imlach, *Hockey Is a Battle* (1969)

Blockbuster for Bathgate

With the Rangers in town for the first of home-and-home games on Saturday, February 22, 1964, Imlach pulled the trigger. He sent slumping Leafs Dick Duff and Bob Nevin, as well as Rod Seiling, Arnie Brown, and Bill Collins, to New York for Andy Bathgate and Don McKenney.

Stafford Smythe told reporters the original deal had just been a discussion of Duff for McKenney.

"All the rest — the other four — were for Bathgate.... Seiling was the clincher. They wouldn't even talk about Bathgate if we weren't willing to give up Seiling.... You know, we've been trying to get [Bathgate] for three years."
— Stafford Smythe to reporters after the trade

"You dream of something like this but it just doesn't happen.... I've been mentioned for a lot of trades but after the one fell through last month, I figured that was it for this season.... This is the biggest break of my life.... Although I've been in the New York organization since I was nine, there's a soft spot in my heart for Leafs. They're a good team and a contender and I think I can help them. On top of everything else, I like Toronto."
— Andy Bathgate

"I feel five years younger already. Leafs skate and move the puck the way we did in Barrie when I was a junior. This is my kind of hockey."
— Don McKenney

"Andy will do two things that'll make a tremendous difference for Leafs. He's an expert on the power play, where Leafs need help, and he has an excellent shot. With those two improvements, they'll be awfully tough to beat. Losing him will hurt us. Bathgate is a great player and McKenney a good one. But we had to do something about our defensive record. That's what's holding us back."
— Rangers coach Red Sullivan

"This deal was made for the present. As far as the future is concerned, we have so many good men in junior hockey, and below, that our farm system is jamming up."
— Leafs vice president Harold Ballard

"There has been a lot of controversy and some criticism of me over that deal since. It was pretty plain that we were going to get the short-term advantage but Rangers would get the long-term advantage. That was okay with me. I thought the addition of Bathgate and McKenney, plus the mental shaking up the trade would give the rest of the Leafs, would win the Stanley Cup — and it did."

— Punch Imlach, *Hockey Is a Battle* (1969)

"Punch Imlach told me about it over the phone. I was pretty disappointed. I had been in their organization for 13 years and I thought they should have told me about the trade to my face instead of calling me on the telephone. If I had time to think about it, I might have quit the game. But I joined the Rangers and that same night we played against the Leafs in Maple Leaf Gardens. I think I just went through the motions, I was that stunned."

— Dick Duff, recalling the trade in later years

The Playoffs

The Leafs went 9–4–2 in their final 15 games of the 1963–64 season. While they still finished in third place (33–25–12, 78 points) they were much closer to the Canadiens (85 points) and Black Hawks (84) and put some distance between themselves and the fourth-place Red Wings (71 points).

Toronto faced Montreal in the semifinals and defeated them in seven tough games. Frank Mahovlich had a strong series, while Johnny Bower and Dave Keon starred in games six and seven as Toronto rebounded from a 3–2 series deficit. Bower made 38 saves and Keon scored a hat trick in the Leafs' 3–1 victory in Game 7.

In the other semifinal, Chicago and Detroit also went seven games before the Red Wings knocked off the Black Hawks. So it was Toronto and Detroit in the Stanley Cup Final for the second year in a row. This was another tight series, with five of the first six games decided by a single goal. The Maple Leafs' 4–3 overtime victory on April 23, 1964, to even the series in Game 6 included a legendary moment.

Bobby Baun's Broken Ankle

In his career, Bobby Baun scored 37 goals in 964 NHL regular season games. He added just three more in 96 playoff games. But like Bill Barilko — another defenceman of a generation before who was otherwise known mostly for his hard hits — Baun scored one of the most famous goals in hockey history.

"You have to pinch yourself. I never scored that many goals. That's how the tilt in life comes. It's like Paul Henderson and the '72 goal," Baun told Scott Burnside of the *National Post* in 2000.

Bob Pulford had put the Maple Leafs ahead of the Red Wings 1–0 with a short-handed goal late in the first period of Game 6 of the 1964 Final. At the end of two periods, the game was tied 3–3. It remained that way midway into the third period when Baun took a hard shot off his right leg just above the ankle. Even at the time, reporters seemed to confuse whether it was Gordie Howe or Alex Delvecchio who had fired the puck. Baun played on, and a short time later there was a whistle to stop the play in the Leafs end. Even then, Baun didn't go off.

"I've got a lot of mileage from [the story].... I stopped a shot at the blue line to start with. I went back into the face-off circle with Gordie Howe. In the old days, defencemen used to take the face-off."
— Bob Baun to Mike Rawn, *Guelph Mercury*, May 11, 2006

"I took [the face-off] with Howe. Then I wheeled and my leg just turned to cream cheese."
— Bobby Baun to reporters at the time after the game

Baun fell to his knees, then struggled back to his feet, but when the puck was cleared over the glass about six seconds later, he was sprawled on the ice in front of Johnny Bower. A few minutes later, he was carried off the ice on a stretcher. The time was either 13:14 or 13:46 of the third period — newspapers at the time reported both.

"An emergency team led by trainer Robert Haggert carted Baun to the Leaf dressing room while the game went on. Dr. Jim Murray of the Leaf medical staff consulted with Dr. Bill Stromberg, a Leaf fan in town from Chicago. The patient was in pain."
— Dick Beddoes, *Globe and Mail*, Toronto, April 24, 1964

"When Baun was hauled off on a stretcher ... the only thing that remained to be decided was whether services for the Leafs should be public or private. Word reached the press box that Baun's right ankle was sprained or broken. In five minutes, he was back. This led to a rumour that Jim Murray, the Leaf doctor, had hacked a leg off Eddie Shack and changed Baun's flat tire."
— Milt Dunnell, *Toronto Daily Star*, April 24, 1964

"'Freeze it,' Baun suggested. Dr. Stromberg took out his hypodermic needle and did the deed. Hypoed to the hip, Baun clumped back to the Toronto bench. He hopped on the ice before Coach George Imlach could restrain him."

— Dick Beddoes, April 24, 1964

"Nothing could have held Baun. He had a charge in him that would have blown up the rink."

— Punch Imlach to reporters after the game

"I want it known that it was my decision to get back into the game after being hurt."

— Baun after the game

When the third period ended, the game was still tied 3–3, so the teams went back to the dressing room to prepare for overtime. "I knew it was broken but I wanted to get out there in overtime. The trainer gave me [another] shot of painkiller and we laced the skate up tight," recalled Baun.

He was late getting back to the bench and the overtime period was already underway. Imlach was about to send Kent Douglas onto the ice, but as Baun told Dough Fischer of the *Kingston Whig Standard* in 2004, "I yelled at Douglas, 'You stay put, I'm goin' out there.' Within seconds the puck came back to me at the Detroit blue line…."

Dave Keon had won a face-off at 1:33 of overtime. He drew the puck back to Carl Brewer, who backhanded it deep into Red Wings territory. Detroit's Al Langlois tried to fire it out, but Baun, pinching in from the blue line, cut off the clearing attempt.

"The puck came to me," Baun told Mike Rawn in 2006, "and I had a good shot on the net. It did what I call a triple flutter blast with a follow-up blooper. It wasn't one of those beautiful goals, as most overtime goals are always strange. It went off [Detroit defenceman Bill] Gadsby's stick, which he still hasn't forgiven me for, and it went the opposite way on [goalie Terry] Sawchuk."

"If I hadn't put my stick up it would have hit me in the face. It might have been better. I didn't try to put the s.o.b. in my net. I don't think Baun ever broke his leg. He had a crappy shot."

— Bill Gadsby to the *Detroit News*, told by Paul Hunter, *Toronto Star*, June 4, 1995

"That's how it goes in this game. I had a good line on that lousy bouncer by Baun. Then at the last minute it hit the shaft of Bill Gadsby's stick and shot to the top corner. I never had a chance."

— Detroit goalie Terry Sawchuk

"I've got a lot of mileage out of that one. Most of the time when I engage in a talk, people bring that up. People have told their children about it. I have little wee ones who know more about it than I know. It makes you realize how much people love their Maple Leafs."

— Bob Baun to Doug Graham, *Kingston Whig Standard*, July 3, 2004

"I never saw it as anything especially brave. I just wanted to play if I could and help the Leafs win the third Stanley Cup. People talk about me scoring the goal in great pain but the really tough part of it was playing the seventh game. It just plain hurt."

— Bob Baun recalling the story for Frank Orr, *Toronto Star*, January 24, 1987

Game 7

Bobby Baun was not the only Leaf nursing a serious injury heading into Game 7. Red Kelly had been forced out of action in the third period of Game 6 after being sandwiched between Gordie Howe and Bill Gadsby. He'd stretched the ligaments in his knee. Don McKenney had already been knocked out of the series with torn knee ligaments in Game 5. Both Baun and Kelly were considered doubtful for Game 7, but both played.

"Bobby Baun was in pain as he undressed, but he had nowhere near the pain that Red Kelly was experiencing. Tim Horton, Allan Stanley, and Ron Stewart carried Kelly from the shower to a stretcher, and he was then transferred to an ambulance that took him to the hospital. As the freezing in his knee wore off, the pain became unbearable. I don't believe that Red would have subjected himself to this kind of personal punishment had we not been playing the Detroit Red Wings. Kelly had played 13 years for the Red Wings and Jack Adams and had then been discarded."

— Billy Harris, *The Glory Years* (1989)

Andy Bathgate put the Maple Leafs on top just three minutes into the game. Only Terry Sawchuk kept Detroit close after that until Toronto finally broke it open with three goals in the third period for a 4–0 victory.

The Leafs gave up a lot of their future to obtain Andy Bathgate, but it paid off in a Stanley Cup victory in 1964. Bathgate never got along with Punch Imlach and would be traded to Detroit in 1965.

"I feel jolted. It's an accomplishment I can't quite realize. It happened so fast, in two months up from the struggle in the valley to the top of the world."

— Andy Bathgate after the game

"I've never seen the team more worked up. There's only one explanation, and the best word I can think of is 'heart.' Think of what Kelly and Baun went through, playing with those injuries. Look at Allan Stanley. Physically, he should be washed up but he's got heart when the games really count. Look at Johnny Bower. How else can you account for him? Hell, he gets tuckered out when we go for a walk in the afternoon. But look at the way he's played. And with guys like that coming through, the others have an example to live up to and they dig in and work."

— Leafs captain George Armstrong

"They told me it wasn't the main bone in my leg that was broken, so I told them I wouldn't worry about it until the series was won. I suppose the leg may be in a cast — but I've got all summer to get over it."

— Bob Baun

"We're still the world's greatest hockey team. And, we save our best game for the finale."

— Carl Brewer

"They were just too much. We gave it our best shot, but it wasn't good enough."
— Detroit captain Alex Delvecchio

1964–65 AND 1965–66

The Leafs would finish the 1964–65 season in fourth place with 74 points. They won four of five games to finish the regular season, but were eliminated from the playoffs in the semifinals when they were defeated by the Montreal Canadiens in six games. Montreal went on to beat Chicago for the Stanley Cup.

Ron Ellis had made his NHL debut this season and had a strong rookie year, playing in 62 games and tying Frank Mahovlich for the team lead with 23 goals.

"I was the first change they made to those three Stanley Cup winners. It was frightening to join that club, but true to the character of that team, they made me feel welcome and part of it, which was likely due to the fact I had been a Marlie. We always practised before or after them, so they were familiar with me."

— Ron Ellis in Ross Brewitt, *Clear the Track* (1997)

Frank Mahovlich was having an increasingly difficult time dealing with Punch Imlach, who was constantly on him. He played just 59 games, missing a month of the season due to fatigue and depression. Andy Bathgate, Allan Stanley, and George Armstrong also missed time due to injuries. The offence struggled, but the defence was solid as ever with Tim Horton, Bobby Baun, and Carl Brewer all playing 70 games, and Kent Douglas seeing plenty of action, too. The beneficiary was Johnny Bower and his new goaltending partner, Terry Sawchuk.

Sawchuk, Bower, and the Vezina Trophy

Despite a solid season and his particularly strong play in the Stanley Cup Final, the Detroit Red Wings had decided to release Terry Sawchuk after the 1963–64 season. They would go with Roger Crozier in goal, and made Sawchuk available in the Intra-League Draft. The Leafs picked him up on June 10, 1964, for just $20,000.

"With Sawchuk in camp we'll have the two goalkeepers who played so well in the Stanley Cup Final last April. Sawchuk gives us a great one-two punch in goal. We've been trying to land him for about four seasons."

— Punch Imlach on the Leafs' acquisition of Terry Sawchuk

"I was knocked for a loop when I heard the news; too stunned to think properly. I had a good year last season and never dreamed Detroit would leave me unprotected. But after a couple of hours I decided it was a helluva break. Toronto has a lot more talent than Detroit. It means moving up one notch right away and I think it will be the way to first place because I believe the Leafs are that good."

— Terry Sawchuk, reacting to his acquisition by Toronto

"It was quite a shock to me, not because I was worried about keeping my job, but because I was really surprised that Detroit would let a goalie of that caliber go. When we got Sawchuk, I told Punch right off the bat, 'I don't know how you got him, but we're going to win another Stanley Cup.'"

— on the Leafs' acquisition of Terry Sawchuk,
Johnny Bower, *The China Wall* (2006)

Plans for how the Leafs would use their two future Hall of Fame goaltenders were outlined early.

"I'll start with Bower and play it by ear. Until proven otherwise, John deserves first crack. But anybody who saw films of the Stanley Cup Final knows why I wouldn't hesitate to use Sawchuk."

— Punch Imlach at the start of training camp in Peterborough, Ontario

"The two-goalie system was an adjustment for me. I guess with me turning 40, Punch was worried about how much game I had left in me, but I thrived on hard work and I wanted to play every game. I felt that at my age, I had to play every game. I wanted to keep playing. Sawchuk was different. Punch knew Sawchuk could sit on the bench for 40 minutes, then come in and play a sensational game. He didn't need a warm-up. That's the way he was in practice, too. He never worked hard, except in the game.

Sawchuk could stand there. He didn't need the warm-ups like I did. He figured he'd save all his good playing for the game, which he did, but in practice he didn't try as much as I did. You'd shoot the puck in practice and if you hit him, you hit him. If you didn't, it went in. He waved at shots more than anything else. Punch knew he could put Sawchuk in at any time, whereas Bruce Gamble and I, we weren't the same until we had a good solid warm-up."

— Johnny Bower, *The China Wall* (2006)

The partnership between Bower and Sawchuk went well right from the start, and by late February it was clear the two might combine to win the Vezina Trophy.

"For the first time in the 39-year history of the award, there may be two winners of the Vezina Trophy this ... season.... The Vezina is awarded to the goalie playing most games for the team allowing the fewest goals. Leafs are leading with an average of 2.38 compared to 2.46 for Chicago Black Hawks and 2.47 for Detroit Red Wings. (Averages are used here because all teams have not played same amount of games.) Bower has played 28 games, Sawchuk 27. And manager-coach Punch Imlach candidly admits 'they'll play 35 each if I have any control over it.' ... The last time such a possibility occurred was in 1950–51, also with Leafs. However, Al Rollins [was awarded the Vezina], playing 39 games to Turk Broda's 31."

— *Globe and Mail*, Toronto, February 23, 1965

"At the start of the season, we shook hands and I said, 'Terry, no matter what happens, if I win the [$1,000] for the Vezina myself, I'll split the prize money with you.' He said, 'Okay, likewise.'"

— Johnny Bower, *The China Wall* (2006)

But the NHL did not yet have a rule in place allowing for two goalies to share the Vezina Trophy.

"The possibility of Leafs winning the Vezina has created a potentially ridiculous situation where Sawchuk will play 36 games and win the award, Bower 34 and win nothing from the league. They'll split the cash [but] the trophy goes to the goalie playing the most games for the team allowing the fewest goals."

— *Globe and Mail*, Toronto, March 27, 1965

"With most teams [now] playing two goalies, there may be a change next season, but nothing can be done this year."

— NHL publicist Ron Andrews, March 27, 1965

When Johnny Bower recorded a 4–0 shutout over Detroit in the final game of the regular season on March 28, 1965, that clinched the Vezina Trophy for Toronto with 173 goals against compared to 175 for Detroit and 176 for Chicago. Terry Sawchuk reiterated what he had been saying for weeks; that he would not accept the trophy unless there was a joint presentation that included Bower.

"It was a team win. But the Vezina belongs to Terry. He played 36 games and won more games than I did."

— Johnny Bower after the season's final game

"Nuts. I'll split the bonus money with him, but John's name belongs on the trophy."

— Terry Sawchuk

Terry Sawchuk (left) and Johnny Bower (right) became the first teammates to share the Vezina Trophy in 1964–65. They're seen here celebrating together after the Leafs' Stanley Cup victory in 1967.

"The league is now forcing all teams to carry two goalkeepers, so it is only sensible that the Vezina should be a joint award. It is ridiculous that a man playing 36 games should get everything and the guy playing 34 games gets nothing."

— Bob Pulford, Maple Leafs player representative

"National Hockey League President Clarence Campbell sees no reason why both Terry Sawchuk and Johnny Bower can't have their names engraved on the Vezina Trophy. The president says it is a matter for the league governors to decide."

— *Toronto Daily Star*, March 30, 1965

But the governors would not meet until June. Meantime, on April 20, 1965, Bower and Sawchuk held a party for their teammates at the Conroy Hotel in Toronto.

"We threw a big party at the end of the season and it cost us more than the money we earned for winning the Vezina. I think it cost us $500–$600 each, but it was worth it."

— Johnny Bower, *The China Wall* (2006)

Six weeks later, a ruling came down from the NHL:

> The National Hockey League Board of Governors ruled yesterday that from now on the Vezina Trophy for goaltending will be awarded to both goaltenders if the winning team has two regular netminders. The monetary reward of $1,000 may be split by arrangement of the netminders involved. The joint award will be made providing each player has participated in 25 or more games. The governors made the change retroactive to last season. Their action means Toronto Maple Leafs veteran Johnny Bower's name will be inscribed [along side] that of teammate Terry Sawchuk for the 1964–65 season.

1965–66

After failing to win their fourth straight Stanley Cup, changes seemed inevitable heading into 1965–66.

"I don't know what players will be back. Maybe I'll be gone. There have to be changes when you lose the Stanley Cup after winning it for three successive years. But I'm sure this will be a better hockey team next season. We had the idea we could take any game we had to win. Canadiens proved we were wrong. Now the fellows know they can't win any time they have to. So those who return will have a better attitude."

— Captain George Armstrong, the day after the Canadiens
eliminated the Leafs from the 1965 playoffs

One big change would see the Leafs get even older. On May 20, 1965, Toronto traded Andy Bathgate, Billy Harris, and Gary Jarrett to Detroit for Marcel Pronovost, Ed Joyal, Aut Erickson, Larry Jeffrey, and Lowell McDonald. The soon-to-be 35-year-old Pronovost was the key player coming to Toronto, while Bathgate was the player Detroit wanted.

"It started out as a 1-for-1 situation. Then Sid [Abel] and I decided we might as well make it a jim-dandy of a trade and he gave me five for three. I think we did very well. Pronovost will help shore up the left side of the defence where we had trouble all last season."

— Punch Imlach on the big trade

"I hated to see Marcel [Pronovost] go. I played with him and coached him, but we had to give up something. I had to give up a valuable player to get a player of the calibre of Bathgate."

— Detroit coach and GM Sid Abel

The acquisition of Pronovost would prove especially useful when Carl Brewer retired unexpectedly at the end of training camp in October. Rookie forwards Brit Selby, Pete Stemkowski, and Wally Boyer all saw regular action for the Leafs this season, but despite a deep farm system, Punch Imlach remained loyal to his veterans. That was made clear at the annual Intra-League Draft on June 9, 1965. With only two goalies from the organization allowed to be protected, it was thought the Leafs would hang on to Johnny Bower and minor-league prospect Gerry Cheevers while exposing Terry Sawchuk. But they didn't.

"I have always rated players who have played in the NHL over those who have not. Sawchuk and Bower have made it. Cheevers has yet to prove he is an NHL goalkeeper. Why should I gamble?"

— Punch Imlach

Bower had another strong season in the Leafs' net, playing 35 games with a record of 18–10–5 and leading the NHL in goals-against average (2.25) for the third straight season. Sawchuk struggled with a record of 10–11–3 and a 3.16 average in 27 games. The Leafs also used goalies Bruce Gamble (10 games), Al Smith (two), and Gary Smith (three) to varying degrees of success.

On offence, Frank Mahovlich rebounded to score 32 goals, which was a distant second in the NHL behind Bobby Hull's record-breaking 54. Bob Pulford (28 — a career high), Eddie Shack (26), and Dave Keon (24) also ranked among the league's best goal scorers, while George Armstrong was among the assist leaders with a team-best 35. Rookie Brit Selby played 61 games and had 14 goals and 13 assists, which was good enough to earn him the Calder Trophy.

"In those days, few players scored 30 goals. Teams just wanted you to check and I was glad to be up there. It was only a six-team league and few clubs brought up more than two rookies a year."
— Brit Selby to Paul Patton, *Globe and Mail*, Toronto, March 7, 1986

The Leafs improved to 79 points this season and finished in third place, but were swept out of the playoffs by the first-place Montreal Canadiens who went on to win their second straight Stanley Cup title over Detroit.

Punch Imlach had one year left on his contract, but there were rumours he would leave the Leafs to begin working for the expansion team in Los Angeles that was slated to enter the NHL in 1967–68. Red Kelly had made it known he was looking for a coaching job and stories had him taking over for Imlach behind the Leafs bench. It was also hinted that George Armstrong and Johnny Bower might retire. But by April 20, 1966, Imlach had signed a three-year extension to remain in Toronto. The players would all be back, too.

1966–67

Most hockey experts dismissed the Maple Leafs as too old to win in 1966–67. Even so, the team had added some younger players. Despite his Calder Trophy win, Brit Selby spent most of the year in the minors, but Brian Conacher would spend his first full season in the NHL and Mike Walton would see action, too. Ron Ellis and Pete Stemkowski both continued to improve. Dave Keon was in his seventh season, but was still just 26 years old — a year younger than Jim Pappin, who would be a key contributor.

The Leafs had a good first half of the season. After a win at home on January 14, they moved past the midway point with a record of 17–11–8. Their 42 points in 36 games had them just three points back of New York and Chicago, who were tied for first place with 45 points. But then the team lost ten in a row and tumbled into fifth place. The Leafs snapped their slide on February 11 with a 4–4 tie against the red-hot Black Hawks, who were pulling away from the rest of the pack. They then climbed up to fourth place with two straight wins.

Then, on February 18, Punch Imlach held his usual 11:00 a.m. meeting with the players prior to their game that evening with the Bruins. Afterward, he complained of chest pains and King Clancy insisted he see a doctor. Clancy would run the team that night, and the Leafs won the game 5–3.

> "I told them [Imlach] couldn't make the game, that everyone would get a chance to play and that I was asking for 100 percent effort, which I got."
> — King Clancy to reporters after the game

There were rumours that Imlach had suffered a heart attack, and later there was a diagnosis of a hiatus hernia. Mainly, though, Imlach was suffering from exhaustion. He would remain hospitalized for a few weeks, while the team rattled off five straight wins en route to a 7–1–2 record in 10 games under Clancy.

> "Everybody remembers 1967 as Canada's Centennial Year. I recall it as the season I got back in to coach again — briefly…. It turned out to be an easy chore to run that club. I wasn't afraid to make a mistake. I gave a little pat on the back to the players who were down … [and] for the next few games the club went on a tear…. Players like Allan Stanley and Ron Ellis said some nice things about my coaching stint. Stanley told a reporter that I was the spark that led the Leafs to another Stanley Cup that spring. But I didn't deserve that kind of credit. That was Imlach's team."
> — King Clancy, *Clancy* (1968)

> "A team is like a musical instrument. You tune it up, and it's as good as it gets. If you tighten it, it will break. And that's what happened to us — we broke. So, in comes Clancy and he was the opposite to Imlach…. He just let the reins go. Everybody did what came naturally."
> — Frank Mahovlich, *The Big M* (1999)

Imlach was back behind the bench on March 12 and remained there for the rest of the season. The Leafs finished the final 11 games with six wins and five losses, ending the 1966–67 season in third place with a record of 32–27–11 for 75 points. They were just two points back of second-place Montreal, but

19 back of the Black Hawks. Chicago ended the season with 94 points on a record of 41–17–12 and finished in first place in the NHL standings for the first time in franchise history.

Bobby Hull led the NHL with 52 goals, while Stan Mikita was tops with 62 assists and 97 points and would win both the Hart and Lady Byng trophies in addition to the Art Ross. The Black Hawks' 264 goals were 52 more than any other team and their 170 goals against gave Glenn Hall the Vezina Trophy by a comfortable margin. Chicago was a heavy favourite heading into the semifinals against Toronto, but Punch Imlach professed not to be concerned.

"I feel great about meeting Chicago. This is a new deal, forget the season. Last year, we had an edge on Canadiens in the regular schedule and they bounced us four straight in the playoffs. You might as well meet the best right off the handle; we're the underdogs and usually do well when downgraded by the experts."

— Punch Imlach, April 3, 1967

Semifinal versus Chicago

The Black Hawks definitely appeared to be the stronger team as the series opened, scoring a 5–2 win at home in Game 1. The Leafs bounced back with two straight wins, but then Chicago took Game 4 to even the series. Terry Sawchuk had been brilliant to this point in the series, but was banged up. The Hawks' Glenn Hall had also been hurt, and while it was known that Denis Dejordy would be in net for Chicago in Game 5, Punch Imlach wouldn't say whether he would go with Sawchuk or Bower. In the end, it was Sawchuk who made the decision to sit out. Bower started, but looked shaky, and so Sawchuk took over at the start of the second period with the score tied 2–2.

"Terry took himself out of the starting lineup before the game. But when Johnny juggled one shot and missed another that fortunately missed the goal, I called him over to the bench and he said he wasn't sharp, didn't have the touch. I asked Terry then, but he said he'd sooner wait until the start of the second period."

— Punch Imlach after Game 5

Shortly after the second period started, Sawchuk took a Bobby Hull slapshot off the shoulder and collapsed to the ice. "I thought he was dead," recalled Leafs trainer Bob Haggert 50 years later in an interview with the *Globe and Mail*'s

Roy MacGregor. "He had a bruise the size of a watermelon," added Larry Jeffrey. "I'm all right. I can go," Sawchuk had insisted, after lying on the ice for a while.

"I almost died when that shot landed. But he came back — you saw it. Words can't describe the marvellous game he played for us."

— Punch Imlach after the game

Sawchuk stopped 37 shots over the final two periods, including 22 in the third as Toronto beat Chicago 4–2.

"I saw him make those saves, but I still can't believe it. That was the most frustrating experience of my careeer…. We had enough chances to win six games, but lately nothing has been going right for us. We're missing too many opportunities and it can't all be good goalkeeping."

— Bobby Hull on Sawchuk after Game 5

"He was that good. He gave us nothing, not a rebound. That, my friend, is perfect goaltending."

— Pierre Pilote on Sawchuk

"Everybody has days like this. Sometimes they go in, other times they don't. Everything broke right for Sawchuk and wrong for us, and mostly it was because he made the right moves. Maybe we'll start getting them in bunches on Tuesday. Certainly we're overdue to break loose."

— Stan Mikita

The Leafs held tight in Game 6, scoring a 3–1 victory to wrap up the series. Brian Conacher had not scored a goal in 25 games, but he got the first one at 5:06 of the first period, and then broke a 1–1 tie with his second of the game at 4:47 of the third.

"I still don't believe they went in. I can't believe it…. You go out there and play as hard as you can. Some nights you don't play too well but you play as hard as you can. I'm just not a consistent hockey player, but I try as hard as I can every night."

— Conacher, after the game

"When I saw Brian flatten [Ed] Van Impe with a bodycheck and retrieve the puck and skate in for the winning goal, it reminded me of the night his

Uncle Charlie led us to victory and into the finals in 1936. Charlie knocked Boston's Red Beatty flat on his pants to gain possession and scored the key goal for us. And, believe it or not, Brian came off the same wing and fired the shot into the same goal as his uncle. The kid has come a long way in two seasons of pro hockey. Like all Conachers, he's great in the clutch."

— King Clancy

"We helped beat ourselves with mistakes, but Leafs got a big series from a lot of guys. You can't knock how Sawchuk played, or [Larry] Hillman and Pronovost. Mahovlich, too. I thought he gave them some big games."

— Bobby Hull

"Chicago was the class of the league that year. Everybody had them pegged as favourites.... But we seemed to hit the playoffs with some momentum.... Getting by Chicago made us all believe that maybe we had a chance to win it all. When you knock off the first-place team, that's big!"

— Ron Ellis, *Over the Boards* (2002)

"If they play like they did against us, they're gonna win more than a couple games. They got the checkers. The way they checked us, you can't say we had any real good chances in the last two games."

— Pierre Pilote on the Leafs' chances for the Stanley Cup

"If the Leafs aren't hurting too badly, they'll win it."

— Chicago's Doug Mohns

Stanley Cup Final versus Montreal

Despite what the Black Hawks were saying, Montreal was a heavy favourite to beat Toronto. The Canadiens were well-rested, having swept the Rangers in their semifinal series, and were on a roll. Counting the four in a row against New York, Montreal had won ten straight games and had 12 wins and three ties in 15 games since their last loss. The Leafs were confident ... but not cocky.

"If we play as well against Canadiens as we did against the Hawks we'll be awfully tough. I'll be very satisfied if we come out of Montreal with a split. That's our objective. If you don't get a split it means you can't lose at home and you've got to get a win on their ice eventually."

— Punch Imlach

One thing that riled Imlach was a quote attributed to goalie Rogatien "Rogie" Vachon of the Canadiens. Vachon had been called up to Montreal from Houston in the Central Pro league. He sparked the team's late season streak and won the playoff starting job over Gump Worsely and Charlie Hodge. Vachon had said he was glad that Toronto had upset Chicago because he figured the Maple Leafs would be easier to beat.

> "You can tell that Junior B goaltender that he won't be facing New York Rangers pea shooters when Leafs open up on him. I just hope [Canadiens coach Toe Blake] doesn't disappoint me by putting somebody else in besides Vachon."
>   — Punch Imlach, at a press conference the day before the 1967 Final began

> "Tell him we're going to send him right back to the Junior B's."
>   — King Clancy

Reporters at the time made it clear that Imlach and Clancy were not really being serious in their criticism of Vachon, but Imlach's "Junior B" remarks would become a lasting memory of the series, with some critics convinced that Blake went with Vachon longer than he should have in an effort to prove Imlach wrong.

But Vachon and the Canadiens were certainly the better team in Game 1. Montreal beat Toronto 6–2 and Imlach pulled Sawchuk during the third period. He wouldn't say whether he'd go with Sawchuk or Johnny Bower in Game 2, but the Leafs claimed to still be confident.

"Why shouldn't we be?" said Clancy. "We beat the best team in the world — the best team in the last 10 years. So what makes everybody think we're going to lose to these fellows just because we dropped one game?"

> "It'll take us maybe six — maybe even seven, but we'll take them all right. The Montrealers will cry before it's over."
>   — Punch Imlach

Imlach decided to play Bower in Game 2, and he was brilliant in a 3–0 victory.

> "The turning point in the series…. Bower shut us out before our own fans. That game took a lot out of us."
>   — Toe Blake, after the series, on Toronto's win in Game 2

Game 3 in Toronto was a tight one that the Leafs finally won 3–2 on a goal from Bob Pulford at 8:26 of the second overtime period.

The double-overtime hero in Game 3 of the 1967 Final, Bob Pulford, enjoys a glass of champagne after the Stanley Cup–clinching victory in Game 6.

"We seemed to pick up momentum as the overtime progressed."

— Frank Mavhovlich

"Us old warhorses are better in a longer race."

— Marcel Pronovost

"Vachon will be in goal Thursday night. It wasn't his fault that we lost. If we'd got the goal he'd have been the hero."

— Canadiens coach Toe Blake

The 42-year-old Bower made 60 saves in the game.

"I don't believe in age. Ability is what counts with me. Age doesn't mean a thing."

— Punch Imlach after the game

Imlach would likely have stuck with Bower for the rest of the series, but the goalie pulled his groin in the warm-up before Game 4 and Sawchuk was forced to take over at the last moment. Sawchuk looked out of sorts in a 6–2 Canadiens victory, but he was back in form for Game 5 in Montreal, and the Leafs scored a 4–1 victory. Vachon wasn't sharp for the Canadiens that night, and was replaced by Gump Worsley after allowing all four goals in two periods.

Worsley would be in net for the Canadiens when the series resumed after two days off, with Game 6 in Toronto on May 2.

"Let's say we made a helluva down payment on the Cup by winning that game on their ice. But we're still that big win away, and I've found it the toughest victory to earn. I know those Canadiens — they're a proud gang and will fly at us Tuesday trying to force a seventh game on their own ice."

— George Armstrong after Game 5

"We had to win at home. We didn't want to go back to Montreal. Could anyone win three games in Montreal? We *had* to win it at home."

— Ron Ellis, *Over the Boards* (2002)

"We'll wind it up here. We don't even have transportation booked for a return trip to Montreal. We haven't even tried. We won't be going to Montreal. I have nothing else to say."

— Punch Imlach the day before Game 6

Sawchuk was strong from the start in Game 6.

"He came up with the key saves and gave them the time to get ahead. There were three or four shots in the early part of the game you could usually count on as goals…. He turned back everything in the first period when we gave it our best. That was the game right there — and the Stanley Cup too."

— Jean Beliveau after Game 6

The first period was scoreless, and then Ron Ellis put the Leafs ahead at 6:25 of the second period. Jim Pappin upped the lead to 2–0 with just 36 seconds remaining in the middle frame.

"We beat Canadiens the only way we can win — playing tough hockey. Let them come at us, then counter-punched to get a goal or two we could protect."

— Dave Keon

But it wasn't as easy as that! Ex-Leaf Dick Duff finally got a shot past Sawchuk at 5:28 of the third period and the Leafs had to hang on as time ticked away.

"Less than a minute remaining, and the Leafs are called for icing; the referee calls for a face-off to the left of Leafs' goal. There's a delay in play and Montreal goalkeeper Gump Worsley doesn't know whether coach Toe Blake wants him to come out of the net. Now Blake has decided to remove Worsley. He's going to the bench. With 55 seconds to play, Montreal will use six attackers and their goal is empty. Canadiens intend to shoot the works. Beliveau is coming on the ice; so are Roberts, Cournoyer, Ferguson, Richard, and Laperriere. It's all or nothing for them now. Leafs, too, are making changes."

— Foster Hewitt's broadcast of Game 6

"I did what some people later called a sentimental thing. I won't argue. We needed to keep those guys from scoring in the last minute. Where better to turn than to my old guard."

— Punch Imlach, *Hockey Is a Battle* (1969)

"Imlach is making his stand with an all-veteran lineup of Stanley, Horton, Kelly, Pulford, and Armstrong. Sawchuk, of course, is in goal."

— Foster Hewitt

"The old men were great out there. That tells the story.... Did you see who was on the ice in the final minute? Sawchuk, Kelly, Armstrong, Stanley, Horton, and Pulford. Say, how did a young guy like Pulford get on the ice?"

— Johnny Bower, after the game

"We had a talk before the face-off and we thought that Jean [Beliveau] was going to try and put it into the corner, and Allan was going to try and stop him from doing that. He played the stick, and Kelly came in behind and got the puck, and up to me, and George was open, and I gave it to him."

— Bob Pulford, after the game

"The puck is dropped. Stanley gets possession. He snaps the puck back to Kelly. Kelly kicks it to Pulford. Pulford passes to Armstrong. Armstrong is driving hard. Army shoots toward the empty net. It's on target. It's in! He scores! Armstrong has scored the insurance goal. It's now Leafs three, Canadiens one."

— Foster Hewitt

The time of the goal was 19:13.

"That was it. They weren't going to get back in."

— Red Kelly on the empty-net goal, to Roy MacGregor,
Globe and Mail, Toronto, February 17, 2007

"That capped the most satisfying Stanley Cup I ever won."

— Punch Imlach, *Hockey Is a Battle* (1969)

"The first three Cups, we were by far the best team and we should have won. But that '67 Cup, we weren't the best team. And for Punch to have his five veterans on the ice, and for George Armstrong to score the winning goal was an incredible feeling."

— Bob Pulford, reminiscing to Ken Campbell, *Toronto Star*, February 13, 1999

"A lot of people don't even know that I scored the game-winning goal. They either think that George Armstrong's empty-net goal was the game-winning goal or it's been such a long time that a lot of people have just forgotten."

— Jim Pappin, reminiscing to Tim Wharnsby, *Toronto Star*, September 16, 2006

"Terry [Sawchuk] made a lot of people eat their words. Nobody wanted to stay with the old pros, but he showed 'em."

— Marcel Pronovost after the game

"Leafs' goalies won this series for them — Bower with the shutout and then in the overtime game, which really killed us, Sawchuk last Saturday and in the first period tonight when we owned the puck."

— Canadiens coach Toe Blake

"The two old fellows in goal were incredible and we did have a few good young guys with strong legs. But mostly, we won because we didn't make many mistakes."

— George Armstrong, recalling the 1967 win in the *Toronto Star*, July 20, 1989

"I don't like ale or champagne and I'm too tired to dance around. But this has to be the biggest thrill of my life. I've had a lot of good moments but nothing compares with this."

— Terry Sawchuk in the dressing room after the game

Sawchuk was considered a strong contender for the Conn Smythe Trophy as playoff MVP, but instead the award went to another Maple Leaf.

"It's a great honour for me, but I think my teammates' names should be on the trophy alongside mine. Ours was a team effort with 18 players playing important parts. We had to have a team effort with every player giving maximum effort in order to win."

— Dave Keon, on winning the Conn Smythe Trophy

Toronto's Stanley Cup victory in 1967 spoiled Montreal's plans to display the trophy in the Quebec Pavilion at Expo 67. Several weeks after the Leafs' parade, the Stanley Cup went on display at the Ontario Pavilion instead.

"It's pretty hard not to get emotionally involved when you're in the Stanley Cup…. When you're a hockey player, this is what you live for…. It was one of my happiest moments I can remember in hockey. We've won the three Cups in a row before, and tonight it was just one of those things, when Army scored that third goal, I actually thought I was going to start crying. There were tears starting to go down my cheeks, and it's never happened like that before."

— Tim Horton on television with Ward Cornell,
Hockey Night in Canada, after the game

"[The great spirit on this club] came about halfway through the year. The guys picked up. The older guys blended with the younger guys. If an older guy did something wrong, there's no shame in a younger guy telling him off. That's the thing that was maybe lacking last year. This year everyone was together, and we all went after one thing and we got it."

— Pete Stemkowski to Ward Cornell, *Hockey Night in Canada*

"This has been a great thrill. This has to be greatest thing to happen to any hockey player, and especially a rookie."

— Brian Conacher to Ward Cornell, *Hockey Night in Canada*

"I'm only sorry that all of us won't be together. With the [expansion] draft coming up, we might lose one or two, or somebody might be going, but jeez this, it's a great thrill for me. It's one of the greatest things in the world. Sometimes there's guys have played twenty years and never won. It's only my third year and I won one, so I'm tremendously happy."

— Pete Stemkowski to Ward Cornell, *Hockey Night in Canada*

"I wanted all my veterans in uniform for what I figured was going to be the last game some of them would play for the Leafs. We were sure to lose some of them in the Expansion draft."

— Punch Imlach, *Hockey Is a Battle* (1969)

1967–68 AND 1968–69

The Toronto Maple Leafs didn't actually lose a lot of key veterans from the 1967 Stanley Cup champions when the NHL held its Expansion Draft for six new teams in Montreal on June 6, 1967. Bobby Baun had not seen much action in recent seasons and was selected by the California Seals, headed up by former Maple Leaf Bert Olmstead. Terry Sawchuk was selected by the Los

Angeles Kings, where — after a wrangle with his rights between Punch Imlach and Kings owner Jack Kent Cooke — Red Kelly would serve as coach.

Aside from his 26-goal season in 1965–66, Eddie Shack had been known more for his comic relief and the devotion of fans, which perplexed Imlach. He was traded to Boston for Murray Oliver in May rather than being given up for nothing in the expansion draft. The Leafs also lost a few minor league veterans, such as Al Arbour, and several young players who might have been part of the future, although neither Brit Selby, Darryl Edestrand, Terry Clancy, Larry Keenan, nor Mike Corrigan went on to become true impact players. (A few of them returned to Toronto in later years.)

Playing in the newly created East Division that first year with the rest of the so-called "Original Six" franchises (the six new expansion teams all played in the West Division), the Maple Leafs didn't have a particularly horrible season with a record of 33–31–10 during the enlarged 74-game schedule, but they finished in fifth place and missed the playoffs.

The big news in Toronto during the 1967–68 season came on March 4, 1968, when the Leafs traded Frank Mahovlich, Pete Stemkowski, Garry Unger, and the rights to Carl Brewer to Detroit for Norm Ullman, Paul Henderson, Floyd Smith, and minor leaguer Doug Barrie. Mahovlich was informed of the trade in a phone call from a reporter at 8:00 a.m. He did not make any comments until later in the day, after King Clancy officially informed him that he had been dealt. Though he'd had his troubles with Imlach over the years, Mahovlich took the high road. "I was always treated well by the Leafs," he said at an impromptu press conference. "This is a good organization and I've made many friends in Toronto. My home is here and it will remain here. I hate to leave…. I think I took the news in stride. Business is business and if I can't please them here, maybe I'll be able to please them there."

"Punch had told me he'd like to get me, so I'm not surprised he did. I like the idea of playing in Toronto. It's near my home [in Lucknow] and I have some business interests in Toronto."

— Paul Henderson to reporters after learning of the deal

"It's no great surprise I've been traded. My play has been a little off this year…. It will be strange to change teams because I've been a Red Wing since I was 12. One of the reasons they got rid of me could be that I held out for four days…. The fact I'm president of the NHL Players' Association doesn't help, either, I suppose."

— Norm Ullman

Punch Imlach was no fan of the Players' Association himself, a fact that contributed to the problems in Toronto in 1967–68 and 1968–69. As Brian Conacher wrote in *As the Puck Turns* (2007):

> My second season with the Leafs was a turbulent one. After our Stanley Cup victory, the NHL doubled in size, expanding to twelve teams, and Al Eagleson formed the NHLPA. Punch Imlach was dead set against the NHLPA and disliked Eagleson intently. Any Leaf player who chose to join the NHLPA was destined for Imlach's doghouse, which was not a place you wanted to be. Eagleson knew he needed the support of the Stanley Cup winners to get the NHLPA off the ground, so he recruited the Leafs aggressively. Many of the older players saw little to be gained from a players' association, and they didn't want to jeopardize their remaining years in the NHL by joining. Eagleson sought support from the younger players like me, Walton, Pappin, Stemkowski and Ellis, and from a few key players like Baun and Pulford. Still an idealist, I thought there was a real need for better player representation, and with a handful of cautious but concerned Leafs, I supported Eagleson and the NHLPA. All that was left was to determine how Imlach would get rid of me and the others who had taken some bold steps.
>
> In the 1967–68 season, the Leafs went from winning the Stanley Cup to missing the playoffs. Imlach had the excuse he needed to get rid of all the players in his doghouse. I was one of them. In the spring of 1968 I was left unprotected, then drafted by the Detroit Red Wings. Within 18 months, Imlach got rid of some dozen players from that championship team, many of them founding members of the NHLPA. Coincidentally, the Leafs began their drift into hockey's wasteland.

With the increased workload in a 12-team NHL, Stafford Smythe wanted Punch Imlach to give up his coaching position to concentrate solely on being GM in 1968–69. The issue came to a head on the afternoon of December 2, 1968. Imlach signed George Armstrong — who'd been absent from the team for seven weeks — to a new contract, but was unclear of his own job status.

"If I don't coach, I don't work," he told reporters as he left Smythe's office.

That night, Smythe insisted that the issue had been blown out of proportion. "Punch has told us that we can make the playoffs and I believe he can get more out of the players than anyone else. I've told him we want more exciting hockey at Maple Leaf Gardens and he says we'll have it. Punch is the best in the business."

Newspapers the next day said Imlach was working under a five-year contract through the 1969–70 season and that he was earning an estimated $38,000 a year. He did get the Maple Leafs into the playoffs in 1968–69, but the team suffered an inglorious sweep in the quarter-finals versus Bobby Orr, Phil Esposito, and the Boston Bruins that included 10–0 and 7–0 losses in the first two games in Boston. Within a few minutes of the end of Game 4 at Maple Leaf Gardens on April 6, Imlach was fired. Jim Gregory, who'd been the Leafs director of amateur player development, was immediately named the new GM. John McLellan, coach of the Tulsa Oilers of the Central Hockey League, would be the new coach.

"That's it, the end of the road; the end of the Imlach era."

— Stafford Smythe announcing the firing

"When Imlach said good luck to me just now, it was the first time he's ever talked to me. But I'll tell you this: He's an egomaniac and I'm glad we knocked him out."

— Boston's Derek Sanderson

"Sanderson's comments will be seconded by many who do not revere Imlach as their pinup boy. He thrives on contention, seems to foster it, seeing issues as all black or white, no shades of grey. 'You're either for me or against me,' is his credo, 'and if you're against me, damn your eyes.'"

— Dick Beddoes, *Globe and Mail*, Toronto, April 7, 1969

When the Leafs had been winning championships, Imlach always had the support of the Toronto fans. And most players knew better than to speak out against him. Even so, resentments had been building up for a while. Frank Mahovlich (whose name he often mispronounced) and Carl Brewer had been particular whipping boys over the years. Reporters knew about many of the issues, even if the fans rarely did. Occasionally there were stories in the newspaper, but mostly it took years for the problems to come to light.

If Punch Imlach had treated players such as Frank Mahovlich (right) better, might he, Billy Harris (left), and captain George Armstrong (centre) have celebrated even more Stanley Cup victories?

Punch Imlach: For Better and For Worse

"We had some terrible battles. I didn't agree with some of the things … Punch did and he probably didn't understand some of the things … I did. I couldn't count the fights we had over salary, and yet, when they were over, we would shake hands. There would be no grudges. I don't think I ever missed a shift on the ice because of them."

— Bob Pulford, Spotlight, Hockey Hall of Fame website

"I got along fine with Punch. I can only speak to the way someone treated me and he treated me fine."

— Johnny Bower, *The China Wall* (2006)

"I got along fairly well with him. I guess you're aware that not everyone does, but I think it's the same with every team. Some players get along with the coach — others don't."

— Dave Keon, Spotlight, Hockey Hall of Fame website

"Punch didn't speak to me for four years. It was terrible. I have no animosity towards Punch today, though. I try to understand the man, why he did the things the way he did. He had a lot of pressure too. He was sincere in the way he tried to get the best out of me. He just went about it the wrong way."
— Frank Mahovlich, after signing with the Toronto Toros of the WHA in 1974

"I was aware that some individuals could do with extra praise, that they really needed it. But would that be fair to the others …? I don't think that would be fair, and in the long run I think it would hurt the team…. Anyway, individual treatment isn't the way to promote my main idea — that this is a team, everybody has to work as a team, be part of the team."
— Punch Imlach, *Hockey Is a Battle* (1969)

"Punch was a very dedicated manager and coach. He expected the same level of dedication from the players and if he felt he wasn't getting it, look out."
— Johnny Bower, *The China Wall* (2006)

"My job is to win hockey games. If I have to bruise a few guys to do it, that's just too bad. I do what I think is necessary to win."
— Punch Imlach, *Hockey Is a Battle* (1969)

"We'd catch a plane back to Toronto on Monday morning, and then he would take us directly to the rink for a practice…. After a while, I began to wonder how long I could take this kind of thing. A day off from hockey does a man a lot of good, but we never seemed to get a day off with Imlach."
— Frank Mahovlich, quoted in Stan Fischler, *Power Play* (1972)

"I figure the same way as those track coaches who say that if you're going to run a mile, you practice for it not by running one mile, but by running ten miles. If you're going to play a hockey game in an hour, you should be able to practice for two hours. That's the way you build endurance."
— Punch Imlach, *Hockey Is a Battle* (1969)

"If the two of them could have quit the bulls**t, they'd have gotten more out of each other. But Imlach wouldn't leave him alone, wouldn't let Frank play his own game. And Frank was always in good shape. He didn't need all that heavy practising and conditioning stuff."
— Eddie Shack in Ross Brewitt, *Clear the Track* (1997)

"Punch Imlach would walk into our dressing room before a game and wave a plane ticket to Pittsburgh under our nose. He'd already have it made out, in your name. That was intimidation, and intimidation of the worst kind. The threat of being sent down again, not knowing if you'd ever be back again; that in itself made an awful lot of chickens courageous."

— Pat Quinn, who'd come up through the Leafs system and played
in Toronto in 1968–69, recalling life under Imlach in 1975

"A good coach doesn't win hockey games but a bad coach can lose hockey games. Imlach was obviously a good coach because he won with a good team. He was loyal. When he had the right mix of people, he knew how to get the most out of them. He was good at that."

— Bob Pulford, Spotlight on the 1961 to 1967 Leafs,
Hockey Hall of Fame website

"With the players and resources we had at our disposal, no one should have been close to the Toronto Maple Leafs during that twelve-year span from 1955 to 1967. And so much of that, it seems to me, was Punch Imlach's inability to control his ego. The old saying goes, there's no *I* in 'team,' but there certainly was an *I* in Imlach."

— Bobby Baun, *Lowering the Boom*

"Imlach was there for eleven years. People said [he] was great because he won four Stanley Cups in eleven years. A lot of us felt that he should have had eight."

— Carl Brewer, Hockey Hall of Fame Spotlight

"Punch returned, as general manager of the Buffalo Sabres, a more knowledgeable hockey person. I have often wondered what might have happened if Punch had handled Frank Mahovlich and Carl Brewer with the same compassion and personal understanding as he did Gilbert Perreault. Perhaps we would have won 10 Stanley Cups in a row."

— Billy Harris, *The Glory Years* (1989)

7

1970s: The Ballard Years Begin

1969–70

There were still a few holdovers from the 1960s' dynasty as the 1970s approached, but the Leafs were getting younger in 1969–70. George Armstrong had retired for the third time prior to the season, but he would come back once again. This time, however, he would no longer be the captain. Armstrong, in fact, had urged the team to name a new captain, and on October 31, 1969, the honour was bestowed upon Dave Keon. Coach John McLellan and vice-president King Clancy made the decision.

Keon As Captain

"There's something special about being captain, all right, but I'm me and I hope that just because I'm captain I don't change."

— Dave Keon to reporters after being given the "C"

"Davey has always been a quiet general on the ice anyway. In his performance, he has always been a leader."

— Leafs GM Jim Gregory

"They couldn't have made a better choice. He's a leader and I don't mean just on the ice. We've had a few important player meetings since I joined this team and Dave always had his say. He had no trouble getting his point across."

— Bruce Gamble

Dave Keon was named captain a few weeks into the 1969–70 season and wore the "C" until the end of his last season in Toronto in 1974–75.

"No one wants to win any more than Keon. He leads us by example, sets the pace for us on the ice."

— Floyd Smith

"He wasn't very vocal, but when he spoke you would be wise to listen because he had a great hockey mind."

— Ron Ellis, *Over the Boards* (2002)

But not everyone was so sure.

"I must admit I was surprised when the Leafs named him captain in 1969.... I didn't think that Davie had it in him.... To me, he was so quiet in the dressing room. Of course, George Armstrong could be quiet at times too. All these quiet guys, they're the ones you have to watch out for."

— Johnny Bower, *The China Wall* (2006)

As the years went by, Keon continued to be the team's best player, but may not have been its best leader.

"Davey was a very intense guy, very abrupt and sarcastic. Despite his acerbic personality, he was a tremendous hockey player."

— Darryl Sittler, *Sittler* (1991)

"[Dave] Keon, the great player, the captain of the Leafs, did me no favours. In fact, he wore me down with his criticism. He never did what I thought a captain should. He never took the new kid to one side and tried to help him. He never encouraged me, never said, 'Hey, that was a hell of a check you threw,' or, 'Good game.' No, he only had criticisms. He would say, 'What the hell are you doing out there,' or 'You couldn't pass the puck if your life depended on it, you son of a bitch.' It didn't seem to occur to him that a young player needed the odd positive comment. Plenty of people had kicked my ass, but no one had ever nagged away at me like Keon."

— Tiger Williams, *Tiger* (1985)

"The veterans haven't taken over with the young guys the way I would have liked. They should be raising hell with the kids and getting them going. I thought Keon should be taking them aside and helping them out. There's nobody in the entire organization to provide spirit and leadership except King Clancy."

— Harold Ballard, quoted by Lawrence Martin, *Globe and Mail*, Toronto, November 20, 1974

The Leafs struggled during the 1969–70 season. They were the only team in the East Division that was never in the playoff picture as Toronto finished last among the "Original Six" clubs with 71 points on a record of 29–34–13 during the 76-game schedule. The season would also see two more veterans depart. Johnny Bower played his last game on December 10, and though he would still sometimes work out with the team, he officially retired on March 19, 1970, to work as a scout and goalie coach. And earlier in March, the Maple Leafs traded away Tim Horton.

Trading Tim Horton

"Horton, a little more than any other player, was the key to the success we had. He was always there, always the same, always giving the effort, the best he had, every night."

— Punch Imlach on Horton's role in the Leafs' success in the 1960s

"He had a large influence on this team. He was never a rah-rah guy, that's sure, but if ever an important matter came up, he'd always speak up…. The first damn thing about him is that he's a great hockey player."

— George Armstrong upon learning of the trade

"Gordie Howe and Bobby Hull, of course, were very strong, but the strongest player in the league in my time was Tim Horton."

— Norm Ullman in Craig MacInnis, *Remembering Tim Horton* (2000)

"Tim would be in my path, nothing dirty, no stickwork, and would stay there, no matter what I did. If I tried to bull between him and boards, forget it because he would just close the gate. Cut to the middle of the ice, and he would be there too, crowding me, forcing me to shoot long-range or pass."

— Bobby Hull in Craig MacInnis, *Remembering Tim Horton* (2000)

"The other players in the NHL were lucky that Horton, with that strength, did not have a mean bone in his body. If Horton had been a nasty guy with even the slightest tendency to hurt people, they probably would have had to pass a rule against him."

— Punch Imlach in Craig MacInnis, *Remembering Tim Horton* (2000)

"He had great reflexes, but he had terrible eyesight. Off the ice he wore glasses as thick as coke bottles…. Tim couldn't fight, but he could squeeze you to death with one of his bear hugs. He didn't know his own strength, and I think he was a bit frightened of what he could do."

— Bobby Baun, *Lowering the Boom* (2000)

Horton was 40 years old, and in his 20th NHL season with the club, when the Maple Leafs traded him to the New York Rangers on March 3, 1970.

"Why did we deal? Why does anybody trade? You try to do the best thing you can to improve your team."

— Jim Gregory to reporters

"It comes as a jolt, to think of leaving Leafs after playing all my hockey for them — 23 years, I believe it is. But I understand their position completely. They have to think of the future now. And if they can get some young fellows in exchange for an older guy like me, they're wise to do it. It's the sensible thing to do, really."

— Tim Horton

"If he had said no, there would have been no deal."

— Jim Gregory, who had kept Horton apprised of the trade talk

"It's flattering, of course, to think that a team like New York would believe you might be able to help them. But at the same time you find yourself thinking that the team you've been playing for apparently doesn't think you've been doing as good a job for them as you yourself thought."

— Tim Horton

"I knew it would have an emotional effect on the team. It had an emotional effect on me, too.... When a man has spent 23 years with an organization and performed the way Horton has, you don't just trade him."

— Jim Gregory

"Our attitude was probably more or less one of awe. Not much was said, really. What can you say? You accept trades as part of being a professional, yet it always comes as a shock. It must have been a very difficult decision for Tim to make."

— Bob Pulford

Pulford, himself, would be the next Leaf veteran traded when he was dealt to the Los Angeles Kings on September 3. He was traded for Garry Monahan and Brian Murphy. It's a little less clear who the Maple Leafs got from the Rangers in the Tim Horton trade. Stories at the time said the Leafs would receive four or five players to be named later, after the season was over. It's not completely clear who they actually received. One player for certain was Denis Dupere. Another was said to be Guy Trottier, although the Leafs had to claim him from the Rangers in the Intra-League Draft in June.

Toronto's deal to acquire Jacques Plante from the St. Louis Blues after the season was also said at the time to be tied into the Tim Horton trade.

1970–71 AND 1971–72

Jacques Plante seemed like a strange acquisition for a team that was obviously getting younger. One of the greatest goalies of all time, Plante starred with the Montreal Canadiens from 1954 to 1963. He had retired in 1965 after two seasons with the Rangers, but made a comeback to play alongside another goaltending legend — Glenn Hall — in St. Louis in 1968. He'd been thinking about retiring again in 1970 when he learned the Leafs were interested in him.

> "How could I think of quitting after playing what I honestly consider to have been my two best seasons in goal?"
>
> — Jacques Plante, *The Jacques Plante Story* (1972)

> "Plante is still a fine goaltender and since we knew he would be available, we decided to go after him."
>
> — Leafs coach John McLellan

> "I had a feeling I was going somewhere, but I didn't know where…. I felt I was wanted [in St. Louis] and if I feel I'm wanted by a team I feel good. Toronto has a young team and I know they are rebuilding. It's an honour to go here."
>
> — Jacques Plante to reporters

> "We felt we could have won a couple more games with steadier goaltending. I think Plante is one of the best goaltenders in the league. We went after him to look after our immediate needs."
>
> — Leafs GM Jim Gregory

Plante was a huge part of the reason the Leafs climbed back into a playoff spot in 1970–71, finishing fourth in a reconfigured seven-team East Division that featured both new expansion teams (the Buffalo Sabres and Vancouver Canucks) while the Chicago Black Hawks were moved out west. Toronto had 82 points in the enlarged 78-game season on a record of 37–33–8. Plante earned a selection as a Second-Team All-Star and finished fifth in voting for the Hart Trophy as NHL MVP after posting a record of 24–11–4 with a league-leading 1.88 goals-against average. He also served as a valuable mentor

Jacques Plante turned 42 during his first season in Toronto in 1970–71 and put up spectacular numbers.

to a midseason acquisition that the Maple Leafs saw as their goalie of the future after they sent Mike Walton, Bruce Gamble, and their first-round draft choice in 1971 to the Philadelphia Flyers for Bernie Parent and a second-round draft choice. It was the first time Toronto had ever traded a draft choice.

> "Juniors are an unknown quantity. In Parent, we got quality. I regard him as the finest young goaltender in hockey."
>
> — Leafs GM Jim Gregory

"Parent could solve our goaltending problems for 10 years. We have been trying to get him for years. He has good size, stands up, and plays the angles well. And he'll learn a lot here from Jacques Plante, the best goal-tender in the world, and Johnny Bower."

— Leafs vice president King Clancy the day after the trade

"It's a good deal for me. I have always liked Toronto.... You know I am a Canadian boy and I like the cold weather. It will be good to have my boys grow up where they can play a lot of hockey.... I think I will be in Toronto for a long time."

— Bernie Parent

As it turned out, Parent would only be in Toronto through the end of the 1971–72 season. But another young player who joined the team in 1970–71 would grow into the Leafs' next superstar. A kid by the name of Darryl Sittler was selected by the Leafs in the first round, eighth overall, in the 1970 NHL Draft.

Drafting Sittler

"In junior hockey I had worn number nine.... All the big shooters in the NHL wore number nine [and] it was flattering to be given that number.... I think the Leafs awarded me number 27 because I was their first draft choice and the number was rather famous in Toronto.... When the Leafs asked me to wear number 27, I felt it meant they had great expectations for me. I knew they were going to give me every chance to do well. I was thrilled to wear that number because Frank Mahovlich was a bona fide star and I had inherited his sweater."

— Darryl Sittler, *Sittler at Centre* (1979)

"We didn't feel we would get Sittler, drafting eighth as we were.... I was amazed and delighted that he was still free when we got our first pick after seven others had been chosen. I thought he'd go in the first five or six. He's a good centre, big, mean, can make plays and score goals."

— Jim Gregory

Sittler jumped directly to the NHL in 1970–71, but was brought along slowly that year. He struggled in 1971–72, but by the 1972–73 season, he was the team's leading scorer and would soon be among the top scorers in the entire league.

Meanwhile, the Maple Leafs made the playoffs again in 1971–72, but went out in the first round for the second year in a row.

1972 TO 1975

Two more teams — the New York Islanders and Atlanta Flames — joined the NHL in 1972–73. The Maple Leafs struggled this season, falling to sixth place in the eight-team East Division and missing the playoffs by 18 points (27–41–10 for 64 points). The best moment for the Leafs came before the season even started, when Paul Henderson scored the winning goal for Team Canada in the last three games of the Summit Series with the Soviet Union, including the series winner with 34 seconds remaining in the final game.

The 1972–73 season also witnessed the arrival of the first pro league to challenge the NHL since the demise of the Western Hockey League (WHL) in 1926. By paying much bigger salaries than NHL clubs were offering, the World Hockey Association (WHA) opened for business with 12 teams stocked with a few big former NHL names and plenty of journeymen looking for a chance.

> "I guarantee you nobody thought a new professional hockey league would get off the ground. That league got started in 1972 with some real big names in the lineups: Bobby Hull, Derek Sanderson, 'Pie' McKenzie, J.C. Tremblay, and Gerry Cheevers, who once played for us. They even stole our best goalie, Bernie Parent, who went to a team called the Miami Screaming Eagles, a team that never played a single game."
>
> — King Clancy, *Clancy* (1997 reprint)

Parent was just one of several players the Maple Leafs would lose to the WHA. Toronto's trouble with the rival league had begun in February of 1972, but in a sense, the root of the problem dated back a few years.

How Harold Ballard Got Control

In October 1968, the RCMP raided Maple Leaf Gardens. As a result, Harold Ballard and Stafford Smythe were charged on July 9, 1969, with tax evasion and for using Gardens funds to pay for personal expenses. Even before the charges were laid, John Bassett convinced the board of directors of the Gardens to fire Smythe and Ballard — but he didn't force them to sell their shares. A year later, Ballard and Smythe staged a proxy war to regain control of the board. On September 1, 1971, the two men bought out their former partner and a few smaller shareholders using a bank loan of nearly $5.9 million. Bassett received about $5.4 million of that, for a pretty good return on his original $900,000 investment back in 1961.

"I've been trying for five months to gain control of the Gardens. Finally, I realized this operation is so much a part of Mr. Ballard and Mr. Smythe there is simply no way. So I told them to take me out."

— John Bassett, explaining his reason for giving up his stake in the team

"It was the first battle he ever lost in his life. He couldn't believe it."

— Harold Ballard

Still facing trial on tax evasion charges, Stafford Smythe was suffering from a bleeding ulcer and died on October 13, 1971, after a major hemorrhage. Ballard was now in control of the team and was officially named president just one week later. He bought up Smythe's shares for about $7.5 million in February of 1972, giving him between 60 and 80 percent ownership of the Leafs, depending on the source.

Ballard was not yet known as the irascible and cantankerous hands-on owner he would become, but he was considered by most people to be crass and commercial-driven. While others ran the hockey side of the business, Ballard had been maximizing profits on other events at the Gardens by jacking up the price of concessions and squeezing in more and more seats. He did this by famously removing the portrait of Queen Elizabeth that had hung inside the arena.

"If people want to see a picture of the Queen, they can go to an art gallery," he said. "[Conn] Smythe didn't like me kicking her out of here, but what the hell, she doesn't pay me, I pay her. Besides, what the hell position can a Queen play?"

WHA Defections

Ballard's own tax evasion case finally saw him convicted on 47 of 49 charges in August of 1972. Two months later, he was sentenced to three years in prison. He only served one year, mostly in a minimum security facility and partly at a halfway house in Toronto, before he was paroled in 1973. But Ballard had already begun to do serious damage to the team back in February of 1972, when the WHA first announced its "negotiation list" and began to draft players.

"Ballard refused to believe that the World Hockey Association was serious, and when WHA representatives came calling, they left with the heart of our team."

— Darryl Sittler, *Sittler* (1991)

"Our organization was one of the hardest hit by the WHA. We lost 14 or 15 players from the entire system."

> — Leafs GM Jim Gregory in Ross Brewitt, *Clear the Track* (1997)

"After Ballard took over, we were all just so sick and tired of the way the team was operating. We couldn't compete with Boston or New York or Montreal. Playing in Toronto is a wonderful experience, but not when you don't have a good team. We lost a lot of our young defensemen to the WHA and we were struggling."

> — Paul Henderson in Ron Ellis and Kevin Shea, *Over the Boards* (2002)

"The trouble's at the top, and you can put that in your paper. You have to start laying the blame on management."

> — Rick Ley, on the Leafs player defections to the WHA

On February 11, 1972, the day before the new league held its weekend-long initial draft, 12 teams in the WHA each selected four NHL players in what was called a pre-draft "Negotiation List." Among the 48 players selected were seven members of the Maple Leafs, which was more than any other NHL team.

"Thank you. This is the first I've heard of it. Other than that, no comment."

> — Dave Keon to Red Burnett, *Toronto Star*, on being
> selected by the yet-unnamed Ontario team

"Is that right? Well, I have a lawyer to handle such matters."

> — Jim Harrison on being selected by the Calgary Broncs

"Isn't that terrific. What a thrill. A $2,000,000 contract, no doubt."

> — Jim McKenny on being selected by the Chicago Cougars

"I'll just have to sit and wait and play it by ear. I have never been contacted by New England, although a representative of the WHA did speak to me."

> — Rick Ley to Red Burnett on being selected by the New England Whalers

"That's interesting.... At the moment, I have no comment to make other than it's good for the hockey player."

> — Norm Ullman on being selected by the Edmonton Oil Kings

Other Toronto players selected were Guy Trottier (Dayton) and Bernie Parent, who was already known by then to be negotiating with the Miami Screaming Eagles.

When Parent arrived in Toronto the year before, he was working under a three-year contract he had signed in Philadelphia. In the fall of 1971, he sat out a week of Leafs training camp in an effort to improve the terms of his deal. According to reports, Jim Gregory and King Clancy approved a new two-year contract said to be worth nearly $80,000. Now, Miami was said to be offering him a five-year deal worth $600,000. (It would later climb to $700,000.) Parent was definitely listening.

"In Philadelphia, I figured I was set as long as I played good goal. But it was not so. I was playing very good when I got traded to Toronto last year and that taught me a lesson — take care of No. 1."

— Bernie Parent, quoted by Stan Fischler in the *Sporting News*

Though NHL president Clarence Campbell vowed that the league would fight in court against any deal Parent signed with the WHA, and Toronto was later reported to have offered $750,000 to woo him back, the Maple Leafs — perhaps because they didn't believe the WHA would ever get off the ground — were not planning to fight for their goalie.

"How could we deny a kid like Parent a chance to pick up $600,000? We can't pay him that kind of money. If Miami can pay it, I want him to have it. All I told him was to make sure he had every penny in advance. Then he won't get hurt if the thing blows up."

— Harold Ballard, as reported by Milt Dunnell, *Toronto Star*, January 24, 1972

"If, after our meeting, I'm convinced that the Miami club is serious, I would have to recommend that Bernie accept the WHA offer because of the fact that, under the Leafs archaic pay standards, Parent couldn't make the same money in Toronto in 15 years."

— Howard J. Casper, Parent's attorney

On February 22, 1972, the Miami club announced that Parent had agreed to terms, now said to be $750,000 for five years. On February 27, Parent and his wife flew down to Miami for a 90-minute press conference.

"Good afternoon. It is an honour and pleasure to be here," announced Parent. "I'm looking forward to next year with the Screaming Eagles. I just like to say, you have great weather here."

Bernie Parent might have solidified Toronto's goaltending for years to come. Instead, he's a symbol of what might have been if the Maple Leafs hadn't lost so many young players to the World Hockey Association.

The Parents returned to Toronto that same night, and he was with the Leafs for practice on Monday morning.

"I plan to play for Toronto as well as I can for the rest of the season. If I'm in goal and they are winning, they'd be stupid not to play me."

Parent did continue to play in Toronto, and as he did, things began to fall apart in Miami. It was soon clear the Screaming Eagles would not have any arena to play in and by mid-April the franchise folded. The team later became the Philadelphia Blazers, and on June 3, 1972, Parent officially agreed to join the new club.

"It's a pleasure knowing I'll be playing for Philadelphia. A year and a half ago I got traded to Toronto and I didn't enjoy that too much. I'm glad to be back. I like the fans and I hope to have my best year."

Parent's signing immediately led to NHL teams increasing their contract offers to keep players. Many signed new and better deals, as Dave Keon eventually did in September when he signed a three-year deal to remain in Toronto for a reported $135,000 per season. Still, the Leafs lost promising young players Rick Ley, Brad Selwood, and Jim Harrison to the WHA in 1972–73. Others, like Paul Henderson, Mike Pelyck, Norm Ullman, and Keon himself, would make the jump in later years.

> "The biggest loss by far was that of Parent. He wouldn't adequately be replaced until the arrival of Mike Palmateer four years later…. Imagine the Toronto team that might have been if we'd been able to keep Ley, Selwood, Pelyck, and others with [Borje] Salming and [Ian] Turnbull in front of a goaltending tandem of Parent and Palmateer."
>
> — Darryl Sittler, *Sittler* (1991)

1973–74

After the Leafs' poor season in 1972–73, and with his contract expiring, John McLellan decided not to return as coach after four seasons behind the bench.

> Coaching in Toronto is tougher than coaching in any other city in the National Hockey League. Sure, it's tough in Montreal. But they have a good team and when you're winning it makes things a little easier. I'm not knocking Toronto when I say it's the toughest place to coach. It's more of a compliment. It's because the fans are more knowledgeable and the press is more knowledgeable than in an American city. Four years here seem like eight somewhere else. It's not hockey for a 78-game season, it's hockey 365 days of the year.

And no, it wasn't sour grapes.

"Yes, I would do it all again," McLellan said.

Speculation about a new coach turned immediately to former Leaf Red Kelly, who, after moving to Pittsburgh following two years as coach of the L.A. Kings, had been fired midway through his fourth season with the Penguins. Even so, Kelly didn't sign in Toronto until August 20, 1973, when he inked a four-year deal.

> "Toronto was where I started my hockey career and where it ended. I grew up 80 miles from Toronto and to me it is the best city I've ever lived in. I have many happy memories here. Coming back to Canada is a great feeling.

"Toronto is an exciting place and ever since I listened to Foster Hewitt broadcasting Leaf games, which is many years ago, I've hoped that some day I'd have the chance to coach in Toronto."

— Red Kelly at the press conference to announce his hiring

Kelly stated that his goal was to get the team back into the playoffs, which he did. Toronto finished fourth in the East Division in 1973–74 with a record of 35–27-16 for 86 points — although they were swept out of the playoffs in a four-game loss to Boston in the quarter-finals. Darryl Sittler continued to improve this season, finishing ninth in the NHL with 38 goals and eighth in points with 84. Lanny McDonald and Ian Turnbull had both been selected in the first round of the 1973 Draft and jumped directly to the NHL. It would take a couple of years for them to make an impact, but two other rookies — one in particular — made an immediate impression.

Salming and Hammarstrom

Gerry McNamara wasn't specifically looking at Borje Salming when the Leafs sent him to scout the Swedish national team at a Christmas tournament in 1972, but Salming made a strong impression on him. McNamara sought him out in the dressing room after the game

"I don't know how he talked his way inside the door. But he gave me his card and asked right away, 'Do you want to play for the Toronto Maple Leafs?'"

— Borje Salming to Lance Hornby, *Toronto Sun*, August 20, 2013

"I trusted Gerry's opinion very much and put Salming on our team list that moment."

— Jim Gregory to Lance Hornby, *Toronto Sun*

The Leafs brought Salming and Inge Hammarstrom to Toronto in May and signed them to contracts.

"We signed both players so they'd keep each other company. We didn't realize until he got here how special Salming was."

— Jim Gregory, Spotlight on Borje Salming, Hockey Hall of Fame website

"Inge and I knew nothing about life in Toronto and the NHL, but said we'd give it everything we've got and, if doesn't work out, we can always go home."

— Borje Salming to Lance Hornby, *Toronto Sun*

"Inge and I arrived in top physical condition. We'd worked out all summer…. We easily outskated the overweight Canadians. At this time, we didn't know that most NHL players reported to camp in poor condition and worked themselves into shape…. I needed only one practice to realize I had a good shot at making the team…. Language was a problem, but I understood the hockey terminology. Besides, we weren't there to gab; we were there to play. Our teammates seemed to appreciate what we could do on the ice, which helped us feel accepted."

— Borje Salming, *Blood, Sweat and Hockey* (1991)

The Swedish imports made their official NHL debut on October 10, 1973. Salming and Ian Turnbull were the Leafs' best defencemen that night as Toronto beat Buffalo 7–4.

"In pre-season games, they were our most reliable defence pair, so I didn't hesitate to use them in any situation."

— Leafs coach Red Kelly after the game

"In the past, NHL people often questioned the intestinal qualities of Swedish players. Nothing in Salming's play indicated a lack in that area. He's not a robust bodychecker but he took his man out solidly, blocked shots adroitly, and rushed well."

— Frank Orr, *Toronto Star*, October 11, 1973

Salming was named first star of the game against the Sabres, but a much bigger test came in Philadelphia the following night when the Leafs faced the Flyers.

"Inge and I arrived in the NHL when the game was at its violent worst…. In Sweden, I was seen by many as a fighter. In North America, I played the same style but I was a pussycat compared to the beasts of the NHL."

— Borje Salming, *Blood, Sweat and Hockey* (1991)

The Broad Street Bullies would win their first of two straight Stanley Cup championships this year and beat the Leafs 2–0 in their early-season matchup. Their rough treatment of Toronto's Swedish rookies was the big story.

"The rugged Flyers made Swedish rookie defenceman Borje Salming their target for the night, but he refused to back off. After Dave Schultz slashed him in the first period, Salming slashed back.... In the third period, Ed Van Impe speared Salming and drew a major penalty."

— Red Burnett, Toronto Star, October 12, 1973

"Early in the first period, we lined up for a face-off in our end. The Flyers players taunted me while their biggest goon, Dave Schultz, stared at me. The puck went in the corner and Schultz and I chased it. We collided. The puck went around the boards, but Schultz didn't follow. He turned and slashed me hard with his stick. I hit him back. Schultz starred at me, his eyes blazing like a madman's. It was humiliating for him to be struck so brazenly by a rookie. Then he slashed me across the chest. I hit him right back, hard, and winded him. A general free-for-all was soon underway. My personal battle with Schultz ended in a draw, but for me it was a clear victory. I showed that I wasn't going to be anybody's punching bag, and if necessary I would give as good as I got. I also knew that I had won the full respect of my teammates when they rushed to my defence after the Schultz attack."

— Borje Salming, Blood, Sweat and Hockey (1991)

"They're new to the league and they're good hockey players. Naturally, they're tested. It wasn't something we set out to do."

— Flyers captain Bobby Clarke after the game

"I think they don't like Swedish boys. They don't play hard, they play dirty. But it's no problem. There will be a next time."

— Borje Salming after the game

"He looks like a real good one if he can stand up to the rugged going in this league. Everyone will try him until he proves he won't back off."

— Bobby Clarke

Salming took heaps of abuse, proving that he was tough enough to take it. By year's end, he was clearly among the NHL's top newcomers. Salming finished third in voting for the Calder Trophy behind winner Denis Potvin of the New York Islanders and runner-up Tom Lysiak of the Atlanta Flames.

"I was more impressed by the fact that Salming finished seventh in the all-star voting for defencemen and Potvin was ninth. Perhaps some writers didn't class him as a rookie because he was an international star for Sweden. I think the all-star rating suggests he was the best first-year man."

> — Leafs GM Jim Gregory when the NHL Award–winners
> were announced in June

"Borje was probably the best and purest athlete on our team, a great hockey player who, had he played with a more successful team like Montreal or Philadelphia, would probably have won a Norris Trophy or two as the league's best defenseman. He was always in top condition, not an ounce of body fat on him, and worked hard in practices and in games. Added to that was a level of skill rarely seen in hockey. How good was Borje? He was up with the very best, and there wasn't a player in the Toronto dressing room who felt otherwise."

> — Darryl Sittler, *Sittler* (1991)

"One of the best athletes ever to play. Something set him apart from the rest of the Europeans — more confidence and more guts…. A fierce competitor. Despises losing. In a battle of any kind, I want Borje on my side."

> — Lanny McDonald, *Lanny* (1987)

"All of us who came after Borje have a lot to thank him for. He really paved the way for all Swedish players and opened the eyes of NHL managers that you know what? Swedes can play in the NHL and do well and be effective leaders. We're not soft."

> — Mats Sundin to Rosie DiManno, *Toronto Star*, November 16, 2014

Salming's star power in Toronto overshadowed Inge Hammarstrom, who averaged 20+ goals per season in his four-plus years with the Maple Leafs.

"Inge was a talented guy. He just didn't have the staying power of Borje. But he was a fine player, a good guy, and had he played for a more established team that fit his style of play, he could have had greater success."

> — Jim Gregory to Lance Hornby, *Toronto Sun*, August 20, 2013

Unfortunately, the most lasting impression of Salming's fellow Swede was the infamous quote from the Leafs' owner during their second season in the NHL.

Borje Salming was unaccustomed to the rough play in the NHL, but the Swedish superstar overcame all obstacles to open the doors to a wave of European players to follow.

"You could send Hammarstrom into the corner with six eggs in his pocket and he wouldn't break any of them."
— Harold Ballard to Lawrence Martin, *Globe and Mail*,
Toronto, November 11, 1974

"While I confronted trouble head on, Inge used the reverse tactic when faced with NHL violence. He sailed into corners at full speed and sailed out neatly and stylishly. He simply skated away from anyone who was chasing him…. Inge was not a coward. His style was just not suited to the NHL at that time. He didn't want to fight…. I am convinced that Inge would have been a big star if he had come to the NHL ten years later. His style of skating and playmaking was perfectly suited to the faster, more artistic game of the 1980s."

— Borje Salming, *Blood, Sweat and Hockey* (1991)

1974–75

The NHL expanded to 18 teams this year, adding the Washington Capitals and the Kansas City Scouts. The schedule was stretched to 80 games and the league was split into four divisions. Toronto played with the Boston Bruins, Buffalo Sabres, and the California Golden Seals in the Adams Division. The Leafs fell under .500 this season, finishing 31–33–16, but grabbed the final post-season spot in a completely revamped playoff format and faced the 42–17–21 Los Angeles Kings in a best-of-three preliminary round. The Leafs upset the Kings in three games, but were then swept out of the play-offs by the Philadelphia Flyers, who were en route to their second straight Stanley Cup.

It was with the Flyers in mind that the Leafs introduced a new rookie this season whom they'd selected in the second round of the 1974 NHL Draft.

Tiger Williams

"The key to making the team is playing my style. My aggressiveness put me here today and it'll keep me here with the team…. I'm not saying I can make a team tougher, but I can make my line tougher. One guy isn't going to make a team — like Dave Schultz with Philadelphia, he can act as tough as he does because they've got [Andre] Dupont and [Bob] Kelly and [Don] Saleski and all the rest."

— Tiger Williams when he was introduced to the Toronto media after signing with the Leafs on August 8, 1974

"The thing we like about Dave, I mean Tiger, I guess that's what they call him out west, is that he's an excellent team man. That's what really impressed us from our scout's reports."

— Leafs coach Red Kelly

"It was thrashing time anytime anyone came near me."

— Williams, explaining how he earned the nickname Tiger for his belligerence as a peewee goalie, to Robin Herman, *New York Times*, May 8, 1978

"Notwithstanding his on-ice reputation, Dave Williams was probably one of the most earnest and businesslike hockey players ever to play for the Leafs. There weren't any shortcuts as far as he was concerned.... Everything he did was full out; Tiger practised as hard as he could and was always in magnificent shape. His greatest strengths were his conditioning and his intensity. Teammates knew they couldn't pull anything over on him."

— Darryl Sittler, *Sittler* (1991)

"I'll fight if it helps the team, but I'm much more concerned with improving as a hockey player.... I'm no fancy Dan. I think I can play in this league, but only if I work my butt off, fight when I have to, and hustle. It's that simple."

— Williams, prior to training camp for 1975–76 season

"When I was a young player with the Leafs, King [Clancy] called me up to the executive office one morning. And he told me to bring some goldfish along. So I ran out and bought a dozen goldfish and when I got up there King showed me some piranhas swimming around in a big tank of water. We threw the goldfish in the tank and ! — those piranhas made short work of them. King turned to me and said, 'Tiger, that's the way I want you to play hockey.'"

— Tiger Williams to Brian McFarlane in King Clancy, *Clancy* (1997 reprint)

1975–76

The Maple Leafs got a lot younger in 1975–76. Veterans Dave Keon and Norm Ullman jumped to the WHA, while Ron Ellis began a short-lived retirement. Lanny McDonald had been a disappointment during his first two seasons in Toronto, but he was still just 22 years old. McDonald began to blossom this year, with 37 goals and 56 assists playing right wing on the team's top line with Darryl Sittler and Errol Thompson, who had a career-high 43 goals. But Sittler was the biggest star. The team's new captain had 41 goals and 59 assists to become the first player in franchise history to reach 100 points. Toronto was barely a .500 team this season, finishing with a record of 34–31–15, but it would be a memorable year for many reasons.

Sittler Gets the "C"

"He's a real team man and all the players respect him."

— Harold Ballard to reporters on Darryl Sittler being the logical choice to replace Dave Keon as captain, July 16, 1975

Darryl Sittler became the face of the franchise during the 1970s.

"Of course, it's an honour to be named captain, but I don't think it will change my approach much. I still have to work hard to play well."
— Darryl Sittler, after being named captain on September 10, 1975

"There are a number of things a captain can do. If a player has a beef, he can talk it out with him or even take the problem to the coach or management. If a player is having communication problems with the coach, then the captain can open the channels between them.... But mostly a captain can lead by example, by having a totally professional approach to the game. If, as captain, I'm not doing things the proper way on and off the ice, then the other players might not do them correctly."
— Darryl Sittler

"He was a perfect team captain, talented and respected as a player, and most of all a great leader off the ice…. Darryl's leadership was our safeguard. He kept us together."

— Borje Salming, *Blood, Sweat and Hockey* (1991)

"Sittler had character like iron. He was right up there with Lafleur and Robinson and Dryden; he was a household name, but he never took anything for granted. He never took his success for granted, nor the people around him."

— Tiger Williams, *Tiger* (1985)

On the day he accepted the "C," Sittler showed he wasn't afraid to speak his mind: "It's no secret there's been poor communication between Red Kelly and most of the players the last two seasons. As captain, I can do something about that. In a meeting I had with Red, he indicated that he wanted me to."

"Red never could see that there was any communications problem, but I think we finally got through to him during the summer. He's had private meetings with 14 players so far, which indicates to me this is something he's really trying hard to improve. I think I'm right in saying there's going to be a whole new atmosphere around the club. And, of course, we're depending on Sittler to help make it work."

— Leafs GM Jim Gregory

Sittler also showed he wouldn't be afraid to take on Harold Ballard either:

I thought the Keon and Ullman situations were handled very badly. I know Mr. Ballard is noted for being outspoken, but in this case I thought it was dead wrong. I don't think it was necessary to come out and say publicly that the Leafs had no further use for Dave Keon and Norm Ullman and were getting rid of them because they were washed up. These are guys who had done a lot for the Toronto club and I thought they deserved more consideration. You don't see that sort of stuff happening in Montreal, for instance. Canadiens might trade a veteran or he just might not appear at training camp. Or he might retire. But the team would never announce that so-and-so is all through and there's no place for him.

Ballard Continues to Criticize

Not feeling at all chastised by Sittler's remarks, Ballard would be critical, as always, throughout the 1975–76 season. In mid-January, the Leafs hit a rough patch with just one win and three ties against four losses in an eight-game stretch. Ballard had some specific targets for his criticism, including backup goalie Doug Favell, who he'd been on for a couple of years.

"What can you do with a guy making that sort of money ($150,000 a year)? Some teams have shown interest in Dougie, but when they hear what he's making they turn and run. There's no use giving him away. He still in my mind is a good goaltender. Sooner or later someone will start to panic and take him from us."

He wasn't thrilled with Red Kelly's coaching either, "Obviously there's no comparison in [Philadelphia Flyers' Fred] Shero's and Red's systems. How many Stanley Cups have we won the last two years?"

Sittler was a target, too, as Ballard said he was determined to find a sensational centre to play between Errol Thompson and Lanny McDonald. "Can you imagine the time bomb we'd set off if we had a hell of a centre in there. Sure, they're hard to find but it would be another Kid Line."

The next night, Saturday, February 7, 1976, the Boston Bruins were in Toronto. The Bruins had won seven in a row, and with a record of 32–10–9, their 73 points had them 20 up on the 21–20–11 Maple Leafs. But it was Darryl Sittler who set off the time bomb.

Sittler's 10-Point Night

The Maple Leafs beat the Bruins 11–4. Darryl Sittler had six goals and four assists that night, breaking the league record of eight points then shared by Maurice Richard (1944) and Bert Olmstead (1954).

> (*Toronto Star*, February 9, 1976)
>
> FIRST PERIOD
>
> 1. Sittler's long pass sent right winger Lanny McDonald down the boards and he beat Bruin goalie Dave Reece with a scorching angle shot. 1 assist.
>
> 2. Sittler's quick move in the centre zone trapped Bruin defenceman Brad Park out of position. He passed to left winger Errol Thompson, who set up defenceman Ian Turnbull for a move into the Bruin zone and a score on a 50-foot slapshot. 2 assists.

SECOND PERIOD

3. A brillian rush by defenceman Borje Salming down the boards into the Bruin end led to a pass-out, which Sittler batted out of the air into the net. 1 goal, 2 assists.

4. Four seconds into a Leaf power play, Sittler won a face-off draw from Gregg Sheppard and fed the puck to Salming at the point for a scoring slapshot. 1 goal, 3 assists.

5. Sittler intercepted a pass in the centre zone, skated across the Bruin line and drove a 50-foot shot through Reece's pads. 2 goals, 3 assists.

6. With Bruins a man short, a delayed penalty was called against them and Sittler replaced goalie Wayne Thomas on the ice. He jammed in a pass from George Ferguson. 3 goals, 3 assists.

7. Sittler passed to McDonald, who drew the Bruin defence to one side and fed a tip-in pass to Salming. 3 goals, 4 assists.

THIRD PERIOD

8. Sittler stuffed in Salming's pass from the edge of the goal crease. 4 goals, 4 assists.

9. The drive which broke the NHL single-game point record was a soft, 40-foot wrist shot which caught Reece off-balance. 5 goals, 4 assists.

10. McDonald passed to Sittler, who was against the boards behind the Bruins net. His attempted pass-out struck Park's skate then bounced in off Reece's skate. 6 goals, 4 assists.

"Undoubtedly, Mr. Ballard will figure his little blast inspired me to set the record, but it just wasn't that way."

— Darryl Sittler to reporters after the game

"Darryl's not afraid to tell the big man to go to hell. Ballard's slams hurt individual players privately, but because of Sittler's attitude and counselling, we're able, as a team, to turn the blasts into a joke."

— an unnamed Leaf player to reporters after the game

"Maybe now he won't have to hunt quite so hard for that centre he wants."
— Darryl Sittler to reporters after the game

"It was greater than what Paul Henderson did in Moscow. We'll certainly reward him for it. We'll give him a gift which can be an heirloom in his family to commemorate the biggest night any hockey player ever had."
— Harold Ballard

"Mr. Ballard congratulated me very warmly and told me how great it was. He gave my wife a big kiss and seemed really happy that I'd done it."
— Darryl Sittler

"You don't like to see something like that happen against your team. But if somebody has to do it, I'm glad it was a player of Sittler's calibre, a guy who works for what he accomplishes."
— Bruins coach Don Cherry to reporters after the game

"The guys on this team wouldn't be happier if they'd done it themselves. He's such a great team man and he works so hard."
— Lanny McDonald

"It was a night when every time I had the puck, something seemed to happen. In other games, you can work as hard and come up empty. That's why hockey is so frustrating. Some games, the puck just goes in the net for you; the next game, it won't do anything you want it to, no matter how hard you try."
— Darryl Sittler after the game

"I don't think many of us realized what was going on until probably half-way through the third period."
— Tiger Williams on the tribute film broadcast when the Leafs celebrated the 40th anniversary of the 10-point game on February 4, 2016

"And then all of a sudden they announce it and the crowd goes crazy."
— Lanny McDonald on the 2016 tribute film

"I didn't know any of that. All I knew was the fans are going berserk and this guy keeps scoring. I'm thinking, 'How many goals does he need?'"
— Bruins goalie Dave Reece, who'd been told before the game that he was going to be sent to the minors, to Lance Hornsby, *Toronto Sun*, February 3, 2016

"The thing I'll remember most about it is the ovation the fans gave me when I got my ninth point. That's something you just never forget."

— Darryl Sittler to reporters after the game

"We were a first-place club. We were on a roll…. They weren't playing a rinky-dink club. Darryl did quite an accomplishment. It wasn't like he was playing Washington or some lower team like that. We were the Big Bruins. So, it was embarrassing."

— Don Cherry on the 2016 tribute film

"Getting 10 points in one game is really a team achievement, not an individual thing. I had plenty of help. Borje Salming played an incredible game and made super plays for two of my goals. Thompson and McDonald played great too."

— Darryl Sittler after the game

"Everyone has those games where nothing goes right. There is nothing you can do to stop the magical momentum. You just have to eat it. It was one of those nights where we were out to lunch and they were hot as hell…. I didn't realize until after the game what he had done. I just knew this is going to take a long, long time to get over."

— Dave Reece to Kevin McGran, *Toronto Star*, February 6, 2016

"It wasn't his fault. Sittler was just hot. One goes in from behind the net. Everything went wrong. There's no way I was putting [Gerry] Cheevers in. I never, ever pulled my goalies. I figured it this way: 'You put us into this mess, now you get us out.'"

— Don Cherry to Kevin McGran

"Everyone always thought after that night was over, if he's got 10 points, and now all of a sudden [Wayne] Gretzky comes along, and then [Mario] Lemieux comes along, and you think, 'Ok, it's just a matter of time. Can it be broken?' All of a sudden it's 40 years. It's unbelievable. That could be a record for a lifetime."

— Lanny McDonald on the 2016 tribute film

The day after the 10-point game, the Minnesota North Stars were in Toronto. The Maple Leafs won 4–1. Sittler had one assist, but he didn't even have an official shot on goal (although one of his drives bounced off the goal post).

"That gets you back to earth," Sittler told reporters after the game. "But it's funny, eh? I think our line had more really good scoring chances against Minnesota than we did against Boston. It shows you need things bouncing for you."

The 1976 Playoffs

The Leafs' 83 points during the 1975–76 season had them well back of Montreal (127), Philadelphia (118), Boston (113), Buffalo (105), and the New York Islanders (101), but comfortably in the playoff picture. They opened the post-season against the Pittsburgh Penguins, who'd had a similar season (35–33–12, for 82 points), and beat them in three games in the preliminary round. That set up a quarter-final rematch against the Philadelphia Flyers, who'd swept Toronto the year before. Toronto hadn't beaten Philadelphia since March 3, 1974 — managing just three ties and 10 losses (14, including the playoff sweep). The Flyers took the first two games 4–1 and 3–1 in Philadelphia this time, and the series turned ugly when the teams got to Toronto for Game 3 on April 15.

Borje and the Brawl

"Hooligans disguised as hockey players made another of their more prevalent feature presentations last night and they chose a Stanley Cup best-of-seven quarter-final game in which to do it. When the gladiators from Toronto Maple Leafs and Philadelphia Flyers finished dragging 16,485 Maple Leaf Gardens fans through a 3 1/2-hour extravaganza marred by [173] minutes in penalties, Leafs escaped with a 5–4 victory and now trail the series 2–1.

"The game featured everything from premeditated assault to back-stabbing tactics with little hockey until the final 10 minutes, when Flyers attempted to tie the score. Flyers, master intimidators, were surly from the game's outset, almost daring referee Dave Newell to exert his authority."

— Don Ramsay, *Globe and Mail*, Toronto, April 16, 1976

"Tonight at Maple Leaf Gardens, Maple Leafs and Philadelphia Flyers will play a game of hockey. At least, everyone concerned — players, coaches, management, the officials and the fans — hope the two teams will revert to hockey…. Following two losses at Philadelphia to open the series, Leafs defeated Flyers 5–4 here Thursday evening in a 3 1/2-hour marathon. It can't be called a hockey game. Fit any degrading word plus adjectives to it and you won't be far wrong.

"The game produced criminal charges against three Flyer players (Joe Watson, Mel Bridgman, Don Saleski), 173 minutes in penalties, which included 107 minutes to Flyers, 66 to Leafs, five game misconducts plus a gross misconduct to Leafs' Kurt Walker for spitting and just about every bad feature which has crept into the game in recent years. Perhaps now the garbage has been cleared from the system of all those involved and the teams can play hockey."

— Frank Orr, *Toronto Star*, April 17, 1976

"I think we showed that we can stand up to them physically."

— Leafs coach Red Kelly

"Maybe now they'll realize that we won't run and hide just because they play it rough, and we can settle this series by playing hockey."

— Darryl Sittler

"Throughout the years, I was involved in other brawls, but not too many…. The most scandalous brawl I ever witnessed was against the … Flyers during the 1976 playoffs. I was paired off with Flyers centre Mel Bridgman. But other Flyers players held on to me, and as they restrained me Bridgman let me have it."

— Borje Salming, *Blood, Sweat and Hockey* (1991)

The fight with Bridgman was the first of Salming's career. Bridgman said he went after the Leafs defenceman because he had tried to spear him: "When a guy tries to spear you, you can't allow him to get away with it. I was knocked down in front of the net and when I got up, another fight was on. Salming was there and he knew I wanted to have a go."

"I know they wanted to take me out of the game if they could. They hacked at me the whole game. I can't go after them every time they do something or I'd be in the penalty box all night. They seemed to want me to fight with them but that's not my nature."

— Borje Salming

"Salming just doesn't know how to fight. He's never learned. But he won't back down from anyone."

— Red Kelly

"They're a tough team which plays very rough hockey…. I get hit and I don't mind as long as it's clean. It's getting cheap shots that I don't like. I prefer to play against Montreal Canadiens and teams like them where it's just a battle of skill."

— Borje Salming

"We check him closely because he's so great. Who in hockey skates better than he does? No one can question his courage or bravery. It would be pretty dumb to say that a guy who dives in front of shots the way he does and battles in the corners lacked courage."

— Dave Schultz

Cooler heads did prevail in Game 4 when Toronto tied the series with a 4–3 victory. Only 10 penalties were called: seven minors against the Flyers (who surrendered two power-play goals) and three against the Leafs. The highlight of the night came late in the second period when Borje Salming — who was playing on his 25th birthday — took a pass from Darryl Sittler and broke in alone to beat former Leaf Bernie Parent. The goal put Toronto up 2–1, giving them a lead they would never relinquish, and the crowd responded with a two-minute standing ovation.

"The feelings went up and down my body. Yes, shivers. That's what it was. Maybe [later] tonight or tomorrow, when I am more calm, it will hit me even more, what it meant. But I appreciate it so much…."

— Borje Salming

Pyramid Power

Amid all the talk of Philadelphia's on-ice violence and Toronto's two victories, another story was quietly beginning to emerge.

"Leafs coach Red Kelly was talking yesterday about a mystical pyramid which gives strange power to those who lurk under its apex. It seems Kelly kept a pyramid under the bench for Thursday's game, and also believes the Gardens' building can serve as one as well."

— Christie Blatchford, *Globe and Mail*, Toronto, April 17, 1976

"Kelly says he devised pyramid power mostly to take the players' minds off statements made by Ballard. Before the series began, Ballard said: 'I'd be terribly surprised if we don't knock the Flyers off in five games' — a strange statement considering the Flyers were the defending champions and the Leafs an average team. That was the kind of pressure Kelly wanted to avoid."

— William Houston, *Ballard* (1985)

"He believed, he said, in pyramids, in the strange powers they have to give energy to those people aware enough to hang around the pyramidal apex. Red continued to praise the pyramid despite continued and vocal protests of ignorance from many of his players."

— Christie Blatchford, *Globe and Mail*, Toronto, April 21, 1976

"Sometimes Kelly would come up with something out of left field — something like pyramid power. He introduced pyramid power as we headed toward a seven-game playoff series with Philadelphia. Red believed that if you had a headache, you could get rid of it by placing a pyramid shape beneath your pillow. Red believed and he got us to believe.... Kelly brought in a guy from the University of Toronto who built four or five special pyramids to put under our bench. I gather it cost the club about $25,000. The university guy would bring them in and line them up to magnetic north."

— Tiger Williams, *Tiger* (1985)

The Leafs lost Game 5 of the series 7–1 in Philadelphia, but bounced back with an 8–5 win at Maple Leaf Gardens that tied the series 3–3 on April 22. It was another fight-filled game in which Darryl Sittler (who'd been held scoreless in the eight previous playoff games before this night) scored five goals.

"Sometimes you go out there and you don't know that's going to happen. I don't know why it happened. I feel lucky. Parent has been great throughout this series. Tonight I think he just had a bad night," Sittler said after the game.

Still, Pyramid Power continued to be the talk of Toronto. Kelly explained that his wife had become intrigued after pyramid-shaped objects had helped their daughter Casey overcome migraine headaches — although Andra Kelly wanted it known that the family didn't actually believe in the occult. Even so …

"When you're going with pyramid power you've got everything on your side. I put the pyramids in strategic locations around the net."

— Red Kelly after the game

"It's working, isn't it?

"I think they can influence events. They must, because without a miracle, there's no way we can beat Philadelphia. That's what I keep hearing, anyway."

— Red Kelly, asked if he really believed in
pyramids after the Leafs win in Game 6

The Leafs would take pyramid expert Thomas Atkins to Philadelphia for Game 7 so that the four-foot pyramid they had for their dressing room and the smaller models for the bench could be set up for maximum power. Darryl Sittler had a three-foot model he said he planned to sit under in his hotel room before the game.

It didn't work. The Flyers put on a solid two-way performance, overcame a 2–1 deficit with three goals in 81 seconds early in the second period, and beat the Maple Leafs 7–3 to win the series.

"We just didn't have it. We just didn't have the depth. Flyers did. We gave it our best shot. I'm proud of the guys and the way they played."

— Red Kelly

"We didn't lose through a lack of effort. We took the Stanley Cup champs to seven games and that, I think, is a remarkable feat. We're on the upswing. We'll improve with experience."

— Darryl Sittler

1976–77

The Maple Leafs had a remarkably similar season to the previous one in 1976–77. Once again, Toronto scrambled to play .500 hockey, finishing the season 33–32–15. Like the year before, they were well back of the NHL's top teams, but comfortably in the playoff picture at the end of the season.

The Popcorn Kid

"Someone came to interview me in juniors and saw me eating popcorn before a game. We used to get to the rink two hours early and would be kind of hungry and the only thing we could get at the concessions was popcorn. They weren't even open yet but we'd knock on the back door and they'd give us some popcorn. So the reporter asked me if I ate popcorn before every game and I said 'Not really.' But when the article came out the next day he called me The Popcorn Kid. The best popcorn was at the London Gardens, but I didn't really eat it every game. To be honest, most of the time when I go to games today I end up getting popcorn."

— Mike Palmateer, mikepalmateer.ca

Mike Palmateer grew up in Toronto and had starred for the Toronto Marlboros, winning the Memorial Cup with them in 1973. The Maple Leafs picked him in the fifth round of the 1974 NHL Draft, 85th overall, and signed him later that summer. He spent the next two seasons in the minor leagues as the Leafs shuffled through goalies Doug Favell, Gord McRae, Dunc Wilson, Pierre Hamel, and Wayne Thomas.

Palmateer was with the Leafs in training camp in the fall of 1976, but began the season in the Central Hockey League with the Dallas farm club Toronto shared with Chicago.

"I might have to spend some time in the minors, but the only reason you come to camp is to make the team. It's awfully tough."

— Mike Palmateer after a strong performance in a 2–1 exhibition game
victory over Detroit, September 23, 1976

"I guess I'd feel cheated if the club wanted Mike Palmateer right away. You know, just based on training camp. I'm not glamorous, but I do think I won a few games for them. But if I start to fall apart in the season, well, I'd guess they would bring him up. That's something else."

— Gord McRae to Christie Blatchford, *Globe and Mail*,
Toronto, October 2, 1976

It didn't take long to make the move. After a 5–3 loss to Minnesota on October 27, 1976, which dropped their early season record to 1–5–3, something had to be done.

"Gord McRae didn't play a bad game, but lately it seems that every time there's a break around our net, the puck goes in…. We're going to need a superb effort in goal to get us turned around, so we'll bring up Mike Palmateer from Dallas Black Hawks to play against Detroit."

— Red Kelly

"Palmy had the reputation of being a cocky little SOB and it was richly deserved. But he was one of those guys his teammates loved. I liked his cockiness, which showed up more in his demeanour than his talk.... Mike was very confident; he didn't have to say a lot in the dressing room."

— Darryl Sittler, *Sittler* (1991)

"Mr. Gregory, your troubles are over."

— remark attributed to Mike Palmateer when he arrived in Detroit for his NHL debut on October 28, 1976

The Leafs beat Detroit 3–1 in Palmateer's first game. The win snapped a seven-game losing streak and marked the first time all season that Toronto had surrendered less than four goals.

"Palmateer did the job, but the guys in front of him played the type of hockey we have to to do anything. We had discipline and control in our play, checking hard and waiting for opposition mistakes."

— Red Kelly

"This was a big night in my life, the chance to show what I could do in the NHL and to get my foot in the door. I wasn't too nervous, but then I'd had a rather hectic 24 hours [getting here] and was a little bit tired. That helped me relax.... I thought I played a pretty solid game, but don't forget that the guys in front of me played a great game."

— Mike Palmateer

Palmateer got the bulk of the starts for Toronto from that point on, solidifying his position as the number-one goalie with a 1–0 shutout against the defending Stanley Cup champion Montreal Canadiens (who had knocked off Philadelphia the previous spring) on November 11, 1976. It was his second consecutive shutout. He made 39 saves in this one game.

"We had the chances. There were some bad breaks around their net, but you can't take anything away from Palmateer's performance. He played exceptionally well."

— Canadiens coach Scotty Bowman

"It was obvious he played well. It was an honest shutout and he earned it."

— Canadiens goalie Ken Dryden

"His confidence is good and he doesn't get rattled. Even in the third period when they came bearing down on him he stood his ground."

— Leafs coach Red Kelly

The Leafs would still struggle to stay above .500, but there would be one very memorable moment this season.

Turnbull's Star Turn

Playing alongside Borje Salming, Ian Turnbull had emerged as a star in his own right in 1975–76, scoring 20 goals to set a team record for defencemen and ranking among the league leaders with a plus-minus rating of +24.

"[Salming] had a much more spectacular style than I did. He would be sliding all over the ice and blocking shots, doing all those sort of things. And I was a little calmer, less spectacular. I went about my business, sometimes to my detriment, I guess. It was said that I almost looked like I wasn't trying, but that's not the truth at all. My style of play was pretty slick. I didn't waste too much effort. I made the game look a little easier than it really is."

— Ian Turnbull to John Iaboni, *Leafs Game Day Program*, issue 3, 2006–07

"Ian Turnbull was another player with great talent, but ... he wasn't conscientious about conditioning or practice; he was the type of guy who'd do as little as he could to get by. I don't think Ian ever reached his full potential because of his lackadaisical attitude, but in his early years with us he had such great skills and natural ability that he contributed a lot."

— Darryl Sittler, *Sittler* (1991)

Heading into a game against Detroit at Maple Leaf Gardens on February 2, 1977, Turnbull was Toronto's plus-minus leader and had 11 goals — but he was in a scoring drought. After recently ending a streak of 30 straight games without a goal, he'd been held scoreless again for five in a row. The slump ended big-time this night. Turnbull scored twice against Ed Giacomin in the Red Wings net during the second period as Toronto jumped out to a 5–0 lead. Jim Rutherford was in goal to start the third period when Turnbull scored two more to tie the NHL record for goals in a game by a defenceman as Toronto built up an 8–1 lead. With time running out, a new record seemed doubtful. Until ...

"Borje Salming pass to Turnbull. He's in the clear! Going in alone. This could be it. Scores! Ian Turnbull has set a record."

— Bill Hewitt's play-by-play call of Ian Turnbull's fifth goal

"Oh, boy. Look at the Leafs pile off that bench. Five goals in a game. A new record by a defenceman. And look at this crowd. Everybody up, up up! ... Oh, what a reaction here at the Gardens with 1:30 left to play.... This is reminiscent of Sittler's big night."

— Brian McFarlane's TV commentary

"Watching Ian tonight brought back memories of that night for me. Even the way Ian's fourth goal went in reminded me of a couple of mine. You have to be a little lucky, too, to have a night like that."

— Darryl Sittler

Seen here battling with Marcel Dionne of the Los Angeles Kings, Ian Turnbull was Toronto's top offensive defenceman in the mid-1970s.

"I guess I just got lucky. You get lucky every now and then."
— Ian Turnbull, after the game

Like Darryl Sittler's 10-point game, Turnbull's record from that night has never been broken. But that doesn't mean that fame has been everlasting, as he found out when he had another big scoring night while playing for the L.A. Kings on December 12, 1981.

"I had just scored my fourth goal of the game. A teammate, Mark Hardy, sat down next to me on the bench. He says something like, 'Ian, wasn't that your fourth goal?' I said yeah. And he says that must be some kind of a record. And I said that no, it wasn't a record. He says back to me, 'It's not a record?' I said simply, 'No.'

"Of course then he asked me what the record was. I said five. He looks at me and says, 'Five? Some guy got five goals in a game?' I just calmly looked at him and replied, 'Yes.' A few more moments went by and he finally looks at me and asked who scored the five goals. I simply looked at him and answered, 'I did.' He couldn't believe it. We just laughed about it. But it just showed me that not everybody in the hockey world knew that I had once scored five goals in a game."
— Ian Turnbull to Randy Schultz, NHL.com, February 2, 2007

The 1977 Playoffs

For the second year in a row, Toronto met Pittsburgh in the preliminary round. The Leafs won the opener of the best-of-three series 4–2 at Maple Leaf Gardens on April 5, 1977.

"Them Penguins are done like dinner."
— Tiger Williams to Brian McFarlane on television after the game

Pittsburgh won Game 2, 6–4 at home, but the Leafs finished them off with a 5–2 win back home in Game 3 and advanced to face the Flyers in the quarter-finals for the third year in a row. Toronto opened the series with two straight wins in Philadelphia.

"The Tiger then suggested that if the Leafs played the same way in the next two, the Flyers were done like dinner."
— Christie Blatchford, *Globe and Mail*, Toronto, April 14, 1977

Tiger Williams was a tough guy who could do more than just fight, and Toronto fans loved him.

But the Flyers won two straight overtime games at Maple Leaf Gardens to get back into the series, and wound up winning it in six games.

"I suspect that more than a few times this summer I'll think back over the season and shake my head when it hits me about what might have happened if we'd just been a little sharper a little longer in those two [overtime] games."

— Darryl Sittler

"What really hurts about losing this series is how very close we came to winning it. I'm proud of my guys because we had seven players injured and we extended a team which finished 34 points ahead of us during the season to six games, lost two in overtime and one by a goal. Take seven players away from the Flyers and see how well they'd do. We battled them right to the end with all we had."

— Leafs coach Red Kelly

Despite what he said, after four years behind the bench, speculation was that Kelly was through as coach of the Maple Leafs.

"My future? I have a contract that runs out in September. I'm a Celt. We don't ask or give any favours. They bury us straight up so we're ready for the fight in the next world."

— Red Kelly, admitting after the game that he'd
received no word yet about a new contract

"Red Kelly's job is as secure as mine and I'm not gonna get fired. There'll be some changes, you can bet on that. We should be in Montreal tonight. We never should have blown two good chances the way we did."

— Harold Ballard

1977-78

As early as May of 1977, there were rumours that Roger Neilson would replace Red Kelly as coach of the Maple Leafs. Neilson had never played pro hockey; never rising above Junior B as a goaltender. He was a teacher who had spent ten years coaching the Junior A Peterborough Petes before taking his first professional hockey job as coach of the Dallas Black Hawks in 1976–77.

"Roger Neilson is in my league, but Red is a good man. I will always have a spot for him in the Leafs organization. There are a lot of things to be worked out in the next couple of weeks. Red is not the most dynamic coach but he did a reasonably good job for us. I will have to sit down with him in the next while and see what he wants…. I have no doubt that Neilson is an excellent hockey man…. But I must emphasize that a decision has not been made on anyone, anywhere. That will be done in a couple of weeks," Harold Ballard announced on May 24, 1977.

At the time, Kelly was nursing a painful back injury as a result of an on-ice collision with Lanny McDonald during a practice in late March. In June, Ballard would use the injury as a reason not to bring Kelly back as coach.

"He told me he had decided on a change and I said fine…. He didn't offer me another chance at the job. My understanding was that I was through. Actually, I'd been considering the situation for quite a while and I'd pretty well made up my mind to get out. Because of that, I wasn't too upset when I met Ballard yesterday. It didn't really fizz on me. I was in that frame of mind when I went in," Kelly told Jim Proudfoot of the *Toronto Star* in June 1977.

"The only thing I don't like," Ballard said, "is the news media using the word *fired*. To me, that word indicates that somebody has done something wrong…. Why, Red could have a job here in our organization anytime. He's a guy who doesn't complain. The word *sickness* is not in his vocabulary. [But]

Red's been bothered by that back for months and it's getting worse. I couldn't afford to take a chance. If surgery is required, he could be on his back for two or three months. He was in excruciating pain when he was here. If he had been in good health, I would have rehired him. But his contract was over anyway and his health helped to make the decision easier."

Kelly's former teammates George Armstrong (who'd been coaching the Toronto Marlboros) and Bob Pulford (who'd recently quit after five years as coach of the L.A. Kings) were also said to be up for the Leafs job, but Roger Neilson was hired on June 27. He was in Johannesburg, South Africa, when he agreed to terms over the phone. It was said to be a one-year deal in the neighbourhood of $40,000 — which was what Red Kelly had been paid.

> "Neilson has been one of the leading candidates for the job all along. We were very impressed with the development of our young players under his coaching last season in Dallas. Neilson has been a coach who has demanded discipline for his players and he's a teacher, both professionally and in hockey. His reports on players in Dallas were the best I've ever seen."
>
> — Harold Ballard

> "I like that he's from the same generation as the players. The ones who were under him in Dallas respected him and improved greatly."
>
> — Harold Ballard

Roger Neilson inherited a team that everyone saw to be on the rise. Jim Proudfoot in the *Toronto Star* compared his situation to that of Punch Imlach in 1958, taking over a team already led by talented young stars (in this case, Darryl Sittler, Lanny McDonald, Borje Salming, and Ian Turnbull) with others (Jack Valiquette, Don Ashby, Randy Carlyle, and John Anderson) thought to be on the brink. In July, it was reported that Harold Ballard and Alan Eagleson had agreed on new five-year contracts for Sittler and McDonald, paying them both about $150,000 per year.

> "I consider Sittler and McDonald the nucleus of the Leaf club and had no reservation whatsoever in renegotiating for contracts of that duration or for that much money. Genuine stars, which they both are, will always command big dollars. It's the unproven player receiving a high salary that doesn't sit well with me."
>
> — Harold Ballard

Neilson got down to work on July 25, 1977, with an approach that was already an old habit with him but something that was new to the NHL — studying video tapes. "I only saw four games all of last season," he said, "so I'll take these back to Peterborough with me and assess them. I can tell who is an offensive player from his statistics, but I really don't know who can check. I wouldn't want to impose a system which will take away from the goal-scoring of this team. However, being able to kill penalties and being able to hold a lead is the requisite of a good hockey club. I want to know who I have that can be sent out when we're ahead 1–0 with two minutes to go."

"[Neilson] said he had not yet considered what changes he might make in the Toronto forward lines, but stressed that he wants a team that plays a tough positional game. He indicated that, although he wants a tough team, there is still room for a player whose ability is offensive ... [but] Leafs' primary problem in failing to reach their potential over the past two seasons was a simple matter of allowing too many goals, in Neilson's analysis."

— James Christie, *Globe and Mail*, Toronto, July 26, 1977

"The Leafs can play a five-man unit, which is as good as any in the NHL. What will decide how well the team does is the strength of the foot soldiers. Montreal Canadiens are [two-time] champions, the team all others are measured against. They have about five super-players, the same as us. But they win because their foot soldiers are so good. Those aren't players with overwhelming talent but they have discipline and desire."

— Roger Neilson

"As a guy, [Roger] Neilson is almost a pacifist; but as a coach they just don't come any tougher. He loves tough players.... From my point of view, Neilson was exactly what we needed as a coach. He could coach the pants of most guys in the league, and he had no toleration for floaters."

— Tiger Williams, *Tiger* (1985)

"I definitely had a better rapport with Red Kelly than I did with Roger when Roger first came to the Leafs. Red was always willing to listen to suggestions, while Roger seemed to have a set way of doing things. It didn't matter at all during Roger's first season because everything clicked into place and there were no major problems that cropped up."

— Darryl Sittler, *Sittler at Centre* (1979)

Neilson set a target for the Leafs of cutting their goals against to under 240 in 1977–78 (down from 285 in 1976–77). They achieved that by allowing just 237. The offence declined from 301 goals to 271, but it was still a big year for the team's top stars. Lanny McDonald was fourth in the league with 47 goals, while Darryl Sittler's 72 assists trailed only New York Islanders star Bryan Trottier (77). Sittler's 117 points were bettered only by Trottier (123) and Guy Lafleur (132), who were also the only players to outpoint Sittler in the voting for the Hart Trophy as NHL MVP.

Despite a few moves during the season, Neilson remained concerned about his team's toughness at the trade deadline in March.

"Tiger was kept very busy that season.... In November, we picked up tough winger Jerry Butler in exchange for Inge Hammarstrom, and Pat Boutette chipped in whenever he could. But the three of them were almost worn out by the end of February. Neilson went to Gregory and laid it on the line:

"'We aren't going anywhere in the post-season unless we can get one more big guy to take the pressure off the skilled players.'

"'Who?'

"'Dan Maloney.'"

— Darryl Sittler, *Sittler* (1991)

The Leafs sent Errol Thompson (whose offence had slumped badly under Neilson's defensive system) and a package of draft choices to Detroit for Maloney. Many critics thought the Leafs gave up too much, but his new team was happy to have him.

"As tough a player as has ever played the game, and no one worked harder than he did. [He] wasn't afraid to grab somebody in the dressing room if he thought they weren't pulling their weight, and he'd lay it on the line."

— Lanny McDonald, *Lanny* (1987)

"Maloney gives our team one of the ingredients we've been missing — that big, aggressive winger who can boss the corners. The only player in the league who's in Dan's class in the pits is [Boston's] Terry O'Reilly."

— Darryl Sittler, who played junior hockey with Maloney in London

"He's a first-rate big leaguer, who works hard and plays tough. With Maloney, Tiger Williams, and Pat Boutette on the left side, the right wingers in this league are not going to have much fun playing against us."

> — Brian Glennie, who'd been viciously attacked
> on the ice by Maloney in 1976

"I have to play aggressive hockey to be effective and that's the style I'll play for the Leafs…. [It's] a great opportunity for me, jumping to a club that's a contender with a good shot at some big things this season."

> — Dan Maloney

The Leafs finished the year with 92 points on a record of 41–29–10. While they were once again third in the Adams Division behind Boston (113 points) and Buffalo (105), they had the sixth-best record in the NHL overall.

1978 Playoffs

The Leafs were in a slump as the regular season concluded. They'd lost 10 of 12 games down the stretch, including four straight to end the schedule. They got back on their game in the playoffs, sweeping the Los Angeles Kings with 7–4 and 4–0 victories in the best-of-three preliminary round.

Lanny McDonald's 47 goals in 1977–78 were one short of Frank Mahovlich's team record at the time. He would score an even more memorable goal in the playoffs that spring.

"In four days, Maple Leafs have advanced from a team in a bad slump to a club that looms as a handful for any foe in the Stanley Cup playoffs. Their efficient, decisive two-game demolition of Los Angeles Kings ... featured the ingredients of a winning playoff team — muscular, aggressive checking, opportunistic goal scoring from all forward lines and strong goaltending by Mike Palmateer."

— Frank Orr, *Toronto Star*, April 14, 1978

"I was impressed by the way Leafs played and they're going to be tough for any club to knock out, if they continue the pattern."

— Kings captain Mike Murphy

It was uncertain yet whether the Leafs would meet Philadelphia once again or the New York Islanders in the next round, as their quarter-final matchup would depend on whether or not Buffalo beat the New York Rangers in their preliminary round series.

"We don't really have a preference as to which team we play. If we can continue to play the style of hockey we used against L.A., we're confident we can give either Islanders or Flyers a big battle."

— Darryl Sittler

"By the spring of 1978, we were so close we could taste the Stanley Cup."

— Tiger Williams, *Tiger* (1985)

Leafs versus Islanders

When Buffalo beat the Rangers, as expected, the Leafs faced the Islanders in the quarter-finals. The New York team had entered the NHL as a laughing stock in 1972–73 with their record of 12–60–6 that season being the worst in modern league history at the time. Building through the draft, the Islanders quickly became a powerhouse behind players such as Denis Potvin, Bryan Trottier, and Mike Bossy. They'd reached the playoffs for the first time by their third season (1974–75) and the 1977–78 campaign marked their third straight year with more than 100 points. They'd reached the semifinals in each of the three previous seasons and were favoured to do so again when they took on the Leafs.

"Islanders are a different story than L.A. — deeper, bigger, stronger, well-coached [by Al Arbour] and very hungry. Leafs must perform at the absolute top of their form to stay close."

— unnamed NHL scout prior to the series

"We've worked hard on conditioning all year and we're in good shape. The longer the series goes, the more confidence our guys will gain.... If we play as well against Islanders as we did against Los Angeles, we'll win."

— Roger Neilson

The series was a rough one, with the Islanders taking the first two games at home. The Leafs bounced back, though, to even things up with two wins at Maple Leaf Gardens. But the Leafs' 3–1 win in Game 4 on April 23, 1977, was a costly one for the team.

"My most serious injury occurred during the 1978 quarter-finals against the Islanders. I was carrying the puck and tried to cut behind Lorne Henning. As I tried to shoot, he spun around to hook me and accidentally struck my eye with his stick. The pain was excruciating."

— Borje Salming, *Blood, Sweat and Hockey* (1991)

"I was trying to check Salming and when I couldn't, I tried to hook him. We fell backward and my stick came around and cut him. It was an accident. I bent over and told him it was an accident, but I guess he was in too much pain and didn't hear me.... There's no way anyone would want to see Salming hurt like that. He's not the type of player you'd try to hurt."

— Lorne Henning after the game

"The stick broke his nose and caused hemorrhaging in his eye."

— Leafs eye specialist Dr. Michael Easterbrook

"I grumbled at the time about having to miss the rest of the playoffs. Looking back, however, I realize how lucky I was not to lose the eye."

— Borje Salming, *Blood, Sweat and Hockey* (1991)

"Throughout the series there had been two constants. The brilliance of Palmateer, and the phenomenal play of Ian Turnbull. When Salming went down, Turnbull took over. He became the quarterback. He wanted the puck the way Salming always did. Ian was like a man possessed. I don't think he ever played as well, before that series or after it."

— Lanny McDonald, *Lanny* (1987)

"Without me, the Leafs battled even harder and extended the series to seven games. Palmateer, Sittler, Turnbull, and McDonald were all superb."

— Borje Salming, *Blood, Sweat and Hockey* (1991)

The Islanders won Game 5 back on Long Island but the Leafs tied them again with a 5–2 win at Maple Leaf Gardens on April 28. That game featured another key injury when the Leafs' Jerry Butler slammed Islanders star rookie Mike Bossy into the boards.

"I didn't know he was hurt until I blew the whistle and there was a stoppage of play. I was concentrating on the puck and the play in front of the Leaf net where [Mike] Palmateer and [Garry] Howatt were going at each other."

— Referee Dave Newell

"I never saw it. All I saw was my teammate down hurt. Look, they can hit as hard as they want to, but not with the stick."

— Garry Howatt, who was later given a game misconduct after fights with Butler, Tiger Williams, and Pat Boutette

"He got me after the whistle. It was a cheap shot."

— Mike Bossy

"I took him with the body in efforts to freeze the puck. It's the kind of play that happens many times during a game. I just glided into him and he went low."

— Jerry Butler

"I heard a little crack and I didn't want to take any chances, so I just lay there."

— Bossy, saying that he was never unconscious but explaining why he stayed down on the ice

Bossy was removed from the ice on a stretcher and was later diagnosed with a sprained neck. Though he would be back for Game 7, the hit may have been a turning point.

"There are times in a series when you know you have the other team, that something has gone out of them. If you had to pick a moment when the balance of power changed in that Islanders series, it was probably the moment when Butler smacked into Bossy. We were sharp in every department, and the longer the series went the more assured we became."

— Tiger Williams, *Tiger* (1985)

"Them Islanders are worse than done like dinner. They're burnt toast."

— Tiger Williams after the game

Game 7 was played on Long Island on Saturday night, April 29. The Leafs came out aggressively but the game settled into a tight-checking affair. Mike Palmateer and the Islanders' Glenn "Chico" Resch were both outstanding, with Palmateer beaten only by Denis Potvin after a mixup in the Leafs' zone early in the first period. The only shot to elude Resch in regulation time was an Ian Turnbull drive that tied the game at 13:42 of the second period. When no one scored in the third, the game headed for overtime, where Lanny McDonald — hampered by a wrist injury and wearing a cage to protect his broken nose — became the hero at 4:13 of the extra session.

"It's a play we've tried a few times in practice, but we needed a little luck to make it work. Turnbull brought the puck up the ice and I cut into the middle to spread the defence. He flipped a high pass to me which hit an Islander [Stefan Persson], hit me and dropped at my feet."

— Lanny McDonald after the game

"For a second [after Turnbull's high pass], I just couldn't find the puck against McDonald's dark blue sweater."

— Chico Resch after the game

"Three players — Clark Gillies, [Denis] Potvin, and Dave Lewis — were all close enough to make the play, but each was thinking the other guy was going to make it."

— Lanny McDonald, *Lanny* (1987)

"All of a sudden, there was nobody between me and Resch and I needed an instant to realize that I was in the clear. Chico came out to cut down the angle."

— Lanny McDonald after the game

"I thought McDonald was going to his backhand and I wasn't completely set for the shot."

— Chico Resch

"I thought about a backhand, but I haven't had much success with it. Then I saw a spot just over top of his glove."

— Lanny McDonald

"Even after the goal went in, it took a long time to register that I had actually scored — that the series was over. It took me all the way from being 25 feet out, to skating past Resch, to circling the net before I finally thought, 'My God, it's over.'"

— Lanny McDonald, *Lanny* (1987)

"We beat the Islanders, who had more talent than we did, because Roger Neilson coached the series brilliantly. He never let up for a second, working the bench, prodding the players, drawing the best out of every one of us. Every night we came to play; every shift we gave the sons of bitches a little more pressure."

— Tiger Williams, *Tiger* (1985)

"We won this series the day we got Dan Maloney."

— Roger Neilson

"There's no way we'd have gone this far without him. [Maloney] has done everything we expected of him and more."

— Leafs GM Jim Gregory

"It appeared they were looking beyond us to the finals. That upset us a little. We're a proud team, after all."

— Darryl Sittler on the Islanders' attitude heading into the series

"Sure, we wanted to play Canadiens again [after losing to them in the semifinals last year] because it would have meant we were in the Stanley Cup Final. But no one can say that we took the Leafs lightly and figured on any breeze. They're just too good a hockey team for us to have that sort of outlook. Leafs got great goaltending from Mike Palmateer, a big effort from every player, and they played strong, disciplined hockey which gave us little room to operate. Sure, they played physically tough hockey with some questionable tactics. But we can't alibi about anything. They beat us. That's all."

— Islanders star Denis Potvin

A cocky kid with a scrambling style, Mike Palmateer was a big reason why the Maple Leafs looked like a team on the rise in the late 1970s.

Leafs versus Canadiens

Instead of the Islanders facing the Canadiens in the Final, it was Toronto and Montreal meeting in the semifinals. It was the first time the two teams had played each other in the post-season since the 1967 Stanley Cup. The Canadiens' Yvan Cournoyer and the Leafs' Ron Ellis were the only players still on their teams from that series.

> "Playing Canadiens is a lift for us because there's something really special about a Toronto-Montreal series … Sure, they're a great team, but I know we'll give them a pretty fair tussle. Beating the Islanders, who are also a fine team, is a big confidence builder for this club."
>
> — Ron Ellis

> "The nucleus of the club is a gang of guys who have been together for about five seasons. Maybe our time has come because we've reached a maturity as players."
>
> — Ian Turnbull

But the Canadiens were just too good, and they swept Toronto in four straight, going on to beat Boston in six games for their third consecutive Stanley Cup championship. They'd make it four straight the following season, sweeping the Leafs again in the 1979 quarter-finals.

1978–79

It would be a long time before Toronto enjoyed another season as successful as 1977–78. Despite having most of the same personnel in place, the Leafs slipped back to the .500 level with a record of 34–33–13 for 81 points in the 80-game season. The poor performance would cost Roger Neilson his job — twice!

"There were a lot of injuries and a lot of losses and a lot of problems to be dealt with. It all came to a head when Roger was fired and then rehired during those bizarre days in early March."

— Darryl Sittler, *Sittler at Centre* (1979)

"We weren't playing hockey as a team. We were playing more as individuals and things were going from bad to worse. Guys would be sulking and complaining about lack of ice time, things like that. Then, suddenly, Roger was fired. Mr. Ballard shook everything up with that announcement and everybody was talking about it."

— Darryl Sittler, *Sittler at Centre* (1979)

"After Roger was dismissed, he approached the players and asked them all to fill out a questionnaire he'd prepared. It was almost as if he wanted us to grade him as a coach…. Roger gave us a choice. We could fill out his questionnaire or we could discuss things privately. Most of the players decided to have a private conversation with him in his office. I'm sure a lot of us pulled no punches because we had no idea Roger would be back with the club a few hours later. We definitely said how we felt. I think we all learned a lot from those candid discussions and the team as a whole was the beneficiary. It was a unique experience for Roger and it would never have happened had he not been fired. I think he became a better coach on that day."

— Darryl Sittler, *Sittler at Centre* (1979)

"Roger Neilson was fired in the middle of the 1978–79 season…. Over lunch, I asked Neilson, 'If Ballard asked you back, would you come?' He said, 'Of course — I like the team and I think it's very close to real success.

Also, I'm unemployed.' I raced home and got on the phone. First I called Sittler and asked him how he felt about Neilson's departure. He said that he was disappointed."

— Tiger Williams, *Tiger* (1985)

"Tiger phoned me on Thursday night.... We agreed to get the players together before practice the next morning, Friday, and we voted."

— Darryl Sittler, *Sittler* (1991)

"We agreed to poll all the players, get them to the rink at nine o'clock the following morning and take a vote. If it was overwhelming, Sittler would go to Ballard as team captain. The vote was about ninety percent in Neilson's favour."

— Tiger Williams, *Tiger* (1985)

"Roger got a ninety percent support rating — Ian Turnbull was one of the few to vote against him."

— Darryl Sittler, *Sittler* (1991)

"We had a long meeting and everybody was serious. We agreed we weren't going anyplace if we didn't change our attitude, if we didn't start pulling together as a team. We agreed it wasn't Roger's fault we were stumbling around and we decided to meet with Mr. Ballard and ask him to reconsider and hire Roger back."

— Darryl Sittler, *Sittler at Centre* (1979)

"Sittler went up to Ballard's office and told him about the team's vote. Ballard came to meet us, listened to Sittler, who could be very eloquent, saying that Neilson had the team's respect and that whatever had gone wrong was the fault of the players."

— Tiger Williams, *Tiger* (1985)

"Mr. Ballard listened to our plea. Then he told us he didn't think his top five players on the team were playing up to their potential. There was something wrong and it was up to us to set things right. He said he would take Roger back, and if any of the players didn't want to play for Roger, Mr. Ballard would arrange to have that player traded to another team."

— Darryl Sittler, *Sittler at Centre* (1979)

"Ballard said, 'Okay, you've got your coach back, but you bastards better make sure you start to do something.' Then he walked out of the room and slammed the door."

— Tiger Williams, *Tiger* (1985)

"I didn't get involved in any of the other business to do with Neilson's re-instatement. I don't know why Ballard suggested that Neilson return with a bag on his head, other than to get the cheapest kind of publicity.... It was a shame we couldn't go on to win the Stanley Cup. It was an even greater shame when Neilson was gonged again that summer."

— Tiger Williams, *Tiger* (1985)

It was unclear for a long while who would replace Neilson behind the Leafs' bench in 1979–80. Ballard was interested in Don Cherry, who would instead wind up with the Colorado Rockies after being fired by the Bruins. There was also talk of Scotty Bowman, but when he left Montreal it was to become coach and GM of the Buffalo Sabres. The names of Flyers' assistant Mike Nykoluk and ex-Leaf Marcel Pronovost (who'd recently been fired as coach in Buffalo) also came up. There was even talk that Ballard would once again re-hire Neilson. But there would be more changes in Toronto before a new coach was named — and they would prove to be disastrous.

8

1980s: Tough Times

1979 TO 1982

The Return of Punch Imlach

The 1980s would be a terrible time to be a fan of the Toronto Maple Leafs. The troubled times started during the summer of 1979 … but Harold Ballard had spoken openly about Punch Imlach returning to Toronto as early as 1975.

> "Sure, I'd hire Punch back, and so would every other club in the NHL if they had the chance. He's a good hockey man and it's a shame he was fired. Stafford Smythe fired Punch not me. My wife became sick during that last game Punch coached. I took her home at the end of the second period. Just as I pulled in my driveway a bulletin flashed over the car radio — Punch Imlach had been fired. I damned near had a fit."
>
> — Harold Ballard, reported by Donald Ramsay,
> *Globe and Mail*, Toronto, October 29, 1975

After building the Buffalo Sabres from an expansion team in 1970 to a perennial power (if never a Stanley Cup champion) by the middle of the decade, Imlach was fired in December of 1978. By March of 1979 — when Ballard had first fired Roger Neilson — rumours began making the rounds that Imlach would return to Toronto.

> "The rumours a few days ago that Punch Imlach's hiring by Leafs was imminent might have been great fun for the fans and media people who

blew this completely baseless report into Topic A for a day or two, but might have been one reason why Leafs skated out Wednesday looking flat and battled."

— Scott Young, *Globe and Mail*, Toronto, March 17, 1979

It turned out the reports were anything but baseless.

"George (Punch) Imlach, fired by Toronto Maple Leafs in 1969, is expected to rejoin the … club next week as general manager and director of hockey operations…. Imlach was offered the job after club owner Harold Ballard failed to hire Don Cherry, who left Boston Bruins to become coach of Colorado Rockies, and Scotty Bowman, who quit Montreal Canadiens to join the Sabres as general manager. Imlach … and Ballard met early last week and ironed out the details that would expedite his return to Maple Leaf Gardens as replacement to general manager Jim Gregory."

— Donald Ramsay, *Globe and Mail*, Toronto, June 23, 1979

On July 3, Imlach and Ballard met again to finalize the deal.

"This is a great day — a great deal. It marks the return of the Imlach era. I've been courting Punch for months. He's the guy I wanted all along."

— Harold Ballard at the press conference to officially
announce Imlach's hiring on July 4, 1979

Not everyone would feel the same way.

"On July 4, 1979, Harold Ballard hired George (Punch) Imlach as general manager of the Toronto Maple Leafs hockey club. With the 1980s only five months away, Harold turned the franchise around and pointed us straight back toward the 1960s. In his own words, our future was our past…. [It was] a gigantic mistake, one which was going to condemn his team to another decade of frustration, poor performances and lack of success."

— Darryl Sittler, *Sittler* (1991)

"Ballard brought in Punch Imlach, and that was more than a shame. It was a goddamned tragedy."

— Tiger Williams, *Tiger* (1985)

1979–80

On July 20, 1979, Imlach hired Floyd Smith as the Leafs new coach. Smith had played under Imlach briefly in Toronto and had coached the Sabres to their greatest successes in the mid-1970s. But it was clear who was in charge of the team. Imlach had set the tone for his return right from the outset.

> "Outside of five or six good players, the team does not have what it takes to go all the way. It's not competitive enough to bring you the Stanley Cup."
>
> — Punch Imlach at the press conference announcing his signing

Obviously there were going to be changes.

> "Right from the start, Imlach had created a new, harsh atmosphere in the Gardens. It was as though we were stepping back in time. One of the first things he did was impose a very harsh dress code…. Imlach also had the phone ripped out of the dressing room; he didn't give any reason for doing it. Anybody could see that he wanted confrontations. He wanted to pick off the main men, and we all knew that it was only a matter of time. We were like guys in the trenches just waiting to be hit by a sniper."
>
> — Tiger Williams, *Tiger* (1985)

One of Imlach's first moves had been to bar Darryl Sittler and Mike Palmateer from taking part in the late-summer filming of "Showdown," a popular skills competition organized by the NHL Players' Association and aired during intermissions on *Hockey Night in Canada*. The two players participated anyway, and the relationship between Imlach and Sittler would never be healed.

> "[Sittler] didn't have any jealousy in him, and that's very important over a long season; jealousy can destroy a club…. Sittler would unify a dressing room, which is something Punch Imlach saw as a big problem when really it could have been Toronto's biggest asset."
>
> — Tiger Williams, *Tiger* (1985)

Darryl Sittler had a no-trade clause in his contract dating back several years. The Leafs would have to pay him $500,000 if he was dealt. But Imlach didn't plan to let that stop him.

"[I thought the revised 1978 contract] constituted a new contract and did not mention the no-trade clause. I thought there was a loophole there and I intended to use it."

— Punch Imlach, *Heaven and Hell in the NHL* (1982)

"For Punch, the trade war was on in earnest. He'd convinced Harold Ballard that I was a cancer on the team and, if he couldn't excise me, he'd be sure all the tissue around me was irradiated."

— Darryl Sittler, *Sittler* (1991)

"There are no untouchables on this hockey club. I'd trade them all if I could improve the team. That includes Sittler, who just doesn't seem to have it some nights. He seems to have lost a step."

— Punch Imlach, quoted by Frank Orr in the *Sporting News*, December 8, 1979

"Communication between the players and the front office? You can't talk about it because there just isn't any. Most players on the team never have talked to Imlach."

— Darryl Sittler, *Sporting News*, December 8, 1979

"If Sittler thinks Punch is going to hold his hand or give him a sucker every time we play, he's wrong."

— Harold Ballard, *Sporting News*, December 8, 1979

"I'm tired of listening to all the horse manure from Imlach. Sometimes I wish they'd trade me so I wouldn't have to put up with it."

— Mike Palmateer, *Sporting News*, December 8, 1979

Imlach couldn't trade Sittler, but he could make it uncomfortable for him to stay. Palmateer wouldn't be dealt until the end of the season, but Imlach started dealing others close to Sittler right after Christmas. First to go was Pat Boutette, a valuable teammate for four years in Toronto who had played junior hockey with Sittler in London. He was dealt on December 27, 1979. An even bigger blow came the next day.

"On December 28, [Ray] Miron and Imlach finalized the trade…. [A]fter practice, Lanny [McDonald] and Joel [Quenneville] were summoned to Punch's office."

— Darryl Sittler, *Sittler* (1991)

Things went bad for Leafs captain Darryl Sittler soon after Punch Imlach returned as general manager. They would only get worse until he was finally traded.

"I left the coach's office. I was numb."

— Lanny McDonald, *Lanny* (1987)

"I was still in the dressing room when Lanny returned, tears in his eyes. 'I've been traded to the Colorado Rockies,' he said. He looked lost. The shock was so palpable; some of the guys fell back or slumped into their seats as if they'd been struck physically."

— Darryl Sittler, *Sittler* (1991)

The trade was Lanny McDonald and Joel Quenneville for Wilf Paiement and Pat Hickey. Hockey-wise, it wasn't a terrible move — but McDonald was part of the heart of the team.

"Leaf players were stunned, almost in shock. Many were speechless. Captain Sittler was in tears."

— Jim Kernaghan, *Toronto Star*, December 29, 1979

"It was like a punch in the face for both Sittler and me. In fact, the reaction throughout the dressing room was one of the most emotional things I've ever seen. McDonald walked into the room after [practice] with a piece of paper in his hand … and it had his flight times typed on it. He didn't say anything. He just handed the piece of paper to Sittler, who read it, then started crying. When it was clear that McDonald was on his way, other guys started to cry. It was really unbelievable. The guys who weren't into crying started throwing things around."

— Tiger Williams, *Tiger* (1985)

"I can't believe it. We just lost the best right winger in the league. Wait and see what he does for Colorado."

— Leafs centre Walt McKechnie

"Imlach had to get rid of one of them to show his strength. He couldn't get rid of Darryl because of that clause in his contract, so they got at him another way by trading Lanny."

— anonymous Leafs player

"To this day, I still believe I was traded out of spite. Punch really wanted to show who was boss…. He saw Darryl and his captaincy as a threat and wanted to trade him, but because of the no-trade clause in Sitt's contract, Punch couldn't deal. Imlach had no way to get back at Darryl, so he did the next best thing: he traded Darryl's best friend instead. That happened to be me."

— Lanny McDonald, *Lanny* (1987)

"Everyone sat down for a minute. They took it hard. Smitty (Toronto coach Floyd Smith) kept saying, 'What? You were traded for who?' Smitty hadn't even been told of the deal."

— Joel Quenneville

"I have to say it was a shock. You get close to an individual and you know how he feels when he is traded. Some of the players felt pretty bad about it. It's a very lonely thing. [McDonald] is one of the classiest guys in the game and his record speaks for itself."

— Leafs coach Floyd Smith

"The whole operation seems to be deteriorating. Instead of building up the players, they're tearing them down. It's not easy to live in that situation, let alone play in it. It's very disappointing after giving seven years of your career.... I'm going to do my best for Colorado and I'm happy as hell to be going to a place that wants me. They've given me a purpose to play the game again."

— Lanny McDonald from Denver before his first game with the Rockies on December 29

That same Saturday night, before the Leafs game at home against the Winnipeg Jets, Darryl Sittler removed the "C" from his sweater following the pre-game warm-up. The following statement was distributed by Leafs trainer Guy Kinnear after the game:

> I told my teammates and my coach before the game that I was resigning as captain of the Toronto Maple Leafs. When I was made captain, it was the happiest day of my life. I have tried to handle my duties as captain in an honest and fair manner. I took player complaints to management and discussed management ideas with players.
>
> At the start of this season, I was personally sued by my own hockey team management. I was told it was nothing personal. I explained my position to Mr. Imlach and Mr. Ballard at that time. I told them that I felt a captain's role was to work with the players and management, not just management.
>
> Mr. Ballard and Mr. Imlach made some negative comments about me and my teammates some weeks ago and I met with them to discuss it. I was told I was being too sensitive. I have had little or no contact with Mr. Imlach and it is clear to me that he and I have different ideas about player and management communication.
>
> I have recently been told that management has prevented me from appearing on *Hockey Night in Canada* telecasts. I am

spending more and more time on player-management problems, and I don't feel I am accomplishing enough for my teammates.

The war between Mr. Imlach and Mr. Eagleson should not overshadow the main issue — the Toronto Maple Leafs. I am totally loyal to the Toronto Maple Leafs. I don't want to let my teammates down, but I have to be honest with myself. I will continue to fight for players' rights, but not as captain of the team.

All I want to do is give all my energy and all my ability to my team as a player.

Sincerely,
Darryl Sittler

Punch Imlach denied that he had anything to do with Sittler's resignation, and claimed that the move "was staged" by Alan Eagleson; something the agent denied.

"I told [Sittler] Friday night not to do anything in the heat of the moment that he might regret and we talked several times for maybe three hours Saturday. I guess he made up his mind during the warm-up."

— Alan Eagleson

"He could have told us earlier in the day. Why did he go out for the warm-up with it and then take it off. Obviously it was staged."

— Punch Imlach

"[Management] should refuse Sittler's resignation and immediately reinstate him as captain. I've played for several captains and Sittler is by far the best. He cares about the players and their problems more than any guy on this team."

— Ron Ellis

"I was never so goddamn mad in my life as when Sittler ripped the captain's C off his sweater. It was traitorous; it was like pissing on the flag of Canada. It was the act of a sulky, spoiled brat. I told Punch Imlach, I said, 'that's it, get that son-of-a-bitch outta here fast, I don't care how you do it.' And, believe me, we're trying. As soon as we can make a deal his ass is gone."

— Harold Ballard on the incident, quoted in William Houston, *Ballard* (1985)

As rumours made the rounds about potential Sittler trades, Imlach continued to deal other players. Another close friend was dealt away on February 18, 1980, when the Leafs sent Tiger Williams and Jerry Butler to Vancouver for Rick Vaive and Bill Derlago.

"Sittler could have been part of this deal, and a while back, he almost was. At that time, Sittler and Williams were offered for Derlago, Vaive, Jere Gillis, and a draft choice. It was scuttled when Sittler rejected the Canucks as a destination.

"Another of the many [rumours] making the rounds had him going to Philadelphia Flyers for Rick MacLeish and Andre Dupont, a proposed transaction said to have been shot down by the Leafs because the Flyers were too old. MacLeish is 30, Dupont 30."

— Jim Kernaghan, *Toronto Star*, February 19, 1980

"According to Buffalo Sabres' associate coach Roger Neilson, former coach of Leafs, Imlach was willing to accept a 29-year-old for Sittler, but that 29-year-old was Gil Perreault. Exit Sabres, at least for now. Imlach wants at least Ken Linseman, a 23-year-old centre, from Flyers. Exit Flyers…. The [Minnesota] North Stars could be the key. They have three excellent young defencemen in Craig Hartsburg, Brad Maxwell, and Greg Smith, so they could afford to give up one…. There's another thing, too. Stars' manager Lou Nanne is convinced someone of Sittler's stature could move the Stars from their present fifth overall into serious Stanley Cup contention. He was upset the Stars didn't get a chance to bid for Lanny McDonald."

— Ken McKee, *Toronto Star*, February 19, 1980

By this time, many Leafs wanted out of Toronto, but not Williams.

"I never wanted to leave Toronto. I like this city. I like the fans…. I got to play on the same team with the league's best player. That's right — Borje Salming. And I got to play for the finest leader — Darryl Sittler. Best goalie, too — Mike Palmateer."

— Tiger Williams after the trade

The Leafs were unhappy to lose Williams, unhappy with the way Imlach broke the news, and unhappy that he hadn't even notified Butler about the trade.

"It's too bad that Jerry had to hear it from Tiger. Tiger was told he'd been traded, went to his room and then had to tell Jerry, his roommate on this trip, that he was gone too."

— Darryl Sittler

"I haven't talked to anybody about this. Nobody's talked to me. Imlach told Tiger about the trade and Tiger told me. I'm gonna get fined if Tiger's fooling around."

— Jerry Butler

"What Imlach's trying to do with the Leafs, well, only time will tell, and I've got no axe to grind. But Punch made a mistake. When he started fooling around with Darryl, he cut into the heart of the team. That's what was causing most of the aggravation on the team — just the treatment Darryl got."

— Tiger Williams

"Messing with Sittler hurt the team in more ways than one. It hurts everyone when they see someone like Sittler, somebody who's given his whole heart and life to the Maple Leafs, get dumped on like he was."

— Jerry Butler

"I have a mandate to fulfill. I've got a puzzle to put together. And I'm working on finding the pieces until it fits."

— Punch Imlach

The NHL had grown to 21 teams in 1979–80 after taking in the Hartford Whalers, Winnipeg Jets, Edmonton Oilers, and Quebec Nordiques from the World Hockey Association. Though the Oilers had been allowed to keep Wayne Gretzky, whom they'd signed as a 17-year-old in 1978, the four top teams from the WHA had been gutted upon their entry into the NHL. Only Edmonton and Hartford managed to eke their way into the playoffs, with Winnipeg and Quebec among the five teams that missed out as 16 of 21 teams qualified for the post-season. The Leafs made it in (they would be swept in the opening round) despite falling below .500 with a record of 35–40–5 (their first losing season in five years). It would be 13 years before the club would climb above .500 again.

The 1979–80 season was a car wreck … literally. On March 14, 1980, Floyd Smith was involved in a car accident while en route from Toronto to his home in Buffalo. The driver and a passenger in the other car were killed. Smith —

who suffered a broken kneecap and various other cuts and bruises — would eventually be cleared of any charges, but he was not able to return as coach. Assistant Dick Duff took over the team for two games, but then Punch Imlach summoned Joe Crozier from his position as coach of Toronto's farm club in New Brunswick to aid him as Imlach appointed himself coach.

"Somebody has to have the job and it might as well be me.... After the film session, I told the players that George Imlach had hired Punch Imlach to coach the team. I told them that all I expect is effort and I better get it. Then I slammed the door and walked out."

— Punch Imlach, March 18, 1980

When Imlach was hired in July, people had expressed concerns about his health. A heart attack had forced him to give up coaching in Buffalo in 1972. Now, the concerns were raised again.

"No, I didn't check with the doctors. Why should I? I think this is the best way to handle the whole goddamn thing and that's all there is to it. I told my wife though, and she just about jumped through my throat."

— Punch Imlach

1980–81

On August 25, 1980, Punch Imlach suffered another heart attack and was rushed to Toronto General Hospital. His doctor, W.F. Greenwood, referred to it as "a good-sized, serious coronary," adding that, "he's now moderately ill, but with any luck he'll be all right. Punch said to say he'll be out of circulation for a month, but if you want my opinion, it will be a lot longer."

Joe Crozier would be the coach and Harold Ballard named himself acting GM in Imlach's place. Though it was believed that Imlach was finally close to negotiating a deal for Darryl Sittler to the Quebec Nordiques, one of Ballard's first moves was to try to mend the relationship with the player he had only recently called "a cancer on the team."

During training camp, Ballard convinced Sittler to take back the captaincy.

"We had a long chat and he asked me if I would put the C back on, and I said, 'I guess I would.'"

— Darryl Sittler, after returning as captain in an exhibition game against Montreal on September 24, 1980

"You can bet he'll never take it off again. It was in frustration that he took it off last year, that's all."

— Harold Ballard

"Of course I said yes. We both made mistakes over the past year but all that is in the past now. We buried the hatchet some time ago."

— Darryl Sittler

"It's the best move anybody could have made. At the moment, it's the best thing that could have happened because Sitt can do so many things. We needed this. We have a lot of young guys and he's so good with them. This will mean a lot to the team."

— Borje Salming

"I was there when he took the C off and it was a downer. A lot of players are pretty happy about it, believe me."

— Leafs goalie Paul Harrison

Imlach recovered and returned to the team on November 13. The Leafs had been playing well to that point, but began to slump. The low point came on January 7, when the woeful Winnipeg Jets (who were 4–29–8 on the season and had just recently snapped an NHL-record 30-game winless streak) crushed the Leafs 8–2. Toronto's record fell to 13–22–5, which had them 17th overall in the 21-team league and sitting outside the playoffs. Two days later, coach Joe Crozier was fired. Mike Nykoluk, a long-time assistant coach under Fred Shero with the Philadelphia Flyers and New York Rangers, was hired as the Leafs' new coach just prior to Toronto's next game. The Leafs tied the Flyers 4–4 that night. They would play .500 hockey under Nykoluk for the rest of the season, going 15–15–10 and climbing into 16th overall with 71 points. Slipping into the last playoff spot, the Maple Leafs matched up against the first overall (and defending Stanley Cup champion) New York Islanders and were crushed 9–2, 5–1, and 6–1 in a three-game sweep.

1981–82

At training camp in September of 1981, Punch Imlach suffered a third heart attack, resulting in quadruple bypass surgery. Although he was never officially fired, when he returned to work in November he found that his parking spot at Maple Leaf Gardens had been assigned to former Leafs scout Gerry

McNamara, who had been named acting GM. Imlach did not return to work and his contract was allowed to expire. He suffered another heart attack in 1985, and died on December 1, 1987.

"He was a great guy and the sporting world, especially hockey, is going to miss him terrifically," Ballard said after Imlach's death. But despite these sentiments, Ballard admitted it was a mistake to bring him back to Toronto.

"He'd lost his effect and I very foolishly hired him when he was washed up. But I don't regret hiring him because he was able to finish in Toronto where he started. He was always, always a Maple Leaf. He played for me as a junior with the Marlboros. We were pretty closely connected for 45 or 50 years."

The End of the Sittler Saga

Even without Imlach, the Leafs were a terrible team in 1981–82. Their record was 6–12–6 at the end of November when Darryl Sittler met with Harold Ballard and Gerry McNamara and told them he would be willing to waive the no-trade clause in his contract if the Leafs would send him to Minnesota or Philadelphia. Sittler would later say that it was something Ballard said that prompted him to reach his decision, although he would not say what it was. Some speculated that it related to Ballard's recent comments that Laurie Boschman's beliefs as a born-again Christian had hurt his play and was harming the team.

Soon, a trade to Minnesota seemed imminent, but Ballard wasn't satisfied with the North Stars' offer of one player off their roster, a player from their minor league system and two second-round draft picks. Ballard apparently wanted centre and team captain Tim Young, defenceman Brad Maxwell, and a first-round draft pick.

> "If Toronto isn't smart enough to realize what a second-round draft pick means, then there won't be any deal. They say they're going to have to bleed a little, so I should have to bleed, too. I'm willing to bleed, but not so much that I need a tourniquet."
>
> — North Stars GM Lou Nanne

McNamara and Nanne met when the North Stars visited Toronto on January 2, 1982.

> "He offered pretty well the same package he's always been offering, but nothing exciting — that's the bottom line. They know what they're getting but what they call a 'front-line' player and what we consider a 'front-line'

player seem to be two different things. That's probably our problem. He's still not playing our tune. It's not a question of him trying to wear me down or me trying to wear him down. It's just a stalemate and I can go on forever."

— Leafs acting GM Gerry McNamara

"What they want [in return] is a Darryl Sittler of eight years ago. Look, we want Darryl Sittler to come with us and be part of the supporting cast that can win a Stanley Cup. We just don't want to give up that supporting cast to get him."

— Lou Nanne

On January 5, Sittler skipped the Leafs' flight to Minnesota for a return engagement with the North Stars. A day later, agent Alan Eagleson said Sittler was "in a state of emotional depression" and had been advised by doctors to get away from hockey for about 10 days. Eagleson also said that Sittler had added the New York Islanders and Buffalo Sabres to the list of teams to which he would accept a trade. Sittler missed eight games (the Leafs went 4–2–2 without him) and had not returned to the lineup when he was finally traded on January 20, 1982. The destination was Philadelphia.

"It's been very difficult for us. Now that it's over, it's a great relief."

— Wendy Sittler, Darryl's wife

"I couldn't sleep after I was told about the trade. I talked to [Flyers' star] Billy Barber at three in the morning and I managed to get some sleep from five to seven...."

— Darryl Sittler

"It has worked out well for both parties. As everyone knows, he has had a great career and I wish him well."

— Harold Ballard

"I'm not proud of leaving the Leafs in this way. If you'd told me three years ago my career here would end like this, I'd never have believed it. But I guess at some point, after seeing what happened to guys like Normie Ullman, Dave Keon, and Ron Ellis, I began to prepare myself mentally for the possibility it would happen to me."

— Darryl Sittler

"I had always figured that I would end my career with the Leafs and never thought about leaving Toronto. Actually, to leave Toronto wasn't as difficult as I thought it would be. If I had known how easy it was, I might have moved earlier. But that's hindsight. The situation in Toronto really got to me. It was affecting my health and causing stress for Wendy and the kids."

— Darryl Sittler, reflecting on the trade a year later

In return for their long-time captain, the Leafs got the rights to promising college player Rich Costello and a second-round draft choice they would use to select Peter Ihnacak, plus future considerations that would turn out to be Ken Strong. Costello would wind up playing just 12 games for Toronto over parts of two seasons — the only action he ever saw in the NHL. Similarly, Strong played just 15 games over three seasons. Peter Ihnacak had a strong rookie season with 28 goals and 38 assists in 1982–83, but would never again match those totals over seven more seasons in Toronto. His brother, Miroslav Ihnacak, would prove an even bigger disappointment after expensive cloak and dagger efforts to get him out of Communist Czechoslovakia landed him in Toronto in 1985.

Rick Vaive Scores 50

There was one bright light in Toronto during the darkness that was the 1981–82 season when the man who replaced Darryl Sittler as captain reached a milestone no other player in franchise history had ever achieved.

Rick Vaive had been a member of the Baby Bulls (a group of seven under-aged free agents) playing with Birmingham in the World Hockey Association in 1978–79 before being drafted by the Vancouver Canucks in 1979. Dealt to Toronto with Bill Derlago in the Tiger Williams trade midway through his NHL rookie season of 1979–80, Vaive scored 22 goals that year and had 31 for Toronto in 1980–81. Despite the team's poor play in 1981–82, Vaive already had 30 goals at the time Sittler was traded. He'd scored 16 times in the Leafs' last 17 games and was on pace to top 50.

"I talked about that stuff my first year. I was going around telling everybody what I was going to get — 25 goals, for instance — then everything got screwed up. Sure, I guess I still have targets but they're in my head. I'll tell you what they are when I get there."

— Rick Vaive to Allan Ryan, *Toronto Star*, January 19, 1982

Rick Vaive replaced Darryl Sittler as Leafs captain and became the first player in franchise history to score 50 goals, which he would do for three straight seasons from 1981–82 through 1983–84.

Serving as captain during Sittler's absence (he would be given the "C" permanently shortly after the trade) seemed to improve Vaive's game.

"It's probably made me play a little better, a little harder. Wearing the C on my sweater makes me feel I have to work a little harder to make everybody else work a little harder."

— Rick Vaive after the Sittler trade

On March 22, 1982, Vaive scored four goals in an 8–5 win over Chicago. He now had 49 goals on the season; breaking Frank Mahovlich's club record of 48 set back in 1960–61.

"When I hit 44 or 45 goals and knew I had eight or nine games left, I started thinking about it. But tonight I just played my usual game and every time I shot it seemed to go in."

– Rick Vaive

"Good for him. I'm happy for him. The way records are being broken these days I felt that sooner or later it would be broken. I'm glad something good has happened for the team this year; that somebody has been able to do something right."

– Frank Mahovlich

"I'd trade a few of my goals for about 15 more points in the standings, because that would give us a playoff spot."

– Rick Vaive

Vaive admitted the burden of going for the team record had begun to affect him, but now that he had it:

"I want to get that 50th goal…. If I don't, I'll be referred to as a 40-goal scorer, not a 50-goal scorer. I've got six games to do it, but as far as I'm concerned, the pressure is over for me now."

– Rick Vaive to Rick Fraser, *Toronto Star*, March 24, 1982

Vaive wasted no time, scoring #50 in Toronto's next game, a 4–3 win over St. Louis at Maple Leaf Gardens that same night. He also set up Miroslav Frycer for the winning goal in the final minute. The win kept the Leafs' dim playoff hopes alive.

"My 50th wouldn't have been half as sweet if we didn't win the game…. The fact that we have to win every game has put enthusiasm into every one of us. We were out there hopping and bumping and shooting."

– Rick Vaive

Fifty goals was no longer considered the magic number it had once been. Wayne Gretzky would set a new NHL record with 92 goals that season, but

Vaive was pleased to be the first Leaf to reach the milestone. "I think it feels just as good as it ever did. The game is different now. But even with that, how many 50-goal scorers were there 10 years ago, three? This year there'll be what, [10]? That's not that much difference. Actually, I wouldn't care if there were 30; I'd still feel just as good."

Vaive scored four more goals over the Leafs' last five games. His total of 54 that season still remains a club record, but Toronto lost all five of those games and finished the season at 20–44–16. Percentage-wise (.350), Toronto's 56 points in 80 games made 1981–82 the worst season in franchise history excluding 1918–19 when the team had just 10 points in 18 games. But things would get even worse in the coming seasons.

1983–89

The Leafs were 28–40–12 in 1982–83 and their total of 68 points was good enough to make the playoffs, although they were eliminated in the first round. Vaive topped 50 goals again with 51 and John Anderson led the team with 49 assists and 80 points. Mike Palmateer was back in Toronto that season, and saw the bulk of the action in goal ahead of Bunny Larocque (in his last of three seasons with the Leafs) and Rick St. Croix (in his first of three). But Palmateer was no longer the acrobatic star he had once been.

A year later, in 1983–84, Palmateer was just 9–17–4 with a career-worst 4.88 goals-against average in what would prove to be his final season. Nineteen-year-old rookie Allan Bester was the best of a weak lot in goal that season. (Nineteen-year-old Ken Wregget also made his debut.) Vaive had 52 goals and a career-best 41 assists and 93 points to lead the offence, but the Leafs sank to a record of 26–45–9. Their 61 points had them last in the Norris Division and put them out of the playoffs. The poor performance cost Mike Nykoluk his job as head coach, but the team would do even worse under Dan Maloney in 1984–85. Going 20–52–8 for just 48 points and a winning percentage of only .300, the Leafs finished last in the overall standings for the first time since the 1957–58 season when there had only been six teams in the NHL.

The Leafs Land Wendel Clark

Having the worst record in the 21-team NHL in 1984–85 guaranteed the Leafs the first pick in the 1985 NHL Draft, which would be held in Toronto on June 15. But unlike in 1984, there was no consensus on the #1 choice in 1985, in what was considered a poor draft year.

Bill Derlago in a game against the Washington Capitals, January 7, 1984. Derlago and Rick Vaive were acquired from Vancouver by the Leafs in 1980 in exchange for Tiger Williams and Jerry Butler.

There was no clear-cut number-one choice when Toronto selected Wendel Clark first overall in the 1985 NHL Entry Draft. His rugged style would forever endear him to Maple Leafs fans, but it resulted in plenty of time lost to injuries.

"Five North American players have emerged as the top prospects for the 1985 National Hockey League entry draft, but unlike last year — when high-scoring centre Mario Lemieux was just about everybody's first choice — the top-rated junior this season is still a matter of speculation.

"When the NHL's Central Scouting Bureau releases its second rating of prospects early next month, the players expected to be ranked in the top five are Craig Simpson, a centre from London, Ontario, who plays for Michigan State University; Wendel Clark, a defenceman with the Saskatoon Blades of the Western Hockey League; Dan Gratton, a centre with the Oshawa Generals of the Ontario Hockey League; Jim Sandlak, a right winger with the OHL's London Knights; and Ryan Stewart, a centre with the WHL's Kamloops Blazers."

— William Houston, *Globe and Mail*, Toronto, January 8, 1985

"No one player sticks out the way [Kirk] Muller, [Mario] Lemieux and [Ed] Olczyk did."

— unnamed NHL scout

"Clark, who grew up on a farm in Saskatchewan, is not overly big for a defenceman. He is 5 foot 11 and 197 pounds, but 'he hits a ton,' according to one scout. He knocked a Soviet defenceman out of the world junior championship with a body check and levelled several other players with open-ice hits. He plays the wing as well as defence and in 31 games with Saskatoon has 12 goals and 21 assists."

— William Houston, *Globe and Mail*

"Clark has that special quality. You can't take your eyes off him when he's on the ice. I like him better at left wing, but at either position he's a quality player."

— unnamed NHL scout

"He's just the best, that's all. He's big, tough, quick, can handle the puck and can be either a defenceman or a winger in the NHL. On defence, Clark plays much like Scott Stevens of Washington Caps, though two ways, and up front, he has a shot that would place him in the top 10 percent of gunners."

— unnamed NHL scout

But would the Leafs pick Wendel?

"All I can say is that we'll show up and we won't pass in the first round."
— Leafs executive assistant Gord Stellick, May 24, 1985

Most experts ranked Craig Simpson as the top prospect by the day of the draft. If the Leafs didn't select him first, it was pretty certain that Pittsburgh would grab him second, but the prospect himself had no idea. "In my talks with Mr. McNamara he hasn't leaned one way or the other whether I'm his pick or not so it's hard for me to have a true gut feeling."

When the time came, the Leafs turned down an offer from the New York Islanders to trade the top pick for the sixth and 13th choices, plus either Bob Bourne or Clark Gillies. Sticking with the number-one choice, Toronto selected Wendel Clark.

"It wasn't up to me, but I would have picked him."
— Wendel's father, Les Clark

"It was a big surprise when the Leafs claimed me but I'm happy that they did."
— Wendel Clark

"You're the guy we wanted."
— Harold Ballard to Wendel Clark

"My goal is to make the Leafs.... I think of myself as a defenceman but I'll go to training camp with an open mind and play wherever they ask me to play."
— Wendel Clark

In four of the previous 10 NHL drafts, a player from the Western Hockey League had been chosen first, but for various reasons Greg Joly (Washington, 1974), Mel Bridgman (Philadelphia, 1975), Doug Wickenheiser (Montreal, 1980), and Gord Kluzak (Boston, 1982) had not really panned out.

"I'm not worried about any jinx. You can't think something's going to happen before it happens."
— Wendel Clark

"He's a pure player, big and strong. He's not tall but solid and tough. He's got talent to burn. He'll survive next year in the NHL on his talent alone."
— former Regina Pats GM Bob Strumm

Negotiations to sign Wendel Clark dragged on throughout the summer. He finally signed late in August and the Leafs staged a press conference to announce it on August 26. Contract terms were not routinely announced it those days, but the deal was said to be three years plus an option and a signing bonus for an estimated total of $650,000 — the richest deal ever given to a Leafs rookie.

"This is probably the greatest moment in my life, other than being drafted number one in June. That has to rank first because so very few players ever get that honour."

— Wendel Clark

The Leafs were not yet sure where Wendel would play, and he was asked again about his preference.

"I have more experience on defence but if they want me to play on the wing, that's fine with me.… Heck, I'd play goal to stay up there."

— Wendel Clark

"If I had one piece of advice to give to Wendel it would be to go out and play hockey and not let anything bother him. That's not easy to do in Toronto but it can be done."

— Leafs captain Rick Vaive

"The pressure I'll be playing with is what I put on myself. I'll just go out and do my best. I'm just preparing myself to come to camp in the best possible shape and hopefully things will work out for the best and I'll stick."

— Wendel Clark

"He certainly comes well recommended by our scouts and with Wendel and a few other changes, I'm certain we'll have a much improved team this year. I know I say at the start of each season we're going to do great things but I've never been more optimistic in recent years than I am right now."

— Harold Ballard

"Things just couldn't go any worse for us than they did last season and it's a straightforward situation here now — we have to get a good club together. Can you imagine the reaction in this city if we could turn it around? It would be unbelievable."

— Rick Vaive

Russ Courtnall had been Toronto's first pick, seventh overall, in the 1983 NHL Entry Draft.

Early in training camp, the Leafs played Wendel at left wing with cen-tre Russ Courtnall and right winger Gary Leeman. All three had played at the famous Notre Dame School in Wilcox, Saskatchewan, and they were dubbed the Hound Line after the school team's nickname. The three-some played together for much of the season and Clark quickly became a fan favourite.

Though only 5 foot 11 and about 194 pounds, Clark didn't back down from anyone on the ice. His aggressive play fired up fans and teammates — though it led to injuries that limited him to 66 games as a rookie, and kept him out of many more over the years. With his powerful wrist shot, he scored 34 goals in his rookie season and would finish as the runner-up to Gary Suter of the Calgary Flames in voting for the Calder Trophy.

> "You can't be 'impressed.' If you are just looking, you stop playing. You'll get beat if you're impressed. I go out and say, 'I dare you to beat me. You'll have to go through me to score'… If they have more skill, then you just have to work harder."
>
> — Wendel Clark to Gare Joyce, *MVP* magazine, April 1986

"That's why I like Wendel. He's got the same attitude as Charlie [Conacher]. Plays like him. The Hound Line and the Kid Line are a lot alike. And he's good people. A tough guy, but a good, fun-loving kid off the ice."

— King Clancy to Gare Joyce

Despite the excitement Wendel Clark helped to generate, the Leafs actually had a pretty poor season in 1985–86. Their record was only 25–48–7, but they did play better in the second half of the season. A truly dismal year by the Detroit Red Wings (17–57–6, 40 points) meant Toronto's 57 points easily qualified them for the final playoff spot in the Norris Division. Once there, they scored a shocking first-round sweep of the Chicago Blackhawks and pushed the St. Louis Blues to seven games in the second round. Even so, the strong finish didn't save the job of their coach.

1987–89

Dan Maloney wasn't fired, but he chose to resign in June after Harold Ballard refused to offer him anything more than a one-year contract with a $5,000 raise. (He quickly signed on to coach the Winnipeg Jets.) John Brophy was given the Leafs' job in July. A long-time minor-league tough guy as a player, Brophy had been coaching — mostly in the minors — since 1967. Hired as a Leafs assistant coach in 1984, he'd been put in charge of the Leafs farm team in St. Catharines midway through the 1985–86 season, but was now back in Toronto as the head coach.

Harold Ballard loved John Brophy's hard-nosed approach to the game, and the Leafs did show improvement under Brophy in 1986–87, but it was short-lived. The team fell to 20th in the 21-team league in 1987–88 with a record of 21–49–10, but their 52 points that season were still enough to make it to the playoffs because the last-overall Minnesota North Stars also played in the Norris Division. Brophy's hyper-intense manner hadn't helped that year.

"He's the first guy behind the bench who panics in situations where you need a guy to calm you down."

— Miroslav Frycer on John Brophy after the final game of the 1987–88 season

When the Leafs posted an 11–20–2 record in 33 games to start the 1988–89 season, Brophy was fired. There was little improvement the rest of the season under Leafs legend George Armstrong (who showed little enthusiasm for the job), and the Leafs once again fell out of the playoffs.

Beginning in 1986–87, Gary Leeman went from 21 goals to 30, to 32, to 51. He never again put up that kind of offensive production after 1989–90.

Toronto returned to the post-season under new coach Doug Carpenter, improving to 38–38–4 in 1988–89 with an offence led by Gary Leeman (51 goals, 95 points), Vincent Damphousse (61 assists, 94 points), and Ed Olcyzk (88 points). Things looked promising for the Maple Leafs as the 1990s dawned — but real improvement was still a few years away.

9

1990s: Cliff, Pat, and Dougie

1990–92

The Death of Harold Ballard

Harold Ballard had suffered for years from heart problems and diabetes and his health concerns were later complicated by kidney disease. He felt well enough to take a vacation during the Christmas holidays in 1989, but became ill and spent most of the next three months in hospitals in the Cayman Islands, Miami, and Toronto. He passed away peacefully on April 11, 1990.

> "I know a lot of people hated him, but he treated me like gold. He was a nice old man. He did a lot of crazy things. But with power like that, you can do that kind of stuff."
>
> — Borje Salming, who had completed his last NHL season in 1989–90 with the Detroit Red Wings after 16 years in Toronto

> "There were a lot of good years. It was enjoyable working under Harold Ballard. There was always talk about our problem — but it was all out of proportion.... I made two recent visits to the Gardens and there were no bitter feelings between us. There was certainly none from me and there didn't seem to be any from him."
>
> — Darryl Sittler

> "He was the opposite of most people. He was pleasant on the inside and negative on the outside."
>
> — long-time employee Gord Stellick, Leafs GM in 1987–88 and 1988–89

"I wish him well — wherever he goes."

— Wendel Clark

Former NHL star and future Maple Leafs president Ken Dryden had described Ballard very well a few years earlier.

"Harold Ballard is the new star of the Leafs. He has become a Toronto, even a national, celebrity. Known locally as jovial and outrageous, nationally above all as outrageous, as owner of the Toronto Maple Leafs he is ipso facto a celebrity, and there is nothing he can say or do, nothing anyone can say or do, to change that. He can be unfair and erratic; he can be unequivocally wrong. It doesn't matter. He is Ballard, owner of the Leafs. What he says, what he does, we pretend is news.

"It is easy to say that a fan can stay home, or at home he can change a channel and watch something else. But it isn't as simple as that. A sports fan loves his sport. A fan in Toronto loves hockey, and if the Leafs are bad, he loses something he loves and has no way to replace the loss. Yet, as his team sinks lower, Ballard continues to parade before us, apparently invulnerable — his Maple Leaf Gardens filled by more and more events, his television revenues increasing, his team selling out as they have since 1946; his celebrity status intact.

"As a member of the Gardens board, as vice president, he was perfect. Likeable, convivial, able to be disregarded at the proper time, without the title that brings platform that brings the rest; but as president, as principal owner, he is very imperfect. And the Leafs' fans suffer."

— *Toronto Star*, October 10, 1983

Ballard left the bulk of his estate (said to be worth less than $50 million) to a charitable trust. Steve Stavro, Don Giffin, and Donald Crump were the executors of the estate and took control of Maple Leaf Gardens. Stavro had been a director of the Gardens since 1981 and became chairman of the board and governor of the Leafs in October of 1991. He eventually became majority owner in 1994.

A New Era Begins

Unlike Harold Ballard, Steve Stavro avoided the spotlight as much as possible and was happy to let the hockey operations staff run the team. Even so, Stavro was opposed to a key move orchestrated by Don Giffin in June of 1991.

After their .500 season and playoff berth in 1989–90, the Leafs had taken another tumble in 1990–91. A 1–9–1 start to the season saw Floyd Smith (who, since the car accident that ended his coaching career, had risen from scout, to chief scout, to general manager) fired head coach Doug Carpenter and replace him with assistant coach Tom Watt. Watt was a long-time University of Toronto coach who'd been an NHL head coach in Winnipeg and Vancouver in the 1980s and was an assistant coach with the Calgary Flames when they won the Stanley Cup in 1989. Watt couldn't do much with the 1990–91 Leafs, as the team finished the season with just 57 points (23–46–11) and missed the playoffs.

Then, in May of 1991, Cliff Fletcher announced his resignation as president and general manager of the Calgary Flames, effective July 1. Rumours began immediately that he would be hired to assume the same jobs in Toronto.

"I felt I was becoming a bit stale. I'm looking for a new challenge, something to get the competitive juices flowing again."

— Cliff Fletcher, May 16, 1991

"Certainly Cliff Fletcher will be on that list."

— Don Giffin, who had been searching for a big-name hockey executive since the fall and had a list of several he planned to present to the Maple Leaf Gardens board in June

"I've had meetings and conversations with two other clubs and I'm not necessarily in a helluva rush to do anything."

— Cliff Fletcher

Despite his claim, Fletcher arrived in Toronto for more meetings on June 3. He clearly wanted the Maple Leafs job — but on his own terms. "I want to be in full control of both the business and the hockey side of things. I know it sounds like a bit of an ego trip to say I want full control, but I'd be looking to be chief operating officer of the Gardens and the hockey club. I think they go hand in hand these days."

But Steve Stavro wanted Toronto businessman Lyman MacInnis as chief operating officer.

"I'm aware of Mr. Stavro's feelings," said Fletcher, "but I hope to meet with him while I'm here and put my perspective across to him. We'll know by Thursday one way or the other, but we'll just have to wait and see what unfolds over the next 48 hours."

Cliff Fletcher brought back a sense of purpose to the Maple Leafs after the Ballard years.

Fletcher did meet with Stavro, but was unable to convince him. Still, when six of seven Gardens directors met in an emergency meeting on June 4, the vote was 5–1 in favour of hiring the ex-Calgary boss. He was signed to a five-year contract worth an estimated $4 million.

"This is the greatest franchise in the National Hockey League. I want to reconfirm the pride and tradition of this great hockey club."

— Cliff Fletcher

"This is a great day in my life, and a great day in the life of the Toronto Maple Leafs."

— Don Giffin

"I am an executive who will be committed to bringing back exciting hockey.... We owe it to the fans to bring back exciting hockey."

— Cliff Fletcher

"Every Leafs fan should cheer."

— Darryl Sittler, whom Fletcher would bring back
into the fold as a special consultant

"Cliff will set a timetable, be it for one year, five years or 10 years, and when that time period is up the team will be exactly where he wanted it to be, or at least very close. It's just a great move for the Leafs."

— Lanny McDonald, who finished his career
under Fletcher in Calgary (1981–89)

"He's been around a long time and done nothing but build winners. It's just great news, from a player's standpoint. Obviously it's a step in the right direction."

— Leafs centre Vince Damphousse

"The job's not going to be easy. There's not going to be any quick cures. You're not going to improve 500 percent overnight. The only thing I can promise you is hard work, dedication from all of us. We're going to have a lot of fun doing it."

— Cliff Fletcher

Fletcher officially took office as president and general manager on July 1, 1991, amid reports that Steve Stavro might well replace him if he got control of the team. (They made their peace on October 4, ahead of Stavro acquiring formal control of the team on October 22.)

Among Fletcher's priorities was to strengthen the off-ice organization, improve the farm system, and to begin negotiations with several Leafs players who were going into their option years. He also wanted to re-sign Wendel Clark, who'd become a free agent.

Hampered by back problems, Clark had averaged only 27 games a season in three years from 1987 to 1990 before playing 63 games in 1990–91. (He would play only 43 games in 1991–92.) Still, on August 8, 1991, Fletcher signed him to the richest contract in team history, agreeing to a one-year deal plus an option year for $600,000 per season. Clark was also named the 16th captain in franchise history.

One of Cliff Fletcher's first priorities was to re-sign Wendel Clark, who was named Leafs captain prior to the 1991–92 season.

"It was humbling and overwhelming at the same time. It's hard to describe the feeling of such an honour. And to this day, it ranks as one of the most memorable moments of my career and my life."

— Wendel Clark, *Wendel* (2009)

"I think Wendel has the respect of his teammates and that's the most important thing a captain has to have."

— Tom Watt, who was returning as Leafs coach

"I'll just go out and play it by ear and be the same person and do the same things I'm doing now. There's no reason to change anything."

— Wendel Clark

The First Big Trade

With the Leafs in training camp and already having begun to play exhibition games, Fletcher pulled off his first big move on September 19, 1991. He sent Vince Damphousse, Peter Ing, Scott Thornton, and Luke Richardson to Edmonton for Oilers Stanley Cup veterans Grant Fuhr and Glenn Anderson, as well as Craig Berube.

The Leafs gave up a lot of promising youth (Damphousse, Thornton, and Richardson were all former first-round picks) for a goalie in Fuhr who had missed most of the previous season after being suspended for cocaine use, and a sniper in Anderson who some believed had lost a step.

"[Fuhr's] good for six or seven years at [his current] level. Twenty-nine is not old for a goalie. [But] I think [Anderson]'s washed up."

— Terry Jones, *Edmonton Sun*

"It's always bad — I mean always — to deal youth. That said, the Leafs did okay, if Anderson can still skate."

— Mark Everson, *New York Post*

"Some people will like the trade; some people won't. But they'll be talking about the Leafs [today].... I think this trade makes a great statement for the ... Leafs."

— Cliff Fletcher

"Right now the Maple Leafs have won the deal. But once again, they've traded for old players. What happens tomorrow?"

— Albert Ladouceur, *Journal de Quebec*

"You could argue that Toronto mortgaged its future, but I think its future looked pretty ugly."

— Al Morganti, *Hockey News*

"It took guts for Fletcher to make the trade. Floyd Smith didn't have it. It's a good sign for Toronto fans. They finally have a GM who's aggressive and willing to do something."

— Pierre Durocher, *Journal de Montreal*

"We'll have to go from last place to being a contender. I like playing on contenders. I had 10 good years in Edmonton, but everyone needs a fresh start. This puts some fun back in the game."

— Grant Fuhr

"Obviously, I'm disappointed."

— Vince Damphousse on being dealt away

But the Leafs would struggle yet again this year. On New Year's Eve 1991, the team had a record of just 10–25–5 through the first 40 games of the 80-game season. They were 21st overall in the NHL and spared last place only by the newest expansion team, the San Jose Sharks. But events elsewhere were conspiring to turn things in Toronto's favour.

The Second Big Trade

On New Year's Day 1992, Doug Gilmour walked out on the Calgary Flames. Gilmour's agent Larry Kelly and Flames GM Doug Risebrough — who had taken over from his mentor Cliff Fletcher — had not been able to work out a satisfactory contract. Gilmour had gone to arbitration seeking $1.2 million (Pat Lafontaine, who had comparable statistics, had recently left the New York Islanders for Buffalo and a $1.8-million contract) but had been awarded only $750,000.

"They said my skills have gone downhill.... They felt my skills had diminished from my first year in Calgary to my last. I was not going to accept that."
— Doug Gilmour after his arbitration hearing in November 1991

"I had just left the Flames after 19 years. And as early as training camp, I knew they were going to have issues with Gilmour and were going to have to do something about it."
— Cliff Fletcher to Steve Simmons, *Toronto Sun*, February 16, 2016

"[Risebrough] has not made any impact trades since he has become general manager. Knowing how unhappy I am, he now has an excuse to trade somebody. And if the trade doesn't work out, then he doesn't have to take the blame for it."
— Doug Gilmour, first asking for a trade on December 9, 1991

"It was mentioned to me in early December that there were problems and it all intensified just before the New Year. Then Dougie was the first star on New Year's Eve for the Flames and, right after that, he walked out on the team. By the next night, we'd made the deal. Funny thing, we couldn't call the league to register the trade on New Year's. No one was in the office. It's not like today. We had to wait 'til the next morning to register. I had to sweat it out all night waiting to make it official."

— Cliff Fletcher to Steve Simmons, *Toronto Sun*, February 16, 2016

Fletcher had quietly been talking to Risebrough about swapping Gary Leeman (who'd fallen off badly since his 51-goal season in 1989–90) for Gilmour, but by the time the deal was announced on January 2 it had grown into a monster 10-player trade. The Leafs gave up Leeman, Craig Berube, Alexander Godynyuk, Michel Petit, and Jeff Reese for Gilmour, Jamie Macoun, Ric Nattress, Rick Wamsley, and Kent Manderville.

"This is a trade of great magnitude, which I felt had to be made with a team that has won 10 of its first 40 games."

— Cliff Fletcher

"I think we gave up a certain amount of youth. But we needed a centre. Gilmour is a playmaking type of centre and a feisty guy. I hope he and the other fellows we got will help some of our other players play better."

— Tom Watt

"I was with Gary for seven years and it's tough to see a good friend go. But the atmosphere was very stable and no one can say they didn't have a chance to show what they could do. That was a difference when Cliff took over compared to how it was. Cliff didn't do anything frantic, only what had to be done."

— Wendel Clark

"Before it came about, I knew I'd be part of a trade shortly.... But it feels really good. Yeah, it does. It's been a long time coming, and as far as my choice goes, this is the number-one team. If there was a wish to come true for me, this is it."

— Doug Gilmour

"He gives the Leafs something they haven't had since Darryl Sittler was traded 10 years ago — an all-purpose, talented, number-one centre who exhibits true grit and determination."

— Bob McKenzie, *Toronto Star*, January 3, 1992

"I'd put him in the top 10 [among NHL centres]. We'd been discussing the possibility of getting Gilmour since last August. We addressed a very glaring weakness on our team.... Gilmour is a consistent 60-assist man in the NHL. I look at that as 60 more goals and we need goals badly."

— Cliff Fletcher

"Obviously, getting Dougie was huge and another big step towards become a legitimate Stanley Cup contender. We all felt we were suddenly at the next level."

— Wendel Clark, *Wendel* (2009)

Gilmour played all 40 games for Toronto in the second half of the season. He had 15 goals and 34 assists for 49 points. The Leafs went 20–18–2, but that still left them with an overall record of 30–43–7. They were fifth in the Norris Division (19th in the overall standings) and missed the playoffs for the second straight year ... but a huge turnaround was coming!

1992–93

On May 4, 1992, Cliff Fletcher relieved Tom Watt of his coaching duties, re-assigning him to the position of director of professional development.

"I have no apologies to make as coach of the Maple Leafs. This wasn't an easy situation. Only two players [Todd Gill and Wendel Clark] are still here since I took over.... This team is on the verge of becoming a pretty decent hockey team and being able to compete with the other teams in this division."

— Tom Watt

"[Watt is] an excellent coach, but for the long-term we want somebody who can grow with the team."

— Cliff Fletcher

Immediate speculation was that the new coach would either be Leafs assistant Mike Murphy or Canadian Olympic coach Dave King. "They are definitely two of a number of people who we will be looking at. We're not going to drag this process out, but we will be thorough," said Cliff Fletcher at the time.

King seemed to be the front-runner. "Eventually Dave and I will have a discussion," said Fletcher. "We're quite familiar with one another from Calgary [where the Olympic team was based]. If you're going to make a coaching change, the one person it behooves you to talk to is Dave King."

But soon another name emerged....

Pat Burns

Growing up in the suburbs of Montreal, Pat Burns had always wanted to be a hockey player, but he didn't have the skill for the NHL. He later got into coaching with a friend's bantam team in Gatineau, Quebec. While working for the Gatineau police force, Burns was hired as a scout for the Hull Olympiques of the Quebec Major Junior Hockey League. He eventually worked his way up to coach and general manager. Convinced by new Olympiques owner Wayne Gretzky that he would coach in the NHL one day, Burns quit the police department. In 1987, he was hired by the Montreal Canadiens to coach their American Hockey League team in Sherbrooke. A year later, he was in the NHL as coach of the Canadiens.

Burns led Montreal to the best record in the Prince of Wales Conference in his first season (1988–89) and to the Stanley Cup Final where they lost to Cliff Fletcher's Calgary Flames. Never quite reaching those heights again, the Canadiens were still among the NHL's best teams under Burns. After a tough seven-game victory over a Hartford Whalers team they should have beaten

When Pat Burns left Montreal to coach in Toronto, he became the first (and only) man to guide both the Canadiens and the Maple Leafs since Dick Irvin in the 1930s, '40s, and '50s.

easily, followed by a four-game sweep at the hands of the Boston Bruins, Montreal players and fans were getting fed up with Burns's defence-first system.

"We, as a team and as an organization, have to be concerned about what's going on. It's not the Montreal Canadiens, the way they played throughout history."
— Canadiens star Denis Savard after the sweep by Boston, May 10, 1992

"Our passing and everything we did was awful. There's a lot of pressure on everyone in this room to win and go far, but we didn't respond to the pressure. There's only so much Pat Burns can do. We have to go out on the ice and play."
— Canadiens captain Guy Carbonneau

"I didn't start all those rumours about [Burns] being fired. But we're going to evaluate every part of this team."
— Canadiens GM Serge Savard

A day later, Savard announced, "Pat has my confidence and he will be back in September." But the media speculation in Montreal wouldn't end. Burns quit the Canadiens and signed with the Maple Leafs on May 29, 1992.

"I wasn't happy about the playoffs, but I was excited about starting things again in September. Then the wagons circled and the arrows started going. It was tough. I had to get away."
— Pat Burns on leaving Montreal

"I had no intention of firing Pat Burns."
— Canadiens GM Serge Savard

"I consider myself to be one of the good coaches in the National Hockey League. I think I've proved that in the past."
— Pat Burns

"It's a welcome surprise. This is a guy with a pretty good coaching record."
— Doug Gilmour

"All I want is to make this hockey club a better hockey club.... I'm here because I want to coach the Toronto Maple Leafs."
— Pat Burns

"His philosophy was defence first and the rest will take care of itself, provided you outwork, outhustle and outhit the opposition for 60 minutes. In Pat's system, there was no room for floaters."

— Wendel Clark, *Wendel* (2009)

"No one who doesn't want to compete will be playing for the Toronto Maple Leafs."

— Burns at training camp before the 1992–93 season

"You know how your dad doesn't even have to yell at you, he just gives you that cop look, and he scares your pants off? That's Pat."

— Doug Gilmour, *Players Tribune*, March 9, 2016

"He genuinely didn't care about what people thought, said, or wrote. That applied to just about everybody right across the board — the fans, the media, and most of all us. His attitude was, 'Boys, here's how we're going to play, no maybes, it's this way or no way.' And we all got the message.... Pat was something else. He'd always be poking or prodding or provoking. Most of the time, it seemed he wanted, maybe even hoped, the players would hate him. It was his way of bringing the team together."

— Wendel Clark, *Wendel* (2009)

The 1992–93 Regular Season and Playoffs

The NHL added two more teams (Tampa Bay and Ottawa) this year and expanded the schedule to 84 games. In Toronto, the Maple Leafs had one of the best years in franchise history. After the first 20 games of the season, Toronto was 10–7–3 and had the NHL's best defensive record.

"Clean up your own end first, and the rest will take care of itself."

— Pat Burns

The team slumped in December, and had fallen under .500 with a record of 16–17–7 in early January, but by season's end, the Maple Leafs had set new franchise records with 44 wins (44–29–11) and 99 points. They had the league's second-best defensive record, while Doug Gilmour set new scoring marks with 95 assists (including six in one game on February 13, 1993) and 127 points.

"Dougie would be the first to admit that he wasn't the most naturally talented player. But nobody ever got more out of himself or gave more of

Dave Andreychuk scored 120 goals in 223 games during his three-plus seasons in Toronto.

himself than Dougie did. His hockey smarts, heart, determination, intensity — they were all completely off the chart. I'm not sure I've ever been around a guy who was more competitive than him. He simply didn't know the meaning of quit."

— Wendel Clark, *Wendel* (2009)

Gilmour finished as the runner-up to Mario Lemieux in voting for the Hart Trophy as NHL MVP and won the Selke Trophy as the league's best defensive forward. Pat Burns won the Jack Adams Award (which he had won previously in 1988–89) as coach of the year.

Toronto's solid defensive play and the strong showing of rookie goalie Felix Potvin led to another big trade on February 2, 1993, when Cliff Fletcher sent Grant Fuhr and a conditional draft pick to Buffalo for Dave Andreychuk, Darren Puppa, and a first-round draft choice. Andreychuk proved a perfect trigger man for Gilmour's slick passes, scoring 25 goals in 31 games in Toronto to give him 54 on the season.

Good as the regular season was, Toronto still only managed to finish third in a competitive Norris Division race behind first-place Chicago (106 points) and second-place Detroit (103). The Red Wings had home-ice advantage when they faced the Maple Leafs in the first round of the playoffs. Detroit had been red-hot to finish the season, winning 14 of its last 17 games, and most experts were ranking the Red Wings as the second-best team in the NHL behind the two-time defending Stanley Cup champion Pittsburgh Penguins as the play-offs began. Detroit was certainly the favourite against Toronto and looked the part in opening the series with 6–3 and 6–2 victories.

"He wasn't playing his game. You really couldn't find him out there on the ice."

— Red Wings tough guy Bob Probert on Wendel Clark's
tame performance in Game 1

"You can question Wendel's ability, or his shot, but no one here can ever question his toughness. Nobody here questions Wendel Clark's courage."

— Pat Burns defending the Leafs' captain

"I'm not that deep. I'm a farmer, for God's sake."

— Wendel Clark, when asked before Game 3 at Maple Leaf Gardens
if the captain should be the team's spiritual leader

The Leafs won Game 3 by a score of 4–2, evened the series with a 3–2 win in Game 4, and then went ahead with a 5–4 victory in Detroit in Game 5. Mike Foligno, who'd missed the end of the 1991–92 season and the first half of 1992–93 with a badly broken leg, scored the game winner at 2:05 of overtime.

"From the moment I woke up in the operating room, I never stopped believing I'd come back."

— Mike Foligno after scoring the OT winner

"It's the biggest goal of my career. I got in the slot, got the puck, and tried to put it on net. One of the biggest pluses with this club has been its ability to play well right up to the end of the game. You saw it tonight."

— Mike Foligno

With a chance to wrap up the series at home, the Leafs were crushed 7–3 in Game 6. They had just one day to regroup before the seventh game in Detroit on May 1.

The Leafs opened the scoring in Game 7 when Doug Gilmour set up Glenn Anderson in the first period, but by 8:44 of the second period, the Red Wings were up 3–2. Toronto held Detroit to just seven shots in the second period, and four in the third, but couldn't get the goal they needed.

> "By the third period, we were basically playing defensive."
>
> — Red Wings coach Bryan Murray

Finally, with just 2:43 remaining in regulation time, Gilmour broke free from Detroit's Steve Yzerman, took a feed from Wendel Clark, and beat goalie Tim Cheveldae for the tying goal. Gilmour had played brilliantly all night with a goal and two assists through regulation time despite behind shadowed by Yzerman and Sergei Fedorov. No Detroit goals had been scored while he was on the ice. Gilmour was playing a double shift, centring Glenn Anderson and Dave Andreychuk on one line and Wendel Clark and Nikolai Borschevsky on another.

> "The more I played, the more I wanted to play. You don't get tired at this time of year."
>
> — Doug Gilmour

Early in the first overtime period, Gilmour dug a loose puck out of the corner deep in the Detroit end and fed it back to Bob Rouse on the point. Rouse fired what looked like a harmless shot until Borschevsky, driving the net, twisted the blade of his stick and redirected the shot past Cheveldae. The time was 2:35 and Toronto had its first playoff series victory since 1987 and its most exciting post-season moment since Lanny McDonald's goal against the Islanders in 1978.

> "This has been an unbelievable turn of events. The Leafs march on. And the Red Wings have been eliminated."
>
> — CBC play-by-play man Bob Cole

> "Unbelievable!"
>
> — Nik Borschevsky, over and over, when asked to describe his feelings by CBC's Ron MacLean

"The doctors told me 10 days, but I say I play today."

— Borschevsky, who had been out since breaking the
orbital bone beneath his right eye in Game 1

"This game was like an apology to our fans for Game 6. They didn't deserve that and I knew tonight if we didn't give Detroit their 10 minutes of glory, we would be all right. And we didn't."

— Pat Burns after the game

"What's so great about this is what it means to the players in there. Wins like this, you just can't understand the impact it has on a developing team…. That was a great team we played…. To beat them in their building in overtime of the seventh game is a hell of a feat."

— Cliff Fletcher

"The best thing about this win, what makes it most satisfying, is the organization is building on such solid ground now. This won't be just a one-time thing."

— Wendel Clark

"I've never been as emotionally high as this moment except for when my kids were born…. We just beat out a club that was supposed to win it all. What more can you ask? Well, I shouldn't say that. We want more. We want to beat St. Louis next."

— nine-year Leafs veteran Todd Gill

After seven games in 13 nights, the Leafs had just one day off before taking on the Blues to open the second round. St. Louis had shocked Chicago with a first-round sweep and hadn't played since April 25, when they took to the ice at Maple Leaf Gardens for Game 1 on May 3.

Blues star Brendan Shanahan had scored 51 goals in the regular season. He'd grown up in Toronto as a Maple Leafs fan watching Darryl Sittler and Lanny McDonald (and would become president of the team in 2014).

"I scored many goals in my driveway that were set up by Borje Salming and Ian Turnbull. I'm trying to forget all that now," Shanahan would tell the *Toronto Star*. "I was saying to some of my friends, 'I'm doing my best to hate the Leafs now.' That's the only way you can approach this thing. I'm trying not to look at the walls and the pictures when I walk in [to the Gardens]…. I'm just trying to treat it like any other city and any other team…. I used to hope that the Leafs would come back to their glory days. Now that I'm in the Norris, they're my enemies, they're my competition, and I want to beat them."

Game 1 was an end-to-end slugfest featuring bad blood and great goaltending. It went into double overtime, with the Leafs firing 64 shots at Blues goalie Curtis Joseph. Felix Potvin faced only 34 Blues shots. The score was 1–1 until 3:16 of the second extra session when Doug Gilmour — who'd been on the ice for about 40 minutes in Game 7 in Detroit, and about 40 minutes more this night — gave Toronto a 2–1 victory.

"Gilmour back of the net. Andreychuk in front with Borschevsky. It is Gilmour waiting. Waiting. Around the net. Waiting! He's out in front … [excited sounds] … Gilmour! Solo job! And he's won it!"

— Bob Cole's call on CBC

"Gilmour started to come out one way, cut back to go around the other, then reversed again to stuff the puck just inside the post beyond the reach of Joseph and St. Louis blueliner Bret Hedican."

— Damien Cox, *Toronto Star*, May 4, 1992

"I didn't know what side to come out on. I'm just happy with the result."

— Doug Gilmour

"I don't have words left. We deserved to win and that's it."

— Pat Burns

But was Gilmour getting too much ice time? Were the Leafs going to burn him out?

"What am I going to do, put my best player on the bench and wait for training camp? What would I save him for? August? Dougie knows, when he's tired he comes off, when he's not tired, he's out there. We talk to each other on the bench and we understand the situation."

— Pat Burns

"I was at the game in Detroit when he played 40 minutes. I figured, well, he's banged up, bruised, he's going to be tired. Then he comes out against us.… I was surprised he was able to play so much against Detroit and then come back against us so strong. I don't know if they're feeding him intravenously or what."

— Blues coach Bob Berry

"He's tireless for a guy his size, but it's all determination, he's almost all heart. He seems to be getting stronger as the playoffs go on."

— Dave Andreychuk

"It's the emotion that keeps you going at this time of year. The adrenalin is flowing, everyone is pretty excited. You don't think about being tired."

— Doug Gilmour

The Blues bounced back with a 2–1 double-overtime win of their own in Game 2, and then went ahead in the series when they beat the Leafs 4–3 in Game 3 in St. Louis. The Leafs took the next two handily, winning 4–1 in St. Louis and 5–1 back at home.

"We haven't won anything yet. It's the same old story, you have to win four and we haven't yet."

— Cliff Fletcher with the Leafs up three games to two

With a chance to wrap things up in Game 6, Toronto played a sloppy game in St. Louis and lost 2–1.

"We played with fire and we got burned. We had no forecheck, only short cuts."

— Pat Burns

The coach hoped for a better effort at home on Saturday night, May 15, in what would be the first Game 7 played at Maple Leaf Gardens since Toronto won the Stanley Cup in 1964. "The guys have to show up and decide whether they want to put the Maple Leafs jerseys away for the summer, or if they want to put them on again Monday night," said Burns.

It wasn't expected to be as easy as that.

"We can't expect that just because we're playing in our building, they're going to roll over and die. They've got momentum. We can't make the same mistake of sitting on [an early lead]. We've got to continue and get the next goal."

— Dave Andreychuk

The Leafs did that and then some! Andreychuk put them up 1–0 at 5:02 of the first period. Wendel Clark made it 2–0 at 10:02 when he flipped a shot into the crease in front of Curtis Joseph and Bret Hedican knocked it into his own net. Mike Krushelnyski put Toronto ahead 3–0 at 15:12, and Clark upped the lead to 4–0 on a classic wrist shot with 20 seconds remaining in the first period. Goals by Kent Manderville and Doug Gilmour in the second period pushed the lead to 6–0 and that's how it wrapped up.

> "I'm just in awe. I still don't understand it. We just won our division."
> — Pat Burns

Wendel Clark had played his best game in a long time. The second-longest-serving Leaf behind Todd Gill had suffered through a lot of tough times in Toronto. His leadership had been called into question earlier in the season, and the Leafs had even considered trading him. But he was having a good time now.

> "It's a lot of fun. It's a lot more fun playing in May than it is in October. Making it to the semifinals is the best feeling. We have a great bunch of guys and we've really come together."
> — Wendel Clark

Next up for the Leafs was Wayne Gretzky and the Los Angeles Kings in the Campbell Conference Final, while in the Prince of Wales Conference the Montreal Canadiens would be meeting the New York Islanders.

> "It's anyone's ballgame now. We're capable of beating any of the teams left and I'm sure they're thinking along the same lines."
> — Leafs defenceman Dave Ellett

> "We'd like to set our sights a little higher now. Maybe one or two more steps."
> — Bob Rouse

> "It's ridiculous to talk about Stanley Cups right now. We have to talk about how to beat the Los Angeles Kings…. I can tell you that by the third period, I was starting to think about who's going to check Gretzky."
> — Pat Burns

> "It should be a good series. They're an older, experienced club and they're very explosive offensively. It's been a fun playoff so far, so we'll see how far we can take it. It'll be back to work tomorrow. We're not satisfied yet."
> — Wendel Clark

Dave Andreychuk is knocked down by Rob Blake while Kelly Hrudey makes a glove save during the 1993 Western Conference Finals against the Los Angeles Kings.

The Kings had not had a great season under rookie coach and former Maple Leaf Barry Melrose, who was Wendel Clark's second cousin. Their record had been 39–35–10, and their 88 points had placed them well back of Vancouver (101 points) and Calgary (97) in the Smythe Division. Shortly before the season started, word came that Wayne Gretzky would be sidelined indefinitely with a herniated disc in his back. It was thought he might miss the entire season, and that perhaps his career was in jeopardy. Gretzky missed the first 39 games of the season. The Kings had actually played well for much of that time, but had suffered six losses and two ties in their last eight games before Gretzky finally returned on January 6. He played all of the Kings' last 45 games, and had 65 points (16 goals, 49 assists). He was in fine form for the playoffs and looking forward to playing his first post-season game in Toronto.

> "I don't think there's anyone that grew up in this area who doesn't dream of one day playing a Stanley Cup playoff game here."
>
> — Wayne Gretzky, the night before the series opener

Gretzky was leading the post-season in scoring with 24 points in 12 games as the Kings upset both the Flames and the Canucks to reach the semifinals against the Maple Leafs.

"I don't think he's meant more to a team than he means to us right now."

— L.A. coach Barry Melrose on Gretzky prior to Game 1 in Toronto

Second behind Gretzky on the playoff scoring list was the Leafs' Doug Gilmour, who had 23 points in 14 games.

"It should be a great series. We'll have to play the way we played during the Detroit series. We can't afford to get into a shootout. They have a lot of great goal-scorers."

— Doug Gilmour

Luc Robitaille had led the Kings in the regular season with 63 goals and 125 points. The offence also boasted Tony Granato, Jari Kurri, and Tomas Sandstrom, and even the defence featured offensive stars in Rob Blake, Paul Coffey, and Alexei Zhitnik.

"We attack all the time and play a wide-open style. Our defence is very mobile and jump up into the play a lot. We don't worry about shutting down guys; we feel they have to worry about us."

— Barry Melrose

"I expect to see a lot of Doug Gilmour. But I can't worry about what they do. I just have to play my game."

— Wayne Gretzky

The Leafs won the opener 4–1. Gilmour was brilliant, scoring the first goal of the game with a one-handed redirection of a shot from Bob Rouse at 17:19 of the first period. After the Kings tied it up in the second period, Gilmour set up two goals and scored one of his own between 9:49 and 15:21 of the third period to put the game away.

"That's the best six minutes I've ever seen anybody play."

— CBC commentator Harry Neale

But perhaps the most memorable moment of the game came a few minutes later when Marty McSorley decked Gilmour with an elbow to the head ... and Wendel Clark made him pay for it.

"I'm pretty sure that what the majority of people will remember most about the series opener wasn't our 4–1 victory, but rather the 'McSorley hit'.... Up until [then], nobody had ever really run Dougie or made him a target."

— Wendel Clark, *Wendel* (2009)

"I came across trying to lay a hit and Gilmour jumped up and left his feet. I couldn't let him get by me.... I wanted to hit him hard but I'm not looking to cheap shot anybody.... I'm not going out to hit Doug Gilmour per se. I'm going out to be a tough, hard-nosed player. That's the way I play."

— Marty McSorley after the game

"All I know is that if Ken Baumgartner did that to Wayne Gretzky, he would have been hung on Parliament Hill."

— Pat Burns

"You want your scorers, your skill guys, to feel comfortable and secure wheeling and dealing around the ice, not looking over their shoulders or worrying about some guy taking their head off. You want them to feel safe to do what they do. So, if a guy takes liberties with your best player, you have to answer the call.... [S]omebody had to respond, answer the bell, and that somebody was going to be me."

— Wendel Clark, *Wendel* (2009)

"I didn't even think about it. He's our best player. It's just part of the game. They're trying to send us a message that they're not going to give up. It was a 4–1 hockey game; it would have been different if it was a one goal game."

— Wendel Clark after the game

Gilmour would be fine, but he was given the day off of practice the next day.

"Dougie had to go back to his planet and rest."

— Pat Burns

In Game 2, the Leafs took an early 2–1 lead but lost 3–2. It was a sloppy and somewhat dull affair.

"We all seemed to sit back and wait for the Doug Gilmour Show to start. Maybe some of our guys still don't realize what this is about."

— Pat Burns

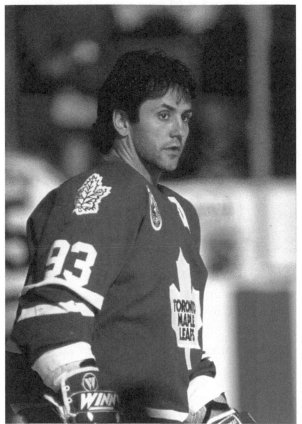

Seen here during his spectacular 1992–93 regular season, Doug Gilmour took his game to incredible new heights during the 1993 playoffs.

In Los Angeles for Game 3, the Kings went ahead in the series with a 4–2 victory, but the Leafs tied it up with a 4–2 win of their own in Game 4. Toronto took the lead again in Game 5 at Maple Leaf Gardens, beating Los Angeles 3–2 when Glenn Anderson whacked a puck out of the air and into the net at 19:20 of overtime.

> "We pulled a rabbit out of the hat, but rabbits are getting scarce. After the first period, I reached down and pulled out a chicken."
>
> — Pat Burns on the Game 5 victory

The Leafs' luck would run out in Los Angeles in Game 6 two nights later.

"Leaf fans will never forget what happened and neither will I. Simply put, Gretz high-sticked Dougie and got away with it. Everybody saw it, except referee Kerry Fraser. Dougie was even bleeding from the chin, but still no penalty."

— Wendel Clark, *Wendel* (2009)

"It should have been five and a game misconduct."

— Doug Gilmour to Rosie DiManno prior to his induction into the Hockey Hall of Fame, *Toronto Star*, November 12, 2011

Toronto had opened the scoring on a Glenn Anderson goal just 57 seconds into the game, but the Kings dominated for most of the evening and led 4–2 with just nine minutes remaining. The Leafs rallied to tie the game 4–4 on a pair of goals by Wendel Clark to give him a hat trick on the evening and send the game into overtime.

"The Kings started on a power play in overtime due to Glenn Anderson's boarding foul on Rob Blake with 13 seconds left in the third period. Thirty-nine seconds into OT, Gretzky clearly, although accidentally, pitch-forked Doug Gilmour in the face, but referee Kerry Fraser and both linesmen missed the incident completely, although the puck had just left Gretzky's stick. Gilmour was cut for eight stitches between his jaw and his neck on the play."

— Damien Cox, *Toronto Star*, May 28, 1993

"Since I was the captain, it was my responsibility to confront Kerry about the call, or in this instance, the non-call. But you know you're never going to win. Referees do not change their minds…. And then, to add more salt to the wound, none other than Gretz scores the winning goal, forcing Game 7."

— Wendel Clark, *Wendel* (2009)

Game 7 back at Maple Leaf Gardens on May 29 would be the Leafs' 21st game in 41 nights. They had also made two 8,000-kilometre round trips to the West Coast in a week.

"I think the travel is getting to Toronto. They looked very tired tonight. They're not used to the travel as we are in the Smythe Division."

— Kings coach Barry Melrose after Game 6

"We're not going to roll over and die. We've got two good hockey teams that are playing at the top of their game. Nobody said this would be an easy series. Whoever scores the most goals in the next game wins. You're upset when you lose, but that's hockey and that's why they have a Game 7."

— Wendel Clark

Despite his controversial winning goal in Game 6, Wayne Gretzky had not played particularly well in this series. Yet with fans in Toronto dreaming of a Stanley Cup Final against the Montreal Canadiens (who'd beaten the Islanders in five games), The Great One stepped up. Gretzky had three goals and set up a fourth as the Kings beat the Maple Leafs 5–4 in a Game 7 thriller.

"We should have won that game, but Gretzky proved what type of player he was."

— Doug Gilmour, recalling Game 7 at the time of his retirement in 2003

"I've taken the roses and I've taken the heat. But tonight I stood up and I answered the bell. I don't think I've ever been more personally satisfied at winning a series. It's the sweetest moment of my career. I've played 14 years and I didn't want to be remembered as the guy who didn't play well in the semifinals versus Toronto."

— Wayne Gretzky after the game

"We fought back…. There is a lot of character on this team. Lots of guts and determination in here. At times on paper we're not as good as the other team, but we have a lot of determination. We've got a good coach who demands a lot and we wanted to win for him. We gave it a good run."

— Doug Gilmour after the game

"What made the loss even harder to take was the fact that deep down we believed we would have beaten the Montreal Canadiens…. One thing I do know for certain is that the Canadiens definitely didn't want to play us. One of their stars, Kirk Muller, told me so. They knew we'd be so pumped mentally and so tough physically that they'd really have their hands full."

— Wendel Clark, *Wendel* (2009)

"I always get asked about it, and I say 'Give me the seventh game at home to go to the Stanley Cup Finals — I'll take it any day. I'd challenge it again.' And then the next question is 'Would you beat Montreal?' What am I going to say? Yes."

— Doug Gilmour, recalling Game 7 on the night the Leafs honoured his #93, January 1, 2009

It was a disappointing end to be for sure, but the Leafs had accomplished so much this season. According to Cliff Fletcher,

> The first goal for a rebuilding club is to become respectable and competitive, and we've done that. The next step is to prove you belong with the top seven or eight teams on a consistent basis. That's the next challenge.

1993–94 TO 1997–98

The NHL reorganized its conferences, divisions, and playoff structure in 1993–94, and Toronto found itself in the Central Division of the Western Conference. The Maple Leafs had another strong season. They opened the schedule with 10 straight wins, which set an NHL record. By season's end, they had a record of 43–29–12 for 98 points, which had them two back of Detroit in the division standings. Doug Gilmour was once again the offensive force, leading the team (and ranking among the NHL leaders) with 84 assists and 111 points. Dave Andreychuk had 53 goals and 46 assists, equalling his 99 points of the year before — although all in Toronto this time. Injuries once again meant Wendel Clark only played 64 games, but he reached career highs in goals (46), assists (30), points (76), and plus-minus (+10). Jamie Macoun and Sylvain Lefebvre anchored the defence in front of goalie Felix Potvin.

For the second year in a row, Toronto reached the Conference Final, knocking off the Chicago Blackhawks in six games to open the playoffs, and then needing seven to subdue the surprising San Jose Sharks. Once again, though, they would not make it through to play for the Stanley Cup, losing in five games to a Vancouver Canucks team led by Pavel Bure, Trevor Linden, and goalie Kirk McLean.

Wendel for Mats

The Maple Leafs had made several trades during the season, the most noteworthy being the deal that sent Glenn Anderson to the New York Rangers (who would win the Stanley Cup that season) for Mike Gartner. The most stunning swap came at the NHL Draft in Hartford on June 28, 1994, when the Leafs sent captain Wendel Clark to Quebec, along with Sylvain Lefebvre, Landon Wilson, and a first-round draft choice for Mats Sundin, Garth Butcher, Todd Warriner, and a first-round pick.

Felix Potvin fends off Vancouver's Murray Craven during the 1994 Western Conference Championship.

"I was shocked by the news like everyone else … but you've got to give up gold to get gold."

— Pat Burns

"This was a very emotional decision to make on our part. We agonized over it for weeks and weeks."

— Cliff Fletcher

"I'm going to a different hockey team — it's not the end of the world."

— Wendel Clark

"This was probably the most difficult deal I ever made, it was very emotional. I knew what we could be getting in Mats. We knew that he was big, strong, durable. I was very attached to Wendel Clark. He had been so important to the franchise. I knew the deal wasn't going to be popular. And I knew what I was feeling. I was kind of sick about it. Ownership was a little shocked at first. But once we explained it, they were very supportive."

— Cliff Fletcher to Steve Simmons, *Toronto Sun*, February 16, 2016

"Oh boy. I guess it really was a big deal. I'm not worried, just a little surprised."

> — Mats Sundin on reading the reports in the Toronto
> papers a few days after the trade

"Coming to Toronto, I didn't know what to expect. And it didn't help that the guy in exchange was Wendel Clark…. You have to be part of the Leafs to understand how important the team is. It took me a while. The whole city breathes and lives the Leafs. The longer you're there, the more you understand what it's like to be part of something that big. Certainly, it was the best part of my life."

> — Mats Sundin, recalling the trade and his time in Toronto, 2012

In 1989, Sundin had been the first European player to be chosen first overall in the NHL Draft. He left his native Sweden in 1990 to make his debut with the Quebec Nordiques and jumped from 23 goals and 59 points as a rookie to 33 goals and 76 points in his second season, and then to 47 goals and 114 points in 1992–93. His numbers declined (32 goals, 85 points) in 1993–94, but he would go on to lead the Maple Leafs in scoring in nearly every one of the 13 seasons he would spend with the team from 1994–95 through 2006–07. He would become one of the greatest Maple Leafs in history, although fans never really warmed to him as they did to Wendel Clark and Doug Gilmour.

Burns Gets Burned

Doug Gilmour was named team captain in 1994–95, but the team would not continue to enjoy the heady days of the previous two seasons. By 1995–96, they had fallen under .500 again. Though the Leafs would make the playoffs that year, an eight-game losing streak in late February and early March helped lose Pat Burns his job.

"It's definitely not the coach. We should be going through the wall for the guy. It's the same exact system we had when we were winning. It's not the coach. It's every guy in this room."

> — Dave Andreychuk after the eighth straight loss on March 3, 1996

"In developments reminiscent of the bad old days, beleaguered president and general manager Cliff Fletcher [on Monday] cashiered two-time NHL coach-of-the-year Pat Burns with only 17 games left in the season. The firing, leaked in the wee hours yesterday and based on a horrendous losing streak, was carried out in clumsy, Ballard-like fashion after Burns had said that he'd be behind the bench tonight against New Jersey."

— Damien Cox, *Toronto Star*, March 6, 1996

"It was done out of deference to Pat. Maybe he just wanted to steal away quietly."

— Cliff Fletcher on why the public had been
misled about the timing of Burns's firing

"When he did it, I said, 'Cliff, I understand, it's not your fault. That's the way it's got to be.'"

— Pat Burns

"The buck stops at my desk. Obviously, I have to accept all responsibility."
— Cliff Fletcher on his expensive and aging roster
that had gone 3−16−3 since mid-January

The Leafs were 25–30–10 at the time of Burns's firing. They went 9–6–2 down the stretch under interim coach Nick Beverly to finish the 82-game season with a record of 34–36–12. In the playoffs, they lost to St. Louis in the opening round.

Gilmour Gone

Mike Murphy was named the new head coach for the 1996–97 season, but he couldn't halt the decline. The Leafs fell to 30–44–8 and finished last in the Central Division, their 68 points ranking them 24th overall in the 26-team NHL. In an effort to salvage something from the season, the Leafs traded their biggest star for younger talent. On February 25, 1997, Fletcher sent Doug Gilmour and Dave Ellett to New Jersey for Jason Smith, Steve Sullivan, and the rights to Alyn McCauley.

"I knew what was going on and I tried to prepare myself as best I could.... I never requested a move from Toronto, but a change had to be made. They needed some younger players here to prepare for the future."

— Doug Gilmour

"Pat Burns couldn't get them going. I couldn't get them going. The personnel on the team had to change. I think this is a step in doing that."

— Leafs coach Mike Murphy

A few weeks later, on March 18, Fletcher would say, "Draft Schmaft"
when he was offered Pittsburgh's first-round pick for Wendel Clark (whom
he'd brought back to Toronto the year before). He wanted players.

* * *

During the summer of 1997, Mats Sundin told Borje Salming that the Leafs
wanted to make him captain, but that he was reluctant to accept.

"The captaincy had been offered to me [in the late '80s] and I'd said no. I
look back on that with regret. At the time, I was worried about my English
and my shyness. Plus, a captain has to give speeches at events and talk
about why the team lost. I didn't want to do that. But I wasn't thinking
about [making] history for a Swedish player. That would have been something. So when Mats asked me, I said right away, 'Do it, it's the greatest
team in the world.'"

— Borje Salming to Lance Hornby, *Toronto Sun*, August 30, 2013

Leafs fans never seemed to appreciate Mats Sundin during his playing days, but he would
become the team's all-time leader in goals and points during the 13 seasons he played in Toronto.

"First heralded as the saviour, later reduced to a budget-slasher, hatchet man, and fall guy, Cliff Fletcher refused to serve as a figurehead and resigned his position as president and general manager of the Toronto Maple Leafs....

"If Fletcher's reputation as an astute judge of hockey talent was damaged by the performance of this year's 30–44–8 team, Fletcher could point his finger at [Steve] Stavro and the board. Although Fletcher tried to minimize the deleterious effects of their demands to slash the team payroll, the Leafs clearly became a less competitive and less entertaining team as they became a cheaper and more profitable enterprise."

— Gare Joyce, *Globe and Mail*, Toronto, May 26, 1997

"We did our best and this past season was just bad hockey. Everything went wrong."

— Cliff Fletcher

"I can't blame Cliff. We're all to blame."

— Steve Stavro

Ken Dryden Comes On Board

Before they hired a general manager, the Leafs made a surprising move in announcing Ken Dryden as their new president on May 30, 1997. Dryden had been a star player as the goalie of the Montreal Canadiens in the 1970s, but he'd been away from the inner workings of the game since his retirement in '79. Dryden had grown up in the Toronto suburbs as a Leafs fan and still called the city home. But it was his personal relationship with Gardens' board members Larry Tanenbaum and Brian Bellmore that resulted in his appointment.

"I want the Leafs to win the Cup. That's why I took the job."

— Ken Dryden

"There's no reason in the world for thinking the Toronto Maple Leafs shouldn't be able to compete at the top. We have to. The loss of a sense of possibility is what kills the fans. You've got to believe that if this can happen, then that can happen, then … wow! That's what we should be able to deliver."

— Ken Dryden

"I don't think it's rocket science or brain surgery. He's here to give the team a sense of direction, a new feeling of what the Toronto Maple Leafs are all about and where they're going, a sense of ourselves and our mission."

— Brian Bellmore

"He'll make mistakes, we know that, but he'll make up for them. He'll learn. He's well qualified…. Ken has the assurances of the board that he will have the resources necessary to build a Stanley Cup–winning team."

— Steve Stavro

"I believe I can do the job…. I don't know how long it will take. I can't promise a timetable. No one can deliver a timetable. What I can deliver is the right goals and the promise that we won't lose sight of those goals."

— Ken Dryden

Dryden's first job was to hire a general manager. He spoke with former NHL GMs John Muckler, David Poile, and Mike Keenan. There were also reports that Glen Sather had discussed the job. Dryden had hoped to hire his former teammate Bob Gainey — the only person, Dryden said, who was offered the job — but Gainey chose to stay on as GM in Dallas. In the end, Dryden hired himself. The announcement came on August 20, 1997.

"I did not think I would be standing here telling you that I was taking on the additional role of general manager. I'm doing it because I want to do this job; because I think I can help make this team … because it's my job to give shape to the organization and direct it where it needs to go."

Drdyen would not be doing the job alone, having assembled a management team to work with him. It included Cliff Fletcher's former assistant GM Bill Watters, who would now be assistant to the president and oversee the Leafs farm club; Anders Hedberg, the Leafs' European scouting director since 1991, who would be assistant GM responsible for amateur scouting; and former Winnipeg Jets GM Mike Smith, who'd be associate general manager in charge of pro scouting and day-to-day hockey management decisions.

"This is not management by committee. The decisions are mine to make."

— Ken Dryden

"Each of them will have a strong voice in the organization. I want them to have a strong voice and those voices will be heard. Whoever makes the most sense on any given matter will carry the day. There will be no problem as long as it's clear who is calling the shots."

— Ken Dryden

Mike Murphy was retained as head coach for 1997–98, but he and Mike Smith would have a difficult relationship and it was another tough season in Toronto. The Leafs went 30–43–9 and missed the playoffs once again. Murphy had another year left on his contract, but it was expected that he wouldn't be back. Still, the axe didn't fall until June 23, more than two months after the regular season had ended.

"You see coaches get fired and the question is: 'Is Jacques Lemaire a bad coach? Or is Mike Murphy a bad coach?' The answer is no. But what happens is they get to a certain point with their teams and find they can't squeeze out as much as they need to get them to the next level."

— Ken Dryden

"We can genuinely look in the mirror and say we did the job the right way."
— Mike Murphy, referring to himself and his assistants,
Terry Simpson, Mike Kitchen, and Rick Wamsley

At his press conference, Dryden said he regretted that the time it took to reach a decision was tough on Murphy and his family, "but I don't regret the ambition of wanting to get to the top."

Everyone knew who the Leafs wanted as their next coach, but it would be a few more days before an announcement was made.

1998–99

Pat Quinn

Pat Quinn had begun his NHL career as a player with the Leafs from 1968 to 1970. He later played two seasons with the Vancouver Canucks and four with the Atlanta Flames, where he served as captain in his final two seasons (1975–76, 1976–77). After his playing career, Quinn became an assistant coach with the Philadelphia Flyers in 1977, and was made head coach midway through the 1978–79 season. In his first full season with the team (1979–80), the Flyers set a record with a 35-game unbeaten streak (25 wins, 10 ties) and reached the Stanley Cup Final. He won the Jack Adams Award as coach of the year. He later coached the Los Angeles Kings from 1984–85 through 1986–87. He then became president and general manager of the Vancouver Canucks in 1987–88, adding coaching duties late in the 1990–91 season. He won the Jack Adams Award again in 1992.

Quinn but gave up coaching after leading the Canucks past the Maple Leafs and into the Stanley Cup Final in 1994. He stayed on as president and GM until being fired in November of 1997. When he was hired in Toronto on June 26, 1998, he was happy to hold just one portfolio.

> "I've been given a very important job at this point. I want to focus on that. Coaching is a full-time job."
>
> — Pat Quinn at the press conference to announce his hiring

Given that the Leafs were, essentially, a younger team, there was some surprise that they hadn't hired a younger coach, such as Marc Crawford, who'd coached the Leafs' St. John's farm club in the early 1990s and won the Stanley Cup as head coach of the Colorado Avalanche in 1996.

> "Pat's a guy who's always been able to relate to people 20 years or more younger than he is. He's very young in terms of energy and enthusiasm. He has seen and done it all, but he doesn't have the jaded quality of some who have seen it all and done it all."
>
> — Ken Dryden

> "What I have to do is like anything, like a car. I have to pick up the hood and look underneath. When it is not running the way you want, then you have to figure out what it is that is maybe holding it back from being the best it can be. And so the next while before training camp, it is my job to find out about players and try to determine in my mind what the best plan is to bring about the things we all want."
>
> — Pat Quinn

> "I think we need to have a deeper lineup, a stronger lineup. Having said that, I am excited about working with Pat."
>
> — Mats Sundin, reacting to the hiring of Quinn

In addition to hiring Quinn, it was clear that while Ken Dryden would retain the title, the Leafs were going to give more authority to Mike Smith with regard to the GM's role. "Mike Smith has, to a great extent this year, [already] taken on those kinds of roles. So I have some involvement that way, but really it's Mike who does most of that," Dryden explained.

Dryden would concentrate mainly on his role as president, and his most visible accomplishment in that role was to have the Leafs moved from the Western Conference to the Eastern Conference this season, where they would now play in the Northeast Division with the Montreal Canadiens, Ottawa Senators, Boston Bruins, and Buffalo Sabres. Mike Smith — who'd been instrumental in the negotiations that brought Quinn to Toronto — would concentrate on improving the roster.

"You never make any major changes without the coach being involved. The coach doesn't want to be blindsided by someone who comes in and says, 'By the way, I made a trade last night, you've got three new players coming in.'"

— Mike Smith

Smith would be responsible for the off-season free agent signings that brought back former Leaf Steve Thomas, secured Garry Valk from Pittsburgh, and — most importantly — gave the team goalie Curtis Joseph from Edmonton. Key trades during the season would see Smith acquire former first-overall draft choice Bryan Berard from the New York Islanders in exchange for Felix Potvin, as well as Yanic Perreault from Los Angeles.

As coach, Quinn chose to accentuate offence, and the results were stunning. The Maple Leafs led the NHL in goals scored (268) for the first time since the 1946–47 season. Six Maple Leafs scored 20 goals or more, including Sergei Berezin, who led the team with 37, and Mats Sundin, who scored 31 and led the team with 52 assists and 83 points. Toronto set a new club record (which they would tie in 1999–2000 and 2003–04) with 45 wins (45–30–7) and finished second in the Northeast Division, and fifth overall in the NHL, with 97 points. The Leafs ranked 21st in goals-against, but it certainly wasn't the fault of Curtis Joseph. He was a key reason behind the Leafs' remarkable turnaround.

As one of the busiest goalies in the NHL this season, Joseph ranked third overall in minutes played and faced the second-most shots of any goalie in the league. Still, he trailed only New Jersey's Martin Brodeur with 35 wins and not only finished second in voting for the Vezina Trophy behind Buffalo's Dominik Hasek, but was also fourth in voting for the Hart Trophy as NHL MVP.

In the playoffs, the Leafs eliminated Philadelphia in six games in the opening round, and then beat Pittsburgh in six to advance to the Eastern Conference Final against Buffalo. With Hasek in goal, the Sabres boasted the NHL's second-best defence in 1998–99. Toronto notched 10 goals against Dwayne Roloson in the first two games of the series (a 5–4 loss and a 6–3

Curtis Joseph was a Hart and a Vezina Trophy candidate during his years in Toronto and helped the Maple Leafs reach the Conference Championship twice in his four seasons.

victory), but when Hasek returned from an injury the Leafs scored only twice in each of the next three games. They were eliminated in five as the Sabres advanced to play the Dallas Stars for the Stanley Cup.

Goodbye MLG, Hello ACC

In October of 1995, shareholders of Maple Leaf Gardens and the hockey team had been told that the organization had no plans to build a new arena. But on March 5, 1996 (the same day it was announced that Pat Burns had been fired), Steve Stavro said that the franchise was actively considering a new home.

While the Leafs explored several possible sites, the Toronto Raptors of the National Basketball Association began construction of the Air Canada Centre in March of 1997 on a site just south of Union Station that had previously been owned by Canada Post. On February 12, 1998, Maple Leaf Sports and Entertainment bought the Raptors. MLSE then ordered major modifications to the basketball-only design of the Air Canada Centre to make it suitable for hockey as well. The new building was finally ready midway through the 1998–99 season.

The NHL had already seen all of its other "Original Six" buildings replaced: the old Madison Square Garden in 1968, Detroit's Olympia in 1979, Chicago Stadium in 1994, Boston Garden in 1995, and the Montreal Forum in 1996.

"You don't replace a Maple Leaf Gardens. It's a special plac[...] never recapture the atmosphere we had in those places. We'll [...] new excitement, new history, I suppose."

— [...]

On Saturday night, February 13, 1999, the Maple Leafs played their last game at Maple Leaf Gardens, closing it as they had opened it, against the Chicago Blackhawks.

"We've slowly lost our shrines, if that's the word. We've moved, especially through the '90s, to a corporate culture. And to me [the Gardens] was the last bastion of the game. And as we move to these monstrous buildings — that are beautiful and great places to showcase our game — we've lost the old element where it was just a place for the everyday guy to go."

— Pat Quinn

"As a youngster growing up, my heroes played on this same ice surface. They dressed in the same seat I dress in. They hoisted the Stanley Cup in the same building I'm playing in. That whole aura and history won't be transferred to the new building no matter how hard they try."

— Leafs backup goalie Glenn Healy

"The fans sit right next to you in the golds and this girl was talking to me. You know, quite a bit. And I guess her boyfriend or husband was on the other side. Next period, he's sitting next to me."

— Curtis Joseph

"It scares me a little bit, the new buildings coming into the league now. A lot of them are just too big."

— Steve Thomas

"He's our only player to have played in the first game at Maple Leaf Gardens and we'd like to turn the score around for him."

— Glenn Healy, joking about veteran Steve Thomas

Having lost the opener at Maple Leaf Gardens to Chicago 2–1 back in 1931, Toronto also fell in the last game, losing this one 6–2. Ex-Leaf Doug Gilmour scored Chicago's third goal of the night, which proved to be the game winner.

Tie Domi surpassed his childhood hero Tiger Williams as the Leafs' all-time leader in penalty minutes. Though he was never quite the scorer that Williams was, Domi could also do more than just fight.

"I was really nervous [today]. I tried to lie down, but I couldn't sleep so I came down about 2:15 in the afternoon to see all the excitement outside the Gardens."

— Doug Gilmour

"They wanted to win very badly tonight. They tried very hard — they just weren't very smart."

— Pat Quinn on the Leafs' effort in the final game at the Gardens

"We're disappointed and we're sorry we let everybody down."

— Tie Domi

"This is a sad night in some ways but it almost feels like a celebration. We're leaving our home, the home we've been in our whole lives and I think the rest of Canada feels the same way. Even if they didn't live here like I did, they did so in their dreams."

— long-time Maple Leaf Gardens' public address announcer Paul Morris

"Mats, take this flag to our new home, but always remember us."

— Red Horner, the oldest living Toronto Maple Leaf, to current captain Mats Sundin at the end of the post-game ceremony

After a 3–3 tie in New Jersey and a 3–2 overtime win in Buffalo, the Leafs were back in Toronto the next Saturday night, February 20, 1999, to open the Air Canada Centre. This time, they came out on top, defeating the Montreal Canadiens 3–2 in overtime.

"It's an incredible feeling to score the winning goal, especially in the first game in this building. If you've ever scored a goal in overtime in any sport, it's an incredible feeling. I was just lucky to be that guy tonight."

— Steve Thomas

Tweaks Toward a New Century

Despite the impressive season on the ice in 1998–99, not all was well behind the scenes. It had seemed that Mike Smith was in position to succeed Ken Dryden as GM, but the two men had not gotten along this season and Smith's contract was not renewed. Pat Quinn's relationship with Dryden had not been the best either, and given that Quinn considered Smith to be the man who'd hired him, he was unsure about his own future. Though he'd claimed that he didn't want to be GM, on July 14, 1999, Dryden confirmed that Quinn would add the GM job to his position as coach.

"Pat's the GM. He has full authority over the hockey operations of the teams — Toronto, St. John's, amateur scouting, player development, and pro scouting. All the things that are normally under the heading of hockey operations...."

— Ken Dryden

"When it came right down to it, I thought, *Wow, this is really something, to be able to have control and influence over the Toronto Maple Leafs.*"

— Pat Quinn

Smith was gone, but Bill Watters would continue to work on player contracts, and Anders Hedberg would stay on as director of player development. Dryden would still be president.

"In Vancouver, I spent so much time on the presidential duties and the business side of things that it took away from my duties towards the hockey operations. I'll be much more effective wearing just the two hats this time around."

— Pat Quinn

Still, he was now the only person in the NHL serving in the dual capacity of coach and general manager. Could he do it?

"I know the job can be done, because I've done it," Quinn said.

And so, with the dawn of a new century just around the corner, everything seemed to be in place for the Toronto Maple Leafs to succeed.

10

2000 and Beyond: Success, Setbacks, and the Shana-Plan

1999–2000 TO 2003–04

In his first season as coach and general manager of the Toronto Maple Leafs, Pat Quinn led the team to the first 100-point season in franchise history. The Maple Leafs were 45–27–7 in 1999–2000 and finished atop the Northeast Division in a close race with the Ottawa Senators. Although they were only seventh overall in the NHL standings, the division crown marked the first time Toronto had finished in first place in anything since the 1962–63 season when the team had finished atop the six-team standings.

Curtis Joseph had another fine season in 1999–2000, setting a team record with 36 wins. Joseph finished third in voting for the Vezina Trophy, behind winner Olaf Kolzig of Washington and runner-up Roman Turek of St. Louis. As usual, Sundin led the offence with 32 goals, 41 assists, and 73 points in 73 games. Tomas Kaberle, in his second NHL season, proved to be an offensive leader from the blue line, while fellow defencemen Bryan Berard and Cory Cross were among the team leaders in plus-minus. Sadly, the 22-year-old Berard suffered a serious injury when he was accidentally clipped in the eye by Ottawa's Marian Hossa on March 11, 2000. It was first thought that the injury would be career-ending. Although Berard would never again play for the Leafs, he later returned to play in the NHL from 2001 to 2008.

Toronto was the third seed in their conference heading into the 2000 playoffs, which matched them up against division rival Ottawa in the opening round.

The Battle of Ontario: 2000

The Leafs and Senators would meet in the post-season four times in the next five years, and while the Battle of Ontario didn't quite measure up to Calgary and Edmonton's Battle of Alberta or the Canadiens' and Nordiques' Battle of Quebec in the 1980s, it still made for some entertaining hockey. Despite finishing five points up on Ottawa in the Northeast Division standings in 1999–2000, the Leafs had been only 1–3–1 in their five meetings with the Senators.

> "Ottawa is a good turnover team. If you turn the puck over to them, you're in trouble. We're a creative team and sometimes in trying to create something, we give up the puck."
> — Toronto's Steve Thomas prior to the 2000 series against the Senators

The Leafs jumped out to an early lead in the series, with Toronto scoring 2–0 and 5–1 wins in the first two games at the Air Canada Centre. But the Senators bounced back to even things with a pair of one-goal wins in Ottawa. Back home in Game 5, the Leafs trailed for most of the night before Steve Thomas evened the score with just 4:30 remaining in regulation time, and then won it at 14:47 of overtime.

> "In two glorious roof-raising moments, in a game in which the Senators had mostly smothered the Leafs, Thomas forever silenced the critics who questioned his continued presence on the top line. Or even in the lineup."
> — Damian Cox, *Toronto Star*, April 23, 2000

> "I use that [criticism] to fuel myself. I didn't want ... to look bad in front of everybody. I didn't want the organization to think they'd made a mistake, and I wanted to do my best for my teammates. I don't think there's any better place to play hockey than in Toronto when you're successful."
> — Steve Thomas

> "I don't know what to say about this guy. It's not in my power to try and explain it. He just comes up with those big plays."
> — Pat Quinn on Steve Thomas

Mats Sundin set up both of Thomas's goals. His quiet leadership was often under-appreciated by the fans, but not by his teammates.

"You know, Mats gets a lot of criticism about his leadership, but I think you guys should start writing about how great a leader he is; he's the best I've ever played with. He doesn't step up and start yelling, but he's unbelievable. He just gave us a sense of, 'Boys, we're going to win this game,' and it had such a calming influence on us."
— Darcy Tucker, who joined the Leafs midway through the 1999–2000 season

"I told them to get going and get their heads out of their asses."
— Mats Sundin, joking about what he told his teammates
between the third period and overtime

In Game 6 in Ottawa, the Leafs trailed 2–0 early in the game, but then Thomas scored his sixth goal of the series at 4:11 of the second period and Sundin tied the game at 7:16 to trigger a four-goal outburst the gave Toronto a 4–2 victory. But the first-round victory over Ottawa was as far as the Leafs got, losing in six games to New Jersey in the second.

2001

The Senators came on strong in 2000–01, finishing atop the Northeast Division and second in the Eastern Conference with 109 points. The Leafs had added players such as Shayne Corson, Gary Roberts, Bryan McCabe, and Wade Belak, but fell back to 90 points on a record of 37–29–10. As the seventh seed in the East, Toronto opened the playoffs in Ottawa. The Senators had won all five games they played against the Leafs during the season, outscoring Toronto 20–10, and were heavy favourites heading into their playoff series. There were rumours that an early playoff exit might lead to the breakup of the Leafs, but the players themselves were confident.

"This year, we're the underdogs. But the fact is, we're here, we believe in ourselves. As players, you can't think about that kind of stuff before a playoff series."
— Curtis Joseph

"You hear the rumours all year. You know, we're still together for a reason, and that's because we've won in the past. And we plan on winning again."
— Garry Valk, who was one of 13 players left on the
team from the 1999 run to the Conference Final

A former 50-goal scorer in Calgary, Gary Roberts brought talent and toughness to Toronto. He was at his best with the Leafs during the 2002 playoffs when captain Mats Sundin was hurt.

The Leafs played with a lot of intensity against Ottawa in Game 1, with Shayne Corson shadowing Alexei Yashin and Toronto using some roughhouse tactics to slow down Marian Hossa and rookie Martin Havlat. Despite taking plenty of penalties, Toronto shut out Ottawa 1–0, the win coming at 10:49 of overtime on a slapshot from Sundin.

> "When you're playing street hockey as a kid, you dream about scoring overtime goals. That's a lot of fun."
>
> — Mats Sundin

The Leafs won the second game 3–0 and didn't allow an Ottawa goal until 16:51 of the third period in Game 3 in Toronto. But then another Ottawa goal at 19:24 tied the score at 2–2.

Toronto had let a 2–0 lead since midway through the second period slip, but the Leafs refused to be downcast heading into overtime.

> "If you had told us last week that we would be one shot away from going up 3–0 in this series, we'd take it."
>
> — backup goalie Glenn Healy to his teammates in the dressing room

Cory Cross proved to be the unlikely hero when he blasted in a 40-foot slapshot for the overtime winner at 2:16. It was his first playoff goal in eight seasons. The Leafs completed their surprising sweep with a 3–1 win in Game 4, and advanced to face New Jersey in the second round for the second year in a row.

In the fourth game of that Eastern Conference semifinal against the Devils, the Leafs were leading 3–1 and were 7.4 seconds away from tying the series when Tie Domi knocked out Scott Niedermayer with an elbow to the face.

"I'd played the best game of my life. I was 17 seconds away from being the first star [of the game] — I saw the list when I came in and they were scratching my name off — and I sat down right where I'm sitting now and said to myself: *What did you do that for?* I wanted to cry. I wished I could have dug myself a hole and crawled in."

— Tie Domi, recalling the incident for Cam Cole of the *National Post*

Domi was suspended for the rest of the playoffs. Niedermayer missed the rest of the series, but New Jersey would win it in seven games and eventually go on to the Stanley Cup Final, where they were beaten by the Colorado Avalanche.

2002

The Leafs bounced back with another solid season in 2001–02, tying the club record set two years before with 100 points. This time, it had them one point back of Boston in the Northeast Division and third overall in the entire NHL — though a long way back of Detroit's league-leading 116 points. Mats Sundin led the way with 41 goals (which tied him for second in the NHL behind Jarome Iginla's 52) and 80 points, which placed him fourth in the scoring race. In the playoffs, Toronto eliminated the New York Islanders in a tough seven-game series and advanced to the second round where they once again hooked up with Ottawa.

"People say there was a lot of hate in the Islander series. Well, at least you saw us shaking hands at the end. There's going to be a lot of hate in the Ottawa series. It's not going to take much to get that rivalry going again."

— Tie Domi

Toronto would face a rash of injuries against Ottawa. Most notable was Mats Sundin, who broke his wrist during the Islanders series and would not play against the Senators. Gary Roberts filled the leadership vacuum, and would top the team with five goals and five assists during the Ottawa series … although no Leaf had a point in Game 1 when the well-rested Senators scored a 5–0 victory.

Roberts was the hero in Game 2, scoring at 4:30 of the third overtime period to give Toronto a 3–2 victory. It was the third-longest game in Maple Leafs history, and the longest since 1943. The game was a big bounce-back for Curtis Joseph, who hadn't been his best this season and had had some weak games in the playoffs. Joseph took a lot of heat after the 5–0 loss, but stopped 54 of 56 shots this night.

"Our whole team felt for him."
— Gary Roberts on the criticism of Joseph

"He came up with a huge game after a lot of people gave him a lot of heat. The guy's one of the best in the world."
— Travis Green

"When he's out there making those big saves, it gives the team a huge lift. But we expected that from him."
— Shayne Corson

"You're always trying to prove yourself."
— Curtis Joseph, denying that the criticism had spurred him on

The next three games were all close, Ottawa winning 3–2 in Game 3, Toronto winning 2–1 in Game 4, and then Ottawa going on top again with a 4–2 win at the Air Canada Centre in Game 5. The Leafs had complained about the officiating throughout the playoffs (Pat Quinn had already been fined $30,000) but they had reason to be angry in this one.

Late in the third period, Daniel Alfredsson hit Darcy Tucker into the boards from behind. It was the kind of hit the NHL was trying to crack down on, but no penalty was called. As Tucker lay on the ice in obvious pain, Alfredsson beat Joseph on a high slapshot at 17:59 to give Ottawa a 3–2 lead. Radek Bonk added an empty-net goal in the dying seconds.

"A bloody joke."
— Travis Green's assessment of the non-call

"I am, quite frankly, full of anger. This should not have been [a call] that gave them any trouble."
— Pat Quinn on referees Steve Walkom and Rob Shick

Darcy Tucker topped 20 goals four times during his seven full seasons in Toronto.

"Everyone is afraid to say anything, but if that was Darcy Tucker making the hit on Alfredsson they would be screaming bloody murder and there would be suspensions to be handed out."

— Travis Green

"They were both adamant [Tucker] did not get hit in the numbers, he got hit on the shoulder and spun into the boards. They are both experienced referees."

— NHL supervisor of officials Dave Newell explaining the non-call

Tucker would be out for the rest of the series, but the Leafs bounced back. Trailing 2–0 early in Game 6, they rallied on a pair of goals from Gary Roberts before Alexander Mogilny scored early in the third period for a 4–3 win in Ottawa that sent the series back to Toronto for Game 7.

"I've just got a feeling that something good will happen."

— Maple Leafs' Alexander Mogilny before Game 6

"I try to say something like that before every game. It's just that it came true this time."

— Alexander Mogilny after Game 6

"I've never thought of myself as somebody who could carry a team offensively. Really, all I'm doing right now is trying to battle hard and have a little success."

— Gary Roberts

"It's been the Gary Roberts show in this series. He's really carried our team and led us offensively, defensively, and in hits. You can't ask for much more from a guy that's 35 or so."

— Alyn McCauley

"It's becoming folklorish in a way. It builds a history of its own. I can only tell you in our room he's been magnificent. I don't want to run off at the mouth with superlatives, but he's been superlative."

— Pat Quinn on Roberts

The Senators had very little experience in Game 7s, whereas the Leafs had just come through one in their victory over the Islanders.

Toronto turned in as dominating a performance as they had in the playoffs, holding Ottawa to just 19 shots and winning 3–0 behind two goals from Mogilny and one from Bryan McCabe.

"It might be about time to start thinking that something special is going on here. Despite the fact that the Leafs have been losing bodies at a prodigious rate to every kind of injury imaginable, they're halfway to the Stanley Cup. Even the injury replacements are getting injured, but the Leafs soldier on to Round 3."

— Ken Campbell, *Toronto Star*, May 15, 2002

"It's weird when you see half your team with suits on when you come off the ice. I've said this many times and I'll say it again; I've never been prouder to be part of a group of guys in my whole career."

— Tie Domi

"Definitely the biggest [moment] since '67. I think '93 was big, but it's the way they're doing this, showing such character. The fans love the Leafs and they have for a long time, but there are non-hockey fans watching this because it's so easy to feel the heart and the enthusiasm of this team."

— 1967 Leafs Stanley Cup champion Ron Ellis

"The Gilmour years. This city got excited then, but now, with the skeleton crew they've got here, the grit, the injuries, the bouncing back, the guys from St. John's. It hasn't been quite like this before."

— Darryl Sittler

"We just put our skates on and play hockey."

— Alexander Mogilny

But despite all the excitement, as in 1993, 1994, and 1999, the Leafs couldn't make it past the Conference Final, losing this time to the Carolina Hurricanes. Even with Mats Sundin returning in Game 2, and leading the team with four points in the five games he played, Toronto fell in a tight six-game series that saw Carolina win games two, three, and six by 2–1 scores in overtime.

"To win the Stanley Cup, you need the stars to line up. It's the hardest championship to win in sports. We didn't have enough stars lining up."

— Curtis Joseph, whose appearance in Game 6 against the Hurricanes would be his last as a Leaf

In his first two seasons in Toronto before the lockout of 2004–05, Ed Belfour gave the Leafs the type of goaltending that earned him his place in the Hockey Hall of Fame.

"There are times when you should not expect to go on and there are times when you should. This year, we had the expectation."

— Pat Quinn

"It was a heartbreak ending this year. This was the best chance of any season we've had. It was there for the taking. Unfortunately, it didn't happen. We'll be thinking about *what if this* or *what if that*. I still really can't believe it."

— Tie Domi

2002–03 AND 2003–04

Curtis Joseph left Toronto when he signed as a free agent with Detroit on July 2, 2002. That same day, Toronto signed Ed Belfour, who'd starred with Chicago and Dallas, winning the Stanley Cup with the Stars in 1999. At the trade deadline during the 2002–03 season, the Leafs acquired veteran Owen Nolan from San Jose for youngsters Alyn McCauley, Brad Boyes, and a first-round draft choice.

Belfour set a new club record with 37 wins (37–20–5) in 2002–03 and the Leafs had another good finish with 98 points, which placed them well back of Ottawa this year as the Senators won the Northeast Division and topped the NHL's overall standings with 113 points. Even so, Ottawa fell in the first round of the playoffs when they were beaten in five games by the New York Islanders. The Leafs fell to Philadelphia in seven games in the opening round.

Speculation of a shakeup in Leafs management had been going on throughout the season, and the early exit from the playoffs only increased the rumours. Talk was that president Ken Dryden wanted Pat Quinn to give up one of his two positions and remain as only the coach or GM. But Dryden had become increasingly less involved in the day-to-day hockey operations of the team over the years, and even his impact on the business end seemed to be lessening as Richard Peddie, president of MLSE and the Toronto Raptors, increasingly spoke for the hockey team as well.

During the summer of 2003, the Ontario Teacher's Pension Fund became the majority owner of the Maple Leafs, Steve Stavro stepped down as chairman and was replaced by Larry Tanenbaum, and Peddie added Maple Leafs president to his other titles. As of June 27, 2003, Ken Dryden (who would soon leave the Leafs to enter politics) reported to Peddie as vice president of MLSE, while Pat Quinn would remain on as coach only.

"As everyone involved has said from the beginning, we anticipated splitting [Quinn's] dual role at a time that was best for the organization.

We all agreed that the time is right to take that step now. We are not satisfied with our current level of success. We expect more and our fans expect more."

— Richard Peddie

"I came to coach. I still want to coach. I think that's what satisfies me the most."

— Pat Quinn in an interview earlier in the month

"We have not interviewed anyone yet despite speculation. We've started to develop a long list and through due diligence and checking up we'll make that a short list. We'll bring those individuals in and the three of us will interview them. We're all [Peddie, Dryden, and Quinn] going to be involved all the way and in the end I see us having a healthy debate."

— Richard Peddie

Steve Tambellini, vice president of player personnel in Vancouver who'd gotten his management start with the Canucks under Quinn, was thought to be a leading candidate. But in the end, it was John Ferguson Jr. — a 36-year-old front office employee with the St. Louis Blues and the son of legendary Canadiens tough guy and longtime NHL front office man John Ferguson — who was hired as the Leafs' new GM.

Toronto had added veteran Joe Nieuwendyk as a free agent earlier in the summer, and would load up with two more veterans — Brian Leetch and Ron Francis — before the trade deadline in March. On the ice, the team remained a success in 2003–04. The Leafs set a new club record with 103 points, which had them one point ahead of the Senators in the Northeast Division standings, but one point back of the Boston Bruins. In the playoffs, Toronto would face Ottawa once again in the opening round. It was the fourth time in five years the two teams had met in the post-season, but there had been a strange new skirmish added to the Battle of Ontario during the season.

On January 6, 2004, during the second period of a game with the Nashville Predators, Mats Sundin broke his stick on an attempted shot. He threw the shaft away in disgust, and it flew over the boards into the crowd. Under NHL rules, Sundin could have been assessed a ten-minute misconduct, or a game misconduct if the referees felt the toss had been deliberate. Sundin received no penalty and later set up Brian McCabe for a pair of third-period goals as Toronto rallied for a 2–1 victory.

"Pitching your stick up into the stands should be a game misconduct. It's sort of ironic he sets up their two goals."

— Predators coach Barry Trotz

"I was getting rid of the stick, you're not allowed to hang onto it once it's broken. I was frustrated. I wanted to get it out of my hands. I thought I was close enough to the boards and it would hit them. I didn't want it to go into the stands."

— Mats Sundin

Sundin received a one-game suspension the following day.

"Regardless of whether Mr. Sundin may have been overcome by the frustration or emotion of the moment, there is no way the league can tolerate his reaction."

— NHL Director of Hockey Operations Colin Campbell

"That was a brain cramp there. I'm just glad nobody got hurt."

— Mats Sundin

Sundin sat out the Leafs' next game, January 8, 2004, at home against the Senators. Ottawa won it 7–1. During the game, Daniel Alfredsson broke his stick and mimed throwing it up into the stands. The Leafs bench broke out in screams of rage.

"I can understand their bench not being too happy. I know Mats, and I don't think he should have had a suspension. It was meant to be a joke, but it was bad timing by me."

— Daniel Alfredsson

"If he thinks that's funny, fine. Players don't bank those things like I remember in our day. If you were going to show someone up, make a big joke, you'd better be ready to pay a price down the line. But I don't think that happens any more. We have a little fun and people will ask me about a stupid situation and I'll have to give a stupid answer. It sickens me, quite frankly."

— Pat Quinn

Leaf players never took any action against Alfredsson, but after that play, and combined with his hit on Darcy Tucker in the 2002 playoffs, Maple Leaf fans would boo him for the rest of his career. In the playoffs, Toronto took a three-games-to-two series lead (winning all of their games by shutout) when Alfredsson — who had guaranteed in January that Ottawa would win the Stanley Cup — further angered Maple Leafs fans by guaranteeing a Senators victory in Game 6.

"We don't even read the papers; we just don't at this time of year. What he says doesn't mean anything to us. We're not clipping things out and pinning them up on our board. We have a veteran group in here and we think we know what it takes to do the job and that's what is most important."

— Toronto's Tom Fitzgerald

Alfredsson and Ottawa made good on the boast, scoring a 2–1 overtime victory and sending the series back to the Air Canada Centre for Game 7.

"It's a tough loss. Everybody worked real hard, [but] I think we have to play a lot better than we did tonight."

— Leafs goalie Ed Belfour

"We sat back a little too much. That's not our game. We have home ice … and we are looking forward to playing in our own building. We're confident."

— defenceman Bryan McCabe

Toronto — once again battling injuries in this series, and playing the final three games without Mats Sundin — eliminated Ottawa with a 4–1 victory. But the Leafs would go no further, dropping their second-round series to Philadelphia in six games. Amazingly, it would be nine years before Toronto returned to the post-season.

2004–05 TO 2007–08

Pat Quinn had coached Team Canada to an Olympic gold medal at Salt Lake City in 2002. It had been Canada's first gold medal in men's hockey since 1952. In September of 2004, he coached Canada to victory again at the World Cup of Hockey. The day after the tournament ended, NHL owners imposed a lockout on the league's players. It would eventually wipe out the entire 2004–05 season.

When the game returned in 2005–06, there were new rules designed to speed up play, and a salary cap supposedly to control expenses and create a better competitive balance. Toronto hadn't won the Stanley Cup — or even reached the Finals — since 1967, and would now lose the financial advantage of being the

NHL's wealthiest franchise. It would no longer be viable to trade for or sign veteran free agents — though they would continue to try, with acquisitions such as Eric Lindros and Jason Allison for the 2005–06 season. The Leafs would definitely have trouble adapting to the new draft-and-develop style of team building.

The Leafs struggled in 2005–06 but finished the season on a 9–1–2 run. Their final record was 41–33–8, but their 90 points left them two back of the last playoff spot in the Eastern Conference. It was the first time Toronto had missed the playoffs under Quinn, and he paid for it with his job — though many fans and media observers felt it was John Ferguson Jr. who should have been let go.

"It's now all about John Ferguson Jr., naked and exposed. With the fired Pat Quinn no longer sharing the limelight or the line of fire, the offspring of one of hockey's most legendary pugilists is going to need a body suit of Kevlar in the coming months…. [I]t is clear Ferguson will now be the one required to answer the hard questions."

— Damien Cox, *Toronto Star*, April 21, 2006

"Quinn's firing was one of the great mistakes of Richard Peddie's run as CEO of [MLSE], maybe the greatest of a mistake-filled time. Peddie didn't want the same man as coach and GM of the Leafs. So he asked Quinn to pick which job he wanted. Quinn stayed as coach and Peddie hired John Ferguson Jr., whom Quinn greeted with the words, 'You're not qualified for the job.' The two didn't last long together. Ferguson stayed. Quinn was shown the door. Pre-salary cap to post-salary cap, the Leafs have never been the same since."

— Steve Simmons, *Toronto Sun*, writing at the time of Pat Quinn's death, November 24, 2016

A few weeks after Quinn was fired, on June 24, 2006, Ferguson acquired goalie Andrew Raycroft from Boston to replace 41-year-old Ed Belfour, whose option would be bought out, as would Tie Domi's a few days later. Raycroft had won the Calder Trophy as rookie of the year in 2003–04, but had struggled badly when the NHL returned in 2005–06 and he lost the Bruins' starting job to Tim Thomas. Raycroft would tie Ed Belfour's club record with 37 wins in goal for Toronto in 2006–07, but he also allowed an NHL-high 205 goals and posted a 2.99 average and .894 save percentage that were among the worst for any NHL starter. Compounding the problem, Ferguson gave up a former first-round draft choice and future star in goalie Tuukka Rask to land Raycroft.

"Ferguson may have had the right idea in trading a young goalie to Boston for Raycroft. He just picked the wrong goalie, preferring Justin Pogge over Rask. That's the Pogge who now stars for Ritten Renon of the Italian Hockey League, if he stars at all. The Rask trade isn't necessarily the worst deal ever made by the Leafs, but it's certainly part of any conversation on the subject."

— Steve Simmons, *Toronto Sun*, March 19, 2013

Mats's Milestones

Paul Maurice replaced Pat Quinn as the Leafs coach in 2006–07 and the team once again finished ninth in the Eastern Conference and just missed the play-offs. One of the high points of the season came early in the schedule, during the sixth game of the season on October 14, when Mats Sundin capped a hat trick in overtime by blowing a slapshot from the blue line past reigning Vezina Trophy winner Miikka Kiprusoff to give Toronto a 5–4 win over Calgary.

"And, oh, did we mention it was the 500th goal of his career. It was magical. The building exploded with the kind of ecstasy usually saved for playoff wins…. The players poured off the bench to swamp the man with the C in a sea of blue sweaters. The fans jumped to their feet, remaining there as they waited for the curtain call. Sundin came out, gloves and helmet off, skating a couple small circles — he's a modest Swede after all — clapping his hands as he beamed at the fans."

— Paul Hunter, *Toronto Star*, October 15, 2006

"It's certainly a fun way to get my 500th goal. It's a special way. I'm very proud of it. It's an achievement not many players have reached in this league and, once I'm retired, I'm going to appreciate it even more. I'll remember this game for my whole life."

— Mats Sundin

Early in the next season, Sundin became the leading scorer in Maple Leafs history, surpassing Darryl Sittler's totals of 389 goals and 916 points, in an 8–1 rout of the New York Islanders on October 11, 2007. In a way, Sundin broke the record twice. First he was credited with an assist he knew he hadn't earned, lifting his stick sheepishly to acknowledge the cheers.

The assist was quickly taken away, and Sundin later broke the record for real midway through the third when a shot he intended as a pass to Jason Blake

bounced off the skate of Islanders defenceman Brendan Witt and past goalie
Wade Dubielewicz. It was a flukey goal, but a legitimate point to break both
of Sittler's records.

> "It was probably better the way it ended. I'm very glad it ended the way it
> did. It would have been embarrassing otherwise."
>
> — Mats Sundin

> "I'm fortunate to have gotten a chance to play for such a great franchise all
> these years. The way the league is now, you don't get a chance to play as long
> as I have with one team. Most important are the fans who have stuck with
> this team that hasn't won a Stanley Cup since 1967. It's a big carrot for us to
> come back every year. We know it hasn't been easy. We've had a couple good
> runs, going to the conference finals. But they've stuck with us. My respect for
> the city has grown every year and I hope they respect me more as a player."
>
> — Mats Sundin

Troubled Times

Leafs management was starting to believe that John Ferguson Jr. was in over
his head. Fans and the media certainly thought so. During the spring of 2007,
Richard Peddie had talked about finding a senior executive to serve as a mentor. Names such as Scotty Bowman and John Muckler were discussed, but by
August the plan was abandoned. Later, as the Leafs struggled during November,
there were rumours that Ferguson wanted to fire coach Paul Maurice, and that
the Leafs wanted to fire Ferguson. Richard Peddie denied both … but hardly
offered his GM a vote of confidence.

> "To be honest, it was a mistake on my part for not fully understanding at
> the time what the job of being [the GM] in this market fully entailed. Let's
> face it. It probably was the wrong place for a rookie general manager to
> start. I mean, all GMs make mistakes, but they are not under the constant
> microscope and scrutiny that you have in Toronto, which is, in our opin-
> ion, the top hockey market there is. That is all hindsight now. John has had
> time to learn a lot since then."
>
> — Richard Peddie in the *Toronto Sun*, November 27, 2007

With that less-than-ringing endorsement from his boss, speculation about
Ferguson's future continued along with the Leafs' poor play. In mid-January came

word that the Leafs had been given permission to speak with Cliff Fletcher, who currently had one year remaining on a contract as a consultant to the Phoenix Coyotes. On January 21, 2008, there were rumours that the eight-member board of MLSE held a meeting to discuss Richard Peddie's plan to re-hire Fletcher.

"I can't say anything about the future of our management. Everybody in the media will find out at the same time as to what we're doing."

— Richard Peddie

"My focus has not changed. And that's to make decisions in the best interest of this hockey club. I'll be in Edmonton today and tomorrow, I'll watch the top prospects game … and we're preparing for the draft, I'm talking to my counterparts around the league, and preparing for February 26 [the NHL trade deadline]. These things are ongoing and they are the focus of my attention."

— John Ferguson Jr.

But the axe fell on Ferguson the following morning.

"It has become clear that change and a new direction is needed … and it's in the best interests of the Leafs and of John to begin the transition immediately."

— Richard Peddie

"I apologize to the fans. In my lifetime, we're going to bring that Stanley Cup back to Toronto."

— Leafs chairman Larry Tanenbaum

Cliff Fletcher signed a contract for 19 months to oversee all hockey operations until the Leafs hired a new president and general manager.

"Cliff will have the autonomy and responsibility for all hockey matters, with focus on establishing a foundation from which the next general manager can build."

— Richard Peddie

"We have big cap issues here, big cap issues that we have to deal with. There won't be any short-term fixes but we'll look to do whatever we can to move the team along as fast as we can. There's going to have to be a lot of creativity."

— Cliff Fletcher

All season long, Mats Sundin had been seen as a bargaining chip that could help jump-start a rebuild. He was just shy of his 37th birthday and had been re-signed prior to the season to a one-year, $5.5 million contract. The contract included a no-trade provision, and despite the team's struggles, Sundin didn't want to leave.

"Mats is driving the engine here. He's an unrestricted free agent at the end of the year and he has a no-trade clause."

— Cliff Fletcher

"When you start in September, you want to be with that group, whether you're fighting to get into the playoffs or you're a team that's cruising into the playoffs. That's what hockey is all about. I never look at other teams and say, 'I wish I was over there.' I've never done that."

— Mats Sundin

Sundin was not the only Leaf to whom John Ferguson Jr. had given a no-movement clause. Far from it. Sundin, Darcy Tucker, Tomas Kaberle, Bryan McCabe, and Pavel Kubina all had similar terms. All were veteran players who may have been useful to a Stanley Cup contender and might have brought a decent return in a trade — but all refused to go. The media dubbed them the "Muskoka Five," painting them as selfish at best, and lazy and unmotivated at worst, preferring the Leafs' country club atmosphere and happy to spend summers in the Ontario cottage country rather than push themselves towards a Stanley Cup somewhere else. Fans felt the five were being disloyal to the team in not allowing themselves to be traded.

"I want to play here and I've always said I want to finish my career as a Toronto Maple Leaf. That hasn't changed. Saying that, though, I understand the position the team is in and that [I'm] in. You miss the playoffs two years and then a third in a row, everybody is screaming for changes and for something to happen.... When you're 37 years old and you sign a year at a time, as I did, you give yourself a chance to make a good decision about your future as a player. I'm going to certainly try to evaluate my own game and what I want to do for next season, sometime in the summer."

— Mats Sundin, after the Leafs were officially
eliminated from the playoffs in 2007–08

At his best, Tomas Kaberle was a solid defenceman with good offensive instincts, but his reputation took a hit when he was one of several players who refused to waive their no-trade clauses to help the Leafs try to rebuild.

Still undecided about his own future when the 2008–09 season started, Sundin would eventually sign as a free agent with Vancouver midway through the schedule; Tucker had been bought-out over the summer; McCabe eventually agreed to be traded in September; and Kaberle and Kubina were moved out in years to come.

Resentment lingered over how Sundin refused to allow himself to be traded, but Maple Leaf fans eventually got over it and were happy to salute him when the team honoured his #13 in February of 2012.

"I always saw myself winning the Stanley Cup in Toronto — I wanted to do that. And also realizing it would never feel the same doing it somewhere else.... There's a business side of hockey, and I have no regrets at all over what went down there. I'm so proud to be back and be honoured. I have no regrets with the Leafs. I think they tried to do everything and anything they could to improve their team, to build a championship team and win a Stanley Cup. That's just part of the business."

— Mats Sundin, February 10, 2012

2008–09 to 2011–12

With Fletcher taking over from Ferguson, several names quickly emerged as potential new Leafs GMs. Brian Burke of the Anaheim Ducks was always near the top of the list, but Ducks owner Henry Samueli wouldn't grant permission to let him go. The Leafs finished the 2007–08 season with a record 36–35–11 for 83 points, which had them 12th in the Eastern Conference and 11 points out of the playoffs. Paul Maurice was fired as coach on May 7, 2008, and Ron Wilson was hired on June 10. Briefly a Leaf at the start of his playing career in the late 1970s, Wilson had had success as an NHL coach with Anaheim, Washington, and San Jose.

"Making the playoffs is not our goal. Our goal is to win the Stanley Cup. Period. That's going to be clear from day one. I can't guarantee we're going to make the playoffs this year. I don't even know what type of team [we're going to be]. The only thing I can guarantee is this team will not accept defeat. If they go down, they'll go down swinging. They'll compete hard every night."

— Ron Wilson at the press conference announcing his hiring

Ron Wilson (standing on the left) came to the Leafs with high expectations, but never seemed comfortable with the media scrutiny in Toronto.

"We might have to take a step back in order to go ahead. But I want to make this team better. I'm not saying it will be 1967 all over again, but don't forget when Pat Quinn was here, this team was close to going all the way."

— Ron Wilson

"Bring it on."

— Wilson, when asked if he was prepared for
the intense daily scrutiny in Toronto

Some in the Toronto media criticized Fletcher for hiring Wilson as coach and signing him to a long-term contract before the team had brought in a new GM. Others saw this as proof that Brian Burke — a long-time friend of Wilson's going back to their days as players together at Providence College in the early 1970s — would soon be on his way to Toronto. There were even those who thought that Burke had, in fact, orchestrated the Wilson signing.

"I'm not ashamed to say that Brian is a good friend of mine, but he's had nothing to do with this process."

— Ron Wilson

Testosterone, Truculence ... and More Trouble

Regardless of whether or not he'd had any input on Ron Wilson becoming the coach in Toronto, on November 12, 2008, Brian Burke stepped down as GM in Anaheim after declining the offer of a contract extension. On November 29, he was introduced as the new president and general manager of the Toronto Maple Leafs. Burke called his new post with the Leafs "a dream job," comparing it to what "the Vatican is to Catholics."

"The man who brings a championship to this city will have schools named after him."

— Brian Burke at his introductory press conference

He promised to bring a tough, new attitude to town.

"We play an entertaining style, we want to justify the price of the ticket every night whether the team is successful or not. We believe in aggressive pursuit and possession of the puck in all three zones. We believe in answering the physical challenges and playing a style that allows our young players to play and develop in a fear-free environment."

— Brian Burke

"We build our team from the net out. We require from our team the proper levels of pugnacity, testosterone, truculence and belligerence. That's how our teams play. I make no apologies for that. Our teams play a North American game. We're throwbacks. It's black-and-blue hockey. It's going to be more physical hockey here than people are used to."

— Brian Burke

"The bigger the better, the faster the better, the more physical the better. But you have to have patience. Just because we hired Brian today doesn't mean we're going to play like the Philadelphia Flyers from 1975. We just don't have that right now."

— Ron Wilson reacting to the hiring

"I don't care what colour a guy's passport is or where he comes from. All that matters is that he can fulfill a role on the team."

— Brian Burke, denying he was anti-European

"[Toronto] haven't drafted that well because they haven't had the high picks. They've never had those top two or three picks because they've had good but never great teams. That perpetuates the inability to get better. Does that mean we're going to tear everything down right away? No. We're going to have to evaluate the team first and see. I do think a team should either be ascending rapidly or descending rapidly. I believe being 'good' is not the solution. This is about having the parade."

— Brian Burke, in an interview with TSN shortly after his hiring

The Leafs were younger in 2008–09, but displayed few of the attributes Burke had described. They finished the season almost identically to the year before with a record of 34–35–13 for 81 points, which was 12th in the East, and 12 points out of a playoff spot.

"It is a day of failure. The yardstick for success in this league is the playoffs, and when you miss it that represents failure."

— Brian Burke after the Leafs were officially eliminated from the post-season

Though his 37 goals in 2011–12 and 2013–14 ranked him among the NHL leaders, Phil Kessel's play in Toronto didn't seem to justify the two first-round picks the Leafs gave up to get him.

In the off-season, Toronto selected Nazim Kadri seventh overall in the NHL Draft and signed defencemen Mike Komisarek and Francois Beauchemin. Then, just before the season started, Brian Burke acquired Phil Kessel from Boston and signed him to a five-year deal worth $27 million.

"I intend to earn every penny and won't let you down."

— Phil Kessel

"I think Phil can be a 45–50 goal scorer in this league."

— Ron Wilson

Still just 22 years old, Kessel had already played three full seasons for the Bruins and had scored 36 goals in 2008–09. He would lead the Leafs with 30 goals and 55 points in 2009–10, but the season was a huge disappointment as Toronto fell to 30–38–14; last in the Eastern Conference and 29th overall in the 30-team NHL. The 2009 first-round draft pick Burke gave up as part of the Kessel trade became Tyler Seguin, and for that and many other reasons, the deal would forever be seen as a bad one. Burke acquired Dion Phaneuf from Calgary midway through the 2009–10 season and installed him as Leafs captain at the start of 2010–11. But Phaneuf, like Kessel, never seemed comfortable with the media attention in Toronto.

> "It is a very tough market to play in … I love playing here. I love the city, the organization, everything about playing in Toronto. But I'd be lying if I sat up here and said there wasn't a lot of [media] scrutiny. But that comes with playing here and you have to accept it and you have to be able to deal with it."
>
> — Dion Phaneuf, June 18, 2014

The Leafs were marginally better in 2010–11, climbing to tenth in the Eastern Conference with 85 points on a record of 37–34–11. It was far from a successful season, but the team came out strong to start the 2011–12 campaign. The Leafs opened with three straight wins and finished October with a mark of 7–3–1. It was early, but Phil Kessel led the NHL with 10 goals and 18 points and Toronto was first in the Northeast Division and second in the Eastern Conference. The team wouldn't maintain that lofty pace, but still seemed comfortably in a playoff spot at Christmas when Ron Wilson announced via Twitter that he'd received a contract extension.

> "This Xmas could be better if Santa stuffs a certain piece of paper in my stocking."
>
> — Ron Wilson

> "'He came! He came!' … I got a new Red Ryder BB gun and a contract extension!"
>
> — Ron Wilson

> "Congratulations to Ron Wilson on his contract extension! Merry Christmas, Ron!"
>
> — Brian Burke via Twitter

Despite the team's improved play, fans and the media weren't convinced Wilson had earned the extension, nor were they particularly pleased with the light-hearted nature of the exchange.

"This is a coach who's earned this … extension. It's not charity. It's not a gift. When the coach goes into the cage, he needs the chair and the whip, not just one. It's not enough to just be the coach for the rest of the season, in my opinion."

— Brian Burke at a press conference on December 26, 2011

"You can ask me that at the end of the season. I'm not interested in hypothetical questions."

— Burke when asked what would happen if the Leafs missed the playoffs again

As late as February 6, 2012, the Leafs were 28–19–6 and their 62 points had them seventh in the Eastern Conference, four points up on ninth-place Washington. But then they hit a 1–9–1 skid, and in a 5–3 loss to Florida on February 28 (Game 10 of the 11-game slide), fans were chanting "Fire Wilson." Burke was listening. Wilson was fired on March 2, prior to a Saturday night game in Montreal.

"It was clear to me it would be cruel and unusual punishment to let Ron coach another game in the Air Canada Centre. I wasn't going to put Ron through that. It was hard to listen to, hard to watch."

— Brian Burke

"The last couple of days have been brutal. I go back with Ronny to 1973. We were freshmen together. We played four years together in college, a more close-knit experience than playing pro. But I have to do what's right for the team."

— Brian Burke

"I've never had a team fall off a cliff like this before. I've had dips, slumps, rough patches, but this is akin to an 18-wheeler going right off a cliff, I don't know what happened."

— Brian Burke

One thing Burke did know was that the team had clearly tuned Wilson out. "They weren't paying attention, they weren't buying it. Every coach has a shelf-life. That time comes for every coach. The harder the coach, the shorter the shelf-life."

And though they were friends, there had always been one big difference in the approaches of Burke and Wilson. "If there was one philosophical difference that Ron and I didn't share, it's that I like a rough team. If you can point to one thing where Ron and I were on a different page, it's that."

That would not be the case with the Leafs' new coach, Randy Carlyle.

"He's demanding, he's hard on players. He likes a physical game.... It became obvious to me in the last week that we needed to make a change if we wanted to salvage this season.... We've got a guy behind the wheel who can get us where we want to go."

— Brian Burke

"I sense this hockey club is very, very tense right now. The confidence level of the group is at a low. My responsibility as a coach is to pick these guys up."

— Randy Carlyle

Despite being chosen seventh overall, Nazem Kadri never really earned the trust of coaches Ron Wilson and Randy Carlyle. He has not only improved his defensive play under Mike Babcock, he scored a career-high 32 goals in 2016–17.

Carlyle, who'd won the Stanley Cup under Burke in Anaheim in 2007 but had been fired by the Ducks earlier in the season, said he'd always been impressed by the Leafs' speed. "They have to get on their horse and skate. First and foremost they've got to feel a lot better about themselves than they do right now. We have to find a way to re-energize the group. We have to re-kindle their spirit. They have an opportunity now to show a new face, a new impression. I'm new here, let's make sure you give me everything you've got, both on and off the ice."

The Leafs won 3–1 in Montreal in Carlyle's debut on March 3, but then lost five in a row and finished 6–9–3 under their new coach. Overall, they were 35–37–10 for 80 points, which left them 13th in the Eastern Conference and 12 points out of the playoffs.

2012–13

It was first reported in December 2010 that Rogers Communication was negotiating to buy the Ontario Teacher's Pension Plan's majority share of the Maple Leafs. In the end, Rogers (owners of Rogers Sportsnet) and rival Bell Globemedia (owners of TSN — The Sports Network) would combine to buy the shares for $1.32 million in a deal that closed in August of 2012.

The new owners took over just in time to preside over another NHL lockout. A new Collective Bargaining Arrangement was finally worked out in January of 2013 and a 48-game season began on January 19. Among the first moves made in Toronto when the lockout was settled was the firing of Brian Burke.

At his final press conference, three days after being fired, Brian Burke explained:

> We didn't win and that's why we're here today.
>
> I want to thank the players. The players might not have gotten the job done for us, but they didn't cheat us on effort. It's a great bunch of guys. I want to thank the media. I think our coverage has been fair, by and large. I want to thank them for that. I want to thank our sponsors. Our season-ticket holders, who are the lifeblood of any team....
>
> Obviously, your job as a GM is to bring in players and win and we didn't win.... I can stand here and say they didn't like my personality. Those all become pretexts and excuses later. If you've won enough games, you can be as obnoxious as you want to be here if you're in first place.... But I wouldn't trade this experience.

You're not sure when you're going to drop dead in the desert but you know it's coming. You can see the vultures. This one here was like a two-by-four upside the head to me. Again, that's not a complaint....

I think ownership has that right to make that call. The people that hired me hired Brian Burke. Maybe the new guys don't like that brand.... They're entitled to that. I'm not changing. I'm not going to change how I view things. That's not possible. I'm Irish. I'm stubborn. I've got to find someone who likes that brand, I guess.

Later, at the annual Conn Smythe Dinner in support of Easter Seals in March of 2013, Burke gave some more insight into what it was like to be the Leafs GM.

You have no privacy. Everybody in that city knows more about running that hockey team than you do. You'd get in a cab, and the cab driver would say, "Your power play sucks." And I'd say, "Drive faster." I was going to a Blue Jays game last year, and a guy who was begging for money yelled at me. Told me I was an imbecile....

I'm pretty sure no one here feels sorry for me. I'm going to go somewhere else and try to haunt this team.

Back to the Playoffs, But ...

The Leafs replaced Burke as GM with Dave Nonis, whom Burke had brought in as assistant GM from Anaheim shortly after he'd arrived back in 2008. Under Nonis and Carlyle, the Leafs finally returned to the playoffs in 2012–13, finishing the abbreviated schedule with a 26–17–5 record, good for 57 points and fifth place in the Eastern Conference standings. Phil Kessel had set career highs with 37 goals and 82 points in 2011–12, both of which ranked him sixth in the NHL, and despite a slow start to 2012–13, he came on strong to finish the 48-game campaign with 20 goals and 52 points and once again placed among the league's top-10 scorers.

In the playoffs, the Leafs faced Boston, which meant they were taking on Tyler Seguin and Dougie Hamilton — the two first-round draft picks they had surrendered in the deal for Kessel. They would also be facing Tuukka Rask from the deal for Andrew Raycroft.

The Bruins got the better of the Leafs in the early part of the series, winning the opening game 4–1 and jumping out to a 3–1 lead through Game 4. But the Leafs bounced back with a 2–1 victory in Boston in Game 5 and another 2–1 win at home in Game 6. That sent the series back to Boston for a seventh game on May 13, 2013. For Leafs fans, those 13s would certainly prove to be unlucky.

The Bruins took an early 1–0 lead in Game 7 after a miscue by Leafs defenceman Cody Franson, who later atoned with two goals that put Toronto ahead 2–1 after two periods. Phil Kessel upped the lead to 3–1 at 2:09 of the third period, and Nazem Kadri pushed it to 4–1 at 5:29.

"I thought we ran out of gas. When you build a 4–1 lead, you want to check, check, check, and as I said, I thought we just ran out of gas as far as our group."

— Randy Carlyle

Nathan Horton scored for Boston at 9:18 to cut Toronto's lead to 4–2, and then, with Tuukka Rask pulled in favour of an extra attacker, Milan Lucic made it a one-goal game with just 1:22 remaining. Thirty-one seconds later, with Rask still out and the Bruins' giant 6-foot-9 defenceman Zdeno Chara setting up a screen in front of James Reimer, Patrice Bergeron tied the game 4–4 at 19:09 of the third.

At 6:05 of overtime, Bergeron scored again to give Boston a 5–4 victory.

"We stayed resilient — I guess that's what I can say. We found a way. Not necessarily the way we would've liked to play the whole game, but like I said, we showed some character coming back in the game and we found a way in overtime. We had the momentum, I thought, and our legs were back. It felt good."

— Patrice Bergeron

"There was a shot from the point and I was tying up [Tyler] Seguin in front. Loose puck, so I tried to clear it and it ended up going right on [Bergeron's] tape. Just an unlucky bounce. I did not see him coming back door like that. Just trying to clear it away as quick as I could."

— Leafs defenceman Jake Gardiner on Boston's winning goal

"That hockey game will haunt me until the day I die."

— Leafs forward Joffrey Lupul, sharing his feelings on Twitter

Though he showed flashes, James Reimer was never able to establish himself as a number-one goaltender during his five-plus seasons in Toronto.

"It's definitely in the top-five lows in your life. There's no way to describe it. Just an empty feeling, really. It's over and there's nothing you can do about it. When you're up 4–1, you want to close the game out. So when you're coming in and you're at 4–4, there's a little bit of shock. But at the same time, we're saying to ourselves that we would have taken overtime coming in this morning. Especially as a goalie, you want to step up and try to make one more save in that situation."

— Leafs goalie James Reimer

"It's probably the toughest loss I've had in pro hockey…. It's just an extremely tough loss."

— Leafs captain Dion Phaneuf

2013–14 TO 2016–17

Six weeks after the Game 7 defeat in Boston, Tim Leiweke became the new president and CEO of MLSE. Leiweke had previously served in the same role for Anschutz Entertainment Group (AEG), owners of the Los Angeles Kings and the

Los Angeles Galaxy of Major League Soccer, and part owner of the Los Angeles Lakers. With MLSE, he would oversee the Leafs, Raptors, and Toronto FC.

The NHL realigned for the 2013–14 season, replacing the three divisions in each of the Eastern and Western Conferences with two larger divisions in each of the two Conferences. Toronto would now be a member of the eight-team Atlantic Division.

The Leafs had acquired goalie Jonathan Bernier from L.A. in a trade on June 23, and would sign free agent David Clarkson to a seven-year, $36.75 million contract on July 5. Clarkson had scored 30 goals for the Devils in 2011–12 and added 15 more in the shortened 2012–13 season. But the Toronto native would turn out to be a bust in his hometown.

And on the day the new season opened on October 1, 2013, Phil Kessel was signed to a new contract paying him $8 million a year for eight years.

> "If you look at his production, he is a top 10 player; he's been in the top 10 in scoring, he's been in the top 10 in goals. He's a player that's put himself in some pretty elite company and he's done that himself.… The one knock that Phil had on him that I thought was totally unfair was that Phil wasn't a great teammate. From the day he got to Toronto, I think we've been able to tell that was completely untrue. He's quiet, he's not as outgoing as some people in a Canadian market would like, but he's a great teammate and well-liked by everybody in our room. We wouldn't have looked to extend Phil if we didn't think he was a great fit in Toronto."
>
> — senior vice president and GM Dave Nonis

> "I've always wanted to be here. It's a place I wanted to play; I want to finish my career here. It's a great city, the organization's unbelievable."
>
> — Phil Kessel

On December 31, 2013, on the eve of their Winter Classic meeting with the Detroit Red Wings in Ann Arbor, Michigan (which Toronto would win 3-2 before a record crowd of 105,491), the Leafs signed Dion Phaneuf to a new seven-year contract worth $49 million to begin the next season.

> "It was an easy decision for me to stay here and be a part of the Toronto Maple Leafs. I think we're building something special. We have passionate fans and a dedicated ownership group. I have great teammates and look forward to growing with them and achieving our goal of winning."
>
> — Dion Phaneuf

Dion Phaneuf was named captain shortly after his arrival in Toronto, but never seemed comfortable as the team's leader and top defenceman.

But 2013–14 proved to be another disappointing season, as the Leafs' record of 38–36–8 was good enough for only 84 points, which left them nine points back of the second wild card spot under the reconfigured playoff system and 12th overall in the 16-team Eastern Conference. As late as 68 games into the season, the Leafs appeared comfortably in the playoff picture, but an eight-game losing streak and just two wins in their final 14 games put an end to that.

A day before the season ended, on April 11, the Leafs named Brendan Shanahan as their new team president. Shanahan had grown up in the Toronto suburb of Mimico. He played in the NHL with five teams from 1987 to 2009, had 656 goals and 698 assists for 1,354 points in 1,524 career games, and had won the Stanley Cup with Detroit in 1997, 1998, and 2002. Shortly after his retirement, Shanahan went to work in the head office of the NHL, where he spent three years before taking the Leafs job. He was officially introduced to the media in Toronto on April 14, 2014.

"Everybody on the hockey side, everybody on the business side for the Toronto Maple Leafs reports in to Brendan Shanahan. He's the boss."

— Tim Leiweke

"This is the time for me to start learning about the organization from top to bottom. It's a time for me to listen, to learn, and get to work.... That's what worked for me when I was done playing hockey and that's what I intend to do here."

— Brendan Shanahan

A few weeks later, Dave Nonis announced that Randy Carlyle had accepted a contract extension to guide the team through the 2016–17 season. All Carlyle's assistant coaches were released, however. Shanahan cleared out assistant GMs Claude Loiselle and Dave Poulin in July, hiring 28-year-old general manager of the Ontario Hockey League's Sault Ste. Marie Greyhounds Kyle Dubas as a new assistant GM. The Leafs would later add former NHLer and long-time London Knights owner and executive Mark Hunter to their Toronto front office, as well. Mostly, though, Shanahan did as he said he would do; watching and learning quietly as the Leafs' 2014–15 season spun out of control.

Early in the season, after a 5–2 win over Tampa Bay at home on November 20, the Leafs didn't raise their sticks to salute their fans. Having just come off a 9–2 home loss to Nashville, the players claimed it was merely an attempt to change up their routine and not a snub to fans who had booed them and thrown sweaters on the ice after a recent string of poor performances.

"To be completely honest with you, it was something about the way we have been playing at home, our record, and just changing up routine. At the end of the day, we did a lot of things different throughout the day, and that was something we decided to change."

— Dion Phaneuf

"No way are we [going after our fans], and I'm sorry if it's being looked at that way."

— James van Riemsdyk

"We didn't think of that. I understand [the fans' reaction], but that [wasn't] our intention. We know we have the best support in the league and I think this is all being blown out of proportion a bit. It was us trying to change things up."

— Tyler Bozak

Through 30 games, Toronto had a record of 18–9–3. Even with seven losses in their next ten games, the Leafs still held down the final playoff position on January 5, 2015, when Dave Nonis made the decision to fire Randy Carlyle.

"One of the things you have all heard me say since training camp is we felt we need to see some level of consistency, and I think we would all agree we've shown some good stretches, but I don't think I can stand in front of you and say we have been consistent. We just felt that at this point that this was the right time to make the change and move ahead and try to get this team playing like we have been during periods of this season."

— Dave Nonis

Assistant coach Peter Horachek was appointed interim head coach, but the team appeared to give up under him. They went just 9–28–5 in the final 42 games of the season, falling to seventh in the Atlantic Division, 15th in the Eastern Conference, and 27th overall in the NHL.

Commitment to Rebuilding the Right Way

Brendan Shanahan ended his silence and came out firing — literally — the day after the season ended. The coaching staff, much of the scouting staff, and Dave Nonis were all let go on April 14. The next day, Shanahan held a press conference.

We need to have a team with more character and one that represents this city the way it deserves. I think people here can understand [losing]. It's a sophisticated hockey market. But what I don't think they can understand is people who go out and give half efforts and people that don't appear to enjoy playing here. You have to give the effort and at least show a happiness in being a Toronto Maple Leaf.… Even if the record is the same record, I think we just have to play differently. That's what had so many people so upset this year.

They are professionals [Nonis and the coaching staff], I'm not here to pile on top of them. It's been a difficult season for them. But they also understand that [Sunday] was just the beginning.

We have some talented parts on this team. As a group, as a mix, they understand and they've shown over the years — not just this year — for whatever reason the mix doesn't work. In spite of the fact we have talented individuals, if the mix doesn't work, there's going to be changes.

"It wasn't a good environment to be around. It wasn't fun to be around the guys, it wasn't fun to go on the road. For the first time in my career, I wanted the season to be over — I was looking forward to the next season, already."
— Joffrey Lupul

"I think sometimes people here try to suggest the reason this can't be done is that the fans of Toronto don't have a stomach to endure what truly needs to be done. I don't believe that. I think they are dying for it to be done."
— Shanahan on the fact that a true rebuild would take several years

On May 20, 2015, Brendan Shanahan hired Mike Babcock as the Leafs' new head coach. Babcock had spent the previous 10 seasons in Detroit, never missing the playoffs and leading the Wings to the Stanley Cup in 2008. He'd also coached Canada to Olympic gold medals in 2010 and 2014. At the end of the 2014–15 season, Babcock (who was still under contract in Detroit until June 30) requested permission from the Red Wings to shop his services to other teams. The Buffalo Sabres were thought to be a leading contender, with St. Louis and San Jose among others in the mix. There was also the possibility that Babcock would return to Detroit. But Shanahan convinced him to come to Toronto and oversee the rebuild from behind the bench. With the salary cap, the Leafs are restricted (as are all teams) in what they can pay for players, but the wealthiest team in hockey signed their new coach to an eight-year contract worth $50 million.

"So if I'm a Leafs fan today, I'm feeling awfully good about the leadership of this organization. One: I think because we got one of the best coaches in the [NHL] to come to Toronto, and he had a lot of choice. Two: More importantly to me, I think Brendan Shanahan just showed us how great he is going to be as a leader, and the commitment and the passion and the vision he has for winning championships here. I'd feel good about that team."
— Tim Leiweke, who would step down as the head of MLSE on December 30, 2015

In his first press conference as the new head coach of the Maple Leafs, Babcock said he was excited about the opportunity to come to Toronto, "Whether you believe it or not, I believe this is Canada's team, and we need to put Canada's team back on the map.... I didn't come here to [just] make the playoffs."

Considered to be the best coach in the NHL today, Mike Babcock left Detroit for the opportunity to lead the Maple Leafs back to greatness.

But he was realistic about the challenges ahead. "If you think there's no pain coming, there's pain coming. It usually takes twice as long and [it's] twice as hard as you think. I believe that."

The Leafs headed into the 2015 NHL Draft with Mark Hunter and Kyle Dubas acting as interim GMs. They opted for smaller, skilled players, headed by Mitch Marner of the London Knights (fourth overall). A few days later, on July 1, 2015, Phil Kessel was traded to the Pittsburgh Penguins. The Leafs also sent Tyler Biggs, defenceman Tim Erixon, and a 2016 second-round pick to Pittsburgh. In return, Toronto received centre Nick Spaling, forward Kasperi Kapanen, defence-man Scott Harrington, plus first- and third-round picks for 2016. Toronto retained $1.2 million of Kessel's salary in each of the next seven seasons.

"Phil's certainly a very talented player, but we knew changes had to come. This is about recognition on our part that what we've been doing here and the group that we assembled here wasn't getting the job done. We are here to build a team that is capable of winning the Stanley Cup and there are no shortcuts to go around doing that."

— Brendan Shanahan

On July 23, 2015, Shanahan announced that the Leafs new GM would be Lou Lamoriello, the long-time leader of the New Jersey Devils and the man who had drafted Shanahan into the NHL back in 1988. "I do think we were lacking in some experience [in the front office]," Shanahan explained, "so if I could map out or draw out a description of the type of person we wanted it would be Lou. I was happy when the Devils gave me the opportunity to talk to him and I was happy when he was interested."

"I'm excited. I don't know any other way to put it."

— Lou Lamoriello

"The thing that has driven me all of my life is winning. The commitment that the ... Leafs have made when they brought Brendan in and brought Mike Babcock in, to me the only thing that can happen is having success. Winning doesn't happen because you say it; winning happens because of everything you do that leads to it."

— Lou Lamoriello

Still, Lamoriello knew it wouldn't be easy, repeating Babcock's warning about pain. "We know the roster needs some work. That's an understatement. That's not saying that the roster cannot have success. There's no question you have to build a foundation before you can go anywhere. Yes it could be slow; there could be more pain, because there could be more subtraction than addition to get that foundation, to get the right culture going forward."

2015–16

There were times during the 2015–16 season when the Leafs looked good. Maybe even good enough to sneak into the playoffs. But that wasn't really part of the long-range plan. With Lou Lamoriello wheeling and dealing to acquire more draft choices, a lower finish would ensure another high pick. The season was really more about seeing what the team's young players could do, and recent draft picks and acquisitions, such as William Nylander, Frederick Gauthier, and Kasperi Kapanen, were among those called up for auditions throughout the year. In the end, the Leafs finished last overall in the NHL for the first time since 1984–85 with a record of 29–42–11 for 69 points.

"The season's lost if you look at it in wins and losses. The season's a long way from lost on an individual basis.... The guys have an understanding of how we are going to play. We need to add skill to the mix."

— Mike Babcock

"This year, more than ever, we really have an idea of where we're going.... We're not where we want to be in the standings, but this year more than

Drafted fifth overall in 2012, defenceman Morgan Rielly was fast-tracked to the NHL as a 19-year-old in 2013–14.

ever I feel as though we had some direction. That really goes a long way in terms of motivating players to want to work hard."

— Leafs defenceman Morgan Rielly

"It's been a long time since I haven't been in the playoffs. This is the most exciting time of the year. You want to be part of this. But in saying that, I like the position we're in better than a lot of teams in the National Hockey League. A lot."

— Mike Babcock

"The ship is at least turned in the right direction."

— Brendan Shanahan

"The real good teams end up with 10-year runs. That's what we're hoping to do. It will take us some time to get to where we want to be, but we're obviously trending in the right direction."

— Mike Babcock

The 2016 NHL Draft

Unlike 1984–85, when last place automatically meant the first-round draft choice (and Wendel Clark), in 2015–16 all the Leafs were guaranteed was the best odds in the draft lottery, which was to be held on April 30, 2016.

"We've taken it on the chin all year to be set up [for] the best chance we can possibly have," Babcock said. In truth, there were several top prospects who would be valuable if Toronto picked anywhere among the top three or four, but winning the draft lottery — which the Leafs did — felt like a symbolic victory.

> "We earned this the hard way. It wasn't a lot of fun this year ... but this will certainly help. It's an important moment for the Toronto Maple Leafs, for our fans."
>
> — Brendan Shanahan

> "I thought it was just a tremendous result for our organization and more important for our fans, who have been so patient throughout this year. It's certainly something everybody feels good about."
>
> — Lou Lamoriello

Auston Matthews, who was born in California, raised in Arizona, trained with the USA Hockey National Team Development Program, and spent his draft season playing in Switzerland, was the top-rated prospect going into the NHL Draft, and the Leafs made him the number-one pick.

> "He's an elite player with an elite drive train. A big-bodied guy who makes players better. I mean, we're going to have to look after him. He's a kid ... that's our job. But he's going to make us better, and he'll develop into a top, top centre in the [NHL]."
>
> — Mike Babcock

> "Hockey is a team game, so there is really no saviour. I know I want to be an impact player. I believe I can be a franchise centreman, a number-one centreman in the NHL, so that's my ultimate goal."
>
> — Auston Matthews

> "Everyone knows he's talented. That's a given. His job is to come in and be a great teammate, be part of a team that wants to win. If you're a great

teammate, great things will happen. And don't try to worry about anything outside the room."

— Wendel Clark

"Those young guys — William Nylander, Mitch Marner — are obviously two pretty special players, so I think it's definitely an exciting time looking forward."

— Auston Matthews

"Obviously, we got a lot better. Lou is a better general manager, I'm a better coach, and the team's way better."

— Mike Babcock

Toronto's first pick, fourth overall, in the 2015 NHL Draft, Mitch Marner had 19 goals and 42 assists in 77 games as a rookie in 2016–17.

2016-17 ...

Leafs fans expected better things heading into the new season — it would be hard not to improve on last place overall! But few people really saw the excitement that was coming. A roster featuring nine rookies (including seven who played in 77 games or more) promised to compete hard every night, but there was bound to be some growing pains along the way. The very first game of the regular season, on October 12 in Ottawa, offered reasons for optimism, as Auston Matthews set a modern NHL record with four goals in his debut.

"It's pretty surreal," Matthews admitted. "I couldn't believe that was happening out there. Our line was clicking tonight. We were really fortunate, we created a lot of opportunities and we were able to cash in on a lot of them. Every line played well tonight. Every line could have had two or three goals apiece. I'm just happy I capitalized on some chances."

But it wasn't a perfect start to the season. The Leafs lost 5–4 in overtime and many faulted Matthews's defensive coverage on the goal that gave Ottawa the victory, but his all-around game would become an impressive part of his rookie season. New goalie Frederik Andersen, acquired in an off-season trade with Anaheim, didn't look sharp that night and struggled in the early going. However, he would soon stake his claim as Toronto's first legitimate number-one goalie since Ed Belfour.

The Leafs were clearly a much more entertaining team to watch, but they showed a disturbing tendency to let leads slip away at the start of the season. With two games to go before a four-day break over Christmas, they sat in last place in the Atlantic Division — although only six points out of third place, which would net them a playoff spot. An 11–2–2 run from December 22 through January 25 put them into the thick of the playoff race. Another solid stretch in March kept them there into April.

Meanwhile, team rookie records piled up. Mitch Marner broke Gus Bodnar's 1943–44 record of 40 assists with 42. William Nylander set a new mark with a 12-game point streak. Zach Hyman scored four short-handed goals. Auston Matthews, playing mainly with Nylander and Hyman on his wings, broke Peter Ihnacak's 1982–83 standard of 66 points with 69, but the real excitement came from his pursuit of Wendel Clark's rookie record for goals, which he broke with his 35th of the season in a 3–2 win over Florida on March 28.

"Just to be in the same sentence as a guy like Wendel Clark is obviously a big honour. A lot of credit to my linemates all season. It's definitely pretty special."

— Auston Matthews

"Second period of the first game."

— Wendel Clark on when he knew his record was in jeopardy

Clearly, the kids were all right.

"You have to find a way to play, and we played our kids. We put them in all sorts of situations, and if we were [going to be] good, it would have to be up to them. We've had a good run: some ups and downs, some silly nights, but we've had a good run."

— Mike Babcock

Still, it took until the 81st game of the 82-game season for the Leafs to nail down a playoff spot. They did it with a nail-biting 5–3 win over Pittsburgh. Kasperi Kapanen, a former Penguin, acquired in the trade that sent Phil Kessel to Pittsburgh and called up from the minors only a few days before, scored his first career goal to make it 3–3 at 14:30 of the third period. "Can't be a better time to score than to tie it up against your old club," he said. "Feels pretty good."

The winning goal, his 20th of the season, was scored by rookie Connor Brown, who'd grown up a Leafs fan in Toronto. "That's a night I'm sure I'll remember for a long time. It's cool it came off my stick."

"It means everything. It's been our goal since the beginning of the year, to make it.... It's a big night for us, a huge clinch.... This is why you play. To play meaningful games like this. So it's a lot of fun."

— Auston Matthews, who scored the clinching goal (his 40th of the season, tying him for second in the NHL) into an empty net with four seconds remaining

"You don't want to sell yourselves short, ever. That being said, you don't really know with all the changes and youth and how that is all going to mesh together. You could always see the potential, but it's nice to see the things coming together this year.... We have put ourselves into the play-offs and that is a pretty drastic jump from last year."

— James van Riemsdyk

"I'm proud of the guys, I'm excited for the guys, they've done a real good job. I told the coaches at the start of the year [that] if we got in, it was going to be tomorrow in Game 82. So we got in one game ahead of schedule, but to be honest with you, I didn't know the kids could be this good."

— Mike Babcock

A win in Game 82 would have moved Toronto into third place in the Atlantic Division and renewed the Battle of Ontario with a first-round matchup against Ottawa. But when Toronto lost 3–2 to Columbus, their record of 40–27–15 for 95 points put them in fourth place and relegated them to the second wild card spot and a playoff date with the Presidents' Trophy–winning Washington Capitals.

"I don't think it changes much. They're the best team in the league. Obviously they're really talented. It doesn't matter to us. We have to be ready to compete, ready to work hard.... They're a good team, but they're not unbeatable."

— Auston Matthews

"You gotta beat the best at some point, so might as well do it in the first round."

— Jake Gardiner

"We're looking forward to playing in the playoffs. Once you get in, anything can happen."

— James van Riemsdyk

Despite Washington's troubles in post-seasons past, few people gave Toronto much of a chance. Still, the Leafs pushed the Capitals into overtime in a 3–2 loss in Game 1, evened things up with a 4–3 double-overtime victory in Game 2, and then returned home to take the series lead with a 4–3 win after 1:37 of overtime in Game 3.

"We're realizing we can play with these guys.... We've been doing this all year. When everybody was writing us off, nobody expecting much, saying how we are young and all that stuff; we were never fazed by that. And we're not just here to show up and have the experience. We want to make it worthwhile to be in the playoffs."

— goalie Frederik Andersen

The Capitals finally seemed to exert their dominance in the early-going in Game 4, jumping out to a 4–1 first-period lead. Toronto fought back, but came up short in a 5–4 loss. Then in Washington for Game 5, the Leafs pushed the Capitals into overtime again but lost 2–1. "They young, but they tough," said Alex Ovechkin afterward. "They never stop."

Hopes were high back at home for Game 6, but in the record-tying fifth overtime game of the series, Washington scored another 2–1 victory. The Leafs were eliminated.

"It's an empty feeling. We've grown a lot and have a lot to be proud of, but it's a very tough feeling right now. It's awesome to be in this community, to be part of this team. The support we have here is unbelievable. There's a lot to build off, but it's tough [now]."

— Frederik Andersen

Auston Matthews and William Nylander talk on the bench early in the 2016–17 season. Their strong rookie seasons are two reasons why the future looks a lot brighter in Toronto.

"It's not the best feeling, but I think we gave it our all; we left it all out on the ice and every one of us is proud of each other. We have a bright future. We played hard, grinding hockey against the best team in the league. I think we definitely gave them all they could handle. We're going to hold our heads up high."

— Auston Matthews

"The loss is tough, for sure, but when we got in here and looked at each other, there's a lot of pride that can be taken. Each guy is motivated to be here, and works hard [to] make this team better. We believe this is just the start. We have goals for the future. We're going to continue to grow, continue to get better and see how far we can take it."

— Morgan Rielly

... AND INTO THE FUTURE

As Mike Babcock admitted in addressing the media the day after the Leafs were eliminated, "In some organizations, if you finish eighth and lose in six games, it's considered a bad year." But, "the guys have had a taste of it now. And they're going to want to have that [again]. In order to have that, we have to get better."

"We all want the Stanley Cup in our hands. We realize we've still got some work to do. But I think that the process has sped up a little bit."

— Nazem Kadri

"We're going to come back next year with a taste of it, and we're just going to want to get better. We expect ourselves to get better."

— Morgan Rielly

"Over the course of my five seasons, there's been some ups and downs [but] the support we get is second to none and that gives you goosebumps.... [The fans] know how far we've come and the effort we've put into this. We're proud to play for this city and these fans."

— James van Riemsdyk

The good feelings from the 2016–17 season continued into the summer, first with Auston Matthews being named a near-unanimous winner of the Calder Trophy which made him Toronto's first NHL rookie of the year since Brit Selby in 1965–66. Then, on July 1, came the signing of two veteran free agents: Ron Hainsey, who had finished 2016–17 playing for the Stanley Cup champion Pittsburgh Penguins, and former Leaf Dominic Moore. The biggest splash came the following day. Though Patrick Marleau would be 38 years old by the time the Leafs opened training camp, the 500-goal scorer who'd spent 19 seasons with the San Jose Sharks was exactly the type of defensively responsible veteran player that coach Mike Babcock craved.

"It was the team, I think. The excitement that's around it, the youth, the coaching staff, the coach, the management, they way they see the game, the players that they have on their roster. It's extremely exciting to be a part of that."

— Patrick Marleau on a conference call after signing

"I can assure everyone that we're not off-course on what the plan is. This just ensures the development process is (going) in the right direction.… You only have one chance to do something like this and we would not have done it if it was not the right player. The timing is perfect for this."

— Lou Lamoriello

"I'm extremely excited and happy to be part of the Maple Leafs organization. It's definitely an honour to be able to call myself a Maple Leaf."

— Patrick Marleau

"If you're not from Toronto and you come to Toronto, you have no idea how spectacular it is. From the … media coverage to the fan base and the love of the team, it's like nothing you've ever seen. If you're a good player and you like winning, this is the best place you could ever play. I've never seen anything like it. It's fantastic. Now we've got to have a team to match that opportunity. That's what we're going to try to grow."

— Mike Babcock

Acknowledgements

I would like to thank Michael Melgaard, who brought this project to me. Also from Dundurn, Allison Hirst for her editorial guidance and Kathryn Lane for her assistance. Thank you to Catherine Leek as well.

Stephen Smith, author of *Puckstruck: Distracted, Delighted and Distressed by Canada's Hockey Obsession*, and the website of the same name, gets a special thank-you for lending me so many books about the Maple Leafs from his huge hockey book collection. Thank you to Phil Pritchard, Craig Campbell, and Miragh Bitove from the Hockey Hall of Fame. I have always appreciated their support. I would also like to acknowledge the Ontario Arts Council Writers' Reserve Program.

Finally, as always, a special thank-you to my wife, Barbara Hehner, my mother, Joyce Zweig, and my entire family for everything they do for me.

Sources

The most important sources used in compiling this book were the newspapers that have covered Toronto's NHL team for 100 years. The *Toronto Star* (previously known as the *Daily Star*) and the *Globe and Mail* (which was just the *Globe* until its merger with the *Mail and Empire* in 1936) were used most frequently, along with the *Toronto Sun* for more recent years and the *Toronto World* and the *Toronto Telegram* in early seasons. From other cities, the *Ottawa Citizen*, the *Ottawa Journal*, the *Montreal Gazette* and *Montreal Herald* often helped to give a well-rounded picture. Additionally, the *New York Times*, *New York Post*, *Edmonton Sun*, *Journal de Quebec*, *Journal de Montreal*, *Hockey News*, *Sporting News*, *Boston Globe*, *Brooklyn Daily Eagle*, *Chicago Tribune*, *Vancouver World*, *Winnipeg Tribune*, *Blueline Magazine*, *Hockey Digest*, *Players Tribune*, and *MVP* magazine were also used. If the spelling of a player name appears inconsistent, it is because the original spelling in the quoted article was kept. If a quote is identified with just a name or a name and a date, it's usually because the same quote, or a variation of it, can be found in many different newspapers. Generally, these are dressing room press conference quotations.

The following books were also used:

Batten, Jack. *Hockey Dynasty.* Don Mills, ON: General Publishing, 1969.
———. *The Leafs in Autumn: Meeting the Maple Leaf Heroes of the Forties.* Toronto: Macmillan of Canada, 1975.
Baun, Bobby, and Anne Logan. *Lowering the Boom: The Bobby Baun Story.* Toronto: Stoddart, 2000.

Brewitt, Ross. *Clear the Track: The Eddie Shack Story.* Toronto: Stoddart, 1997.

Clancy, King, and Brian McFarlane. *Clancy: The King's Story.* Toronto: ECW Press, 1997. First published 1968 by McGraw-Hill Ryerson.

Clark, Wendel, Scott Morrison, and Jeff Jackson. *Wendel: My Life in Hockey.* Aurora, ON: Jackson Events, 2009.

Conacher, Brian. *As the Puck Turns: A Personal Journey Through the World of Hockey.* Toronto: John Wiley, 2007.

Duff, Bob, and Johnny Bower. *The China Wall: The Timeless Legend of Johnny Bower.* Wayne, MI: Immortal Investments, 2006.

Duplacey, James, and Dan Diamond. *Maple Leaf Magic: The Complete Story of Toronto's Magical Ride in the 1993 Stanley Cup Playoffs.* Toronto: James and Dan Diamond, 1993.

Ellis, Ron, and Kevin Shea. *Over the Boards: The Ron Ellis Story.* Bolton, ON: Fenn, 2002.

Fischler, Stan. *Power Play! The Story of the Toronto Maple Leafs.* Chicago: Henry Regnery Company, 1972.

———. *Those Were the Days: The Lore of Hockey by the Legends of the Game.* New York: Dodd Mead, 1976.

Fitkin, Ed. *Come on Teeder!* Toronto: Baxter, 1950.

———. *The "Gashouse Gang" of Hockey.* Toronto: Baxter, 1951.

———. *Max Bentley: Hockey's Dipsy-Doodle Dandy.* Toronto: Baxter, 1951.

———. *Turk Broda of the Leafs: The Story of a Great Net Minder.* Toronto: Baxter, 1950.

Harris, Billy. *The Glory Years Memories of a Decade, 1955–1965.* Scarborough, ON: Prentice-Hall Canada, 1989.

Hewitt, Foster. *Foster Hewitt: His Own Story.* Toronto: Ryerson Press, 1967.

Hodge, Charlie, and Howie Meeker. *Golly Gee It's Me! The Howie Meeker Story.* Toronto: Stoddart, 1996.

Houston, William. *Ballard: A Portait of Canada's Most Controversial Sports Figure.* Toronto: Seal Books, 1985.

———. *Maple Leaf Blues: Harold Ballard and the Life and Times of the Toronto Maple Leafs.* Toronto: McClelland & Stewart, 1990.

Imlach, Punch, and Scott Young. *Hockey Is a Battle.* Toronto: Macmillan of Canada, 1969.

———. *Heaven and Hell in the NHL.* Toronto. McClelland & Stewart, 1982.

Leonetti, Mike. *Defining Moments: Maple Leafs Edition.* Markham, ON: Red Deer Press, 2014.

MacInnis, Craig. *Remembering Tim Horton.* Toronto: Stoddart, 2000.

Mahovlich, Ted. *The Big M: The Frank Mahovlich Story.* Toronto: HarperCollins, 1999.

McDonald, Lanny, and Steve Simmons. *Lanny.* Toronto: McGraw-Hill Ryerson, 1987.

Melady, John. *Overtime, Overdue: The Bill Barilko Story.* Trenton, ON: City Print, 1988.

O'Brien, Andy, and Jacques Plante. *The Jacques Plante Story.* Toronto: McGraw-Hill Ryerson, 1972.

Oliver, Greg. *Written in Blue & White: The Toronto Maple Leafs Contracts and Historical Documents from the Collection of Allan Stitt.* Toronto: ECW Press, 2014.

Oliver, Greg, and Richard Kamchen. *The Goaltenders' Union: Hockey's Greatest Puckstoppers, Acrobats and Flakes.* Toronto: ECW Press, 2014.

Podnieks, Andrew. *Return to Glory: The Leafs from Imlach to Fletcher.* Toronto: ECW Press, 1995.

Salming, Borje, and Gerhard Karlsson. *Blood, Sweat and Hockey: 17 Years in the NHL.* Toronto: HarperCollins, 1991.

Selke, Frank. *Behind the Cheering.* Toronto: McClelland & Stewart, 1962.

Shea, Kevin. *Barilko: Without a Trace.* Bolton, ON: Fenn, 2004.

Sittler, Darryl, Chrys Goyens, and Allan Turowetz. *Sittler.* Toronto: Macmillan of Canada, 1991.

Sittler, Darryl, and Brian McFarlane. *Sittler at Centre.* Toronto: Collier Macmillan of Canada, 1979.

Williams, Tiger, and James Lawton. *Tiger: A Hockey Story.* Toronto: Seal Books, 1985.

Young, Scott. *Conn Smythe: If You Can't Beat 'Em in the Alley.* Toronto: McClelland & Stewart, 1981.

———. *The Leafs I Knew.* Toronto: Ryerson Press, 1966.

Image Credits